Also by William D. Griffin
A PORTRAIT OF THE IRISH IN AMERICA

The Book of Irish Americans

The Book of Irish Americans

William D. Griffin

TIMES BOOKS

RANDOM HOUSE

All rights reserved under International and Pan-American
Copyright Conventions. Published in the United States by
Times Books, a division of Random House, Inc., New York,
and simultaneously in Canada by Random House of
Canada Limited, Toronto.

Library of Congress Cataloging-in-Publication Data

Griffin, William D.
  The Book of Irish Americans/William D. Griffin.
    p.   cm.
  Includes index.
  ISBN 0-8129-1264-0
  1. Irish Americans.   I. Title.
E184. I6G739   1990
973'. 049162—dc20   88-40167
                                                         CIP

Manufactured in the United States of America
9   8   7   6   5   4   3   2
First Edition

DESIGNED BY BARBARA MARKS

Permissions Acknowledgments appear on page 383.

To P.J.L.

ACKNOWLEDGMENTS

Many thanks to the editorial team at Times Books, especially Hugh O'Neill and Kathleen Becker, whose patience and diligence did so much to bring this project to fruition. An even more special acknowledgment goes to Michael W. Griffin, whose assistance as a researcher and whose advice as a student of social history have been of the greatest value.

CONTENTS

INTRODUCTION

*T*he Irish discovered America. They discovered it first in their imagination. On the westernmost fringe of Europe, from the island they
called Eire, the Irish of ancient times gazed out over the Atlantic and
wondered what lay beyond the broad expanse of water. Their earliest
legends and poems repeatedly speak of "enchanted isles to the west" or
a "land of eternal youth" far out in the ocean. Some say that St. Brendan
of Kerry sailed to the New World in the seventh century, or that a man
from Galway accompanied Columbus in 1492.

The plain fact is that the Irish have been coming to America ever
since they knew there was an America to come to. They were here in
Colonial days, they fought in the Revolution, and they came in ever
growing numbers to help build the new nation. During the Famine time
they came by the hundreds of thousands seeking a new life. And during
the past century, they have continued to come, seeking new opportunities. They were America's first immigrants and probably its most numerous.

And America discovered the Irish. It saw them first as diggers of
canals, pavers of roads, layers of tracks. Later it saw the Irish appear as
the engineers of great bridges and the constructors of mighty skyscrapers. It saw the Irish as outcasts, pioneers of the American ghetto,
and then as insiders, rulers of the nation's cities.

The Irish, their fellow Americans noted, had, within a generation or
two of their arrival, produced the country's leading architect (Louis Sullivan), its finest novelist (Henry James), and one of its most remarkable
thinkers (Henry's brother William). The sons of immigrants from Ireland
included America's greatest dramatist (Eugene O'Neill) and the founder
of its greatest industry (Henry Ford). The military theorist who taught
the generals of America's Civil War (Dennis Mahan) was the son of Irish
immigrants, as was one of his ablest pupils (Philip Sheridan). And the
son of Dennis Mahan was the naval theorist who laid the basis of America's maritime power—until the submarine (invented by the Irish-born
John Holland) altered naval strategy.

MAY THE ROAD RISE
TO MEET YOU. MAY
THE WIND BE
ALWAYS AT YOUR
BACK, THE SUN
SHINE WARM UPON
YOUR FACE, THE
RAIN FALL SOFT
UPON YOUR FIELDS,
AND UNTIL WE
MEET AGAIN MAY
GOD HOLD YOU IN
THE HOLLOW OF HIS
HAND.
Traditional Irish Toast

Irish-American enthusiasm in Philadelphia has at times reached elephantine proportions.

When Americans count up the number of their presidents and legis-
lators, jurists and administrators, politicians and teachers, lawmen and
outlaws, entertainers and artists, they discover that the Irish have made
a greater contribution to the United States than any other people.

The Irish experience is in many ways unique in this "nation of nations." Alone among America's ethnic groups, they are more numerous
in their new land than in their old. There are five (by some counts, ten)
times as many people of Irish descent in America as in Ireland. The
posterity, the future, of the Irish has been transferred to the United
States. But, as unique as they may be, the Irish share the experiences of
their fellow Americans. Like the Indians, they have suffered loss of their
ancestral land; like the blacks, they have endured bondage; like the Jews,
they have tasted religious persecution; like the Asians, they have been
scorned because they looked and acted "different"; like the Italians and
the Slavs, they have been despised as "poor and ignorant"; like the Hispanics, they have been denounced as violent and disruptive.

The story of the Irish in America is, then, both unique and universal.
It commands the attention of Irish Americans and deserves the attention
of all Americans. It is sometimes amazing, often amusing, frequently
distressing, but always inspiring. It tells us not only who the Irish in
America are, but also what America itself is all about. ◆

From Ireland to America

The North Star

*Y*ou landsmen all, on you I call, and gallant seamen too,
   Till I relate the hardships great that lately we went through;
On board the North Star, from Ireland we set sail,
To meet our friends in America—our loss they may bewail.

We had near five hundred souls on board, likewise a gallant crew.
For fifteen days we ploughed the seas, the wind tremendous blew
But still no danger we did fear bound for our native shore,
Our gallant ship nigh the Welsh coast she sunk to rise no more.

Through all the rage and tempest our good ship glided on,
She crossed the proud Atlantic without the slightest wrong,
Each heart was joyful, they thought from danger they were free
But the coast of Wales . . . that dreadful spot—soon proved their destiny.
On the 8th day of December, most dreadful to deplore,
Our gallant ship, alas! she ran too close to the Welsh shore,
Not thinking any danger near she got a dreadful shock,
And the North Star struck that night upon a fatal rock.

The screams of those poor passengers would reach the lofty skies.
The storm raged, the billows foamed, most dismal were the cries,
The captain and his noble crew they strove their lives to save,
But all their efforts were in vain—they met a watery grave.

Before the gallant ship went down they fired signal guns,
And sent up rockets in the air, but no relief did come,
Their screams and cries for mercy would pierce your heart full sore,
But these unhappy passengers they sank to rise no more.

The scene was dreadful to behold when daylight did appear,
To see their mangled bodies float for them you'd shed a tear,
The mothers held their children, as in death's grave they lay,
And husbands with their loving wives washed in by the sea.

On the 8th day of December last, they met their awful fate,
On board the North Star (it's heart-rending to relate),
Out of near 500 passengers but twenty-nine were saved,
The rest was lost nigh the Welsh coast—they met a watery grave.

Oh! may the Lord their souls receive, they met an awful doom,
They sunk beneath the foaming wave far from their native home,
If they had reached America their friends would happy be,
But, alas! those sons of Erin's isle sleep in the briny sea. ◆

The First
Irishmen in
America

That the Irish were among the first immigrants to the New World there is no doubt. The question of which of them came first is more debatable.

Certainly they had been looking in the right direction for a long time. Pre-Christian Irish legends repeatedly refer to "enchanted islands to the West," lying far out in the ocean—*Tir na-Og*, the land of eternal youth, and *Hy Brasil*, the island of great desire. According to tradition, St. Brendan the Navigator, sailing westward in search of new mission fields before A.D. 600, reached inhabited lands and preached the Gospel to the natives. Whether or not Brendan discovered America, it is certain that his fellow monks reached the Faeroe Islands in the mid-seventh century and settled in Iceland about a hundred years later. Norse sagas dating from A.D. 1000 refer to "Great Ireland," lying to the southwest of Greenland and inhabited at this period by white-skinned people descended from early Irish voyagers.

A more substantial contender for the title of first Irishman is William Eris, or Ayers, a native of Galway who is supposed to have sailed with Columbus in 1492. He is said to have been one of the forty volunteers left behind in Hispaniola who were killed by the Indians before Columbus's return. Nearly a hundred years later, during one of the abortive English attempts to settle North America, Captain Ralph Lane wrote (1586) that "an Irishman serving me, one Edward Nugent, volunteered to kill Pemisapan, king of the Indians. We met him returning out of the woods with Pemisapan's head in his hands, and the Indians ceased their raids against the British camp." As this camp was near present-day Edenton, North Carolina, Nugent would seem to qualify as the first Irishman within the present boundaries of the United States. Close runners-up were "Two Irishmen, Darbie Glaven and Dennis Carrell," who accompanied Captain John White to Virginia in 1587. They were put ashore on St. John (Virgin Islands) to collect supplies and fill water barrels. For some unrecorded reason they were left behind when the ships sailed and were never heard of again. ◆

The history of the Irish in America does not begin with the Famine Years. Traditional textbooks notwithstanding, there was an Irish presence on this continent long before the great stream of immigrants flowing westward during the Hungry Forties. Notable among these earlier generations were the Men of '98, who sought in America the liberty that the failure of their own rebellion had denied them at home. And preeminent among these refugees of revolution were two leaders of the United Irishmen—Thomas Addis Emmet and William James MacNeven. Drawn into political collaboration and personal friendship by a shared love of Ireland, these two men of differing background and religion risked all for freedom's sake, and suffered the tragedy of banishment. Boldly encountering the pitfalls and opportunities of the New World, each made a distinguished place for himself in his adopted country, and the two worked together once more to counsel and protect the next generation of immigrants arriving from the old land. Their story is worth remembering.

Ireland in the latter half of the eighteenth century was a country deprived of religious and political freedom. The harsh Penal Laws had reduced the Catholics, who constituted the vast majority of the population, to virtual serfdom; totally bereft of civil rights, they were allowed bare survival merely on the sufferance of their overlords. The status of the Ulster Presbyterians and other Protestant dissenters from the Established Church was little better. But even those who conformed to the Church of Ireland enjoyed few practical advantages, for English rule lay heavily upon this colonial dependency, and Irishmen of all creeds were viewed as an inferior species, fit only to be governed and economically exploited.

THE EYE OF A FRIEND IS A GOOD LOOKING-GLASS. *Traditional Irish Proverb*

Thomas Addis Emmet belonged to the privileged stratum of this hierarchical society. Born in 1764, he was the son of Dr. Robert Emmet, a descendant of English settlers whose kinsman, Lord Temple, viceroy of Ireland, had granted him the lucrative sinecure of State Physician. Educated at Trinity College, Thomas acquired a medical degree from the renowned University of Edinburgh and commenced his career in Dublin in 1789. But the death of his elder brother, who had already gained a great reputation as a barrister, induced him to turn to the legal profession, and within two more years the young physician had completed his studies at London's Temple and been admitted to the Irish Bar.

William James MacNeven, by contrast, sprang from the old Celtic stock and from a family that had managed to retain both its Catholic faith and its small landed property in the west of Ireland. Barred by the Penal Laws from gaining an education at home, MacNeven was obliged, like most of the Catholic gentry, to evade the regulations that forbade him to seek it abroad. While his near-contemporary Emmet was attending the leading institutions of the British Isles, MacNeven resided with an expatriate uncle in Prague. Having pursued the study of medicine there and in Vienna, he returned to Dublin—for, by an anomaly of the statutes, an Irish Catholic might practice medicine, though he could not legally study it, or enter any other profession, or hold any public office.

Hope had been awakened in 1782 when England, hard pressed by American rebels and Irish patriots, granted home rule to the Kingdom of Ireland. But the years between the end of the American Revolution and the outbreak of the French Revolution saw the fading of that hope, as the cause of religious liberty and political equality was stifled by a parliament too corrupt and unrepresentative to welcome change.

Despite their dissimilar backgrounds, both young men were moved by the same liberal instincts and the same passion for social justice. MacNeven threw himself into the work of the Catholic Committee and helped replace the timid and compromising leadership of that lobbying group with activists of his own aggressive breed. Emmet, turning his back on privileged security, rapidly won a reputation as the defense counsel for prosecuted reformers. When the Protestant radical Theobald Wolfe Tone was chosen secretary of the Catholic Committee, his friend Emmet followed him and here met a kindred spirit, MacNeven. The two were early adherents of the Society of United Irishmen, founded by Tone in 1791.

The aims of this society were "to promote a brotherhood of affection and union among Irishmen of every religious persuasion" and "to procure a full, equal, and adequate representation for all the people of Ireland." The United Irishmen sought at first to attain these goals by constitutional, peaceful methods, only to be frustrated and calumniated by those with a vested interest in the prevailing system. Then, like their predecessors in America, they turned to independence and republicanism as their only remedy. By 1795 they were proscribed revolutionaries, conspiring for an uprising that would separate Ireland from the British Empire. After Tone had been exiled to the United States—whence he made his way to France to enlist support—Emmet and MacNeven shared, with Lord Edward Fitzgerald, the high command of the organization. Emmet was described by a government informer as "the most dangerous man in Ireland, from the standpoint of zeal, bearing, power of speech, and ability." MacNeven, who had been raised on the Continent, turned his experience and linguistic talents to advantage, journeying to France and Holland to confer with Tone and to concert plans with Ireland's allies. A hundred thousand men were enrolled in an underground army, ready to rise all over Ireland at a signal from the supreme directory.

Then, on March 12, 1798—disaster. Betrayed by a trusted comrade, Emmet, MacNeven, and several dozen leading United Irishmen were arrested. With these chieftains imprisoned and Fitzgerald slain while resisting capture, the United Irish revolution was doomed. When insurrection burst forth a few weeks later, it was leaderless and swiftly degenerated into a sectarian agrarian revolt—bloody, directionless, and easily crushed. The belated arrival of an inadequate French invasion force, its defeat, and Tone's death sealed the fate of the nation for another century. The Act of Union was forced through a frightened parliament and Ireland was degraded from the rank of an autonomous kingdom to that of a British province.

At first condemned to hang for treason, then reprieved, Emmet, MacNeven, and the other "State Prisoners" were passed from one jail to another during the next five years, finally being lodged at remote Fort George in the Scottish Highlands. Yet when a peace treaty between Britain and France brought their release, the first thought of these determined nationalists was to persuade Bonaparte that Ireland was still ripe for revolution. The failure of Robert Emmet's rebellion and his death upon the scaffold in 1803 disillusioned his older brother. Convinced that France would do nothing more for Ireland, Thomas Emmet "turned his thoughts to the only secure refuge from oppression" and in October 1804 sailed for America. During the next few years, MacNeven and many other Men of '98 were to follow his example.

Emmet, accompanied by his wife and children, arrived in New York in November 1804. The long waiting period required in this state before admission to the bar inclined him to try his fortunes on the "free frontier" of Ohio. He knew, moreover, that he would be unacceptable to conservative Eastern Federalists, who had denounced earlier refugees as "Irish Jacobins" and "wild Irishmen come to stir up sedition." Among men of the Jeffersonian persuasion, however, the name of Emmet was well known and esteemed. "Mr. Emmet's strong and decided attachment to democratic principles," wrote one of them, "was known even before he reached the American shores. Coming to a country where he may breathe and speak freely, he should not find it necessary to suppress those bold and ardent sentiments which animated his bosom while toiling for the emancipation of Ireland." Thanks to the intervention of Governor George Clinton and of his nephew, DeWitt Clinton, mayor of New York (themselves descendants of an Irish immigrant), the State Supreme Court waived its rules and admitted Emmet at once to the practice of

There lurks in the Irish psyche, I am convinced, a profound skepticism about the fashionable compassion of the American do-gooder. We are inclined to think their compassions are just a bit phony, and we wonder where they were when we needed help. We also find it just a bit ironic when they demand that we feel guilty for what their ancestors did to the blacks and the American Indians. They do not seem to display much guilt for what happened to us at the hands of their ancestors here and in Europe.

Andrew Greeley,
The Most Distressful Country (1973)

law in New York in recognition of "his great talents and his sufferings."

The confidence of the Clintons in Emmet's abilities was fully justified. In the words of a contemporary, "Mr. Emmet now commenced that splendid career at the American bar that has not only elevated the character of the profession, but reflected back a lustre on his native land. The Irish bar have reason to be proud of the exile who has so essentially aided in giving immortality to Irish genius." Despite Federalist attempts to isolate and thwart him in his professional career, Emmet prospered, and within a few years had gained such a standing among his colleagues that he could put all opposition at defiance. By 1812 the immigrant had become attorney general of New York. Emmet regarded this office as a mark of honor to his professional attainments, however, rather than as a political stepping-stone. Though consistently identified with the party of Jefferson and Madison, he sought no other public title and declined all nominations to elective or appointive office. By 1824 the exile had become "one of the great pillars and ornaments of the American bar." "Mr. Emmet walks on in life," declared a writer of that date, "amid the eulogiums, the admiration, the enthusiastic regard of a great and enlightened community. Without the glare and influence of public office, without titles and dignities, who fills a wider space, who commands more respect than Thomas Addis Emmet? Like a noble and simple column he stands among us proudly preeminent—destitute of pretensions, destitute of vanity, and destitute of envy." His renown was nationwide. As a New Orleans attorney attested, "Thomas Addis Emmet is the great luminary whose light even crosses the western mountains. His name rings down the valley of the Mississippi, and we hail his efforts with a kind of local pride."

NEITHER MAKE NOR BREAK A CUSTOM.
Traditional Irish Proverb

When, in later years, Irish friends urged him to return to his native land, or at least send his children there, Emmet replied: "My principles and my sufferings were my first passport and introduction here, and they procured me that effective regard of the leading characters of this State, and in the Union at large. In proportion as I cherish these principles I am respected, and every day's reflection and observation makes them dearer to me. Ought I go where they are treasonable and sufficient ground for perpetual proscription? . . . As to my children, I hope they will love liberty too much ever to fix a voluntary residence in an enslaved country."

MacNeven landed in New York on the Fourth of July, 1805, in the midst of the celebrations marking America's independence from Britain, and immediately felt at home among his new brethren. The *New York Medical Gazette* of August 11, 1841, reviewed his subsequent career: "He immediately entered upon the practice of his profession, and in 1808 was appointed professor of obstetrics in the College of Physicians and Surgeons. In 1811 he exchanged his chair for that of chemistry. In 1812 he was appointed Resident Physician of the City. . . ." In 1826 he joined in founding the Duane Street School (later Rutgers Medical School). In 1832 he supervised the hospitals during the cholera epidemic. "As a lecturer he was simple, clear, and animated—as a practitioner, judicious and efficient—as a man, amiable, honest and kind-hearted—as a patriot, ardent, active, bold, disinterested."

During the thirty-six years of his residence in New York, MacNeven was an active, valuable, contented member of the community—all the more so after his marriage in 1810 to a lady of the long-established Riker family gave him not only companionship and children but an intimate connection with Old New York. Nevertheless, his dearest friends were those who had shared the struggles of his young manhood—United Irishmen like the brilliant barrister William Sampson, the editor Thomas O'Connor (whose *Shamrock*, founded in 1810, was the first American-Irish newspaper), and, of course, Thomas Addis Emmet.

The Men of '98 were concerned with more than nostalgic socializing. They knew that the end of the protracted revolutionary wars in Europe and of "Mr. Madison's War" with England would open the way for Irish immigrants seeking the freedom and opportunities that these men had found. And they wholeheartedly committed themselves to aiding and guiding their kindred in this new land of theirs. Emmet and MacNeven were the prime movers in setting up a free employment service for Irish immigrants. The office opened in 1816 on Nassau Street not only found jobs in the city and its vicinity but directed the newcomers to "places in the interior where employment had been previously engaged for them." In the following year, the leading Irish residents of New York met under MacNeven's chairmanship to plan for "the settlement of Irish agriculturists in American lands." The Irish Emigrant Association, with Emmet as president, petitioned Congress to set aside public lands in Illinois to which the new immigrants might go rather than remain in the "crowded and corrupting cities of the Eastern seaboard." Congress was asked to "sell land, on fourteen years' credit, to deserving Irishmen, who would serve as a frontier guard against marauding Indians." The petition was rejected by an 83 to 71 vote in the House of Representatives. Another employment agency was organized by Emmet and MacNeven in 1827, even though their request for municipal backing was unsuccessful.

On November 14, 1827, almost twenty-three years to the day after his arrival in America, Thomas Addis Emmet suffered a fatal stroke while addressing the United States Circuit Court. On the news of his death, both Congress and the state legislature adjourned as a mark of respect. Delegations from Washington and Albany joined city officials and citizens of New York in his funeral cortege. No one was more moved by his passing, however, than William MacNeven, who commented sadly: "Emmet's first speech at the bar in the United States was in defense of a slave; his last effort in a court of law was in behalf of a charitable institution. That was as it should be with his career." Emmet's

*The first pota-
toes to reach
North America
arrived in Vir-
ginia in 1622,
imported by col-
onists who were
Irish or had
lived in Ireland.
The first potato
cultivation in
what is now the
United States
dates from
1719, when
Irish immigrants
planted potato
fields in New
Hampshire.*

professional colleagues placed a marble bust and tablet to mark the spot in the courtroom where he died. His fellow exiles, led by MacNeven, raised an obelisk to his memory in St. Paul's Churchyard. But for his old comrade, the happiest memorial was undoubtedly the marriage of Thomas Addis Emmet, Jr., to his daughter, for it was in their home that he spent his last years.

For the remainder of his long life, MacNeven carried on his labor on behalf of his fellow Gaels. He set up yet another free registry office, this one for domestic servants, at Broadway and Canal Street, where it long rendered aid to the new arrivals. He wrote and published a pamphlet, "Advice to Irishmen Arriving in America," that included directions for naturalization prepared by Emmet. In 1828 he was elected president of the Friends of Ireland and enlisted American support for the cause of Catholic Emancipation. In 1837 he was active in promoting Irish settle-ment in Texas. "There is great jealousy of them in the United States," he wrote sadly, "and it is increasing daily, for their numbers are multiply-ing very fast, and the natives think that these foreigners, as they call them, interfere too much. There actually exists a dislike to them, not-withstanding the immense good they do. It would be a great matter for those who might remain here if there was another good place to which they would be welcome. . . . Texas would form an invaluable settlement for rich and poor."

At the time of his death, on July 12, 1841, MacNeven, holding an office that Emmet had held before him, president of the Irish Emigrant Association, was still profoundly concerned with those bonds of flesh and spirit that held his two countries in a unique relationship. The last sur-vivor among the leaders of '98, he had lived long enough to see the problems that the rising tide of immigration would bring to his Irish brethren and to his adopted compatriots. He and his fellow pioneers had done their best to pave the way; the new problems would have to be met by new generations.

The memorial to Emmet at St. Paul's has been matched by a second obelisk, commemorating MacNeven. It is fitting that these United Irish-men, united in their life's work, should be remembered together by those who pass their monuments on the busy thoroughfare they themselves trod on their first days in America. Both in Ireland and in the United States they stood together for the noblest of civic and human virtues. "With him the love of country was a passion as well as a principle; and when that country shall cease to cherish his memory she will be utterly unworthy of him"—so wrote a New York editor of William James MacNeven. He might have said the same of Thomas Addis Emmet. He did not specify whether the "country" was Ireland or America. He might well have meant both. ◆

The great flood of immigration from Ireland swept over America after the Great Famine of the 1840s. But for at least two centuries before the Hungry Forties, Irish immigrants had been making their way to the New World. Coming at first as individuals or in small groups, they settled throughout the thirteen colonies. After the independence of the United States, to which the Irish made significant contributions, the number of immigrants grew steadily and their involvement in the affairs of the new nation became ever more varied. The following chronology highlights various aspects of the Irish presence in America during the two hundred years before the famine.

1644

Daniel Gookin the Younger (1612–1687), son of an early Irish settler in Virginia, moved to Massachusetts, where he became a member of the Governor's Council, major general of militia, and superintendent of Indian affairs.

1645

Teague Jones (died 1676), native of Ireland, freeholder and resident of Yarmouth, Massachusetts. He was fined in 1660 for refusing to take an oath of fidelity to the Crown.

Dutch Colonial records list "Jan Andriessen de Iersman van Duglingh" (John Anderson, the Irishman

from Dublin) as a resident at Beverwyck, near Fort Orange (Albany). He died in 1664, the year of New Amsterdam's capture by the British.

1652

Oliver Cromwell, victorious in his campaigns in Ireland, began large-scale confiscation of Irish land. Thousands of Irish men and women were dispossessed and many of them enslaved and "transported" as laborers to the West Indies. Some of the "transported" Irish (especially those in Barbados) subsequently found their way to British colonies on the North American mainland.

1653

James Butler, a native of Ireland, settled in Massachusetts. At his death in 1681 he was the "largest landowner" in what is now Worcester, Massachusetts.

1657

Thomas Lewis, from Belfast, arrived in New Amsterdam as a carpenter under contract to the Dutch West India Company. Under the name of Thomas Lodewicksen he became captain of a cargo vessel plying the Hudson River between New Amsterdam and Fort Orange (Albany). He was a special protégé of Governor Stuyvesant, and is mentioned in Stuyvesant's

(continued)

correspondence as "Thomas the Irishman." He died in 1685, leaving a son, Thomas, who married the daughter of Governor Jacob Leisler.

1662

Town of Kinsale was founded in Virginia by Irish settlers from Cork.

1669

Michael Kelly, a "native of Ireland," was commissioned by the Council of Rhode Island to prepare "defensive works" against Indian attacks.

1670

English and Irish emigrants established a settlement at Charleston and began the colonization of South Carolina. One of the ships in the first fleet was commanded by Captain Florence O'Sullivan, who was named surveyor-general of the new province and commander of the militia. Sullivan's Island in Charleston harbor is named after him.

1672

Robert Pollock, from Donegal, and his wife (a native of Londonderry) arrived in Maryland. Their son, William, who contracted the name to Polk, was the great-grandfather of President James K. Polk.

1677

Charles McCarthy, from Cork, led a party of forty-eight Irish immigrants in

the founding of East Greenwich, Rhode Island.

1678

About 100 Irish families sailed from Barbados to Virginia and the Carolinas.

1680

George Talbot, "an Irish gentleman," received a land grant in Maryland, which he named New Ireland and subdivided into estates called New Munster, New Leinster, and New Connaught. It included what is now Hartford and Cecil Counties, Maryland, and part of Newcastle County, Delaware, and was settled by Irish immigrants.

1682

Dennis and Mary Ruchford, from Wexford, accompanied William Penn on his first visit to Pennsylvania. Dennis was named a member of the Pennsylvania Assembly in 1683.

Sir Thomas Dongan (1634–1715), born in Kildare, was named governor of New York. He held the post until 1688, and was subsequently created Earl of Limerick.

1683

Irish immigrants from Tipperary settled in Salem County, New Jersey.

1684

Richard Kyrle, "an Irish gentleman," was named governor of South Carolina. During his term there was a considerable influx of Irish settlers.

1685

James Moore (1640–1703), a native of Ireland, was appointed a member of the Governor's Council. He subsequently served as acting governor, chief justice of the province, and attorney general. His son James became governor of South Carolina in 1719.

1688

Anne Glover was hanged as a witch in Boston. A native of Ireland, she had been sold as a slave in Barbados in Cromwell's time and subsequently was brought to Massachusetts.

Charles Carroll was named attorney general of Maryland by Lord Calvert, the proprietor. He was the grandfather of Charles Carroll of Carrollton, a signer of the Declaration of Independence, and was the founder of one of the most distinguished and prosperous Irish-American families of the Colonial era.

1690

Andrew Meade, from Kerry, settled in Nansemond County, Virginia, and later became a burgess, judge, and colonel of militia. Among his descendants was General George Meade, victor of the Battle of Gettysburg.

Daniel Sullivan, from Cork, settled in Nansemond County, Virginia, and was subsequently elected to the House of Burgesses. His descendants, who spelled the name Sullivant, were pioneers in the settlement of Ohio.

1691

Daniel MacCarthy, from Cork, settled in Virginia, becoming a burgess in 1705 and Speaker of the House, 1715–1720. His son Denis married (1724) Sarah Ball, a first cousin of Mary Ball, George Washington's mother. Washington was a neighbor and intimate friend of his MacCarthy cousins.

1692

William O'Brien, from County Clare, settled in North Carolina. He was the first American ancestor of William Jennings Bryan.

1696

Irish immigrants from Waterford settled in Burlington County, New Jersey.

1699

James Logan (1674–1751), from Armagh, came over as secretary to William Penn. He subsequently became a member of the provincial council, mayor of Philadelphia, acting governor (1736–1738), and chief justice of Pennsylvania. While mayor, he authorized his fellow Irishmen to attend the first public Mass in Philadelphia.

1703

Daniel Dulany (1685–1753), born in Queen's County, Ireland, arrived in Maryland as an indentured servant. After gaining his freedom, he won admission to the Maryland bar (1710). He became a judge, attorney general of the province, a member of the legislature (1722–1742) and of the Governor's Council (1742–1753), and championed the Colonial cause in his pamphlet "The Rights of the Inhabitants of Maryland to the Benefit of English Laws" (1728). His son, Daniel (1722–1797), was secretary of the province of Maryland (1761–1774) and a leading opponent of the Stamp Act.

1704

Laws discouraging the entry of Catholics into Maryland were passed by the legislature this year and again in 1715. They excluded or imposed duties upon the importation of all "Irish servants." A similar law had been passed in South Carolina in 1698.

1706

Reverend Francis Makemie (1658–1708), from Donegal, organized the first American Presbytery, in Virginia. He had been a "wandering evangelist" since his arrival from Ireland in 1683, and is regarded as the founder of Presbyterianism in America.

1710

Settlers from the north of Ireland, including McDowell, McDuffie, and McGruder families, settled in the Blue Ridge region of Virginia.

1718

The earliest organized band of emigrants to leave Ireland in the eighteenth century sailed from Donegal. The group included about one hundred families, who settled in New Hampshire, at the town of Londonderry.

1720

Noting that some 2,600 Irishmen had arrived in Boston during the past three years, the governor of Massachusetts complained of the "public burden" imposed by the coming of "so many poor people from abroad, especially those that come from Ireland." The General Court of Massachusetts warned immigrants from Ireland to leave the colony within seven months.

1721

Between this date and 1742, over 3,000 immigrants came to America from the province of Ulster alone.

1722

Members of the Presbyterian congregation at Voluntown (near Hartford), Connecticut, petitioned for the removal of their minister, Reverend Samuel Donance: "He came out of Ireland," and since his coming, "The Irish do flock into town."

Matthew Watson, a native of Ireland, settled at Barrington, Rhode Island, and engaged in brickmaking. He supplied

(continued)

much of the brick for New York's "urban expansion" during the eighteenth century, as he remained active in business until over one hundred years of age.

1729

Charles Clinton (born 1690 at Corbay, County Longford) landed at Cape Cod. He and his wife, also a native of Ireland, later settled in New York. Their son James (1733–1812) became a brigadier general during the Revolutionary War, and his son, DeWitt (1769–1828), served as governor of New York, 1817–1821 and 1825-1828. James's younger brother George (1739–1812) held the governorship 1777–1795 and 1801–1804, and served as vice president of the United States, 1805–1812.

1736

James Patton (born Londonderry, 1692) received a grant of land west of the Blue Ridge Mountains. Augusta County, Virginia, was settled largely through his efforts. He crossed the Atlantic twenty-five times bringing Irish settlers. Patton was killed by Indians in 1755.

A band of settlers from Binbridge, County Down, established themselves on the banks of the Opequan River in the Shenandoah Valley of Virginia.

1737

The Charitable Irish Society was founded on St. Patrick's Day in Boston by twenty-six Irish immigrants "to aid unfortunate fellow countrymen, to cultivate a spirit of unity and harmony among all Irishmen in the Massachusetts colony and their descendants, and to advance their interests socially and morally." This is the oldest Irish society in the United States.

Jeremiah Smith, born in Ireland in 1705, came to America in 1726 and began operating the first paper factory in this country, at Dorchester, Massachusetts.

1738

William Johnson (1715–1774), a native of Meath whose original family name was MacShane, settled in the Mohawk Valley, New York. In 1755 he was created a baronet and named superintendent of Indian Affairs. On his death he was succeeded by his nephew Guy Johnson (1740–1788), also born in Ireland, who directed Iroquois attacks against the colonists during the Revolutionary War.

1740

At about this date, Edward and William Patterson, natives of Dungannon, County Tyrone, began the first manufacture of tinware in America, at New Britain, Connecticut.

1743

Travelers' accounts refer to "the Irish Tract," a district in the lower Shenandoah Valley occupied by Irish settlers.

1752

Hugh Gaine (1726–1807), from Belfast, who came here in 1745, founded the New York *Mercury*, which became one of the leading Colonial newspapers.

1760

John Lynch, from Galway, settled in Virginia, where his elder son, John, founded the town of Lynchburg and his younger son, Colonel Charles Lynch, was a commander of irregular forces during the Revolution and, by his drastic treatment of Loyalists, gave rise to the term "lynch laws." Colonel Lynch's son, Charles, became governor of Louisiana.

1762

First recorded celebration of St. Patrick's Day in New York City "in the house of John Marshall at Mount Pleasant, near the College" (King's College, later Columbia).

1764

Thomas Burke (1747–1783) and his brother Aedanus (1743–1802) arrived in America. Thomas represented North Carolina in the Continental Congress from 1776 to 1781, when he was elected governor of North Carolina; captured by the British, he died shortly thereafter. Aedanus was chief justice of the South Carolina Supreme Court in 1778 and represented his state in the First Congress, 1789–1791.

1765

Matthew Lyon (1750–1811), a native of Wicklow, arrived in America. Settling in Vermont, he aided Ethan Allen in the capture of Fort Ticonderoga (1775), and represented Vermont in Congress, 1797–1801. After moving south, he was elected congressman from Kentucky, 1803–1811.

1768

A band of Irish Methodists, led by Philip Embury (1728–1773), a native of Ballingane, founded the Wesley Chapel on John Street in New York City, the first Methodist church in America.

The Friendly Brothers of St. Patrick, a fraternal organization largely composed of Irish-born officers serving in the British forces in North America, began its existence, which extended to the end of the Revolutionary War. Its annual meetings were usually held on St. Patrick's Day in New York City.

1770

Patrick Carr, a native of Ireland, killed in the "Boston Massacre."

1771

The Friendly Brothers of St. Patrick founded in Charleston, South Carolina, by a group of Irish Americans, including John and Edward Rutledge, both of whom subsequently became governors of South Carolina.

1771

The Pennsylvania Packet commenced publication. Its owner, John Dunlap (1747–1812), came to America from County Tyrone in 1757, and in 1776, as printer to the Continental Congress, printed the first copies of the Declaration of Independence. *The Pennsylvania Packet*, at first a weekly, was transformed in 1784 into the first daily newspaper published in the United States.

1772

A decline in the linen trade and exorbitant rents spurred a new wave of emigration from the north of Ireland. Some 30,000 Ulstermen sailed for America in the five years preceding the Revolutionary War.

1774

A British contingent under Colonel Andrew Lewis (1720–1781), a native of Ireland, defeated the Shawnee Indians at Point Pleasant on the Ohio River, opening the way for American penetration of the Northwest Territory during the Revolutionary War. Lewis, who had come to America in 1732 and settled in Virginia, joined the patriots in 1776 and was named a brigadier general in the Continental Army.

John Sullivan (1740–1795), whose father had emigrated from Limerick in 1723, led a band of New Hampshire militiamen in the seizure of Fort William and Mary, Newcastle, New Hampshire. The gunpowder captured here was later used at Bunker Hill. Sullivan, hailed as "the first to take up arms against the King," was commissioned a major general in the Continental Army and in 1779 broke the power of the Iroquois and Loyalists in New York State. He served as governor of New Hampshire from 1786 to 1789.

1775

Daniel Boone, accompanied by other pioneers of Irish origin, including McGrady, Harland, and McBride, commenced the settlement of Kentucky.

Jeremiah O'Brien (1744–1818), whose father was a native of Cork, captured the British schooner *Margaretta* in Machias Bay, Maine, on June 12. This first naval action of the Revolution has been called "the Lexington of the Seas." Jeremiah and his brother John commanded American privateers during the war.

General Richard Montgomery (1736–1775), a native of Dublin, who had come to America in 1772, led a contingent of Continental troops in an invasion of Canada. He captured Montreal, but was killed leading an assault on Quebec City (December 31).

1776

Samuel Loudon (1727–1813), a native of Ireland, founded *The New York*
(continued)

Packet and American Advertiser, a weekly newspaper.

British troops evacuated Boston on March 17, and General Washington prescribed "St. Patrick" as the password of his army for that day. Among his staff officers during the war were Colonel Stephen Moylan, a native of Cork, Colonel John Fitzgerald, born in Wicklow, and Colonel Francis Barber, whose father, Patrick, had emigrated from Longford.

Declaration of Independence was signed in Philadelphia (July). Irish-born signers were Matthew Thornton (1714–1803) of New Hampshire, George Taylor (1716–1781) of Pennsylvania, and James Smith (1719–1806) of Pennsylvania. Signers of Irish origin included Edward Rutledge, Thomas Lynch, Thomas McKean, George Read, and Charles Carroll. The secretary of the Congress from 1774 to 1789 was Charles Thomson (1729–1824), who came to America as an indentured servant after being orphaned at the age of ten. By 1760 he was a prosperous merchant in Philadelphia. It was his duty to read the Declaration before the Congress for the first time and to notify George Washington of his election to the presidency in 1789.

1777

Battle of Saratoga (October 7). Sharpshooter Timothy Murphy of Morgan's Rifle Corps picked off two British commanders—a major factor in the American victory. Murphy (1751–1818), son of Irish immigrant parents, was the most famous marksman of the Revolution.

Hercules Mulligan, an Irish-born tailor in New York City, was appointed Washington's chief "confidential agent." While posing as a collaborator during the British occupation of the city, he provided the American commander with vital information on the enemy's plans and movements.

1778

General Sir Henry Clinton, reporting on the American rebels to the colonial secretary in London, declared that "the emigrants from Ireland are in general to be looked upon as our most serious antagonists." Men of Irish birth or descent have been calculated to have formed between one-third and one-half of the Revolutionary forces, including 1,492 officers and 26 generals (15 of whom were born in Ireland).

1779

First St. Patrick's Day parade in New York City, sponsored by the Volunteers of Ireland, a Loyalist regiment commanded by Lord Rawdon, an Irish peer.

1782

Great Britain recognized Ireland's legislative autonomy and her right to regulate domestic affairs through her own parliament. The so-called Revolution of 1782 that brought this about was facilitated by Britain's preoccupation with the American war. Exchange of congratulations and felicitations between United States Congress and Irish parliament in recognition of their common interests and grievances.

1784

James Duane (1733–1797) was elected first post-Colonial mayor of New York City. A former member of the Continental Congress (1774–1784), he held office until 1789. His father, Anthony Duane, had emigrated from Ireland in 1717.

Friendly Sons of St. Patrick was organized as a fraternal and charitable body in New York City. Daniel McCormick, a native of Ireland and a director of the Bank of New York, was elected first president.

Mathew Carey (1760–1839), a leading Dublin newspaper editor, fled to America to escape prosecution for criticism of the British government. He founded the *Pennsylvania Herald* in 1785 and the *Columbian Magazine* in 1786, and became a prominent publisher and bookseller in Philadelphia. His son, Henry Charles Carey (1793–1879), won renown as an economist.

1785

Dominick Lynch (1754–1825) arrived in New York from his native Galway and soon established himself as one of the leading merchants of the city. His son, Dominick II (died 1844), was a leader of New York society and a patron of the arts.

1789

General Henry Knox (1750–1806), son of Andrew Knox, an Irish immigrant, was appointed secretary of war in Washington's cabinet. He had served as chief of artillery throughout the Revolutionary War, succeeded Washington as commander in chief from 1783 to 1784, and acted as secretary of war under the Articles of Confederation, from 1785 to 1789. He was a member of the Charitable Irish Society of Boston, and of the Friendly Sons of St. Patrick in Philadelphia.

1790

The Hibernian Society of Philadelphia was founded. Thomas McKean (1734–1817), the son of Irish immigrants and signer of the Declaration of Independence, was elected the first president.

The first census of the United States recorded 44,000 Irish-born residents, more than half of them living south of Pennsylvania. Some historians regard this figure as far too low, estimating two or three times as many Irish-born Americans at this date.

1791

James Hoban (c. 1762–1831), a native of Kilkenny who had settled in Charleston after the Revolutionary War and acquired a reputation as an architect, produced the design for a "President's Palace" in the new Federal City (Washington, D.C.). The "Palace," subsequently known as the White House, was modeled upon Leinster House in Dublin.

1793

The Society for the Relief of Emigrants from Ireland was founded in Philadelphia by Mathew Carey and other leading members of the Irish-American community.

1795

William Duane (1760–1835), a graduate of Trinity College, Dublin, began editorship of *The Aurora* in Philadelphia. This newspaper was a leading mouthpiece of Thomas Jefferson's Democratic Party. Duane was named adjutant-general during the War of 1812. His son, William John Duane (1780–1865), was secretary of the treasury in President Jackson's cabinet.

1798

Revolutionary uprising of the Society of United Irishmen against British rule in Ireland. After the destruction of their movement many rebels took refuge in the United States. Among these were: Patrick

Rogers, whose four sons were eminent scientists, notably William Barton Rogers (1804–1882), who became first president of the Massachusetts Institute of Technology; Robert Adrian, who became professor of mathematics and natural philosophy at Columbia College; and John Daly Burk, author of a four-volume *History of Virginia* and political protégé of Jefferson. James McKinley, grandfather of President William McKinley, also emigrated from Antrim at about this time. His brother Francis had been hanged as a United Irish rebel.

1801

The Act of Union between Great Britain and Ireland abolished Irish legislative autonomy and created the United Kingdom of Great Britain and Ireland. Repeal of this act became a major goal of Irish and Irish-American political aspirations.

1803

The Benevolent Hibernian Society of Baltimore was organized. Its first president was Dr. John Campbell White, a United Irishman who had fled Belfast in 1798.

1804

Thomas Addis Emmet (1764–1827), a leader of the United Irishmen, arrived in America, having been banished from Ireland. He was admitted to the New York Bar by a special act of

(continued)

the legislature and in 1812 became attorney general of New York.

1805

William J. MacNeven (1763–1841), like T. A. Emmet a member of the United Irish Directory, exiled after the 1798 rebellion, settled in New York City. He became professor of obstetrics at the College of Physicians and Surgeons and "made many distinguished contributions to the advancement of medicine." President of the Irish Emigrant Society until his death and "elder statesman" of the Irish American "community." Among his works was "Advice to Irishmen Arriving in America," a pamphlet that contained an appendix on the naturalization laws by T. A. Emmet.

1806

Harman Blennerhasset (1765–1831), member of a Kerry land-owning family, whose republican sympathies had led him to emigrate, was involved in Aaron Burr's conspiracy, and his estate, on Blennerhasset's Island in the Ohio River, was the assembly point for Burr's "army," which (according to various versions) was intended for the invasion of Mexico or the overthrow of the United States government. Blennerhasset was arrested with Burr, but released without being brought to trial.

1807

James Sullivan (1744–1808) was elected governor of Massachusetts. He was a son of John Sullivan, who had come over from Limerick in 1723, and a brother of Major General John Sullivan, the conqueror of the Iroquois.

1808

Joseph Carless, a native of Westmeath, who had settled in St. Louis after the failure of the 1798 Rebellion, established the *Missouri Gazette*, the first newspaper west of the Mississippi River.

1810

The Shamrock, the first Irish-American newspaper, was published in New York City. It was edited by Thomas O'Connor (1770–1855), a United Irish refugee, who became a leader of Tammany Hall, a city commissioner, and (1842) candidate for mayor of New York.

1811

The American Review of History and Politics, the first quarterly journal in the United States, was started by Robert Walsh (1784–1859), son of an Irish immigrant. Walsh also edited the *American Register* (1817–1818), the *National Gazette* (1819–1836), and the *Magazine of Foreign Literature*. He served as American consul in Paris, 1845–1851.

1812–1815

During the war between the United States and Britain, a number of officers of Irish parentage played notable roles: Andrew Jackson, the victor of New Orleans, and later the president of the United States, was the son of County Antrim emigrants; the mother of Commodore Oliver H. Perry, victor of Lake Erie, was born in Newry, County Down; Commodore Thomas Macdonough, who defeated the British at Plattsburgh, was the grandson of John Macdonough, who came over from Kildare in 1730. In addition, Commodore John Shaw (1773–1823), who emigrated from Ireland in 1790, commanded the United States Naval Squadron in the Mediterranean during the war.

1814

Irish Emigrant Society was founded in New York City by Dr. Robert Hogan, president of the Friendly Sons of St. Patrick. Its purpose was to meet new arrivals from Ireland, protect them from being exploited by swindlers and boardinghouse keepers, and aid them in establishing themselves in America.

1815–1835

Great era of road and canal building in the United States, carried out largely by Irish labor drawn from the rising flow of immigrants.

(continued)

THE SHAMROCK;

OR,

HIBERNIAN CHRONICLE.

"FOSTERED UNDER THY WING, WE DIE IN THY DEFENCE."

VOL. I. NEW-YORK, SATURDAY, MAY 11, 1811. NO. 22.

THE SHAMROCK;

or, Hibernian Chronicle,
By EDWARD GILLESPY,
24 *William-street, nearly opposite the Post-Office.*

Is published every SATURDAY, at the price of three dollars per annum, payable half yearly, in advance.

Subscribers at a distance, who receive their papers by mail, are to be accountable for the postage thereof.

Subscriptions, Advertisements, and *Communications,* will be thankfully received and carefully attended to.

Rate of Advertising in the Shamrock.
For one advertisement not exceeding one square, first insertion, 4s. and every succeeding one 2s. and so in proportion for any number of squares.

In consequence of the extraordinary increase of subscribers, particularly from the interior of the country and from parts very remote, where the expense of going to collect would far exceed the annual subscription, we are obliged to adopt the following conditions. No paper can be forwarded to any part where there is not an agent appointed, unless *one year's advance* is forwarded free of postage. Where agents are or shall be appointed, 6 months advance will only be required.

AGENTS.

Mr. N. H Wright, Editor of the Whig, Newburyport (Ms.)
Mr. Patrick Mathews, Albany.
Mr. Michael Muldon, Hudson.
Mr. George Gordon, Newburgh.
Mr. John Gillespy, Philadelphia.
Mr. William D. Conway, 238 Market-street, Baltimore
Mr. John Hoff, bookseller, Charleston, S. C.
William Armstrong, jun esq. Romney, Virginia.
Mr John O. Lynch, Printer, Richmond, Virginia.
Daniel Redmond, esq. Post-Master, Tarborough, North Carolina.
Wm. W. Worsley, editor of the Reporter, Lexington, Kentucky.
John Kincaid, Esq. Alexandria, Columbia.
John D. Byrne, Esq Canajoharry, Montgomery County, New-York.
Mr. Thomas Orr, Chillicothe. Ohio.
Mr. James Mac Clary, Washington City and Georgetown.
Charles Kenny, Esq. Westchester, P.

⁂ *We entreat our friends at a distance not to put us to the expense of postage, as our profits cannot possibly bear it—We shall forward our paper to such as comply with this request, but discontinue it after the second paper is sent, unless the advance is remitted free of expense.*

☞ The Editor of the Shamrock begs leave to inform his countrymen arriving in the United States, and those already resident here, who wish to find out the residence of their friends, that he will insert the substance of their inquiries in the form of advertisements, at a very small expense, by applying either personally, at the office, or by letter post paid,—but, no attention will be paid to such inquiries, or the answers thereto, which will subject him to any expense—the names of passengers arriving, will always be inserted as an article of news.

EMIGRANTS OFFICE.

To Proprietors of Vacant Lands.

The Editor of the Shamrock in order to render every possible service to his native countrymen on their arrival at the port of New-York, and to facilitate their immediate settlement in this country, informs the proprietors of vacant lands, that he has opened a book where a full and minute description of lands for sale may be registered, at a very trifling expense. The advantages resulting to proprietors will be, that on the arrival of emigrants, the book will be exposed to them, and the general and local advantages of the several lands clearly pointed out. Maps will be also taken charge of and exhibited, and persons wishing to purchase, referred to the proprietors or their agents, so that no commission on sales at this office will be incurred by either party—a wish to serve those from his native country, and promote the population, and consequently add to the strength and protection of our beloved adopted country, being the principal object.

The exertions of the Catholics of Ireland to attain the same rank, and possess the same privileges as their Protestant brethren, has excited considerable agitation in the public mind. So large a mass as near five millions of a brave people, degraded below their fellow men, in the centre of an enlightened world, ought to be a matter of serious concern to the votaries of liberty. How far the complaints of that great body may be considered well founded, will appear from the following statement of the political and civil disabilities of the Catholics. But these are not all. There are many other heavy grievances experienced alike by the Protestant desenter and Catholic, of which they all appear now to be truly sensible. A common calamity has excited a common sympathy, and it is gratifying to learn, that religious distinctions, in a *political* sense, are gradually dwindling away. When this hideous monster of division, which was let loose by their task-masters disappears, we shall then behold the sun of Irish liberty rising in splendor. The good sense of Irishmen can accomplish this WITHOUT ARMS.

Mr. O'Connel's calculation, of the number of public situations from which persons professing the Roman Catholic religion, are excluded.

The first thing that offered itself was the Parliament. From seats in both houses the Catholics were excluded, amounting to 900.

Next came the offices in Corporation. We are in Dublin excluded from the offices of

Lord Mayor and Aldermen	24
Sheriffs and Sub Sheriffs	3
Sheriffs Peers	38
Common Council	96
Recorder	1
Treasurer	1
Town Clerks	2
Masters and Wardens of Guilds	78
	245

There are, I think, 86 other corporate cities and towns in Ireland, which, at the low average rate of 32 officers in each from which Catholics are by law excluded,

Amount to	2840

Giving a total, under positive exclusion, of 3083

But, if a more accurate view of the other offices in the gift of the corporations, or confined to them, be taken, it will be found that Catholics are, by the spirit and operation of the law, if not by the letter of it, excluded from those latter offices—as, for example, in Dublin :—

President of the Court of Conscience, his Secretary and Clerk, (worth 2000*l* per annum)	3
Lord Mayor's Secretary	1
Police Justices	12
Their Secretaries and Clerks	12
City officers, as Constables, Sword Bearer, &c. (*See Red Book*)	27
Cranes	4
Pipe Water Board	22
Public Money—Yards, &c.	3
Ballast Officers	16
Paving Board and Officers	13
Grand Jury, with *very very* few exceptions, and other public boards, offices, and clerks	50
	173
Add to these, similar offices in the other 86 Corporations of Ireland, averaged at only 22 to each—amounting to	1892
Total	2065

Thirdly—There are in the profession and administration of the Law Officers, from which we are directly excluded :

Lord Chancellor	1
Master of the Rolls	1
Law Judges	12
Serjeants	3
King's Counsel (now)	28
Masters in Chancery	4
Attorney and Solicitor-General	2
Counsel to the Commons	2
Chairman of Kilmainham	1
Sheriffs of Counties	32
Sub-Sheriffs	32
Advocates in the Spiritual Courts	20
Proctors in Dublin	9
Do in the Country	56
Law Officers in the Spiritual Courts—the jurisdiction of those Courts extend over temporal matters	100
Total	343

Add to those a number of officers under the patronage principally of the foregoing, which, although the profession of the law is most unequivocally liberal, yet Catholics are almost uniformly excluded from such as assistant Barristers of counties, assistant Counsel, Coroners, Law Clerks in the Law and Equity Offices in Counties—(*See Red Book,*)

Amounting at least to	700
Total	1043

The next class I shall mention is that of the officers in the army and navy. It is notorious that the Catholics contribute very largely in money and men, to those services.

The number of officers may be thus estimated. In the army the regiments are :

Life-Guards	2
Horse-Guards	1
Dragoon Guards	7
Dragoons	24
Foot Guards	3
Foot	101
Artillery	4
Irish Militia, from several of the Commissions in which Catholics are absolutely excluded	38
	180

Several of the regiments have 2, 3, or more battalions, so that the entire may be estimated at 200 battalions, and must contain 7500 commissioned officers, from which deduct 100 for Catholic officers in the Irish militia,

It will leave	7400

And it is quite manifest that the proportion of 100 Catholic officers in the Irish militia, is a great exaggeration.

Add the Paymasters, Commissariat Department the Staff, Storekeepers, Contractors, &c. &c. under the same patronage, amounting at least to	1600
Amounting in the entire to	9000

In the navy the officers may be thus estimated—there are in commission about 900 ships.

At a very moderate average, there are 10 officers to a ship, being	9000
Admirals, &c. about	200
Add the Dock-yard Establishments, the companies of Marines, the Pursers, and the other offices dependent on the Naval Departments, amounting to	3800
	13,000

There are other offices of trust, honour and emolument, from which the Catholics are excluded :

Lord Lieutenant	1
Lords of the Treasury	8
Governors of Counties (now)	38
Privy Counsellors, present number, including Duigenan	90
Fellows of Trinity College	23
Postmasters-General	2
Teller of the Exchequer	1
Chancellor of the Exchequer	1
Keeper of the Privy Seal	1
Vice-Treasurer	1
Auditor-General	6
Custodes Rutulorum	11
Secretary of State	1
Secretary to the Lord Lieutenant	2
	286

I am sure I can be reproached only with having too far diminished the dependent offices from which the Catholics are excluded under this head, when I state them

Only at	2000

Catholics are excluded from the following offices :—

	Directly.	Indirectly.
1st. Parliament	900	
2d, Corporations	3084	1829
3d. Law	349	700
4th, Army	5400	1600
5th, Navy	9200	3800
6th, Other offices enumerated	296	2000

Thus giving a total of offices from which Catholics are excluded, by positive enactment,

Of	21,167

And of offices from which they are almost with equal certainty excluded by the spirit and operation of the law,

Amounting to	9929
Amounting in the entire to	31096

Let it be recollected, that in giving this statement, we abstain altogether from the situations which belong of right to the Established Church—we should be sorry to see any similar law created for our clergy, and we most assuredly do not seek to disturb those that exist.

From the Belfast Magazine.

RETROSPECT OF POLITICS

For February.

As a subject of prime importance, we shall notice in the first place, the sentence passed in this month by the court of King's Bench in London, on Peter Finnerty, for a libel on Lord Castlereagh, by which he has been added to the list of those, who are now suffering a long imprisonment in several gaols in England. It may be recollected that in 1809, he accompanied the unfortunate expedition to Walcheren, for the purpose of publishing an account of the transactions there, but was sent home in consequence of orders transmitted from government. Suspecting that Lord Castlereagh had been the cause of this order being issued, on his return he published some severe observations on him, and to account for the minister's enmity towards the author, he adduced some instances of former conduct towards himself in Ireland, and reprobated Lord Castlereagh's general conduct while he was in office in this country, as secretary to the Earl of Camden, and the Marquis of Cornwallis. A prosecution for a libel was instituted against him, and finding he would not be permitted to bring forward the truth of the libel as a justification, he suffered judgment to go against him by default. The law of libel is founded on a curious fiction, that libels have a tendency to provoke to breaches of the peace. Hence arises the strange maxim, that the greater the truth, the greater the libel, and the consequent greater danger of the peace being broken, or as a woman once sarcastically and wittily observed; that a person with a red nose would feel greater anger on being reminded of that circumstance, than if she were conscious that the reproach did not apply to her.

On being brought up to receive sentence; Peter Finnerty adduced an affidavit comprising a number of others, which he had lately collected in Ireland, as to the conduct of Lord Castlereagh in 1797 and 1798, that as he was not allowed to justify, he might have those affidavits received in mitigation. But he was over-ruled by the court and sentenced to be imprisoned for 18 months in the gaol of Lincoln, and find security for his good behaviour for five years, himself in 500*l*, and two sureties in 250*l* each, and be further imprisoned, till that security be procured.

The attorney general in his speech in aggravation of punishment is stated to have asked, who is this Peter Finnerty, who sets himself up against Lord Castlereagh? Leaving this question to be answered by our readers; we will say that there are those who would prefer Peter Finnerty's feelings on the evening of the trial, and in his prison, to those of the prosecutor, smarting under the exposure, which the reading of those affidavits produced

"And more true joy exil'd Marcellus feels,
Than Cæsar with a senate at his heels."

But do the people of Ireland, find that nothing more is due to their intrepid supporter, and the unfolder of former scenes than bare thanks? Governments do not so reward their advocates, and the people should be no less generous. A man dependent on his literary exertions, must forcibly feel that his means are lessened by imprisonment, and a generous country should solace "the prison hours," of those who risque much in vindication of liberty. On the Irish people, Peter Finnerty has strong claims, and we earnestly recommend to them liberality to subscribe to his support.—It is a debt of honour and of justice.

We may soon expect some decisive issue to the long protracted warfare in Portugal. What that issue will be, has been often foreboded in these retrospects, and the prospect certainly does not at present become any brighter. Poets, who have been proverbially characterised, as dealing in fiction, and who may seek to turn the efforts of their muse to some profit, may find themes of panegyric in the bravery of Irishmen, although they are suffering in an unvailing contest on a foreign shore, and may chant the praises of Lord Wellington, but these scenes require other reflections from the bards of freedom, while the politician will contemn, and the philanthropist will lament the unprofitable waste of blood and treasure, the sufferings of the actors, and the folly of the planners in such ruinous expeditions*. This sentiment of disapprobation of the measures adopted in Portugal, remains in full force, notwithstanding the praises put by the ministry into the speech of the Regent in favour "of the consummate prudence and perseverance of Lord Wellington."

The speech of the Regent announces a deficiency in the Irish revenue. This may be considered as a notice of fresh taxes to be shortly imposed. Since the union, the debt of Ireland has increased from 23 to 81 millions. Irish prodigality remains unchecked: the debt increases, and we are again to feel with diminished resources, and a bad trade,

* It is painful to perceive that poets, who erewhile have sweetly sung in the cause of liberty, should give room to fear that by falling in with the temper of the times they have turned, or are in danger of turning, apostates to the cause they once so virtuously espoused. If any such there should be, *the grave of liberty* would silently administer self-reproach, and in their own case they might write *an epitaph on the living.* May such see the danger in time, before they are further ensnared.

1816

Irish Emigrant Society opened an office on Nassau Street, New York City. Dr. William MacNeven organized this service to procure employment for the new wave of Irish refugees that followed the end of the wars in Europe and America.

Archibald Mellon, from County Tyrone, settled in Pennsylvania with his son Andrew, who married Rebecca Wauchop, also born in Ireland. Their grandson was Andrew Mellon (1855–1937), secretary of the treasury, 1921–1932, and ambassador to Britain, whose family remains prominent in industry, finance, and art patronage.

1817

The Irish Emigrant Society petitioned Congress to set aside public lands in Illinois to which new arrivals might go rather than remain in the "crowded and corrupting cities of the Eastern seaboard." Congress was asked to "sell land, on fourteen years' credit, to deserving Irishmen, who would serve as a frontier guard against marauding Indians." The petition was rejected by an 83 to 71 vote in the House of Representatives.

1818

Erin Benevolent Society was founded in St. Louis. St. Patrick's Day was first celebrated there by Irish immigrants on March 17, 1820.

1820–1830

During this decade some 50,000 Irish immigrants entered the United States.

1823–1829

Campaign for Catholic Emancipation in Ireland, led by Daniel O'Connell, won sympathy and support of the Irish in America.

1823

James Shields (1810–1879), a native of Tyrone, settled in Illinois. He served as a brigadier general in the Mexican War and held the same rank during the Civil War. In addition to serving as governor of the Oregon Territory in 1848, he was United States senator from Illinois, 1849–1855, from Minnesota, 1858–1859, and from Missouri, 1879—the only man ever to have represented three different states in the United States Senate.

Alexander T. Stewart (1803–1876) a native of Lisburn, County Antrim, who arrived in the United States in 1820, opened a small dry-goods shop in New York City that developed into the great retail store A. T. Stewart and Company.

1824

The National Gazette listed seven Irish Americans currently serving in the House of Representatives: Jeremiah O'Brien of Maine, George Cassaday of New Jersey, Samuel McKean of Pennsylvania, Louis McLane of Delaware, Henry Connor of North Carolina, Henry Conway of Arkansas, and Patrick Farrelly of Pennsylvania (who was born in Ireland). McKean and McLane later became United States senators, and the latter was secretary of state under President Jackson.

1824

John McLoughlin (1784–1857), whose father was born in Donegal, became chief factor for the Hudson's Bay Company at the fur-trading post of Fort George near the mouth of the Columbia River. In this capacity he ruled (until 1846) an area now occupied by Oregon, Washington, Northern California, Idaho, and adjacent portions of Nevada and Wyoming, as well as northwestern Canada as far as the Yukon.

1828

Two colonies of Irish immigrants were established in Texas, then a province of Mexico. James Power and James Hewitson brought 200 families to Refugio, and another 200 families settled at San Patricio under the leadership of John Mullen and Patrick McGloin.

The Friends of Ireland, an association supporting Daniel O'Connell's campaign for Irish Catholic Emancipation, was formed in New York under the presidency of Dr. William

A rare photograph of Philadelphia during the riots. This daguerreotype, taken by William and Frederick Langenheim on May 9, 1844, shows a crowd at Third and Dock streets, outside the Girard Bank, which was occupied by the military at the time.

MacNeven. Branches were established throughout the United States, and in Mexico, and large sums of money were collected and forwarded to Ireland to aid the "cause."

1830–1840

During this decade 540,000 immigrants entered the United States, of whom 44 percent were Irish. At this time the United States had a population of only 13 million.

1833

At this date there were an estimated 40,000 Irish-born residents of New York City.

1834

Anti-Catholic riot in Charlestown, Massachusetts, where an Ursuline Convent was burned. Growing anti-Catholic and antiforeign feeling in the United States was stimulated by increased Irish immigration and competition in the job market.

Charles O'Malley, a native of Mayo and fur trader on Mackinac Island, promoted a large-scale immigration of settlers from his native county into Michigan.

1835

Thomas Jefferson Rusk (1803–1857), son of an Irish immigrant stonemason, born in South Carolina, settled in Texas. In the following year he was a member of the convention that proclaimed Texas an independent republic. He served successively as secretary of war, commander in chief of the army, and chief justice of the supreme court. In 1845 he was president of the convention that voted for annexation to the United States, and, along with Sam Houston (also descended from Irish immigrants), he was one of this state's first United States senators.

1837

Edmund O'Callaghan (1797–1880), a native of Mallow, County Cork, settled in Albany and devoted himself to historical research. Among his writings: *A History of New Netherlands* (1846), *A Documentary History of New York* (1849–1851), *Documents Relative to the Colonial History of New York* (1853–1861).

Bond Street Riot in Boston, resulting from continued friction between Irish immigrants and "Yankees" who feared the growing numbers of the newcomers.

1840–1850

During this decade nearly 800,000 Irish immigrants entered the United States.

1841–1846

Campaign for Repeal of the Act of Union between Britain and Ireland, led by Daniel O'Connell (died 1847). O'Connell's insistence on nonviolence and his willingness to maintain an Anglo-Irish connection under the Crown alienated many Irish Americans and led to a divided attitude toward the Repeal movement in America.

1843

Anti-Irish nativism inspired formation of an "American Republican Party" pledged to securing a twenty-one-year-residence requirement for naturalization.

Art 5 Photo Philadelphia

1844

Anti-Catholic riots in Philadelphia. Irish neighborhoods invaded by nativist mobs: 30 killed, 150 wounded, 200 families burned out, 3 churches destroyed.

1845

The phrase "Manifest Destiny," as an embodiment of the American concept of expansion, was coined by John L. O'Sullivan, editor of the *Democratic Review*, 1836–1845. O'Sullivan, son of an immigrant, was one of the first Irish Americans to receive a diplomatic appointment, serving as minister to Portugal, 1854–1858. ◆

The Sale of
Indentured
Servants,
Described by
Dr. Williams,
an American
Colonist, to a
Committee of
the House of
Commons

BELFAST NEWS LETTER, MARCH 22, 1774

It appeared that a trade was carried on in human flesh between Pennsylvania and the province of Ulster. Such of the unhappy natives of that part of Ireland as cannot find employment at home, sell themselves to the masters of vessels, or persons coming from America to deal in that species of merchandise. When they are brought to Philadelphia . . . they are either sold aboard the vessel, or by public vendue, which sale on arrival there is public notice given of, either by handbill, or in the newspapers. They bring generally about fifteen pounds currency at market, are sold for the term of their indentures, which is from two to four years, and on its expiration, receive a suit of clothes, and implements of husbandry, consisting of a hoe, an axe, and a bill from their taskmasters. Several gentlemen in the committee expressed their abhorrence of such a barbarous traffic. . . . ◆

The Wild Geese

*J*ust as the Irish emigration to the newly independent United States was beginning, another epoch of Irish emigration was coming to an end. Just as the door was opening to what would become a great flood of Irish exiles into America, the door was closing on what had once been a steady stream of Irish exiles into Europe. The link is more than coincidental. It was precisely this long-established habit of leaving Ireland, of venturing forth into distant lands and unfamiliar societies that gave the Irish the courage and the confidence to embark for the New World. To an extent unparalleled among any other European people, the Irish had experience in emigration, and a record of notable successes abroad to inspire them. The story of this earlier emigration, of the "Wild Geese" who flew away from their homeland, deserves to be better known. In a very real sense, it is part of the history of the Irish in America.

The Irish have always been an inquisitive and venturesome race—witness the ninth-century German chronicler who wrote of "the Irish nation, with whom the custom of traveling into foreign parts is now become almost second nature." The flow of Irish refugees to the Continent began in the late sixteenth century and increased significantly in the seventeenth. Yet it was in the hundred years between the Treaty of Limerick and the collapse of the Old Regime that the greatest exodus took place, and it was in the eighteenth century that the Irish émigrés emerged as a distinct element in European society. During this span of three generations, the greater part of Ireland's natural leadership class lived in exile.

Why did Irishmen and -women leave their homeland in the eighteenth century? Loyalty to the Jacobite cause was the principal motive of the first wave of émigrés. In the conviction that they had lost several battles but not the war, the partisans of James II rallied on the Continent, constituting His Britannic Majesty's army in exile, preserving the red coat and English as the language of command even while passing temporarily into the service of their king's Bourbon allies. Down to mid-century the hope of a Stuart restoration continued to animate the Irish Catholic aristocracy and to attract fresh recruits—the so-called Wild Geese—who flew away to join those Irish Brigades abroad from which the Jacobite invasion army would be formed. To this motivation, the imposition of "antipopery" legislation at the turn of the century added a longing for religious freedom and individual opportunity. The Penal Laws imposed on the vast majority of the Irish population what Edmund Burke called "penalties and modes of inquisition not fit to be mentioned to ears that are organized to the chaste sounds of equity and justice." Catholics were forbidden to acquire land, vote, hold office, seek an education, engage in the professions (including that of arms), keep weapons, or even own a horse. Hence the clergy and the gentry were obliged to go abroad for schooling, and while many of the priests returned to risk imprisonment or martyrdom in the "Irish mission," there was little inducement for others to go home when they might fulfill their aspirations in another land. On the other hand, the Catholics of the towns who prospered in trade and industry—the only sphere left open to ambition at home—often did so through overseas contacts, and sent younger sons to promote the family's business interests on the Continent. These upper- and middle-class elements in the emigration were reinforced by the large number of discharged Jacobite soldiers and sailors who found humbler occupations in civilian life abroad.

Where did these exiles settle? The Irish colleges on the Continent, founded during the sixteenth and seventeenth centuries for the training of priests, provided the nuclei for the initial colonies. They included some thirty institutions, the more important being those at Douai, Alcala, Salamanca, Lisbon, Bordeaux, Paris, Santiago, Louvain, Lille, Rome, Madrid, Antwerp, Toulouse, Poitiers, and Nantes. In addition, the Irish Franciscan seminaries in Prague, Capranica, and Boulay in the Duchy of Lorraine were significant rallying points for the Irish abroad. Most of these, while essentially clerical in character, welcomed lay students for secondary or even advanced schooling. Although there were no specifically Irish religious houses for women overseas, there were numerous convents in France, Spain, and Belgium where a contingent of Irish nuns or the presence of an Irish abbess led them to welcome Irish girls, either as novices or as pupils. Irishmen seeking medical training congregated at the universities of Prague, Rouen, and Montpellier. The influx of Irish soldiers and sailors made the capitals and the principal garrison towns and seaports important rendezvous, and a "Street of the Irish" dating from this period can be found in Paris, Madrid, Prague, and several other cities. Certain commercial centers, especially those serving the seaborne trade, attracted large numbers of Irish merchants. Nantes and Bordeaux had the largest Irish communities, though Rouen and St. Malo received their share of settlers. In Spain, Seville and Cadiz were thronged with Irish exiles, while in Italy Naples and Parma drew Irish swordsmen and their families. The Belgian provinces, newly transferred from Spanish to Austrian rule, had their Irish colonies at Brussels and Antwerp. France was undoubtedly the favorite "new land" of Irish emi-

Of all the tricks which the Irish nation have played on the slow-witted Saxon, the most outrageous is the palming off on him of the imaginary Irishman of romance. The worst of it is that when a spurious type gets into literature, it strikes the imagination of boys and girls. They form themselves by playing up to it; and thus the unsubstantial fancies of the novelists and music-hall song-writers of one generation are apt to become the unpleasant and mischievous realities of the next.

George Bernard Shaw, *Essays* (1906)

grants—"the asylum of our poor fugitives," an Irish scholar wrote near the end of the century, "for seventy years past." But the establishment of a common dynasty in both France and Spain had put an end to the dilemma of earlier Irish refugees, who had been obliged to choose irrevocably between one or the other of the hostile Catholic powers. Now Spain, and the later Bourbon acquisitions of Naples and Parma, were linked to France in a "Family Compact," and the Irish moved freely and frequently among the civil and military services of the allied states. The Hapsburgs still claimed the allegiance of many Irishmen who were prepared to travel farther afield, while even in non-Catholic countries occasional Irish families were to be met with, such as the Lacys and O'Rourkes in Russia, the O'Reillys in Hessen-Kassel, and the O'Briens (O'Breens) in Holland.

What careers did the Irish on the Continent pursue? The British historian William Lecky provides some notable examples:

Lord Clare became Marshal of France; Browne, who was one of the very ablest Austrian generals, and who took a leading part in the first period of the Seven Years' War, was the son of Irish parents; and Maguire, Lacy, Nugent, and O'Donnell were all prominent generals in the Austrian service during the same war. Another Browne, a cousin of the Austrian commander, was Field Marshal in the Russian service and Governor of Riga. Peter Lacy, who also became a Russian Field Marshal and who earned the reputation of one of the first soldiers of his time, was of Irish birth. . . . He sprang from an Irish family which had the rare fortune of counting generals in the services . . . of Austria, Russia and Spain. Of the Dillons, more than one attained high rank in the French army, and one became Archbishop of Toulouse. The brave, the impetuous Lally of Tollendal, who served with such distinction at Dettingen and Fontenoy, and who for a time seriously threatened the English power in Hindustan, was the son of a Galway gentleman. Among Spanish generals, the names of O'Mahony, O'Donnell, O'Gara, O'Reilly and O'Neil sufficiently attest their nationality. . . . Wall, who directed the government of Spain with singular ability from 1754 to 1763, was an Irishman. . . . By parentage MacGeoghegan, the first considerable historian of Ireland, was chaplain to the Irish Brigade in the service of France. The physician of Sobieski, King of Poland, and the physician of Philip V of Spain were both Irish; an Irish naturalist named Bowles was active in reviving the mining industry of Spain in 1752. . . . In the diplomacy of the Continent Irish names are not unknown. Tyrconnel was French Ambassador at the Court of Berlin. Wall, before he became chief minister of Spain, had represented that country at the Court of London. Lacy was Spanish ambassador at Stockholm, and O'Mahony at Vienna.

THE THREE SHARPEST THINGS OF ALL—A THORN IN MIRE, A HOUND'S TOOTH, AND A FOOL'S RETORT.
Traditional Irish Proverb

Service in the armed forces of the Continental princes was undoubtedly the route by which the majority of Irishmen made the transition from the old country to the new. Even after the massive reduction in troop strength following the Treaty of Utrecht, France retained five regiments in its Irish Brigade and Spain three, with a fourth Spanish regiment transferring to the Neapolitan establishment in 1740. Although there were no Irish units as such in the Austrian forces, hundreds of Irish officers held commissions under the emperor. In all of these realms, the profession of arms, to which the Irish gentry turned almost instinctively, was the avenue to the titles and rewards, civil as well as military, that their religion denied them at home. Of the fifty-four patents of nobility conferred upon Irishmen in France down to the Revolution, the majority were earned by military or naval prowess, and the record is comparable elsewhere. Count Taaffe, chancellor to the duke of Lorraine, Count Wall, foreign minister to the king of Spain, and Baron O'Connell, chamberlain to the Holy Roman Emperor, among other statesmen, all started out as fighting men. For other ranks, the evidence is less abundant. Many enlisted men seem to have spent their entire working lives in the army or navy and to have raised their sons to follow in their footsteps. Others, procuring their discharge, turned to a variety of trades, though two commoners who emerge from historical obscurity were both shoemakers: Joseph Kavanagh, a leader of the attack on the Bastille (where two of the seven prisoners were Irishmen) and later a police inspector under the Terror, and Daniel Murphy, whose daughter, Marie Louise, became mistress of Louis XV and mother of an Irish-Bourbon daughter.

The merchants and bankers of the great Continental seaports also formed an important component of the Irish abroad. From the time of the early confiscations, many of the dispossessed Catholic landowners drifted into the cities and towns of Ireland and there applied themselves to trade. The mercantile element in Ireland was thus in part composed of families having ties to the Catholic landed gentry and to the émigré families abroad. These merchants, in turn, often found it expedient to send younger sons to the Continent, not to be soldiers but to be businessmen. The Blakes of Seville, the Coppingers of Bordeaux, and the Fitzgibbons, Kellys, and Moores who settled at Lisbon, Bilbao, and Alicante were all branches of this Irish mercantile elite. Certain fields of business in particular seem to have attracted the Irish: in Spain the Wisemans of Seville, the O'Neales of Jerez, and the Lynches of Cadiz were wine merchants, and in France the Byrnes and O'Quinns of Bordeaux followed a similar trade, while Richard Hennessy founded the distillery in Cognac that still bears his name. Both Anthony Walsh of Nantes and Walter Rutledge of Dunkirk became wealthy from West Indies privateering, and the Clarkes and Shiels of Nantes were great shipowners as well, operating half the vessels of that port engaged in the lucrative slave trade. As early as 1718, Irish shipowners in the Low Countries took a leading part in planning the Ostend East India Company, and the advice of men like Count O'Gara of Brussels and General Plunkett, governor of Antwerp,

MAY YOU HAVE NICER LEGS THAN YOUR OWN UNDER THE TABLE BEFORE THE NEW SPUDS ARE UP.
Traditional Irish Toast

One wonders if by the year 2000 Jews will have forgotten Hitler's extermination camps. That the rest of the world wants to forget is understandable, but that the Jews would let them forget it seems very unlikely. Yet the Irish have cooperated, one might almost say enthusiastically, in blotting out the memory of the Great Famine. Perhaps it is too horrible to remember; perhaps we were so eager to become Americans that we quickly shed the memories of a non-American past; perhaps we so wanted to prove ourselves capable of respectability that we thought

was eagerly welcomed by the Hapsburgs. Throughout the eighteenth century many Irish families were involved in banking in France, including the Quains, Woulfes, Darcys, and Arthurs; George Waters of Paris was the confidential agent and banker of the Stuarts and the chief financial supporter of the Jacobite Rising in 1745.

During the Penal Era, and in defiance of the prohibitions against seeking education abroad, the Catholic clergy of Ireland received its training on the Continent. Each year, graduates of the Irish colleges would return to their native land via the same clandestine route by which they had left it. Fully half the priests of eighteenth-century Ireland were educated in France, with Spain, Portugal, and the Low Countries providing most of the rest; even the college of far-away Prague produced 115 alumni (including two future bishops) in the last three decades before the anticlerical Joseph II closed it in 1783. A considerable number of Irish students, however, did not return to Ireland—at least, immediately—finding positions as chaplains in noble households or in the armed forces. Others settled down to parish or monastic life, or found a niche in the Continental hierarchy. Most notable among these prelates was the Franco-Irish ecclesiastical magnate Arthur Richard Dillon, who became, successively, bishop of Evreux, archbishop of Toulouse and of Narbonne, and president of the states of Languedoc, France's largest province. Irishmen in the influential office of vicar general, such as Abbé Kearney at Tarbes and Abbé Walsh at Clermont, were not uncommon. Perhaps the most remarkable ecclesiastical career was that of Patrick Curtis, educated in Spain and a chaplain in her navy during the American Revolutionary War, then rector of the Irish College of Salamanca and royal professor of philosophy and astronomy at the university there, a friend and helper of the duke of Wellington (a fellow Dubliner) during the Peninsular War, and then, after an absence of nearly sixty years, appointed archbishop of Armagh and primate of Ireland in time to take an active role in the Catholic Emancipation campaign of the 1820s.

Irishmen distinguished themselves in a variety of professions, particularly medicine: Philip V of Spain and his successor had Irish physicians, as did Louis XIV, XV, and XVI. Dr. John MacMahon, a native of Limerick and graduate of the faculty of medicine at Rouen, acquired the title of Marquis d'Eguilly and founded a line that included a son who served as ambassador to the United States and a grandson who became president of France. Irish scholars in France and Spain attained distinction in the more controversial aspects of philosophy and theology, both as university professors and as writers. While Dr. Brady of Lisbon and Dr. Birmingham of Salamanca were credited with reviving Greek studies in Iberia, Richard Cantillon, the Paris banker from Ballyheigue, author of the "Essai sur la nature du commerce en général" has been called "the father of political economy," and Bernard Ward, economic reformer and minister of commerce, was one of the outstanding figures of the Spanish

Enlightenment. The economist Ward belonged to a dazzling constellation of Irishmen who strove to achieve administrative and fiscal modernization in Spain. It included William Bowles, geologist, naturalist, and royal counselor, Alfonso O'Crouley, geographer and historian, Bernardo O'Connor, governor of Barcelona and initiator of social reform, Count Lacy, diplomat and patron of scientists, and the indefatigable Dr. Timoteo O'Scanlan, who introduced vaccination into the country.

To what degree did the Irish on the Continent retain their distinctive identity? Although there was no bar to Irish integration into the host nationalities, and despite the fact that a sizable minority married outside their own community, the majority of eighteenth-century Irish émigrés seem to have remained firmly committed to a distinctive identity. Congregating in certain cities, marrying their compatriots, and attending by preference their own churches and schools, they remained a breed apart. Even when traveling on the Continent, the Irish liked to break their journeys at the homes of kinsmen, or at least fellow Irishmen. Some comfortably situated exiles, such as the Abbé Griffin, canon of the Cathedral of Cambrai, provided what amounted to a hotel and mail-forwarding service for their wandering brethren. The affluent followed the practice of providing burses, or scholarships, at the Continental colleges for Irish students, sometimes limiting them to particular clans or particular native countries. In many families it was customary to send expectant mothers back to Ireland so that children might be born in the old country though they would be brought up in the new home. Some families preserved distinctively Irish given names through the generations, as did the Kindelans in Spain, who have honored their patron, St. Ultan, by christening the eldest son Ultano down to the present. The Continental Irish customarily used English within their own community, and were regularly employed as interpreters, intelligence officers, and envoys during the wars and negotiations of the era. Major O'Reilly of the Hessian army, for instance, acted as provost marshal of New York during the British occupation, because he could communicate with equal facility with British and German troops; General O'Donoju served as Spanish liaison officer with Wellington during the Peninsular War. Most families also passed on a knowledge of Gaelic to the younger generation: the six O'Donnell brothers, who won distinction in the Napoleonic struggle, though born in Spain were all fluent Gaelic-speakers. The ancestral tongue was used in everyday conversation by the rank and file of the Irish Brigades, at least through midcentury.

The most striking manifestation of Irish identity and solidarity on the Continent is their invariable determination to look after their own. Irish officers made frequent trips to the homeland to reinforce the depleted ranks of their regiments. (Those in the service of the Bourbon princes, who were usually at war with Britain, did so secretly, and at peril of their lives; neutral and friendly states, like Austria, were gen-

it expedient to dismiss the injustices which had been visited upon our predecessors. Maybe part of the price of acceptance into the American society was that we forget the past. In any case, we have forgotten it. . . . ❥

Andrew Greeley, *The Most Distressful Country* (1973)

erally given tacit permission to seek volunteers.) In seeking out and sponsoring cadets of Catholic gentry stock, some senior officers, like Count Daniel O'Connell of the French army, were virtual one-man recruiting bureaus, and O'Connell's concern for the advancement of his kinsmen and fellow Kerrymen were characteristic of the Irish abroad. Well-placed Irishmen in the military, in government, and in business were ever alert to procure places and opportunities for their brethren. Ambrose O'Higgins, for instance, who came to Spain originally as an apprentice in a banking house, procured a commission in the royal engineers through the influence of Colonel John Garland, who also got him started on a career in South America that culminated in his becoming viceroy of Peru, the highest-ranking position in the colonial service. O'Higgins, in turn, brought his nephews over from Ireland and appointed them to provincial governorships and military commands; his son, Bernardo, became the founder of the Chilean Republic.

Florida was another happy hunting ground for Irishmen in search of advancement: the Hibernia Regiment captured Pensacola in 1782, its colonel, Arturo O'Neill, was appointed governor, and four other Wild Geese ruled East and West Florida in succession. American frontier provinces were usually placed under the direction of army officers, and the Irish in Madrid proved adept at securing these governorships for kinsmen such as Hugh O'Connor in Texas, Philip Barry in Nueva Vizcaya, and Charles Murphy in Paraguay.

The Irish, for all their demonstrated loyalty to their adopted countries, clearly preferred to have their own kind about them, and to fill up the jobs at their disposal with their relatives. Nepotism was deemed a virtue. Colonel Henry O'Shea, for example, military secretary to the duke of Orleans, procured a commission for his nephew, Henry Clarke, from the duke and the latter acted as the young man's patron until the Revolution, during which Clarke became successively a general, minister of war, and duke of Feltre in the imperial nobility; Clarke, in his turn, obtained for his nephew, Andrew Elliott, a colonelcy and the post of aide-de-camp to Bonaparte. Regimental commands in the Irish Brigades were handed down from father to son, and choice commissions were reserved for the colonel's clansmen—whence the numerous generals and colonels bearing the surnames of such powerful houses as Dillon and Walsh. The large number of admirals and naval bureaucrats named MacNamara in France and MacDonnell in Spain testifies to the prevalence of similar practices in the sister service. The existence of virtual dynasties like the Comyns and O'Reillys in medicine and the houses of Cantillon and Waters in banking confirms that the system was followed in civilian circles as well. Nor were national boundaries a consideration: the influence of Wall and O'Reilly in Spain secured the importation of the Irish economists Ward and Bowles from France; John Vincent Dillon, of the Neapolitan branch of that family, transferred to the French army as chief

HE WHO CAN FOLLOW HIS OWN WILL IS A KING.
Traditional Irish Proverb

engineer for the construction of the Seine bridges. Many officers moved through three or four different countries in search of advancement, usually following the summons of some relative or friend who had paved the way for them. A network of communication and collaboration extended across the Continent—one almost expects to find complaints about an "international Irish conspiracy."

The Irish abroad, then, preserved a vigorous social self-consciousness. But what was their attitude toward Ireland itself? Among the exiles as a whole, the preservation of tradition was supplemented by correspondence and visits, often clandestine, through which they maintained their ties with those left behind and with the scenes of their youth. Not infrequently youngsters born abroad were sent for a brief sojourn with kinsfolk in Ireland, and there are many instances of foreign-born Irish who had reached maturity without making such a trip seeking the opportunity "as the Muslim yearns for Mecca." News from Ireland was closely followed through the press and through private informants. Erin's past, present, and future were matters of interest and concern. Literary men among the overseas Irish demonstrated their preoccupation with such volumes as *The History of Ireland, Ancient and Modern* by the Abbé MacGeoghegan, *The Elements of the Irish Language* by Hugh MacCurtin (who also published an Irish-English dictionary and a book on the antiquities of Ireland), *Nomenclatura Hibernica* by Hervy Morres, and the Marquis de Lally-Tollendal's *Tuathal-Teamar, or the Restoration of the Monarchy in Ireland*. On a different level, there were gatherings of the sort described in the *Annual Register* under the heading for March 1767:

On the 17th of this month his Excellency, Count Mahony, Ambassador from Spain to the Court of Vienna, gave a grand entertainment in honour of St. Patrick, to which were invited persons of condition, that were of Irish descent; being himself a descendant of an illustrious family of that kingdom. Among many others were present Count Lacy, President of the Council of War, the Generals O'Donnel, McGuire, O'Kelly, Browne, Plunket and McEligot, 4 Chiefs of the Grand Cross, 2 Governors, several Knights Military, 6 staff officers, 4 Privy Councillors, with the principal officers of state; who, to show their respect for the Irish nation, wore crosses in honour of the day, as did the whole Court.

For some exiles there was a lasting bitterness, a desire for revenge: General O'Reilly longed to lead a Spanish invasion army to Ireland and strike down the Protestant cousins who had usurped his patrimony; exiles in France produced invasion plans each time during the century that France went to war with England. For others, there was the hope that an enlightened toleration might prevail, and that one day they or their children might be accorded the full rights of free men, so that they could return to Ireland and live as contented and loyal subjects.

The second half of the eighteenth century was a time of change for

MAY YOUR DOCTOR NEVER EARN A DOLLAR OUT OF YOU AND MAY YOUR HEART NEVER GIVE OUT. MAY THE TEN TOES OF YOUR FEET STEER YOU CLEAR OF ALL MISFORTUNE, AND, BEFORE YOU'RE MUCH OLDER, MAY YOU HEAR MUCH BETTER TOASTS THAN THIS.
Traditional Irish Toast

the Irish communities abroad. Following the Jacobite disaster at Culloden (where a contingent of the Franco-Irish Brigade stood and died covering the retreat of Prince Charles Edward), the prospects of a Stuart restoration languished, and the unifying force that the dynasty represented faded away. On the death of James III in 1766, the Pope refused to recognize his son as king, and the appointments to Irish episcopal sees, which had hitherto been made on the nomination of the pretender, became a purely papal concern. The frustrated and increasingly dissolute Prince Charlie ceased to extend the patronage that his father had always granted the Irish exiles, and gradually lost their loyalty and even their interest. The decline of Jacobitism was paralleled by a falling off of recruiting in Ireland. The unjust condemnation and execution of the Irish hero Count Lally, after his defeat in India, was a further blow to morale, and even his posthumous rehabilitation—won by his son with Voltaire's crusading aid—did not cancel out the impression of royal ingratitude, or restore the flow of recruits. The Irish Brigades of France and Spain were presently filled up by a rank and file who were predominantly non-Irish, though the officers remained Irish-born or -descended. During these years the growing disinclination of the Irish peasantry to enlist for foreign service, and a tendency of the lower social class to integrate more readily and more thoroughly into the host population, served to emphasize the elite character of the Irish communities abroad. Irishmen continued to seek their fortunes on the Continent, but they were usually young gentlemen who expected direct commissions or "junior executive" status.

The year 1793 brought two developments that proved decisive for the fate of the Irish on the Continent—the downfall of the French monarchy and the passage of the Catholic Relief Bill. The former led to a general European war and two decades of political anarchy. The latter opened a wide range of civil and military offices to the Irish Catholic gentry and permitted them to carve out careers in their own country.

Most of the Irish in France remained loyal to the unfortunate Louis XVI—indeed, it was the Abbé Henry Edgeworth who gave him the last consolations of religion on the scaffold—and they frequently paid the supreme penalty for their identification with the Bourbons. The abolition of the Irish Brigade as "the mercenary instrument of monarchical tyranny" drove many Franco-Irish officers into a new exile. Some, like Count Daniel O'Connell or Colonel Edward Stack, who had fought against George III in the American War, now received commissions from a belatedly tolerant British government and raised regiments among the Catholics of Ireland to fight for the same king. Others, like Colonel Brian O'Toole, who commanded successively Germans, Corsicans, and Portuguese, drifted from one country to another. Those Irish generals who tried to survive the transition to a French Republic were regarded with suspicion: "He is an Irishman," wrote a police official about one victim of the Terror, "and they can't get Republicanism into their skulls."

'TIS A VERY GOOD STORY THAT FILLS THE BELLY.
Traditional Irish Proverb

Ward, O'Moran, and Arthur Dillon all died under the guillotine's blade, Theobald Dillon was murdered by his own troops, and Admiral Henry MacNamara was lynched by a mob. But some younger men, like Harty, Kilmaine, Blackwell, and the O'Meara brothers, flourished with the New Order; Robert Arthur, Jacobin and member of the Commune, won the nickname of "Little Robespierre"; and Jean Baptiste O'Sullivan conscientiously inflicted his own Reign of Terror upon Nantes.

Spain, too, was divided by the spreading revolution, with General O'Donoju heading the loyalist War Ministry at Cadiz while General O'Farril served King Joseph Bonaparte as war minister at Madrid—the one supported by Irishmen like Generals Blake and Sarsfield, the other by men like General Vincent Kindelan. Some, like General Luis de Lacy, fought in turn on both sides. Similar dislocation beset the Irish in Italy and the Low Countries. Like many other European institutions, the Irish "nation in exile" was shattered by the earthquake of Revolution.

For the Continental Irish, a way of life had come to an end. The abolition of foreign regiments in one country after another ended their distinctive military role, and while many families continued to follow the profession of arms during the nineteenth century, they did so as individuals, without the old esprit de corps. The Irish radicals who fled to France after the collapse of the French-sponsored Irish rebellion in 1798 were never really accepted by the surviving old-regime families, and for the most part did not mingle with them. The growth of opportunities for the Catholic gentry at home, especially after Emancipation in 1829 removed the remaining disabilities, made emigration unnecessary, while for the poorer classes the gold-paved streets of the United States and the dominions proved more enticing. Maynooth now provided the priests for the Irish Catholic Church. Mercantile ties with the Continent were not renewed after the war. Without the stimulus of new arrivals and the inspiration of unfulfilled dreams, the Irish on the Continent gradually lost their identity, marrying outside their nationality group, spreading beyond their traditional centers, abandoning their cultural heritage and both their languages. In time they became merely Frenchmen, Spaniards, or Austrians with incongruous last names, having little notion of what brought their ancestors to alien shores and sustained them in their adversity.

The Wild Geese never returned to liberate Ireland, as the poets had prophesied. Yet they played a vital role in the history of the Irish people. At a time when the Irish at home were economically degraded and politically oppressed, there was scarcely a Catholic country in Europe where the Irish exiles or their children might not be found in posts of dignity and power. The Irish abroad inspired pride and hope among those who remained behind. And when the great new land of opportunity in the West beckoned, they set forth in the bold spirit of the Wild Geese, to build a better life for themselves beyond the seas. ◆

Although it may appear extravagant, it is nevertheless a serious truth, that a large portion even of those who pride themselves on their literary acquirements are as ignorant of the affairs of Ireland as they are of the affairs of the Arabians or the Japanese.

Mathew Carey,
*Vindicae Hibernicae;
or Ireland Vindicated*
(1819)

The Glorious Victory of Seven Irishmen, Over the Kidnappers of New-York

All you that love the shamrock green attend both young and old,
I feel it is my duty those lines for to unfold,
Concerning those young emigrants that lately sailed away,
To seek a better livelihood all in America.
On the 18th day of April their gallant ship did sail,
With 55 young Irishmen, true sons of Granuaile,
They landed safe all in New York on the 19th of May,
To meet their friends and relatives all in America.

Some of them met acquaintances as soon as they did land,
With flowing bumpers drank a health to poor old Paddy's land,
Though many of them had no friends their hearts were stout and bold,
And by those cursed Yankees they would not be controlled;
As seven of those Irishmen were going thro' George's-street,
One of those Yankee gentlemen they happened for to meet,
He promised them employment in a brickyard near the town,
To which they were conducted their names for to take down.

He brought them to an ale-house and called for drink galore,
I'm sure such entertainment they never got before,
But when he thought he had them drunk then to them he did say,
You're listed now as soldiers to defend our country;
They looked at one another and then to him did say,
It's not to list that we did come unto America,
But to labour for a livelihood as many done before,
That we have emigrated from the lovely shamrock shore.

Twelve Yankees in soldier's dress came in without delay,
And said my boys you must prepare with us to come away,
This is one of our officers he listed you complete,
You need not strive for to resist we will no longer wait;
The Irish blood began to rise one of those heroes said,
We only have one life to lose therefore we're not afraid,
Although we are from Ireland this day we'll let you see,
We'll die like sons of Granuaile or keep our liberty.

Our Irish boys got to their feet, which made the Yankees frown,
As fast as they could strike a blow they knock'd the soldiers down,
The officer and all his men they left them in crimson gore,
They proved themselves Saint Patrick's sons throughout Columbia shore;
A Frenchman of great fame that seen what they did do,
He says I will protect you from those Yankee crimping crew,
I'll bring you to Ohio where I have authority,
And keep you in my service while you're in this country.

You'd think it was a slaughter-house where the Yankees lay,
The officer and all his men on carts were drawn away,
With bloody heads and broken bones they'll mind it evermore,
The spring of sweet shillelagh that was brought from Erin's shore;
Before I do conclude those lines let young and old unite,
To offer up a fervent prayer both morning, noon and night,
In hopes the Lord he will protect our friends that's away,
And keep them from all danger while in America. ◆

The Emigrant's Farewell

Farewell, dear Erin, I now must leave you,
And cross the seas to a foreign clime,
Farewell to friends and to kind relations
And to my aged parents I left behind.
My heart is breaking all for to leave you,
Where I've spent many a happy day,
With lads and lasses and sparkling glasses,
But now I'm bound for America.

Farewell green hills and sweet lovely valleys,
Where with my love I did often rove,
And fondly told her I ne'er would leave her,
Whilst walking thro' each silent grove.
But I must leave you my charming Mary,
Was fortune kind sure at home I'd stay,
So do not mourn for I'll soon return,
And bring you off to America.

Oh lovely Willy, now do not leave me.
I love you dearly, right well you know.
Pray do not stray to a foreign nation,
Or leave me here, love, in grief and woe.
I know right well that the times are changed
Which causes thousands to go away,
But if you wait until the next season
We'll both sail over to America.

My love, I'm bound for a foreign nation,
If the lord be pleased to bring me o'er,
To seek promotion and look for labour
Since all things failed on the Shamrock shore.
But if you have patience—if fortune favors
To crown my labours, believe what I say,
I will come, love, with gold in store,
And bring you over to America.

When I am rolling upon the ocean,
Sweet Mary dear, you will run in my mind,
So do not mourn for I will return,
If you prove constant, love, I'll prove kind.
I pray have patience, my charming Mary,
Farewell, adieu, now I must away.
I do intend it, let none prevent it,
To seek adventures in America.

Unknown to parents, friends and relations,
My dearest Willy, with you I'll roam,
For I have plenty to bring us over,
As you won't consent, love, to stay at home.
He then consented—straightway they went
And they got married without delay,
Full fifty pounds there she did lay down,
Saying our joys we'll crown in America. ◆

Emigrants from Ireland to the United States During the Nineteenth Century

*A*side from the years 1800–1802, when a brief interval of peace and a simultaneous decline in the Ulster linen industry combined to stimulate an annual emigration of about 6,000, relatively few Irish came to the United States during the Napoleonic Wars, and practically none from 1812 to 1814, when Britain and the United States were at war with one another. There were approximately 1,500 emigrants to the United States in 1815, and increasingly large numbers during the next five years. Reasonably accurate (though by no means definitive) figures are available from 1820 on.

1820	3,614	1841	36,428	1862	33,521	1883	82,849
1821	1,518	1842	49,920	1863	94,477	1884	59,204
1822	2,267	1843	23,597	1864	94,368	1885	50,657
1823	1,908	1844	37,569	1865	82,085	1886	52,858
1824	2,345	1845	50,207	1866	86,594	1887	69,084
1825	4,826	1846	68,023	1867	79,571	1888	66,306
1826	4,821	1847	118,120	1868	57,662	1889	60,502
1827	9,772	1848	151,003	1869	66,467	1890	52,110
1828	7,861	1849	180,189	1870	67,891	1891	53,438
1829	9,995	1850	184,351	1871	65,591	1892	48,966
1830	12,765	1851	219,232	1872	66,752	1893	42,122
1831	13,598	1852	195,801	1873	75,536	1894	39,597
1832	15,092	1853	156,970	1874	48,136	1895	52,027
1833	14,177	1854	11,095	1875	31,433	1896	39,952
1834	16,928	1855	57,164	1876	16,432	1897	32,822
1835	13,307	1856	58,777	1877	13,991	1898	30,878
1836	15,000	1857	66,080	1878	18,602	1899	38,631
1837	22,089	1858	31,498	1879	30,058	1900	41,848
1838	8,149	1859	41,180	1880	83,018	1901	35,535
1839	20,790	1860	52,103	1881	67,339		
1840	25,957	1861	28,209	1882	68,300		

NOTE: Figures do not include Irishmen entering the United States from Great Britain, who formed a significant proportion of the "British" listings in U.S. immigration records, or those who entered (legally or illegally) through Canada.

Famine

During the Hungry Forties, hundreds of thousands of refugees crossed the Atlantic to escape a situation described with quiet intensity in the following essay. It appeared in the Dublin University Magazine *in April 1847, and was written by Isaac Butt, who in later years became leader of the Home Rule movement. The "calamity" of which Butt speaks marks a watershed not only in the history of Ireland but in the history of Irish America.*

Ireland is now, in one sense, in the midst, in another sense, we fear, in the beginning of a calamity, the like of which the world has never seen. Four millions of people, the majority of whom were always upon the verge of utter destitution, have been suddenly deprived of the sole article of their ordinary food. Without any of the ordinary channels of commercial intercourse, by which such a loss could be supplied, the country has had no means of replacing the withdrawal of this perished subsistence, and the consequence has been, that in a country that is called civilized, under the protection of the mightiest monarchy upon earth, and almost within a day's commmunication of the capital of the greatest and richest empire in the world, thousands of our fellow-creatures are each day dying of starvation, and the wasted corpses of many left unburied in their miserable hovels, to be devoured by the hungry swine; or to escape this profanation, only to diffuse among the living the malaria of pestilence and death.

As we proceed, we trust it will be seen that we have no inclination either to exaggerate or unnecessarily to alarm; but it were criminal to disguise the extent of the calamity, or to shrink from telling all the hideous truth. We must presume that there are none of our readers to whom the evidences upon which this statement rests are not familiar, in the appalling narratives that have filled the journals of the empire for the last few months. It is long since the coroners gave over in despair the task of holding inquests upon the bodies of those whom starvation had stricken down. Our journals have become unable to record, our people to communicate, the deaths which in some districts result from insufficient food. "Death by starvation" has ceased to be an article of news, and day by day multitudes of our population are swept down into the pit—literally into the pit—in which the victims of the famine are interred.

We will not take up our space by repeating the testimonies, which prove incontestably that this is no exaggeration. It is not, perhaps, the least appalling feature of this calamity, that it is difficult, if not impossible, to obtain accurate information upon the extent of devastation that has already taken place. Nearly a month ago the deaths that had resulted in one shape or other from starvation were estimated at 240,000. Long before the same period, the deaths that were occurring each day in Ireland beyond those of the same period in the preceding year, were estimated at 1,000—1,000 each day—a number we apprehend below the truth. In many of the workhouses deaths occurred in numbers that would lead to a much greater estimate of the loss of life in the entire country. In one electoral poor-law division of the county Cork—one not within the fatal district of Schull or Skibbereen—out of a population of 16,000, the deaths in the early part of March were averaging 70 a day, a rate of mortality that would sweep away the entire population in about eight months. There are parts of Mayo, Galway, and Sligo, in which the deaths were nearly in the same proportion. It is impossible, however, to form more than an approximation to the real extent of the calamity. . . .

In the autumn of 1845, it was discovered that a disease had attacked the potato in Ireland, and in several other parts of the world. Of the actual existence of such a dis-

SEARCHING FOR POTATOES IN A STUBBLE FIELD.

ease there was no doubt. Its extent was, like most questions in Ireland, made a party one—and, we grieve to say, the Tory party were in the wrong. Some of the journals in Ireland, supposed most to represent the aristocracy, persisted in vigorously denying the existence of any failure to more than a very partial extent. The question of the corn laws, then pending, gave this question an imperial interest. The potato famine in Ireland was represented as the invention of the agitators on either side of the water. So far was party feeling carried, that the conservative mayor of Liverpool, honestly, we are sure, refused to convene a meeting for the relief of Irish distress. A committee which sat at the Mansion House, in Dublin, and first declared their belief in the approach of an overwhelming calamity, were stigmatised as deluding the public with a false alarm. Men's politics determined their belief. To profess belief in the fact of the existence of a formidable potato blight, was as sure a method of being branded as a radical, as to propose to destroy the Church.

Thus in the very outset of this sore trial did Ireland encounter that which has ever been her bitterest curse—that questions of fact are made party questions, and the belief or disbelief of matters of fact is regulated in each man's mind, not by the real state of the case, but by his own political prejudices or opinions.

Sir Robert Peel was then at the head of affairs, and the ministry certainly foresaw the coming calamity. Inquiries were made as to the substance that would be the best and cheapest substitute for the potato. Indian corn was adopted, and without any public excitement on the subject, orders were given by the government for the importation of Indian corn to the amount of $1,000,000. This timely precaution, and the subsequent judicious distribution of this store, had the effect of bringing the people through the winter that closed the year 1845, without exposing them to any very severe privations. Arrangements were made by the government for the supply of provisions in biscuit and rice, to a much greater extent, if needed. However men may differ as to the merits of Sir Robert Peel as a politician, whatever estimate may be formed of his measures, it is impossible to deny that for the limited distress that existed consequent upon the partial failure of the potato crop of 1845, provision was made with the most consummate skill—at least with the most complete success. Uninfluenced by party representations, the minister had evidently accurately informed himself of the nature of the calamity, and clearly foresaw its extent. That he erred in fixing too early a period for its full realization, subsequent events have proved; but this was an error on the right side; and all that Sir Robert Peel predicted of the fearful extent of calamity which he anticipated in the summer of 1846, has been more than realized in the spring of 1847. . . .

The destruction of the potato crop entailed a double misery upon the poor. It destroyed their food, and at the same time it took from them

From what I have read and heard, and particularly from my own observation, I am persuaded that the national character of the Irish is inferior to no other people. To me they appear not to be surpassed in native activity of the mind, sprightliness, wit, good nature, generosity, affection, and gratitude. Their peculiar defects and vices, I am persuaded, are owing to the want of education, or a bad one.

Timothy Dwight, *Travels in New England and New York* (1822)

41

their income. Let the corn of England fail, and you have indeed the distress among her population that a scarcity of the means of subsistence will occasion, but the capacity of the great mass of people to purchase that subsistence, were it offered at the accustomed price, is left unimpaired. Far different, however, was the effect of the withering of the potato gardens and the corn-acres of Ireland. The poor man's store was altogether gone—a purchaser of his provisions he never had been—the means of purchasing he never had.

The new year opened gloomily on Ireland. By this time the appalling extent of the calamity, and the inefficiency of the measures adopted to meet it, were, at least, partially understood. . . . Men who have hated democracy all their lives, began seriously to reflect whether the people had influence enough upon a Parliament in which their sufferings were so little heeded. Irishmen, too, began to feel that they were legislated for by men ignorant of the condition and circumstances of their country. ◆

Perils awaiting immigrants include the temptress, the confidence man, those who would steal baggage or money, and dubious friends from the "Old Country." The Irish immigrant at the upper left has already been entrapped by a "runner" from one of the seedy boardinghouses that catered to "greenhorns."

Mary from Dungloe

Oh then fare thee well, sweet Donegal,
The Rosses and Gweedore
I'm crossing the main ocean
Where the foaming billows roar
It breaks my heart from you to part
Where I spent many happy days
Farewell to kind relations
I am bound for Amerikay.

Oh then Mary you're my heart's delight
My pride and only care
It was your cruel father
Would not let me stay here
But absence makes the heart grow fond
And when I am over the main
May the Lord protect my darling girl
Till I return again.

And I wish I was in sweet Dungloe
And seated on the grass
And by my side a bottle of wine
And on my knee a lass
I'd call for liquor of the best
And I'd pay before I'd go
And I'd roll my Mary in my arms
In the town of sweet Dungloe. ◆

Kathleen Mavourneen

Kathleen Mavourneen! the grey dawn is breaking,
The horn of the hunter is heard on the hill;
The lark from her light wing the bright dew is shaking,
Kathleen Mavourneen! What, slumbering still?
Oh! Hast thou forgotten how soon we must sever?
Oh! Hast thou forgotten this day we must part?
It may be for years, and it may be forever,
Then why art thou silent, Kathleen Mavourneen?

Kathleen Mavourneen! awake from thy slumbers,
The blue mountains glow in the sun's golden light,
Ah! where is the spell that once hung on thy numbers,
Arise in thy beauty, thou star of my light.
Mavourneen, Mavourneen, my sad tears are falling,
To think that from Erin and thee I must part;
It may be for years, and it may be forever,
Then why art thou silent, thou voice of my heart?
It may be for years, and it may be forever;
Then why art thou silent, Kathleen Mavourneen? ◆

MAY YOU HAVE WARM WORDS ON A COLD EVENING, A FULL MOON ON A DARK NIGHT, AND A SMOOTH ROAD ALL THE WAY TO YOUR DOOR.
Traditional Irish Toast

*Another emigrant ship has foundered and 248 of our fellow creatures
have been launched, unshrived, into eternity. And another, and
another, will share the same fate unless a strict and searching inquiry
be instituted to ascertain if man is not guilty in some measure of
causing so great a sacrifice of human life. The tale of one unfortunate
vessel is the tale of many. . . . A few days and the circumstance is
forgotten—it is only the foundering of an emigrant ship—remembered
but by relatives. Of the 251 passengers (the supposed number on
board) only three escaped. The rest were drowned "between decks" or
washed from the wreck. No agonising cry was heard—no piercing
scream for help arose above the howling of the waves—all were silent,
speechless, and sank into the sleep of mute death. . . . O God! it is a
most harrowing picture.*

The year was 1847 and the ship was the *Exmouth*, out of Londonderry; bound for America, she got no farther than the coast of Scotland. As this indignant lament published in a Liverpool newspaper
indicates, the foundering emigrant ship was an all-too-familiar contemporary image. Nor was there any change for the better in subsequent
years. Between 1847 and 1853, no fewer than 59 emigrant ships were lost
en route to America.

Thousands of Irish men, women, and children seeking the "Golden
Land of the West" perished in their attempt to cross this stormy Atlantic.
Some died within sight of their goal: the screams of *Powhattan*'s drown-
ing passengers could be heard by horrified spectators on the New Jersey
shore. Others were lost in far, sub-Arctic waters, like those who sailed
from Newry aboard the *Hannah* and were crushed by icebergs; in that
same year, 1849, the *Maria*, from Limerick, was also sunk by a massive
ice floe. The *California Packet*, having sprung a leak, was abandoned by

her crew, leaving her passengers—including a large number of children—to their fate.

To the danger of wind and wave was added that of fire. The *Ocean Monarch*, carrying a large number of Irish—as well as British—emigrants burst into flames when she was barely out of her Liverpool anchorage. The fire, variously attributed to a careless smoker or an overturned candle, swept rapidly through sails and rigging; many passengers, emerging from the depths of steerage, were felled by spars crashing to the deck, or swept overboard when the foremast collapsed. Many of those who fell or jumped into the sea were dashed against the sides of the ship and sank unconscious beneath the waves.

The survivors of this disaster owed their lives to the fortunate arrival of the Brazilian frigate *Affonso*, whose crew plucked them from the water. One survivor was a girl from Leitrim, who later told how she had been standing on deck amid a mass of panic-stricken emigrants, some cursing, others praying, when a woman, driven mad with fear, seized her and hurled her overboard. She floated in the water, dazed and gasping.

Sometimes she was ascending, and at others descending. At length she caught hold of a hand. It was the hand of a dying woman. They seized each other with a sort of death grasp, and for some time it was a kind of struggle with them as to who should be the conqueror or last survivor of the two. The dying woman, however, who had been shattered about the head, from having been no doubt frequently driven against the hull of the burning vessel, breathed her last. Her head sank but her body floated on the water. The girl held on by that dead body and was absolutely saved by it. It bore her up for a considerable length of time, until at length she was taken on board the Affonso, *where she was put into a warm bed, and had brandy and other restoratives administered to her.*

The struggle for survival sometimes ended in murder. In May 1841, the *William Brown*, five weeks out from Liverpool with a cargo of emigrants for Philadelphia, struck an iceberg. Most of the steerage passengers went down with the ship, but thirty-three of them, along with nine crew members, crammed themselves into a lifeboat. At nightfall, with the waves rising and the boat taking on water, the mate ordered the sailors to lighten the load. Six emigrants, too numbed by the cold to realize what was happening, were put over the side without protest. But Frank Carr insisted that he was strong enough to help bail and even offered his life savings—five pounds—if they would spare him; the sailors forced him, struggling, over the side. Trying to soften their hearts, his sister Mary called out, "Oh! don't put out my brother—if you put him out, put me out." Taking her at her word, the crewmen hurled her overboard as well. Then, in a ghoulish version of keeping the family together, they threw Ellen Carr into the icy water to join her brother and sister in death. The next day, the remaining occupants of the boat were

THE DEVIL IS GOOD
TO HIS OWN IN THIS
WORLD AND BAD TO
THEM IN THE NEXT.
*Traditional Irish
Proverb*

THE "EUROPA," MAIL STEAM-SHIP, AND BOATS, RESCUING EMIGRANTS FROM THE BRIG "CHARLES BARTLETT."

picked up by a passing ship; the passengers recounted their horror story before a British court, and the mate was imprisoned for manslaughter.

There were times, too, when none was left to tell the tale. The *City of Glasgow* sailed for America in the summer of 1854, carrying 480 emigrants. The ship, her crew, and her hopeful passengers vanished without a trace in mid-Atlantic.

By 1855 the sufferings of the emigrants had become such a scandal that a parliamentary committee was appointed to look into conditions on transatlantic vessels. John Ryan, a laborer from Limerick who had attempted the voyage to America, was among the witnesses summoned to testify on his experiences. Ryan had crossed from Dublin to Liverpool on a small steam launch, expecting to travel to New York on the emigrant ship *Commerce*, a sizable craft with accommodation for several hundred passengers. Instead, he was put on board the *E. Z.*, a small ship carrying only a handful of passengers. His account of their fate is told in the simple language of an illiterate, unsophisticated—and thoroughly disillusioned—country lad:

Did you come across from Dublin to Liverpool?—Yes.

Upon the deck of the steamer?—Yes.

Was it a bad night?—It was a very bad night indeed.

Had you any shelter?—None, except as a man can shelter himself.

Then you were taken to the E. Z.?—Yes.

And then you were given sleeping places, where; on the upper deck? —Yes, on the upper deck, in the bows. . . . We had a house made with boards over the hatchway.

There were fourteen of you?—There were.

And several were of one family?—There was eight of one family, and another girl who joined them, which made nine.

What was the name of that family?—Fitzgerald.

Now, when you were some time out, it happened that those houses were knocked away by a sea?—Yes, quite away.

And there were persons carried away with them and drowned?— There were; drowned altogether.

You saw no more of them?—I saw no more of them than of a man that was at Cork.

Were you all washed overboard?—Thirteen were washed away; every one but myself.

Had you good food?—They gave me no drink but water, and the biscuit was too hard for me.

Do you know the tonnage of the vessel; what size it was?—There were three masts in it.

Were you ever at sea before?—No.

Not till you came over to Liverpool?—No.

The vessel put back to Liverpool?—Yes, the same vessel.

Of the Fitzgerald family, how many of them remained alive?—None.

You lost all your clothes?—Yes, everything, and every one that was with me.

Supposing no disaster had happened to the E. Z., and your passage had been completed successfully, should you have had reason to complain of not being carried on the Commerce?—I had a great deal to complain of; nearly every day you would have the water up to your knees.

Was the weather so rough?—Yes, it was no sooner in it than out of it; the water would come in and go out. If we were under deck, we should not have had that; we should be saved from it; it used to come under the bedclothes; they used to be wet at the bottom, under us.

How large was this place where the fourteen lived; how many feet long, and how many feet wide?—I could not tell that.

When it was washed away, was there nothing over your head but the sky?—Nothing in the wide world, nothing but the sky.

Were you all in this place at the time that the sea washed away this

THE DOORSTEP OF A GREAT HOUSE IS SLIPPERY.
Traditional Irish Proverb

house where you lived; were you all inside at the time?—All the passengers but me; at the time of the accident, I was outside.

And that was the reason you were saved?—Yes, I believe so.

When you got back to Liverpool, did you tell anybody there that they had not put you on board the vessel they had promised to put you in?—I do not think I did say anything; I did not care, if I could come home.

You would not like to go to sea again?—Not if I could help it.

Such parliamentary investigations in Britain and public outcry in the United States led to some official attempts at regulating emigrant ships, particularly with regard to health and sanitary conditions and supply of provisions. Nevertheless, until steam replaced sail, the Atlantic crossing remained a hazardous and frightening prospect for emigrants.

British steamship lines—which began transatlantic service during the 1840s—at first scorned the emigrant trade as unprofitable, and limited themselves to mail, cargo, and a few well-to-do cabin passengers. By the late 1850s, they had discovered that many emigrants were prepared to pay extra (the fare was double that of sailing vessels) for a faster and safer voyage to America. When Confederate raiders virtually drove American shipping from the high seas during the early 1860s, British steamships multiplied to take advantage of this opportunity, and the era of the transatlantic crossing under sail was definitely over.

The steamships of the 1870s reduced the length of the American voyage to less than two weeks. The crossing became safer, too, for the danger of fire virtually disappeared as wood and sail yielded to iron and steam: after 1858, no emigrant ship was destroyed by fire.

But shipwrecks, though less frequent in the steamship era, still occurred; because the new, larger ships carried more passengers, the loss of life in individual sinkings was greater than ever. In April 1873, for example, the *Atlantic*, fleeing a fierce storm, ran onto the rocky coast of Nova Scotia and began to break up almost at once: 546 emigrants were drowned or dashed to death on the jagged outcroppings of the New World. Those who had survived the first minutes of the wreck clung to the shattered vessel's rigging, hoping for rescue from the nearby shore. During the night, many of them died of cold or were washed away by towering waves. A young Irishman, Patrick Leahy, perched precariously above the raging sea, gazed down at break of dawn:

"It was just gleaming day; a large mass of something drifted past the ship on the top of the waves, and then was lost to view in the trough of the sea. As it passed by, a moan—it must have been a shriek, but the tempest dulled the sound—seemed to surge from the mass, which extended over fifty yards of water; it was the women. The sea swept them out of the steerage, and with their children to the number of 200 or 300, they drifted thus to eternity."

With daylight, the storm subsided and the sea calmed; local fishing boats came out to rescue Leahy and his fellow survivors.

The new century brought navigational improvements and wireless

We, as a people, are intolerant of ragged garments and empty paunches. We are a people who have had no experience in physical tribulation. As a consequence, the ill-clad and destitute Irishman is repulsive to our habits and our tastes. We confound ill-clothing and destitution with ignorance and vice.

Christian Examiner (1848)

communications to further reduce the perils of the ocean. Despite all safeguards, however, the Atlantic continued to claim its toll. In 1912, the *Titanic*—newest, fastest, safest of all the great liners—struck an iceberg on her maiden voyage to New York. The Belfast-built, "unsinkable" ship went down with 673 crew and 825 passengers: many of them were Irish sailors and Irish emigrants. Almost forgotten in the shadow of the *Titanic* disaster was another wreck, two years later, off the coast of Canada, in which over 1,000 people drowned. With grim symbolism, the ship was named *Empress of Ireland.*

With the sinking of the *Empress of Ireland* in the spring of 1914, both the great age of Irish emigration to America and the most perilous epoch of transatlantic travel came to a close. A few months later, the Great War broke out and the patterns of life in both Europe and America changed forever. The next great ocean liner to go down in the Atlantic would not be the victim of nature's rage or men's incompetence: it would succumb to the scientific ingenuity of the new century, as torpedos, fired by a lurking undersea craft, tore it in half. Ironically, as some of the *Lusitania*'s 1,000 corpses washed onto the nearest shore, the old pattern was reversed: instead of wretched Irish emigrants cast upon the rocky shore of America, it was now the remains of affluent American travelers that were littering the peaceful strands of Ireland.   ◆

Patrick Pearse, leader of the Easter Rebellion, the 1916 rising in Ireland, is shown here (*on the right*) with his brother William, in a card autographed by their mother. Both men were executed by the British as part of the brutal reprisals that aroused such indignation in the United States.

VERSE 1:

We'll sing a song, a soldier's song,
With cheering, rousing chorus,
As round our blazing fires we throng,
The starry heavens o'er us;

Impatient for the coming fight,
And as we wait for the morning's light,
Here in the silence of the night,
We'll chant a soldier's song.

CHORUS:

Soldiers are we, whose lives are pledged to Ireland;
Some have come from a land beyond the wave,
Sworn to be free, no more our ancient sireland
Shall shelter the despot or the slave.

Tonight we man the bearna bacghail,
In Erin's cause, come woe or weal;
'Mid cannons' roar and rifles' peal,
We'll chant a soldier's song.

VERSE 2:

In valley green on towering crag,
Our fathers fought before us,
And conquered 'neath the same old flag,
That's proudly floating o'er us;

We're children of a fighting race,
That never yet has known disgrace,
And as we march, the foe to face,
We'll chant a soldier's song.
(CHORUS)

VERSE 3:

Sons of the Gael! Men of the Pale!
The long watched day is breaking;
The serried ranks of Inisfail
Shall set the Tyrant quaking.

Our camp fires now are burning low,
See in the east a silv'ry glow,
Out yonder waits the Saxon foe,
So chant a soldier's song.
(CHORUS) ◆

Conditions on Emigrant Ships, 1847

MINULES OF
EVIDENCE
BEFORE THE
SELECT
COMMITTEE
(LORDS) ON
EMIGRATION
FROM IRELAND.
*Testimony of
Robert Smith
(London, 1847)*

The fearful state of disease and debility in which the Irish emigrants have reached Canada must undoubtedly be attributed in a great degree to the destitution and consequent sickness prevailing in Ireland, but has been much aggravated by the neglect of cleanliness, ventilation and a generally good state of social economy during the passage, and has afterwards been increased and disseminated throughout the whole country in the mal-arrangements of the Government system of emigrant relief. Having myself submitted to the privations of a steerage passage in an emigrant ship for nearly two months, in order to make myself acquainted with the condition of the emigrant from the beginning, I can state from experience that the present regulations for ensuring health and comparative comfort to passengers are wholly insufficient, and that they are not and cannot be enforced, notwithstanding the great zeal and high abilities of the Government agents.

Before the emigrant has been a week at sea he is an altered man. How can it be otherwise? Hundreds of poor people, men, women and children of all ages, from the drivelling idiot of ninety to the babe just born, huddled together without light, without air, wallowing in filth and breathing a fetid atmosphere, sick in body, dispirited in heart, the fever patients lying between the sound, in sleeping places so narrow as almost to deny them the power of indulging, by a change of position, that natural restlessness of the disease; by their ravings disturbing those around, and predisposing them, through the effects of the imagination, to imbibe the contagion; living without food or medicine, except as administered by the hand of casual charity, dying without the voice of spiritual consolation, and buried in deep without the rites of the Church. The food is generally ill-selected and seldom sufficiently cooked; in consequence of the supply of water, hardly enough for cooking and drinking, does not allow washing. In many ships the filthy beds, teeming with all abominations, are never required to be brought on deck and aired; the narrow space between the sleeping berths and the piles of boxes is never washed or scraped, but breathes up a damp and fetid stench, until the day before the arrival at quarantine, when all hands are required to "scrub up," and put on a fair face for the doctor and Government inspector. No moral

DINNER IN THE FORECASTLE.

The cramped quarters on board early-nineteenth-century immigrant ships forced passengers to take their meals in the same space in which they spent their nights and most of their days. The food was cooked in the ship's galley and carried back by each immigrant to his bunk. It was sure to be chilled, spray-soaked, and perhaps half spilled by the time he got there.

53

We can see in the history of the Irish nation the sources of the tenacious pride, the poetic temperament, the rich mosaic imagination, the quick feeling, the intense nationality of the Irish people.

Samuel G.
Goodrich, *Ireland and the Irish* (1841)

restraint is attempted, the voice of prayer is never heard; drunkenness, with its consequent train of ruffianly debasement, is not discouraged, because it is profitable to the captain, who traffics in the grog.

In this ship which brought me out from London last April, the passengers were found in provisions by the owners, according to a contract and a furnished scale of dietary.

The meat was of the worst quality. The supply of water shipped on board was abundant, but the quantity served out to the passengers was so scanty that they were frequently obliged to throw overboard their salt provisions and rice (a most important article of their food) because they had not water enough both for the necessary cooking and the satisfying of their raging thirst afterwards.

They could only afford water for washing by withdrawing it from the cooking of their food. I have known persons to remain for days together in their dark, close berths because they thus suffered less from hunger, though compelled at the same time for want of water to heave overboard their salt provisions and rice.

No cleanliness was enforced, and the beds were never aired. The master during the whole voyage never entered the steerage, and would listen to no complaints; the dietary contracted for was, with some exceptions, nominally supplied, though at irregular periods; but false measures were used (in which the water and several articles of dry food were served), the gallon measure containing but three quarts, which fact I proved in Quebec and had the captain fined for. Once or twice a week ardent spirits were sold indiscriminately to the passengers, producing scenes of unchecked blackguardism beyond description; and lights were prohibited because the ship—with her open fire-grates upon deck—with lucifer matches and lighted pipes used secretly in the sleeping berths—was freighted with Government powder for the garrison at Quebec.

The case of this ship was not one of peculiar misconduct; on the contrary, I have the strongest reason to know, from information I have received from very many emigrants well known to me, who came over this year in different vessels, that this ship was better regulated and more comfortable than many that reached Canada.

Disease and death among the emigrants, nay, the propagation of infection throughout Canada, are not the worst consequences of this atrocious system of neglect and ill-usage. A result far worse is to be found in the utter demoralisation of the passengers, both male and female, by the filth and debasement and disease of two or three months so passed. The emigrant, enfeebled in body and degraded in mind, even though he should have the physical power, has not the heart, has not the will to exert himself. He has lost his self-respect, his elasticity of spirit; he no longer stands erect; he throws himself listlessly upon the daily dole of Government, and in order to earn it carelessly lies for weeks on the contaminated straw of a fever lazaretto. ◆

Love Them
or
Loathe Them

Some nineteenth-century views on the Irish:

How gallantly, indeed, do Irish wit, and cheerfulness, and hospitality, and patriotism ride on the wreck of individual hopes, and sparkle through the very waves of adversity!"
—*Samuel G. Goodrich, 1841*

The Irish position "is one of shame and poverty. . . . 'My master is a great tyrant,' said a negro lately, 'he treats me as badly as if I was a common Irishman.' "
—*Patrick Murphy, 1851*

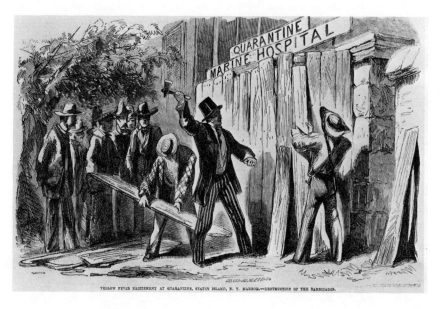

YELLOW FEVER EXCITEMENT AT QUARANTINE, STATEN ISLAND, N. Y. HARBOR.—DESTRUCTION OF THE BARRICADES.

A mob of local residents attacks the government quarantine station at Staten Island, New York. They had long complained about this "pest-hole" in their midst, and the danger of disease spreading from the (mostly Irish) immigrants confined there. Finally, on the night of September 11, 1858, a band of "disguised and armed residents" seized the hospital, removed the patients, and burned down the buildings.

*O*ut of these narrow lanes, dirty streets, damp cellars, and suffocating garrets, will come forth some of the noblest sons of our country, whom she will delight to own and honor."   —*Orestes Brownson, 1854*

*T*he Irish soon acquire the sentiments of self-respect common to the American character. . . . They become more Americanized than the Americans."   —*William Chambers, 1854*

I am sorry to find that England is right about the lower class of Irish. They are brutal, base, cruel, cowards, and as insolent as base . . . my own theory is that St. Patrick's campaign against the snakes is a Popish delusion. They perished of biting the Irish people."
                                     —*George Templeton Strong, 1863*

*T*housands of my countrymen at this time fill with dignity and invulnerable fidelity, various situations of trust and emolument in the land of their adoption.   —*Jeremiah O'Donovan, 1864*

*O*f all the tricks which the Irish nation have played on the slow-witted Saxon, the most outrageous is the palming off on him the imaginary Irishman of romance. The worst of it is that when a spurious type gets into literature, it strikes the imagination of boys and girls. They form themselves by playing up to it; and thus the unsubstantial fancies of the novelists and music-hall songwriters of one generation are apt to become the unpleasant and mischievous realities of the next."
                                       —*George Bernard Shaw, 1896*

◆

South Water
Street, west from
Dearborn, Chicago
(c. 1900).

Did St. Patrick Drive Them Out?

*L*egend has it that St. Patrick banished the snakes and toads from Ireland. Alas, like many Irish stories, this one has more charm than truth to it.

Certainly Ireland's zoology is deficient in the area of amphibia and reptilia. Unlike the rest of Europe, where such creatures abound in a multitude of species, the amphibians of Ireland include only one native species each of frog, toad, and newt. Among reptiles, there is only one species—the viviparous, or common, lizard. There are, indeed, no snakes at all. This anomaly, however, is due to natural circumstances.

When the last great Ice Age ended, some 13,000 years ago, the British Isles were still linked to the European Continent by land bridges. As the climate in northwestern Europe grew warmer, animals able to tolerate the still relatively cold environment began to migrate there from the overpopulated southern lands. The cold-blooded amphibians and reptiles lagged behind.

But they put off their trip a few thousand years too long. As the ice sheets melted, the sea levels rose, and the land bridges were inundated. The link between Britain and Europe was submerged by 5000 B.C., but the Irish Sea had been created before that: Ireland was cut off from Britain as early as 8000 B.C. A few amphibians had braved the less-than-ideal conditions of Ireland before 8000 B.C., but the snakes had lagged behind in the sunny south. A few of these reptiles made it to Britain before the continental link was severed in about 5000 B.C. But by then it was too late for them to migrate on to Ireland, for the western isle had long since ceased to be joined to Britain. Hence, no snakes reached Ireland. They got to the departure point too late to make the crossing.

St. Patrick did not drive the snakes out of Ireland—because there were no snakes there for him to drive out. The legend of his miraculous expulsion order was devised to explain a phenomenon that science can now elucidate in its usual prosaic fashion. Without the story, however, art and literature would have been the poorer all these centuries. And Brendan Behan would not have been able to make the quip that when St. Patrick banished the snakes from Ireland, they crossed the Atlantic and became Irish-American judges. ◆

The interior of Castle Garden, New York. First a fort, then a concert hall, this building was used as a reception center for immigrants from 1856 until the Ellis Island facilities were opened in 1892.

Outside the Castle Garden processing station, immigrants are recruited for the Union Army. Prior to the start of conscription in July 1863, volunteers were obtained by offering bounties for enlistment. Many Irish immigrants, attracted by the prospect of $600 (if not by the martial music) signed up immediately.

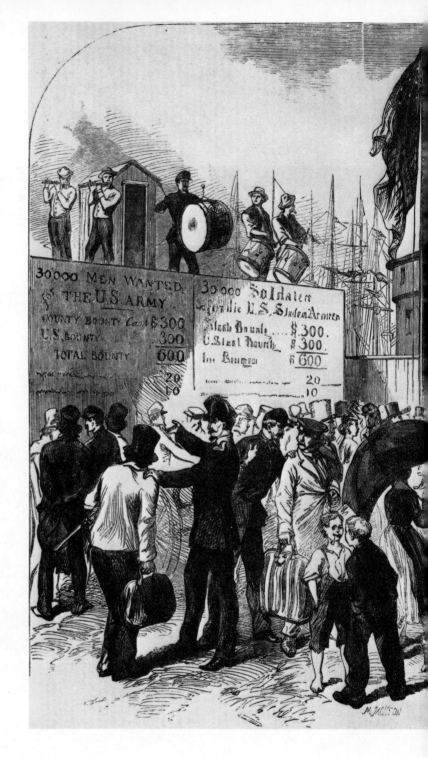

The Irish in the Military

Naval
Notables

*A*mericans of Irish origin have distinguished themselves in the naval service of their country throughout its history. Here are ten of the most eminent Irish-American seamen.

1. JEREMIAH O'BRIEN
An ardent patriot, residing in Machias, Maine, O'Brien boarded and captured the British warship *Margaretta* on June 2, 1775, in the first naval battle of the Revolution. Commissioned as a privateer, he continued to harass the enemy during the war that he, in a sense, had inaugurated.

2. JOHN BARRY
This Wexford-born officer was in the thick of the fighting at sea from 1776 onward. His long and valuable service earned him the designation "father of the United States Navy."

3. OLIVER HAZARD PERRY
Perry, whose mother was born in Ireland, became the greatest naval hero of the second Anglo-American war when he defeated a British fleet on Lake Erie in September 1813. His victory is remembered through his laconic announcement: "We have met the enemy and they are ours." His younger brother Commodore Matthew C. Perry was the man who "opened Japan to the West" in 1852.

4. THOMAS MACDONOUGH
A year after Perry's victory on Lake Erie, the British made another attempt to move their forces south from Canada. Macdonough's defeat of the enemy's squadron on Lake Champlain, in September 1814, saved New York and Vermont from invasion and hastened the negotiations that concluded the War of 1812.

5. MATTHEW FONTAINE MAURY
A Virginian of Irish Huguenot descent, he was the first head of the U.S. Naval Observatory and virtual founder of the modern science of oceanography. Upon the outbreak of the Civil War, this internationally re-

nowned scientist followed his native state and organized the Confederacy's naval defenses.

6. STEPHEN C. ROWAN

A Dubliner who came to America at the age of eleven, he began his long naval career a few years later. Rowan played a major role in the conquest of California during the Mexican War, and was one of the most active commanders during the Civil War. His most significant victory was the defeat of a Confederate force under the Irish-American commodore W. F. Lynch in North Carolina coastal waters in February 1862. During the postwar years Admiral Rowan held most of the top offices in the navy.

7. ALFRED T. MAHAN

This grandson of Irish immigrants became the navy's outstanding sailor-scholar. His *Influence of Sea Power Upon History* (1890) and other works established him as a world-recognized authority on naval strategy.

8. WILLIAM D. LEAHY

After service in the Spanish-American War and World War I, he rose to the highest position in the U.S. Navy in 1937, as chief of naval operations. Following retirement, he was governor of Puerto Rico and ambassador to France before being called back to duty in World War II. As chief of staff to Presidents Roosevelt and Truman, he provided liaison between the commander in chief and the armed forces and presided over the then informally constructed Joint Chiefs of Staff. Promoted to fleet admiral in 1944, Leahy was the first officer to hold that five-star rank.

9. DANIEL J. CALLAGHAN

Serving as President Roosevelt's naval aide at the beginning of World War II, he was appointed chief of staff, South Pacific Forces, in 1942. In November of that year, the admiral took command of the cruiser-destroyer squadron that intercepted a Japanese attack against Guadalcanal. In a fierce, close-fought engagement, the enemy fleet was routed, but Callaghan was killed.

10. DANIEL V. GALLERY

Gallery, who played an important part in developing naval aviation, held key commands in both the Atlantic and the Pacific during World War II. On June 4, 1944, his antisubmarine forces intercepted the U-505 off the North African coast, and he gave a command not heard since the War of 1812: "Away boarders!" Gallery thus carried out the navy's first capture of an enemy vessel in the high seas since 1815. The admiral, in addition to holding important postwar assignments, had considerable popular success as a writer on naval topics. ◆

Englishmen, Scotchmen, Jews do well in Ireland—Irishmen, never; even the patriot has to leave Ireland to get a hearing.

George Moore, *Ave* (1920)

The Father of the United States Navy

True to the seafaring tradition of his native Wexford, John Barry shipped out as a cabin boy at an early age. By 1761—when he was fifteen—he had crossed the Atlantic, to Philadelphia, which would henceforth be his home port. He advanced rapidly in his profession: at twenty-one he was captain of a schooner, and at twenty-nine he commanded one of the finest ships in the transatlantic trade.

An ardent patriot, he offered his services to his adopted country at the outbreak of the Revolution. He was given command of the *Lexington*, and was the first captain in the Continental navy to capture a British vessel—the tender *Edward*—on April 7, 1776. During the war he fought several ship actions, harassed British communications, and took part in at least one battle on land. Just as he had commenced the naval war, so he fought its last sea battle, in March 1783, when his *Alliance* engaged the British frigate *Sybill*.

Like most of those who served on land and sea during the Revolution, Barry returned to private life at the end of the war. However, after the adoption of the Constitution and the establishment of the new government, it was decided that the United States ought to have a regular navy. Barry was appointed senior captain of the fleet, with a commission dated June 4, 1794. While he held a seagoing command (the forty-four-gun frigate *United States*), he was also the first head of the United States Navy, with the title of commodore.

Barry directed operations in the West Indies during the crucial years of the quasi-war with France and maintained the security of American commerce in those waters during a period of revolutionary disturbances and increasing piracy, from 1797 to 1801. He was about to lead an expedition to the Mediterranean to chastise the Barbary corsairs when he was overtaken by a fatal illness and died on September 13, 1803.

The most distinguished Irish American of his day, Barry was buried with full honors in the graveyard of St. Mary's Church. His services to the United States are commemorated by statues in Philadelphia and Washington. The land of his birth displays its pride in his achievements with a statue of the commodore that gazes out over the harbor of Wexford. ◆

The
Irish Spy

*I*t's hard to be objective about spying. One group's heroic "intelligence agent" is another group's treacherous villain. Ireland's history in particular is full of infiltrators and informers, and double—and even triple—agents abound. The Irish in America have produced fewer practitioners of this art, but a few of them—with all their ambivalences—deserve to be noted here.

Hercules Mulligan, an Irish-born tailor residing in Colonial New York City, seemed to be a good Tory. Like many others in this Loyalist stronghold, he profited from its being the headquarters of the British forces throughout the Revolutionary War. Officers gossiped freely about military movements as they gathered at his shop to be fitted for new uniforms. From these conversations, and other sources, the supposedly faithful Mulligan compiled regular reports for the American army that proved invaluable to the success of their operations. When independence was finally achieved, and the troops of the newborn United States entered the city, General Washington publicly acknowledged the services that Hercules Mulligan had rendered to the cause and hailed him as an outstanding patriot, a "true friend of liberty."

The Confederate states probably would have said much the same about Michael O'Laughlin. Although his background is obscure, he seems to have served in a Southern regiment during the early period of the Civil War, then deserted and made his way to Washington. Whether or not O'Laughlin's defection from his unit was real or feigned, he evidently found plenty of opportunities for spying in the federal capital. Like other Confederate soldiers living in and about the District of Columbia, he kept in close touch with the rebels across the Potomac. When, despite their efforts, the Confederacy collapsed, O'Laughlin was among those who joined in John Wilkes Booth's assassination plot. Sentenced to life imprisonment as a co-conspirator in the murder of Abraham Lincoln, O'Laughlin was pardoned after a few years and faded from view.

James McParlan, from County Armagh, has been described as "the epitome of the swashbuckling, generous, roguish, charming devil-may-care Irishman." He was also an agent of the Pinkerton Detective Agency, sent to the coalfields of western Pennsylvania in the early 1870s to infiltrate the Molly Maguires. This secret society of Irish miners had been waging a campaign of terror against the oppressive mine owners and managers of the region, and the authorities were convinced that only an Irishman could penetrate their organization. McParlan succeeded so well that he became the intimate friend of the group's leaders. As a result of his spying, nineteen of the group were hanged in 1876.

And now for a red herring: Sidney Reilly. Many people who have heard about the exploits of this daring "ace of spies" have picked up the idea that he was an Irish American. But he was actually born in Russia, worked during most of his espionage career for the British Secret Service, and previously went under the name Sigmund Rosenblum (although what name he bore during childhood remains unknown). He adopted his first wife's surname with the explanation that "few people would completely trust anyone with a Jewish name, but everybody likes the Irish." Apparently the Bolsheviks didn't; for Reilly disappeared while on a mission inside Russia, and, after sixty years, the wizards of Whitehall still have not been able to learn the fate of their greatest spy.

Ironically, it was this same British Secret Service that inspired an eminent Irish American to become spymaster-in-chief of the United States. General William J. Donovan possessed splendidly "green" credentials as a soldier-politician. He had commanded the "Fighting Irish" of New York's 69th Regiment in the A.E.F., and had run for governor of New York. But Donovan was a thoroughgoing Anglophile and acted as President Roosevelt's confidential agent in London on the eve of World War II. He came back convinced that America needed an intelligence organization similar to that of Britain. The outcome was the Office of Strategic Services, which General Donovan directed during the war. The range of OSS activities in the realm of espionage and sabotage was wide and included some genuinely dirty tricks. But all is forgiven to those who win, and the United States emerged from the conflict firmly committed to spying as a way of life in the Nuclear Age. Among the many bright, ruthless young Irish Americans whom "Wild Bill" Donovan recruited into his apparatus was William Casey, destined to be a spy master himself. But that is another story. ◆

It is the plain duty of every Irishman to disassociate himself from all memories of Ireland—Ireland being a fatal disease, fatal to the Englishmen, doubly fatal to Irishmen.

George Moore, *Ave* (1920)

A Hessian
O'Reilly

*A*mong the more mysterious figures that may be glimpsed in the pages of Irish-American history is one Maximilian Wilhelm O'Reilly, who served throughout the war for American independence in the Hessian mercenary forces. His name turns up at regular intervals in the records of the time, without any clear indication of who he was or where he came from. He is listed in 1776 as a captain in Von Lengerke's Grenadier Battalion. He was wounded in the fighting near Flatbush during the Battle of Long Island (August 1776). He was apparently taken prisoner in 1777 but was soon exchanged. By October 1780 he had been promoted to major in the Von Bose Infantry Regiment that was dispatched from New York in that month to reinforce Cornwallis in the Carolinas. The campaign of 1781 culminated in the surrender at Yorktown, at which time O'Reilly was acting commander of his regiment. He was subsequently released on parole, returned to New York, and presumably sailed for home during the following year.

During 1778–1779, O'Reilly served as Town Major of New York, having been chosen in preference to other Hessian officers because of his "very good knowledge of English." This position, which made him, in effect, chief of military police, involved him in the supervision of both British and German occupation troops in their relations with the American civilian population.

O'Reilly's origins are not clear, although an otherwise uninformative letter from him in the Hessian dispatches is written in French, suggesting a lack of fluency in written German and a non-German birthplace. Who was this wandering Irishman? Where did he come from? Where did he go? We have no answers. He simply plays his role in the birth of the United States and, like so many others among the far-ranging Celts, disappears into the mists. ◆

Who Was That Irishman at Yorktown?

*A*s every schoolchild knows, Cornwallis surrendered at Yorktown. Well, not exactly. The British commander may have signed the document, but the man who actually surrendered His Majesty's forces to General Washington was Charles O'Hara. It is he who appears in Trumbull's famous painting of the event. But what was an Irishman doing in such a role? Surely someone with a name like O'Hara would be a deadly enemy of all things British? Again, not exactly. Major General Charles O'Hara, second in command to Cornwallis, spent his life in the service of King George III. It is a life worth noting, if only because, on that October day in 1781, this Irish soldier acknowledged the triumph of the American Revolution. He thus played a part in the birth of the United States.

Charles O'Hara represented the third generation of generals in his family, which is said to have originated in Sligo, although his grandfather, Charles (1640–1724), was born in Mayo. The latter was a protégé of the Butlers of Ormonde, rising from captain in Lord Ossory's regiment to the lieutenant colonelcy of the First Foot Guards and a knighthood in 1689. He served with William III in Flanders, with the duke of Ormonde at Virgo, and at Guadalajara and Almanza under Lords Galway and Peterborough, attaining the rank of lieutenant general in 1704 and that of full general ten years later. In the meantime he had been created Baron Tyrawley in the peerage of Ireland in 1706, and had withstood a parliamentary inquiry into the conduct of the war in Spain. Lord Tyrawley served as commander in chief of the forces in Ireland from 1714 to 1721 and later as governor of the Royal Hospital, Dublin, in which city he was buried. His only son, James (1690–1773), served under his father in Spain, and under Marlborough in the Low Countries, being wounded both at Almanza and at Malplaquet. In 1714 he succeeded the elder O'Hara as colonel of the Royal Fusiliers, and in 1722 was created an Irish peer in his own right as Baron Kilmaine. Two years later he became the second Baron Tyrawley as well; like his predecessor, he was a member of the Privy Council and, like him, survived a parliamentary inquiry. Lord Tyrawley served as envoy to Portugal from 1728 to 1741, to Russia from 1743 to 1745, and to Portugal from 1752 to 1755, rising in military rank from brigadier in 1735 to field marshal in 1763.

A BAD WIFE TAKES ADVICE FROM EVERY MAN BUT HER OWN HUSBAND.
Traditional Irish Proverb

●*We sensed the bitter antipathy, scarcely concealed, which nearly all these good women in charge of the schools felt toward those of us who had Catholic faith and Irish names. For any slight pretext we were severely punished. We were made to feel the slur against our faith and race, which hurt us to our very heart's core. As all the teachers were of this same stamp, it was little wonder that from my fifth to my twelfth year school life meant nothing to me but a dreary drive, with a feeling of terror lest, for any reason, or no rea-*

Although the second Lord Tyrawley left no issue by his marriage to a daughter of the second Viscount Mountjoy, he had numerous illegitimate children, being, according to Horace Walpole, "singularly licentious, even for the courts of Russia and Portugal." On his return to England in 1741 (again according to Walpole) he was accompanied by "three wives and fourteen children." While this is undoubtedly an exaggeration, the actress George Anne Bellamy (who was Tyrawley's daughter by an earlier liaison) describes the Stratton Street residence of the ambassador, his Portuguese mistress Doña Anna, three girls by three different ladies, and assorted swarthy boys, as having "more the appearance of a Turkish seraglio than the home of an English peer."

Charles O'Hara was one of the youngest of this brood, presumably born at Lisbon in 1740. He seems to have been his father's favorite, and was much in Lord Tyrawley's company, which explains his choice of career as well as his exuberant, extravagant style of life, so much resembling the older man's. Educated at Westminster, Charles was made an ensign in the Eighth Foot in 1751 and a cornet in the Third Dragoons in 1752, but his active service began after he was appointed "lieutenant and captain" in his father's newly acquired regiment, the Second (Coldstream) Foot Guards, on January 14, 1756. Tyrawley was home on leave from his governorship of Minorca; when he sailed in June 1756 to assume command at Gibraltar Charles went with him as aide-de-camp, and remained there until April 1757—his first visit to the Rock where he was to end his days. After the Battle of Minden he joined the marquess of Granby's staff as an aide-de-camp, and in Germany became acquainted with Charles Cornwallis (then Lord Brome) and Henry Clinton, his future chiefs in the American war.

The threat of a Spanish invasion in 1762 impelled Portugal to seek British aid, and Lord Tyrawley returned to familiar terrain as plenipotentiary and commander of an 8,000-man expeditionary force. Charles, with the brevet rank of lieutenant colonel (February 10, 1762), accompanied him in the capacity of quartermaster general. Their army icluded, at Tyrawley's suggestion, a contingent of Irish Roman Catholics, whom he called upon to show by their conduct their appreciation of the relaxation of anti-Catholic legislation by the king, as well as regard for the people of Portugal, with whom they were now joined in arms. Tyrawley accomplished little, however, and was criticized at home as being too old and lacking experience in the field, while hostile circles at the Portuguese Court labored to undermine his position. Both O'Haras returned to England in disgust early in 1763.

With the end of the Seven Years' War, newly acquired territories had to be integrated into the Empire. In 1765 the Senegal forts and dependencies were combined with the old Gambia holdings as the Province of Senegambia, and Captain O'Hara of the Coldstream Guards had the good fortune (or influence) to be named governor, at a salary of £1,200 per annum. In addition, he was appointed lieutenant-colonel-commandant of His Majesty's African Corps of Foot, a unit comprising three "Independent Companies" of "military delinquents," pardoned on condition of accepting life service in Africa. He and his troops sailed from Portsmouth in March 1766 and landed at Fort St. Louis on April 14 to find the defenses of Senegambia's "capital" in a decayed state.

Paying little attention to civil administration, O'Hara rebuilt fortifications, drilled his shiftless garrison, and antagonized many of the local traders by compelling them to quit the island for the mainland in order to make military improvements. His reports to the Colonial Office were at first voluminous, pointing out the danger of French interference with trade, complaining that he had been forced to go into debt to pay for necessary construction because official funds were inadequate, and demanding reinforcements after an epidemic in 1767 killed half of his officers and all but 90 of the 300 "Independents." O'Hara regarded his verbal reports, delivered during visits to England in 1770 and 1774, as adequate accounts of his stewardship, and went heedlessly on with his military preoccupations, neglecting the promotion of trade and the establishment of a model colonial government, two duties laid down in his original instructions. This led to an investigation into O'Hara's administration by the Board of Trade, and his failure to carry out his instructions or to submit regular reports was adjudged ground for dismissal. The formal order to this effect was dated June 16, 1776.

But meanwhile war had broken out in America. O'Hara had maintained his seniority in the Guards, becoming lieutenant colonel in 1769, and when he quit Senegambia for England, it was only for a brief stay. He reached Howe's headquarters at New York in March 1777.

O'Hara saw little action at first, being retained at New York and Philadelphia on prisoner exchange duties, even after receiving a brevet colonelcy on August 29, 1777. When Howe was succeeded by Clinton in May 1778 his prospects improved. As Clinton reported to the War Office: "The necessity of paying particular attention to Sandy Hook whilst the French fleet lay off this Harbour inclined me to appoint Colonel O'Hara to that Command, and as the Duty was extraordinary and the trust great, I thought the appointment of him to the rank of Brigadier General a just recompense." The brevet brigadier found the peninsula on the Jersey shore (at that time it was actually an island) a great threat to the security of New York so long as D'Estaing's squadron was in the vicinity. On July 15 he informed Clinton that "as so many formidable attempts may be made . . . I conceive that it would be immediately necessary that a very considerable reinforcement of not less than fifteen hundred men with six pieces of field artillery would be requisite for its defence." Within four days, Clinton had sent O'Hara 1,800 men and a battery of guns, and the anchorage of Admiral Lord Howe's fleet, which lay behind the Hook, was secure. This smooth cooperation between the two generals does not seem

son, the teacher might vent her ill feeling upon our defenseless persons.

William Cardinal O'Connell, recalling his school days in Lowell, Massachusetts, during the 1860s, *Recollections* (1934)

to have lasted long. Clinton later commented that he had given O'Hara this assignment because he was considered a good engineer and was well known to Lord Howe, "but I soon found he was the last man I should have sent with a detached corps—plans upon plans for defence, never easy, satisfied or safe; a great, nay plausible, talker." The departure of D'Estaing and the cooling of Clinton's esteem ended O'Hara's duties at Sandy Hook. During the fall he was temporarily in command on York Island (Manhattan), and in December again served as commissioner for prisoner exchange. Seeing no immediate chance of active duty, he obtained leave and sailed for England in February 1779.

O'Hara evidently employed his time in England to good advantage, for when he arrived back at New York in October 1780 it was with the full rank of brigadier general "in North America" and command of the Guards brigade scheduled to join Lord Cornwallis's southern campaign. After the usual delays, O'Hara reached the earl's advanced camp at Winnsboro, South Carolina, on January 18, 1781. The next day the entire British force set out after the retreating Americans. At the hard-fought crossing of Cowan's Ford (where he was plunged into the rushing waters of the Catawba when his horse was hit) on February 1, on the banks of the Yadkin (where he routed the local militia) on February 4, and in the headlong pursuit of the rebels to the Dan—which they managed to cross, with the last boats, scant hours ahead of him on February 14—O'Hara led the advance guard and drove his men and himself beyond the point of exhaustion. When contact was resumed at Guilford Court House on March 15, O'Hara was wounded early in the fighting and handed over the Guards to Lieutenant Colonel Stuart. Seeing Stuart killed, O'Hara struggled to his feet and rallied his men for the charge that drove the enemy from the field. "The zeal and spirit of Brigadier-General O'Hara," wrote Cornwallis in his dispatch, "merit my highest commendations, for after receiving two dangerous wounds, he continued in the field while the action lasted. . . ." The battle was a tactical victory, but a strategic defeat, for so heavy were the British casualties (the Guards lost 11 out of 19 officers and 206 out of 462 men) that Cornwallis had to retreat to the coast, with the gravely wounded O'Hara carried in a horse litter.

By the time O'Hara returned to duty in the summer of 1781, the fate of the earl's army had already been sealed. Cornwallis had moved into Virginia, clashed indecisively with Lafayette, and then taken up a "defensive post" at Yorktown. His messages to O'Hara, who was still in Portsmouth, scarcely reflected confidence. "Dear Charles," he scrawled hastily on August 2, "after a passage of four days we landed here . . . without opposition. The position is bad, and of course we want more troops. . . ." And on August 4: "I am not easy about my post . . . and am in great want of negroes to work, as the heat is too great to admit of the soldiers doing it. . . ." By August 22 O'Hara was at Yorktown—the only other general officer present—doing his best to raise his chief's spirits and to put the defenses of the place in order. But Cornwallis seemed overcome by lassitude and indecision, and as for the town itself, little could be done with the resources at hand. Within a few weeks a Franco-American army under Rochambeau and Washington was besieging the garrison, whose only hope was relief from the sea. O'Hara, as second in command, was forbidden to lead a sortie, and those that were attempted accomplished little. When it became evident that Yorktown could neither be held nor evacuated, and that help could not arrive in time, Cornwallis, with O'Hara's reluctant concurrence, capitulated on October 20.

The formal surrender of the British army took place at noon on the twentieth. Cornwallis, pleading illness, sent his deputy to preside over this unhappy ceremony. O'Hara was conducted to the surrender field by Colonel Mathieu Dumas, Rochambeau's aide-de-camp, who described how the "dark, ruddy-faced Irishman" sought to make his submission to the French commander, displaying the reluctance shared by most British officers to accept defeat at the hands of the "Yankees." Rochambeau gestured toward Washington, who in turn indicated General Lincoln, his own second in command, as the proper person to receive O'Hara's surrender. Then followed the laying down of arms and the departure of the rank and file into captivity. O'Hara, like the other officers, was promptly paroled and, making the best of a bad business, dined cheerfully that night with Washington and the next evening amazed all by his conviviality as a guest at Rochambeau's table.

General Patrick Cleburne, a native of County Cork, was one of the Confederacy's most able commanders. Although comparatively few Irish settled in the South, many of them fought valiantly under the "Stars and Bars." Cleburne was killed in action in 1864.

Unlike Cornwallis, who went home in December, O'Hara remained in New York even after his exchange (for the American Brigadier Lachlan MacIntosh, captured at Charleston) had been ratified on February 9, 1782. He served on several boards of general officers, having been promoted to major general as of October 19, 1781, and in March was one of the four-to-two majority in a council of war that rejected Clinton's proposal for a new campaign up the Delaware. In April he sailed to Charleston, picked up two infantry regiments, and proceeded south to reinforce Jamaica, then threatened by French naval operations. The invasion did not come, however, and after his troops had been distributed among the Carribean garrisons, O'Hara returned to New York in the fall and departed for England. The war was as good as over.

O'Hara had inherited his father's improvident habits: by the end of 1783 he had been compelled to withdraw to the Continent until he could put his tangled finances in order. He spent much of 1784 in Italy in the company of his friend General Conway. On December 7, Cornwallis wrote to his cousin, Lord Sydney, a secretary of state, on behalf of the exile: "I inclose to you a letter which I have received from my old friend

Charles O'Hara. . . . His zealous service under my command . . . give him a just claim, independent of our old friendship, to my strongest representations in his favour." By the summer of 1785 O'Hara's affairs were in order and October found him back in London. He could undoubtedly have procured an appointment under Cornwallis when the earl went to India as governor-general in the following year, but O'Hara, having tasted Europe, Africa, and America, had no desire to add Asia to the list. In 1787 he was appointed to the staff at Gibraltar, and remained there as commandant of the garrison.

By this time, Britain was on the verge of a new war. Once hostilities commenced with Revolutionary France early in 1793, O'Hara could expect to see action again. In September 1793 he was directed to proceed to Toulon, which had raised the banner of the Bourbons, and assume the office of military governor. For the first time during an actual war, O'Hara had been given a major independent command, and with it went a promotion to lieutenant general. He arrived at Toulon on October 27 and set about improving the defenses of the city against the besieging Republican army.

O'Hara had at his disposal nearly 15,000 Neapolitans, Sardinians, Spaniards, and French royalists, in addition to 2,000 British infantry brought from Gibraltar and the seamen and marines of Lord Hood's fleet. Sickness and the strains of the siege left him with no more than 12,000 effectives, however, and the quarrels and rivalries within his multinational garrison added another dimension to his problems. The French, numbering about 25,000, had been more hampered in their operations by political interference and inept leadership than by the Allied forces, but O'Hara's arrival at Toulon coincided almost exactly with the appointment of General Dugommier to direct the siege. This clever and capable veteran soon intensified the bombardment of the outlying forts to the point where their fall seemed imminent.

Undoubtedly O'Hara remembered the fatal outcome of Cornwallis's inertia at Yorktown. Then he had been powerless to avert the consequences of passivity; now, as commander in his own right, he determined on a policy of counterattack. After several preliminary blows against the besiegers, O'Hara led a sortie in strength on November 29 that overran the key Battery of the Convention on the left of the French line. Dugommier fought back desperately to keep O'Hara from pressing on to the artillery parks and stores in the French rear. One of his columns reached the foot of the captured battery through an unnoticed supply trench and opened fire on the Neapolitans, who volleyed back blindly. O'Hara climbed up on the breastwork to discover the enemy's position and was hit in the right arm by a French sharpshooter. He toppled off the breastwork, rolled down the slope, and was seized by the French. They at first believed him to be a colonel, and were amazed to discover that their prisoner was the Allied commander, whose brave but imprudent involve-

THE FOUR DRINKS—THE DRINK OF THIRST, THE DRINK WITHOUT THIRST, THE DRINK FOR FEAR OF THIRST, AND THE DRINK AT THE DOOR.
Traditional Irish Proverb

ment in a task that ought to have been confided to a subordinate left Toulon without its governor. O'Hara's captor was none other than *chef de bataillon* Napoléon Bonaparte, who courteously returned his sword and saw to it that he was well treated.

Unfortunately, these civilities from the future emperor did not set the tone of O'Hara's captivity. He was regarded not as a military prisoner but as a political criminal for having proclaimed Louis XVII at Toulon and promoted insurrection. His subsequent treatment at the hands of the French Republic was very different from that accorded him after Yorktown. En route to face "Republican justice" in the capital, he was obliged to sample his probable fate by being stood in front of a guillotine at Lyons while forty "enemies of the people," mostly women and young girls, were beheaded. In Paris, O'Hara was paraded back and forth through the streets to receive the insults of the mob before being imprisoned in the Luxembourg. He was allowed to retain two servants and a surgeon to attend to his wound, but these three, as well as an English drummer boy, a Spanish officer and his servant, a German officer, and two other prisoners all shared the general's small room. They were allowed no eating utensils. Their food, usually "offals of the market, like dog's meat," was deposited in troughs and they were led out at stated hours "to feed together in droves, like cattle." Constantly abused and insulted, he was kept in suspense as each day a few dozen of his fellow prisoners were taken away to be executed. Finally, "articles of accusation" were drawn up against him, and he was on the point of being brought before the Revolutionary Tribunal when, on July 27, 1794, Robespierre was overthrown and the Reign of Terror came to an end. After this the conditions of O'Hara's imprisonment were eased, and he was even allowed to walk about in the streets of Paris, though always under guard. Nevertheless, it was more than a year before he was exchanged, in August 1795.

While O'Hara had been in prison, Toulon had fallen, British arms had suffered new reverses, and—perhaps most interesting to him—Sir Robert Boyd, governor of Gibraltar, had died in May 1794. Clinton had been awarded the governorship ("God forbid I should interfere with O'Hara," he had written, "but I never thought Gibraltar was intended for him"). But Clinton had been in ill health for the past year and had never gone out to Gibraltar. By the time O'Hara returned to England in August 1795 it was evident that Sir Henry would never recover and that the governorship would go to the "great, plausible talker" after all. O'Hara was still suffering from the aftereffects of the wound he had sustained at Toulon, but despite his discomfort and the prospect of a return to duty, he found time to pay court to Mary Berry, the authoress and protégée of Horace Walpole, whom he had first met in Rome in May 1784. A "tender attachment" had developed during the intervening years, and now O'Hara, the man-about-town, was prepared to spend his

This tidal wave of Irish corruption is too much for you and I to do much about. This brutalized, shovel-faced Mick underclass of Moon Mullins types are usually three sheets in the wind. There will always be taxpayer-supported jobs for these morons and a gutless nonentity like Massachusetts Governor Dukakis to put them on the payroll.

Anonymous letter in the *Boston Herald* (1987)

mellowing years in married tranquillity. They became engaged, but when, at the end of 1795, he had to leave for Gibraltar (Clinton died on December 23), Miss Berry declined to leave her family. She was to join him later, but doubts and recriminations led to estrangement, and they never met again.

O'Hara spent the remaining six years of his life as governor of Gibraltar. It was a post of high responsibility at a time of grave danger, but although there was a great deal of activity and alarm in the Mediterranean during this period, life in the citadel was routine and orderly. O'Hara (who became a full general on January 1, 1798) was a strict disciplinarian and apparently regarded his fellow Celts as a troublesome lot. In March 1799 Cornwallis—then lord lieutenant in Dublin—was warned not to send him any Irish militia regiments, as he had "too many Irish in Gibraltar already." Admiral Sir William Hotham, who knew him at this time, recorded: "O'Hara was not a good-tempered man; and, though he had the manners of one very conversant with the world, and was considered a very good officer, he was frequently subject to fits of ill-humour which he was at no pains to conceal. This was partly attributed to the suffering and privations he had undergone while in the Luxembourg, which had permanently soured his disposition."

Yet O'Hara was popular with the garrison, who called him "Old Cock of the Rock," and acknowledged the justice and fairness of his regime. Despite the pain he suffered from his old wounds in his last years, he offered lavish hospitality at his residence, the Convent, and exerted on the local merchants and their families the same charm he had displayed throughout his career. Still a tall, handsome man, "with his face as ruddy and black and his teeth as white as ever," he retained the dazzling smile and the dandified habits of his younger days.

In August 1801 O'Hara's health suddenly worsened, and there ensued "an illness of six months, during which he suffered the most excruciating tortures from his wounds breaking out afresh and a dreadful strangury which followed." He placed his estate in the care of three trustees, one of whom was his regimental agent, Mr. Bowmas, another of Tyrawley's sons. Despite his financial vicissitudes in the past, he had amassed a considerable fortune in his later years, and some $70,000 was placed in trust to provide annuities for his own natural children. On February 21, 1801, his sufferings ended in death.

"The General's death is much felt and lamented at Gibraltar," recorded his obituary. "Few men possessed so happy a combination of rare talents. He was a brave and enterprising soldier . . . and a polite accomplished gentleman." True enough, for even if Charles O'Hara was not a commander of the first rank, his fifty-year career had been a distinguished one. Yet the obituary omits O'Hara's greatest claim to fame: the unique experience of being captured personally by both George Washington and Napoléon Bonaparte. ◆

MAY YOU BE POOR IN MISFORTUNE, RICH IN BLESSINGS, SLOW TO MAKE ENEMIES, QUICK TO MAKE FRIENDS. BUT RICH OR POOR, QUICK OR SLOW, MAY YOU KNOW NOTHING BUT HAPPINESS FROM THIS DAY FORWARD.
Traditional Irish Toast

Thomas Conway's "Bum Rap"

*A*merican history textbooks invariably sing the praises of the heroic foreign volunteers who fought for liberty during the Revolutionary War. Lafayette, Pulaski, DeKalb, and others have their names commemorated by everything from forts to high schools. Yet no one has a good word to say for Thomas Conway. On the contrary, the Irish-born general is portrayed as the leader of a plot against George Washington. References to the "Conway cabal" and its efforts to oust Washington as commander in chief of the Revolutionary army have perpetuated the Irishman's name in dishonor. The record needs to be set straight.

Thomas Conway was born in Kerry in 1735 and taken to France for his education six years later. While still in his teens, he was commissioned in the Irish Brigade of the French army; by 1777, after distinguished service on campaign in Germany, he had attained the rank of colonel. In 1776, the American representatives in France recommended him, along with a number of other French officers, for service in the Revolutionary forces. On his arrival in the New World he was appointed brigadier general in the Continental Army. Conway soon justified his reputation as a skilled tactician and an outstanding administrator. His brigade of Pennsylvania troops became one of the best-drilled and most-admired units in the army. During the Brandywine and Germantown operations Conway aroused "a respect that amounted almost to awe" in the minds of his superiors. In December 1777—a mere seven months after his arrival—Conway was promoted to major general, over the heads of twenty-three senior brigadiers, and named inspector general of the army.

The so-called cabal with which Conway's name has been linked had, in the meantime, arisen because of reverses suffered by the forces under Washington's direct command during the same period that General Horatio Gates was defeating the British in the Saratoga campaign. Some argued that Gates was the better general and should replace Washington; Gates himself did nothing to discourage this talk. While no actual conspiracy ever materialized, such senior officers as General Charles Lee and General Thomas Mifflin were highly critical of Washington, and their position found support in Congress.

Into the midst of this intrigue and gossip blundered Thomas Conway, whose chief faults were frankness and loquacity. He had been offended by Washington's reluctance to see him promoted so rapidly and did not bother to conceal his professional impatience with the sometimes amateurish conduct of military operations. Anonymous criticisms favoring Gates over Washington came to the commander in chief's attention and he erroneously believed that they were authored by Conway. He did not confront the Irish officer directly, but chose to have an accounting with Gates, who disowned all disloyal talk. Lee, Mifflin, and the others immediately denied any hostile intent and pointed the finger at Conway.

Conway now found himself the scapegoat for the so-called cabal, of which he had been, at worst, only a peripheral associate. Lafayette, indignant over the "treacherous" behavior that he attributed to his fellow soldier of fortune, refused to accept him as his second in command, and several other "loyal" generals likewise repudiated him. In April 1778 Conway appealed to Congress for an independent command appropriate to his rank and threatened to resign. The anti-Washington faction had no further use for him as a front now, and to his "surprise and chagrin," his resignation was accepted.

Conway's troubles in America were not yet over, however. Colonel John Cadwalader, supposedly angry over Conway's aspersions on Washington, picked a quarrel with the Irishman that resulted in a duel fought on July 4, 1778. Conway was shot in the face.

Perhaps believing himself at death's door and wanting to clear his reputation, Conway wrote a letter to Washington, with whom he had had no direct communication throughout the course of the "conspiracy."

"I find myself just able to hold the pen during a few minutes," he explained, "and take this opportunity of expressing my sincere grief for having done, written, or said anything disagreeable to your Excellency. My career will soon be over; therefore justice and truth prompt me to declare my last sentiments. You are in my eyes the great and good man. May you long enjoy the love, veneration and esteem of these States, whose liberties you have asserted by your virtues."

Washington, no doubt deeming this an exercise of blarney, did not reply.

Conway returned to France, where he recovered and resumed his career in the Royal army, rising to the rank of general and becoming governor of French possessions in the Indian Ocean. At the outbreak of the Revolution his conservative sympathies stirred up resentment among the colonists, and he was called home. He fared no better in the French Revolution than he had in the American. Denounced as a monarchist intriguer, he was forced to flee from France. Ironically, he found refuge in Britain, where he was commissioned colonel of an Irish regiment raised to fight the French Republic. He died in his British exile in 1800.

Clearly, Conway was neither a military genius nor a patriotic hero. But he was a competent, experienced field commander and a strict disciplinarian with a gift for training officers and men. Under different circumstances he might have become the drill master of the Revolution that Steuben, his successor as inspector general, eventually became. He might well have transformed the raw recruits of the Continental Army into first-class soldiers, as he did with his own brigade, and thereby shortened the war. But he fell into the midst of personal and political intrigues he did not fully understand, and his vanity and indiscretion made him the dupe of those who did not challenge Washington themselves. When their maneuvers were uncovered, they threw the blame on the "foreigner"—and the blame has stuck for the last two centuries.

It is doubtful that there was anything substantial enough under way in 1778 to be termed a cabal. In any case, there was certainly no such thing as a "Conway cabal." In the vernacular of contemporary criminal justice, Thomas Conway got a bum rap. ◆

General Philip Sheridan and his senior officers gather in front of headquarters tent during the 1864 campaign in Virginia.

I thought it was all so much damned tomfoolery and humbug. That was at first. But I found that the most pious of them were the very bravest—and that astonished me more than anything. I saw these men tried in every way that men could be tried, and I never saw anything superior to them. Why, sir, if I wanted to storm the gates of hell, I didn't want any finer or braver fellows than those Irishmen. . . . I saw how their religion gave them courage to meet death with cheerful resignation.

U.S. Army colonel quoted by John F. Maguire, *The Irish in America* (1868)

Officers, but Not Gentlemen?

The following "efficiency report," dated August 15, 1813, was sent to the War Department by General Lewis Cass, and contains "all the observations I deem necessary to make." Cass, who later became a senator and served as secretary of war and secretary of state, was the Democratic nominee for president in 1848. Presumably, by that time he had learned to disguise his anti-Irish prejudices.

27TH REGT. INFANTRY

Alex Deniston, Lt. Col. Comdg.   *A good-natured man.*

Clarkson Crolins, First Major   *A good man but no officer.*

Jesse D. Wadsworth, Second Major   *An excellent officer.*

Captain Shotwell   *A man of whom all unite in speaking ill. A knave despised by all.*

Captain Thomas Earle   *Indifferent, but promises well.*

Captain Allen Reynolds   *An officer of capacity, but imprudent and a man of violent passions.*

Captain Daniel Warren, Captain Porter   *Strangers but little known in the Regiment.*

1st Lieut. Jas. Kerr, 1st Lieut. Thomas Carling   *Merely good, nothing promising.*

1st Lieut. Wm. Perrin, 1st Lieut. Dnl. Scott, 1st Lieut. Jas. Ryan, 1st Lieut. Robt. McElwrath   *Low vulgar men, with the exception of Perrin. Irish and from the meanest walks of life—possessing nothing of the character of officers and gentlemen.*

1st Lieut. Robert F. Ross   *Willing enough—has much to learn—with small capacity.*

2nd Lieut. Nicholas O. Garner   *A good officer but drinks hard and disgraces the service and himself.*

2nd Lieut. Stuart Elfer   *An ignorant unoffending Irishman.*

2nd Lieut. McConiley   *Raised from the ranks, ignorant, vulgar and incompetent.*

2nd Lieut. James Carrey   *A stranger in the Regiment.*

2nd Lieut. Darrows   *Just joined the Regiment—of fine appearance.*

2nd Lieut. Piercy, 2nd Lieut. Thomas G. Spicey   *Raised from the ranks but behave well and promise to make excellent officers.*

2nd Lieut. Oliver Vance, 2nd Lieut. Royal Geer, 2nd Lieut. Miars, 2nd Lieut. Crawford, 2nd Lieut. Clifford   *All Irish, promoted from the ranks, low vulgar men without any one qualification to recommend them—more fit to carry the hod than the epaulette.*

2nd Lieut. John G. Scholtz, 2nd Lieut. Francis T. Wheeler   *Promoted from the ranks. Behave well and will make good officers.*

Ensign Rehan   *The very dregs of the earth. Unfit for anything under heaven. God only knows how the poor thing got an appointment.*

Ensign John Brown, Ensign Byron   *Promoted from the ranks—men of no manner and no promise.*

Ensign Charles West   *From the ranks. A good young man who does well.*

Luckless Leatherneck

*A*nthony Gale was born in Dublin, emigrated to the United States after the Revolution, and by 1798 had obtained a commission in the United States Marine Corps. Evidently a man of strong temper, he killed a naval officer in a duel a few months later. Nevertheless, he served uneventfully thereafter, and after long sea duty was given the choice appointment of barracks commander at Philadelphia in 1815. Gale soon became involved in a dispute with his superiors, however, and the commandant, Colonel Wharton, ordered a court of inquiry. Although the Irishman was cleared, Wharton transferred him to a less desirable post in New Orleans. There he began to drink heavily.

When his antagonist, Colonel Wharton, died, in September 1819, Gale found himself the senior serving officer of the Marine Corps. Many officers felt that, despite his rank, he was not fit to be commandant. Led by Major Arthur Henderson, they blocked his appointment, and the position remained vacant for six months. Finally, in March 1819, at the age of thirty-six, Major Anthony Gale became fourth commandant of the Marine Corps. His troubles, though, were just beginning.

Gale (now promoted to colonel) was probably not the most competent of administrators, and he was certainly intemperate, in every sense of the word. Nevertheless, his downfall was not solely of his own making. The corps at this time was deeply split into warring factions, led by ambitious careerists like Henderson and the adjutant, Samuel Miller. Gale, who had few friends, became the target of vicious allegations and outright conspiracies, in which ethnic prejudice seems to have played a part. A running battle developed between the commandant and the secretary of the navy over questions of prerogative and financial accountability. Finally, in August 1820, Gale was placed under arrest and a court-martial ordered.

The outcome was a foregone conclusion. The court-martial found Gale guilty of malfeasance; President Monroe ratified the findings. In October, Gale was dismissed from his office and from the corps.

The chief intriguer at headquarters, Major Henderson, became commandant—a position he held for the next thirty-eight years. The disgraced Colonel Gale withdrew to Kentucky, where he died in 1843. ◆

The wonder is not that the Irish hate the English, but that they really don't hate them.

Andrew Greeley, in the Chicago *Sun-Times* (1987)

The San Patricio Deserters in the Mexican War, 1847

In September 1959 a memorial was erected in the Plaza de San Jacinto in San Angel, Federal District of Mexico, to the San Patricio Battalion. The memorial is a tablet in the wall of one of the buildings in the square, and the inscription on it reads:

En memoria de los soldados Irlandeses del heróico batallón de San Patricio mártires que dieron su vida por la causa de México durante la injusta invasión Norteamericana de 1847.*

Capitán John O'Reilly	Peter Neil	James Speers	Martin Lydon
Henry Logenhamer	Kerr Delaney	Abraham Fitzpatrick	Dennis Conahan
Henry Venator	Patrick Antison	Henry Ocker	Auguste Morsrtaft
Francis Rhode	Harrison Kenny	Henry Whistler	James Mcdowel
John Kiager	Roger Hogan	William H. Keeck	Gibson Mcdowel
Alfred K. Fogal	John Sheehan	Edward Mcherron	Hugh Mcclelland
George Dalwig	John A. Myers	Andrew Nolan	John Mcdonald
Berney Hart	Richard Parker	Patrick Dalton	John Cavanaugh
Thomas Millet	Lemmuel Wheaton	John Cuttle	Thomas Cassidy
Hozekiah Akles	Samuel H. Thomas	John Price	John Daly
John Bartely	David Mcelroy	William Oathouse	Martin Miles
Alexander Mckee	John Benedick	William A. Wallace	Parian Fritz
F. W. Garretson	John Rose	Elizier S. Lusk	James Kelly
John Bowers	Lachiar Mclachlen	Herman Schmidt	John Murphy
M. T. Frantius	Patrick Casey	Thomas Riley	John Little
Henry Mewer	John Brooke	James Mills	Lewis Preifer
Francis O'Connor	Roger Duhan	Lawrence Mackey	

Con la gratitud de México a los 112 años de su sacrificio Septiembre de 1959†

*Translation: In memory of the Irish soldiers of the heroic San Patricio battalion, martyrs who gave their lives for the cause of Mexico during the unjust North American invasion of 1847.

†Translation: With the gratitude of Mexico on the 112th anniversary of their sacrifice, September 1959.

The Irish Americans in the Mexican War, as Described by General Winfield Scott, in a Letter to the Journalist W. E. Robinson

JULY 2, 1850

*I*n Mexico, we estimated the number of persons in the army, foreigners by birth, at about 3500, & of these more than 2000 were Irish. How many had been naturalized I can not say, but am persuaded that seven out of ten had at least declared their intentions, according to law, to become citizens. . . .

It is hazardous, or may be invidious, to make distinctions; but truth obliges me to say that, of our Irish soldiers—save a few who deserted from General Taylor, and had never taken the naturalization oath—not one ever turned his back upon the enemy or faltered in advancing to the charge. Most of the other foreigners, by birth, also behaved faithfully and gallantly. ◆

The Irish Brigade

One of the most famous units of the Northern army during the Civil War was the Irish Brigade. This name has been used so frequently at various times and in various places that some confusion has arisen over exactly what forces constituted this most renowned of all Irish Brigades.

As originally created, the Irish Brigade included the 63rd, 69th, and 88th New York infantry regiments. In the fall of 1862 the 28th Massachusetts and the 116th Pennsylvania were added. Also, the 29th Massachusetts was attached to the brigade during the campaigns of the Peninsula and Antietam. The surviving fragments of the 7th New York were attached in September 1864 shortly after the 116th Pennsylvania was transferred.

The most famous fight of the brigade took place during the Battle of Fredericksburg, when it suffered enormous casualties in repeated gallant charges at Marye's Heights.

The successive commanders of the brigade were Brigadier General Thomas F. Meagher, Colonel Patrick Kelly (killed at Petersburg), Colonel Thomas A. Smyth (killed at Farmville), Colonel Richard Byrnes (killed at Cold Harbor), and Brigadier General Robert Nugent.

The brigade served throughout the war in the First Division of the Second Corps, Army of the Potomac. ◆

This recruiting poster for a Massachusetts Irish regiment dates from early in the Civil War. Later enlistment bounties were much higher. General Michael Corcoran, the first commander of the Irish Brigade ("Our Irish Hero") was killed in a battlefield accident and succeeded by General T. F. Meagher.

IRISH IN THE UNION ARMY, 1861–1865

New York	51,206	Missouri	4,362	Kentucky	1,303
Pennsylvania	17,418	Wisconsin	3,621	Vermont	1,289
Illinois	12,041	Indiana	3,472	Minnesota	1,140
Massachusetts	10,007	Michigan	3,278	Kansas	1,082
New Jersey	8,880	New Hampshire	2,699	District of Columbia	698
Ohio	8,129	Maine	1,971	Delaware	582
Rhode Island and		Iowa	1,436	West Virginia	550
Connecticut	7,657	Maryland	1,400		

These 144,221 men of Irish birth constituted one-fourth of all foreign-born volunteers in the Union army.

THIRD IRISH
REGIMENT

From Massachusetts, and First Irish Regiment for Nine Months' Service.

25 ABLE-BODIED MEN

Wanted to fill up the Company to be commanded by

CAPTAIN WILLIAMS,

Formerly of the MASS. 24th; now of the 55TH (IRISH) MASS. REG'T.

Come with us and our IRISH HERO,

CORCORAN

Let us carry the American Eagle over the Potomac, down like an avalanche through the land of Dixie, emulating

THE GLORY of the other IRISH REGIMENTS.

$150 Bounty

And all who Enlist will receive the STATE AID.

All Recruits to this Regiment, on signing the Muster Roll, will go at once into comfortable quarters, and receive full rations of the best the market affords. Apply immediately to

Captain WILLIAMS, or, Lieut. LEONARD!
No. 109 CAMBRIDGE STREET, BOSTON.

Herald Job Office, No. 4 Williams Court, Boston.

"Irish Bridget"

Mathew Brady, already admired as a portrait photographer, won his greatest renown as the camera chronicler of the Civil War. This picture was made at the siege of Petersburg, Virginia.

Bridget Divers became a famous figure in the Union army during the Civil War. When her husband enlisted in the First Michigan Cavalry, she followed him on campaign and served as a nurse. She often rode into action, and had several horses killed under her. On more than one occasion, she helped to rally the regiment. At the Battle of Fair Oaks, she reportedly looked up from attending her wounded husband, and yelled, "Arragh, go in, b'ys! Bate the bloody spalpeens and revinge me husband." This halted a retreat and drove the men back into a charge. At the Battle of Cedar Creek she galloped through the enemy lines after they had surrounded her, and tales were told of even more daring escapades on other fields.

Mrs. Divers, who was nicknamed both "Irish Bridget" and "Michigan Bridget," continued her military career after the war, during the Indian campaigns. The regiments serving in the West were authorized to have four laundresses per company, usually wives of the enlisted men. In this modest but congenial role, Bridget was able to continue her soldiering for the rest of her life. ◆

Irish Soldiers
in Gray

uring the siege of New Orleans, in May 1862, Forts Jackson and St.
Philip were defended by several companies of Irish-born troops in
Confederate service, commanded by officers with names like Quigley,
Mullen, Ryan, and Kennedy. Though full of inaccuracies and exaggerations, this ballad gives an idea of Irish interest in the deeds of their
kinfolk in America.

A NEW SONG ON THE DREADFUL
ENGAGEMENT WITH A TREMENDOUS
LOSS OF IRISH IN AMERICA

You Irishmen and women too draw near both young and old,
A doleful lamentation now to you I will unfold,
One hundred gallant Irishmen we are left for to deplore
Whose bodies fell a victim upon fair Columbia's shore.

It was at the siege of New Orleans upon the 9th of May,
Our countrymen they suffered sore upon that fatal day.
They were engaged by five to one when charged on with the steel,
But Erin's sons did loudly cry, "We'll die before we'll yield."

They were repulsed—they could not stand—exertion proved in vain,
They strove to break the enemy's force and drive them off the plain,
But alas, their number was too small and gave them no fair play,
Not one of them did there escape upon that awful day.

To see the streets that evening each heart would rend with pain,
The human blood in rivers ran like any flood or stream,
Men's heads blown off their bodies most dismal for to see,
And wounded men did loudly cry with pain and agony.

The Federals they did then advance and broke in through the town,
They trampled dead and wounded men that lay upon the ground.
The wounded called for mercy, but none they did receive,
They numbered them among the dead and threw them in a grave.

HERE'S TO YOU, AS
GOOD AS YOU ARE.
HERE'S TO ME, AS
BAD AS I AM. AS
GOOD AS YOU ARE
AND AS BAD AS I AM,
I'M AS GOOD AS YOU
ARE, AS BAD AS I AM.
Traditional Irish Toast

Three hundred killed and wounded that day lay in their grave
One half of them were Irishmen far from their native shore.
Poor orphans now may weep and cry and parents rue the day
They let their lovely children go unto America.

All you that hear those doleful lines do not neglect to toil
And labour for a livelihood on bless'd St. Patrick's Isle,
And think upon our countrymen that left their native shore;
Their friends may mourn for their loss, they'll never see them more.

Now to conclude in these few lines, with grief I'll say no more,
You know it was through poverty they left their native shore.
They had no one to heal their wounds; may angels them surround,
Before the throne of Heaven may they wear a brilliant crown. ◆

Father Abraham Corby, chaplain of the Irish Brigade, gives his benediction to the soldiers of New York's Fighting Sixty-ninth before they carry their green regimental banner into the battle of Gettysburg (July 1863).

Lynch's Law

*C*harles Lynch (1736–1796) was a planter and justice of the peace in Colonial Virginia, residing near the town that his Irish immigrant forebears had founded, Lynchburg. He joined the Revolution and commanded a volunteer regiment under General Nathanael Greene at the battle of Guilford Court House. During the disturbed and lawless times when rebels and loyalists were struggling for control of Virginia, Lynch presided over an extralegal court that dispensed arbitrary justice. Conviction was followed by summary punishment, usually flogging, but in more serious cases hanging. The terms *lynch law* and *lynching* derive from the drastic methods of this Irish-American judge. ◆

Father and Son

wo members of an Irish American family, the Mahans, profoundly influenced American military and naval policy in the nineteenth century.

Dennis Hart Mahan (1802–1871) was born in New York City, to parents who had left Ireland after the failed rebellion of 1798. He had a brilliant academic career as a cadet at West Point and was appointed acting instructor in mathematics while still a student. Following graduation at the head of his class, he was given a regular appointment on the West Point faculty, and spent the years 1826–1830 in France pursuing advanced studies. He then returned to the military academy, where he spent the rest of his life, becoming professor of civil and military engineering in 1832 and dean of the faculty in 1838. To meet the need for suitable textbooks, he wrote *Complete Treatise on Field Fortification*, *Course of Civil Engineering*, and *Treatise on . . . Service of Troops*, all of which long remained standard works in the field of military science. Not only did these and his other books serve as texts for the academy, but Mahan's exacting instruction, combined with his grand concept of the need of military education, raised the standards of the West Point curriculum to a new height. Mahan was the teacher and guide of almost all the senior commanders on both sides of the Civil War.

His son, Alfred Thayer Mahan (1840–1914), was born at West Point, where his father had already established his dominance as the mentor of America's future military leaders. Alfred, however, chose a naval career and, after graduation from Annapolis in 1859, served on blockade duty throughout the Civil War. During twenty years of postwar cruises and routine assignments, he devoted himself to the study of naval history and theory. In 1885, due to his reputation for scholarship, Captain Mahan was appointed lecturer on history and strategy at the new Naval War College. He became president of that institution in 1886, holding the post until 1889. The next year his lectures were published as *The Influence of Sea Power upon History*, a book that revolutionized the study of international affairs and the role of the armed forces in shaping them. By the time his second major work, *The Influence of Sea Power upon the French Revolution and Empire*, appeared in 1892, he had already won

❝Ours was a picked lot. They came mainly from the Irish County Societies and the Catholic Athletic Clubs. A number of the latter Irish bore distinctly German, French, Italian, or Polish names. They were Irish by adoption, Irish by association, or Irish by conviction.❞

Father Francis P. Duffy, chaplain of the Fighting Sixty-Ninth Regiment, *Diary* (1918)

worldwide recognition, and this further analysis of naval power also became a classic. Mahan's books and articles continued to appear throughout the remainder of his life, and exercised a tremendous influence among both American and foreign leaders. The worldwide growth of naval forces in the period before the First World War owed much to the impact of Mahan's thought upon American, British, and German strategists. Mahan served another term as president of the Naval War College, and was a member of the naval strategy board during the Spanish-American War; he retired with the rank of rear admiral. His civilian honors range from honorary doctorates at Oxford and Cambridge to the presidency of the American Historical Association.

The Mahans, father and son, guided the thinking of generations of American military and naval leaders from the Mexican War to the Great War. In that sense, they were perhaps the most important soldier and sailor among the hundreds of thousands of Irish Americans who have worn the uniform of the United States. ◆

During the relatively quiet early days of the Civil War, members of the Sixty-ninth New York Regiment and their guests gather for Sunday Mass. The Fighting Sixty-ninth was encamped during the summer of 1861 in northern Virginia, just across the Potomac from Washington, D.C., and was frequently visited by wives and other civilian friends.

Irish-
American
Heroes in
World War II

*A*mong the tens of thousands of Irish Americans who distinguished themselves during World War II, several names gained special attention. The first hero of the war was Captain Colin Kelly, pilot of a bomber that destroyed a Japanese warship in the Philippines on December 9, 1941. When his plane was damaged by enemy fire, he ordered his crew to bail out, and he flew on until the plane crashed. He was posthumously awarded the Distinguished Service Cross.

Thomas B. McGuire was born in New Jersey in 1920 and entered the army air corps in 1941. During his service in the Pacific he shot down a total of thirty-eight Japanese planes, making him the second-highest-ranking American fighter ace of the war. On January 7, 1945, while aiding a comrade under attack, Major McGuire crashed in the Philippines. He was awarded a posthumous Medal of Honor in December 1944 and January 1945. McGuire Air Force Base in New Jersey is named for him.

Edward H. O'Hare was born in St. Louis in 1914 and graduated from the Naval Academy in 1937. Early in 1942, he was serving as a naval aviator on the carrier *Lexington*. When the ship was attacked by Japanese bombers, and the rest of his squadron was heavily engaged, O'Hare found himself alone, opposed by an entire enemy squadron. He attacked the nine heavily armed bombers single-handed, shooting down five and damaging three others. The surviving attackers fled. O'Hare had saved the *Lexington* and become the Navy's first ace of the war. He was awarded the Medal of Honor and promoted to lieutenant commander. By November 20, 1943, he had shot down a total of twelve enemy planes; on that date he was listed as missing in action. O'Hare International Airport in Chicago is named in his honor.

Audie Murphy was born in 1924 to a poor Texas Irish sharecropping family. He enlisted in the army in 1942, and during the next thirty months rose from private to lieutenant, serving in Tunisia, Sicily, Italy, France, and Germany. Wounded three times, he was repeatedly cited for gallantry in action. He won the Medal of Honor for single-handedly holding off a German force of half a dozen tanks and over 200 men. With a total of twenty-eight American and foreign medals, he was the most highly decorated United States serviceman of World War II. ◆

Irish-Born Recipients of the Congressional Medal of Honor

The Medal of Honor is the highest decoration awarded to members of the American armed forces. It is conferred by the president, in the name of Congress, upon one "who, while serving in the armed forces distinguished himself conspicuously by gallantry and intrepidity, at the risk of his life, above and beyond the call of duty."

Instituted by Abraham Lincoln, the medal was first presented in 1861. The 202 Irish-born recipients constitute the largest group of immigrants to receive this award.

CIVIL WAR

David L. Bass
Terrence Begley
Felix Brannigan
Christopher Brennan
John Brosnan
Michael Burk
Thomas Burke
William Campbell
Hugh Carey
David Casey
Thomas Connor
James Connors
John Cooper
Thomas Cosgrove
John Creed
Thomas Cullen
Timothy Donoghue
Patrick Doody
William Downey
Thomas T. Fallon
Thomas Flood
Christopher Flynn
George Ford
William Gardner
Richard Gasson
James H. Gribben
John H. Havron

John Highland
Patrick Highland
Michael Hudson
Patrick Irwin
Andrew Jones
William Jones
John Kane
Joseph Keele
Thomas Kelly
John Kennedy
Hugh Logan
John Lonergan
Richard C. Mangam
Edward S. Martin
James Martin
Peter McAdams
Charles McAnally
Bernard McCarren
Michael McCormick
Patrick H. McEnroe
Patrick McGinley
Owen McGough
John McGowan
Thomas McGraw
Patrick McGuire
Alexander U. McHale
George McKee

Michael McKeever
Patrick Monaghan
Robert Montgomery
Charles Moore
Charles W. Morton
Dennis J. F. Murphy
John P. Murphy
Thomas C. Murphy
John J. Nolan
Peter O'Brien
Timothy O'Connor
George C. Platt
Thomas Plunkett
John Preston
Peter Rafferty
John Rannahan
George Reynolds
Thomas Riley
John Robinson
Thomas Robinson
Peter J. Ryan
Patrick Scanlon
Bernard Shields
William Smith
Timothy Spillane
Joseph Stewart

Never were men so brave. They ennobled their race by their splendid gallantry on that desperate occasion. Though totally routed, they reaped a harvest of glory. Their brilliant, though hopeless, assaults on our lines excited the hearty applause of our officers and men.

General Robert E. Lee on the conduct of the Irish Brigade at Fredericksburg (1862), quoted in Michael Cavanagh, *Memoir of T. F. Meagher* (1892)

Timothy Sullivan
William Toomer
George William Tynell
M. Emmett Urell
John Walsh
Richard Welch
Thomas Wells
Edward Welsh
Christopher W. Wilson

INDIAN CAMPAIGNS

Richard Barrett
James Bell
Edward Branagan
James Brogan
Patrick Burke
Richard Burke
Edmond Butler
Denis Byrne
Thomas J. Callen
Thomas Carroll
George Carter
John Connor
Charles Daily
Charles H. Dickens
Cornelius Donavan
John S. Donelly
James Dowling
William Evans
Daniel Farren
James Fegan
John H. Foley
Nicholas Foran
Michael Glynn
Patrick Golden
Frank Hamilton
Richard Heartery
Thomas P. Higgins
Henry Hogan
Bernard J. D. Irwin
Daniel Keating
John Keenan
Charles Kelley
Philip Kennedy
Thomas Kerrigan
David Larkin
James Lenihan

Patrick Leonard
George Lloyd
Patrick Martin
William McCabe
Bernard McCann
Michael A. McGann
Michael McLoughlin
James McNally
William McNamara
Robert McPhelan
John Mitchell
John J. Mitchell
John Moran
James L. Morris
Myles Moylan
Edward Murphy
Jeremiah Murphy
Phillip Murphy
Thomas Murphy
Thomas Murray
John Nihill
Richard J. Nolan
Moses Orr
John O'Sullivan
William R. Parnell
Frederick Platten
James C. Reed
Joseph Robinson
David Roche
Patrick Rogan
David Ryan
Dennis Ryan
Thomas Sullivan
John Tracy
William Wallace

INTERIM, 1866 TO 1870

Thomas Burke
James Carey

KOREAN CAMPAIGN, 1871

John Coleman
James Dougherty
Patrick H. Grace
Michael McNamara

INTERIM, 1871 TO 1898

Thomas Cramen
John Dempsey
John Flannagan
Hugh King
Patrick J. Kyle
John Laverty
John O'Neal
Patrick Regan
Thomas Smith
James Thayer
Michael Thornton

WAR WITH SPAIN

George F. Brady
Thomas Cavanaugh
Thomas M. Doherty
John Fitzgerald
Philip Gaughan
Michael Gibbons
Michael Kearney
John Maxwell
Daniel Montague
John E. Murphy
Edward Sullivan

PHILIPPINE INSURRECTION

Cornelius J. Leahy
Thomas F. Prendergast
Patrick Shanahan

CHINA RELIEF EXPEDITION— BOXER REBELLION

James Cooney
Martin Hunt
Joseph Killackey
Samuel McAllister

INTERIM, 1901 TO 1911

Thomas Cahey
Edward Floyd
John King
Patrick Reid
Thomas Stanton

WORLD WAR I

Joseph H. Thompson ◆

Besides those who inhabit the United States of America, there are other Americans—those who live in Latin America. And just as the Irish have played a major role in the history of the United States, so they have contributed, albeit on a lesser scale, to the history of Latin America.

Although men of Irish descent had served in the Spanish army and administration during the colonial period (Ambrose O'Higgins had been viceroy of Peru, the highest-ranking office in all of Spanish America), Irishmen won the gratitude of the colonial peoples by joining in the wars of independence during the early nineteentth century. An Irish Legion recruited by John Devereaux in Dublin brought hundreds of volunteers to aid in the struggle for liberty. Devereaux, the redoubtable John Thomond O'Brien, and Morgan O'Connell, son of the great "Liberator," Daniel O'Connell, were in the forefront of Simón Bolívar's struggle against Spanish forces in what is now Colombia and Venezuela. Daniel Florence O'Leary played the role of statesman as well as soldier, helping to draft the constitution of the Republic of New Granada and representing Bolívar's government in Washington.

Farther south, Edward Sandes became a national hero and postindependence political figure in Ecuador, while Francis O'Connor played a similar role in Bolivia. William Brown, a Galway soldier turned adventurer, created and led the Argentine navy against the Spanish fleet. The long succession of Argentine warships named *Almirante Brown* in his honor testify to the esteem in which this Irish admiral is held in his adopted country. Bernardo O'Higgins, the Chilean-born son of Ambrose, led his nation's revolt against European rule, and was joined by naval and military commanders who included Raymond Morris, George O'Brien, and Charles O'Connor. Following the expulsion of the Spaniards, O'Higgins became the first head of the newly created republic of Chile.

In Mexico, while scarcely a freedom fighter, Juan O'Donojú made a decisive contribution to that country's freedom. Although the Spanish government had sent him, as captain general of New Spain, to repress the Mexican rebels, he negotiated a settlement with them (the Plan of Iguala, 1825) that virtually recognized their independence. He died

Bernardo O'Higgins, son of the Irish-born Spanish colonial viceroy, Ambrose O'Higgins, led Chile in revolt against colonial rule during the early 1800s. He became the Republic of Chile's first president, and is here pictured on one of its stamps.

Juan O'Donojú, a Spanish general of Irish descent, was Spain's last viceroy in Mexico. Defying instructions from the Madrid government, he recognized Mexico's independence from Spain in 1825. He is buried in the National Cathedral in Mexico City, and is regarded as a hero by Mexicans.

shortly afterward, and is buried in Mexico City's Cathedral, alongside other national heroes.

Brazil had won its independence from Portugal with relatively little bloodshed, by 1825. An exotic plant among the republics of South America, the new Brazil was a monarchy, with a son of the king of Portugal as emperor. Deciding to form an imperial guard that would include foreign troops, the government recruited large numbers of Germans and Irishmen. The volunteers were encouraged to bring their wives and children with them, for the ultimate purpose of the Brazilian authorities was to increase the "European" population of the country by establishing military colonies in the outlying provinces. The arrival of these "aliens" provoked hostility in Rio de Janeiro, however. The local militia, in particular, resented the threat to their military monopoly posed by the outsiders. The crisis came when the newly formed Irish battalion was marching through the streets of Rio and found itself under attack by an armed mob. Only the timely arrival of their German comrades saved the Irish from being overwhelmed. At length the authorities yielded to public opinion, and the Europeans were repatriated. Thus the vision of an Irish settlement in Brazil was quickly swept away.

Several decades after the departure of the Irish from Brazil, Brazilian troops were engaged in a bloody war with Paraguay, in which an Irishwoman played a notable part. Eliza Lynch had linked her fortunes to those of Francisco Solano López, president of Paraguay, a dictator who built up a huge army in his landlocked nation and aspired to dominate South America. His plans—and his life—came to an end in a bitter struggle (1865–1870) that devastated the country and virtually annihilated its male population. Eliza Lynch in her role as First Lady organized women's battalions that fought fiercely against the Brazilian invaders. Dismissed as an adventuress by some historians, she remains a heroine in Paraguay.

The twentieth-century Irish presence in Latin America has generally been modest and scattered, though names of note in the library world, like O'Gorman in Mexico and McKenna in Peru, mark the random footsteps of earlier Irish expatriates. In Argentina, however, the story is quite different and distinctive.

During the 1850s and 1860s, the underpopulated Argentine Republic actively sought European immigrants. Among those who came in large numbers were the Irish, with 10,000 to 15,000 families settling under the Southern Cross by the time of the First World War. Although most of them have developed marriage ties outside their community, and have become patriotic (and Spanish-speaking) Argentinians, they preserve a strong consciousness of their heritage. Prominent Argentinians of Irish ancestry range from General Edelmiro Farrell, who was president from 1944 to 1946, to Norma Nolan, a beauty queen who went on to win the Miss Universe title. Even the Argentine-born hero of international revolution, Ernesto "Che" Guevara, was of partly Irish origin.

The Irish who voyaged to the "other" America were few, but their impact was by no means insignificant. ◆

Ambrose O'Higgins (1720–1801) had one of the most spectacular careers of the Irish "Wild Geese." Rising from clerk in a Seville winemerchant's office to viceroy of Peru, the highest-ranking post in the Spanish colonial empire. Here he presides over a meeting (in what is now Chile) in which pageantry is provided by viceregal guards and Arucanian Indians.

97

Irish Footsteps
in Puerto Rico

Visitors to Puerto Rico often come across distinctly Irish names among the local population, though they sometimes appear in surprising forms: a singer named Megenes, a businessman named Sollevan, a policeman named O'Rourke, a teacher named Purcell, and a beauty queen named Carty. An Irish presence in Puerto Rico does, in fact, extend well back into the island's history.

According to tradition, a sixteenth-century plague of vermin that had proved impervious to practical remedies was ended when a learned clergyman remembered an Irish saint who drove out snakes, and led the people in successful prayers to St. Patrick. As Irish involvement with Spain increased during the Reformation era, an occasional Irishman turned up in Puerto Rico, such as Manuel Gilligan, who was a major trader in the island during the late 1600s.

A significant Irish presence really began in the mid-eighteenth century, when the Irish-born General Alejandro O'Reilly was sent to inspect conditions in Puerto Rico and to report on the state of its fortifications and general economy to the Spanish Crown. Not only did O'Reilly produce an analysis that remains a major source on the history of the island, he also made recommendations for the development of its commercial activity and the increase of its population. Among the new settlers who arrived there in the late 1700s were the O'Neill family, who were to have a lasting influence in business and educational activities; Miguel Conboy, a tobacco merchant who carried on an extensive trade throughout the Caribbean; and Juan Kennedy, who operated the principal slave market. The most important of these new Irish colonists was undoubtedly Colonel Tomás O'Daly, a protégé of O'Reilly, who was made chief engineer and given the task of modernizing and expanding the defenses of San Juan. The great fortress of San Cristóbal stands as a monument to his professional skill. The neighborhood in the capital known as San Patricio remains as a monument to his family estate, the Hacienda San Patricio, which lay on what was then the outer fringe of San Juan.

The descendants of these settlers continued to play a prominent part in Puerto Rico's affairs well down into the nineteenth century. Ramón Power, an officer in the Spanish navy, was the island's first representative in the parliament at Madrid. He was succeeded as delegate to that body by Demetrio O'Daly, a general in the Spanish army who was a relative of Tomás O'Daly. Luis O'Neill combined the sinecure of director of prisons with his journalistic and literary activities. Although Puerto Rico was off the main track of Irish emigration in the 1800s, a few families joined the Hibernian community there during the last years of Spanish rule.

Ironically, some Americans opposed to the annexation of the island in 1898 saw Puerto Rico in "Irish" terms. As one anti-imperialist put it: "Puerto Rico will become the Ireland of the United States." If nationalism in this "colony" has never become quite as grave a problem for the United States as it has been in British-ruled Ireland, the perceived resemblance is not entirely irrelevant. For the time being, however, the Irish touch continues to be provided by those Celtic surnames, occasional incongruous physical reminders like the "Hugh O'Neill Memorial Presbyterian Church" in San Juan, and, in recent years, a St. Patrick's Day parade through the streets of the capital. ◆

MAY YOU HAVE AS MANY CHILDREN AND MAY THEY GROW AS MATURE IN TASTE AND HEALTHY IN COLOR AND AS SOUGHT AFTER AS THE CONTENTS OF THIS GLASS.
Traditional Irish Toast

Many Irish immigrant girls found employment at restaurants like this one at the turn of the century. This tile-and-marble-adorned Child's was on Forty-second Street in New York. The work was respectable and offered the added advantage of free meals.

The Irish in America

Poverty
Amidst Plenty

Mathew Carey (1760–1839), a radical Dublin newspaper editor, came to America in 1784 as a political refugee. Although he prospered as a bookseller and publisher in Philadelphia, Carey was acutely aware that not all immigrants had fared so well. His Appeal to the Wealthy of the Land *(1833), from which these extracts are taken, is the work of an Irish-American humanitarian warning the citizens of the new republic of a growing gap between rich and poor, of the evils of hardheartedness, and of the folly in allowing the class divisions of Europe to reappear in the United States.*

*S*hould it appear, as it probably will, to some of my readers, that I have expressed myself with too much warmth, in discussing the sufferings of the seamstresses, etc., let it be borne in mind, that I have been pleading the cause of probably 12,000 women in Boston, New York, Philadelphia, and Baltimore (with souls as precious in the eye of heaven as the most exalted females that ever trod the earth—as a Maria Theresa, a Princess Victoria, a Mrs. Washington, a Mrs. Madison, or a Mrs. Monroe) who are grievously oppressed and reduced to the utmost penury, in a land literally flowing with milk and honey, while many of those for whom they toil, make immense fortunes, by their labours.

We are assured, as I have stated, by ladies fully competent to judge on the subject, that nine cotton shirts a week are as much as the great mass of seamstresses can make. Those shirts are frequently made for 6, 8, and 10 cents, leaving 54, 72, and 90 cents a week for the incessant application of a human being, during thirteen or fourteen hours a day, for the payment of rent, the purchase of food, clothes, drink, soap, candles and fuel!

Deplorable as is the condition of the poor in the crowded cities of Europe, there are few females there who earn much less than this—and therefore, it must follow, that there is frequently as intense a degree of distress suffered here, as in London or Paris. The principal difference is not in the intensity, but in the extent of the distress. Compared with London or Paris, there are few who suffer in this way here. But it is no alleviation of the misery of an unfortuate female in Philadelphia or Boston, who makes shirts for 6 or 8 cents, or even 10, that is to say, who earns from 9 to 16 cents per day, that there are fewer similarly circumstanced here than in those cities.

It is often triumphantly asked, respecting the case of the women who are so very inadequately remunerated for their labours, what remedy can be applied to such an inveterate evil? Does not the proportion between supply and demand, in this, as in all other cases, regulate prices? And while there is such an overproportion of labour in the market, must not competition reduce prices, as it has done, to the lowest grade, even below the minimum necessary to support existence?

I am well aware of the superabundance of female labour—of the direful effects of ever-driven competition, not only on the comfort and happiness, but on the morals of the labouring classes of society, in every quarter of the globe. But I contend for it, that every principle of honour, justice, and generosity, forbids the employer to take advantage of the distress and wretchedness of those he employs, and cut down their wages below the minimum necessary to procure a sufficiency of plain food and clothes to guard against the inclemency of the weather. Whoever passes this line of demarcation, is guilty of the heinous offence of "grinding the faces of the poor." The labour of every human being ought to insure this remuneration at least. And I am persuaded that there are thousands of honourable men who give inadequate wages to males as well as females, merely because they have never thought sufficiently on the subject; and who, therefore, have no idea of the real state of the case. They would scorn to give the wages they do at present, were they aware of the distress and misery thus entailed on those by whose labours, I emphatically repeat, they not only enjoy all the comforts of life, but many of them make immense fortunes. My object is to induce upright men thus circumstanced, to scrutinize the affair, and obey the dictates of their better feelings as soon as they have ascertained the truth. Of the honourable issue I cannot entertain a doubt.

Let me most earnestly, but most respectfully, conjure the ladies, into whose hands these lines may come, to ponder deeply, and frequently, and lastingly, on the deplorable condition of so many of their sex, who are ground to the earth by an inadequate remuneration for their painful labours. Let them raise their voices, and exert their influence in their defence, and urge their male friends to enter the lists in the holy cause of suffering humanity. I am not so enthusiastic or deluded as to suppose that a complete remedy can be applied to so enormous and so inveterate an evil—an evil, the remedy of which requires more generosity and disinterestedness than usually fall to the lot of mankind. But by proper

ALWAYS TOUCH A NEWBORN BABY, OR WHEN IT GROWS UP IT WILL LIFT ITS HAND AGAINST YOU.
Traditional Irish Proverb

efforts, the oppression of the mass of the sufferers may at least be mitigated, and a portion of them may be completely relieved.

The ladies will, I hope, pardon me for an observation which applies to some of them, but I hope to only a few. I have known a lady expend a hundred dollars on a party; pay thirty or forty dollars for a bonnet, and fifty for a shawl; and yet make a hard bargain with a seamstress or washerwoman, who had to work at her needle or at the washingtub for thirteeen or fourteen hours a day to make a bare livelihood for herself and a numerous family of small children! This is "a sore oppression under the sun," and ought to be eschewed by every honourable mind.

"Let it be reformed altogether." . . .

. . . My object is to consider the case of those whose services are so inadequately remunerated, owing to the excess of labour beyond the demand for it, that they can barely support themselves while in good health and fully employed; and, of course, when sick or unemployed, must perish, unless relieved by charitable individuals, benevolent societies, or the guardians of the poor. I use the word "perish" with due deliberation, and a full conviction of its appropriate application . . . for as these people depend for daily support on their daily or weekly wages, they are, when those wages are stopped by whatever means, utterly destitute of wherewith to support their existence, and actually become paupers, and therefore, without the aid above stated, would, I repeat, "perish" of want.

The crisis of suffering through which this class about three years since passed there and elsewhere, and the occurrence of similar suffering in all hard winters (and, in other seasons, from sickness and destitution of employment), often without receiving that extra aid which such a state of things loudly demands, appears to require a sober and serious investigation, in order to probe to the bottom so deplorable a state of things, whereby the comfort and happiness of such a large portion of human beings are so cruelly shipwrecked, and to ascertain what are the causes of the evil, and whether it be susceptible of any remedy.

The erroneous opinions to which I have alluded are—

1. That every man, woman, and grown child, able and willing to work may find employment.

2. That the poor, by industry, prudence, and economy, may at all times support themselves comfortably, without depending on eleemosynary aid—and, as a corollary from these positions.

3. That their sufferings and distresses chiefly, if not wholly, arise from their idleness, their dissipation, and their extravagance.

4. That taxes for the support of the poor, and aid afforded them by charitable individuals, or benevolent societies, are pernicious, as, by encouraging the poor to depend on them, they foster their idleness and improvidence, and thus produce, or at least increase, the poverty and distress they are intended to relieve.

Scene in Irish tenement district of New York City, about 1890.

These options, so far as they have operated—and, through the mischievous zeal and industry of the school of political economists by which they have been promulgated, they have spread widely—have been pernicious to the rich and the poor. They tend to harden the hearts of the former against the sufferings and distresses of the latter—and of course prolong those sufferings and distresses.

"Posterity will scarcely credit the extent to which the popular feeling has been *worked upon and warped by the ravings of some of our modern economists.* They truly, have done all that in them lay, TO EXTINGUISH IN THE BOSOMS OF THE MORE OPULENT CLASSES, EVERY SPARK OF GENEROUS AND BENEVOLENT FEELING TOWARDS THE DESTITUTE AND NEEDY PAUPER. *In their eyes, pauperism is a* crime, for which nothing short of absolute starvation can form an adequate punishment."—*London Quarterly Review*, July, 1828.

Many wealthy individuals, benevolent and liberal, apprehensive lest by charitable aid to persons in distress, they might produce evil to society, are, by these pernicious and cold-blooded doctrines, prevented from indulging the feelings of their hearts, and employing a portion of their superfluous wealth for the best purpose to which it can be appropriated —that purpose which, at the hour of death, will afford the most solid comfort on retrospection—that is, "to feed the hungry; to give drink to the thirsty; to clothe the naked; to comfort the comfortless." The economists in question, when they are implored by the starving poor for "bread," tender them "a stone." To the unfeeling and uncharitable of the rich (and such unhappily there are), those doctrines afford a plausible pretext, of which they are not slow to avail themselves, for withholding their aid from the poor. They have moreover tended to attach a sort of disrepute to those admirable associations of ladies and gentlemen, for the relief of the poor. . . .

WHO LIES DOWN WITH DOGS WILL GET UP WITH FLEAS. *Traditional Irish Proverb*

The higher orders of society have generally enjoyed the advantages of a good education and good examples: the censorial eye of the public is on them, and serves as a curb to restrain them from guilt: regard to character has a powerful operation. Nevertheless, do we not unfortunately see considerable numbers of them who lapse from the paths of rectitude? How powerfully do such lapses tend to extenuate those of the poor, who are under no such controlling or restraining circumstances, and have so much stronger incentives to aberration!

The population of Philadelphia is about 160,000 souls, of whom about 100,000 depend on the labour of their hands: 40,000 are probably laborers, hodmen, seamstresses, families of workmen on the canals and rail-roads. The utmost industry and economy they can employ will scarcely suffice to sustain them, if not unremittingly employed; and few of them are so fortunate as to be employed through the year. These last descriptions of persons are those whose case I have undertaken to consider. ◆

A Call
to Arms

The "exiles of Erin" who left their homeland by the hundreds of
thousands in the middle of the nineteenth century fled not only the
horrors of famine, but also the desolation of political defeat. The Young
Ireland rebellion of 1848 was quickly put down by the British
authorities, as a population exhausted by hunger and disease failed to
follow the idealistic Young Irelanders. Banished to the penal colonies of
Australia, many of the rebel leaders eventually found their way to the
United States, where they found a more fertile ground for their ideas.
The following editorial, printed in their newspaper, The Nation, on July
22, 1848, was their call to arms—a call that would echo among
generations of Irish Americans.

THE HOUR OF DESTINY

The last plank has now, indeed, been shivered, to which we clung
with such despairing faith. The last drop added to the full cup of
insult and misery, it has overflowed. Men of Ireland, the hour of trial and
deliverance has at last been struck by Providence. Only contemplate all
that God, humanity, and your outraged country demand of you, and then
resolutely dare, heroically conquer, or bravely die. What have you to
fear? Nothing in Heaven, for you are justified before God. You may kneel
by your lifted battle flag and call upon Him to witness how you have
patiently endured every wrong, suffered, unrevenged, every infamy, and
sought redress only with streaming eyes and clasped hands, and passionate prayers for Justice!

Justice. That cry has gone up to Heaven and entered into the ears of
the Lord of Sabaoth, but it could not move the hearts of men. We appeal
to God, then, on the day of battle. We claim His vengeance for our
wrongs, for has He not said, "Vengeance is mine, saith the Lord?"

Do you fear the judgement of men? Look round the Earth—every

30,000,000 IMMIGRANTS

THE PLACES THEY LEFT BEHIND THEM

During the period 1856–1910, the following ten counties in Ireland had the highest rate of emigration. The county of Dublin had the lowest rate of emigration.

1. Kerry
2. Cork
3. Clare
4. Longford

5. Leitrim
6. Galway
7. Limerick

8. Mayo
9. Tipperary
10. Cavan

nation cheers you on with words of hope, and sympathy, and encouragement. Uplift your battle flag, and from the two hemispheres and from across the two oceans, not words alone but brave hearts and armed hands will come to aid you.

Ireland! Ireland! It is no petty insurrection, no local quarrel, no party triumph that summons you to the field. The destinies of the world—the advancement of the human race—depends now upon your courage and success, for if you have *courage*, success must follow. Tyranny, and despotism, and injustice, and bigotry are gathering together the chains that have been flung off by every other nation in Europe, and are striving to bind them upon us—the ancient, brave, free Irish people. It is a holy war to which we are called—a war against all that is opposed to justice, and happiness, and freedom. Conquer, and tyranny is subdued forever.

It is a death struggle now between the oppressor and the slave—between the murderer and his victim. Strike! Strike! Another instant and his foot will be upon your neck—his dagger at your heart. Will *he* listen to your prayers? Will *he* melt at your tears? God help us! We have looked to Heaven and to Earth and asked, "Is there no way to save Ireland but by this dark path?" We have taken counsel of Misery, and Famine, and Plague, and said, "Will ye plead for us?" Will not Horror grant what Justice denies? But they die!—They die! The strong men, and the mothers and the pale children, down they fall, thousands—a death ruin of human corpses upon the earth, and their groans vibrate with a fearful dissonance through the country, and their death-wail shrieks along the universe, but no pity dims the stern eye of the murderer who watches their agonies.

Then rose a band of martyrs, and they stood between the living and the dead, and preached the *truth*, such as the world has known from the beginning, only they preached it more eloquently, for they were young and gifted, and genius burned in their eyes, and patriotism in their hearts —and God had filled these noble young spirits with a lofty enthusiasm for the divinest purpose—the redemption of their country. But what care they for genius or virtue or patriotism, those iron machines called Governments who "grind down men's bones to a pale unanimity"? So they trembled at the voices of these young preachers, and strove to crush them by cunning and ingenious tortures that made life more terrible even than death, and soon there were noble hearts writhing in prison, and proud hearts beating in ignominious exile; and now with the groans of the dying there went up from our fated land the shrieks of despairing mothers, and the weeping of young wives, desolate by their lonely hearth, and

IRISH-BORN POPULATION OF PRINCIPAL U.S. CITIES IN 1870

CITY	TOTAL POPULATION	IRISH-BORN
New York, N.Y.	942,292	202,000
Philadelphia, Pa.	674,022	96,698
Brooklyn, N.Y.	376,099	73,986
St. Louis, Mo.	310,864	32,239
Chicago, Ill.	298,977	40,000
Baltimore, Md.	267,354	15,223
Boston, Mass.	250,526	56,000
Cincinnati, Ohio	216,239	18,624
New Orleans, La.	191,418	14,693
San Francisco, Calif.	149,473	25,864
Buffalo, N.Y.	117,714	11,264
Washington, D.C.	109,200	6,948
Newark, N.J.	105,059	12,481
Louisville, Ky.	100,753	7,626
Cleveland, Ohio	92,829	9,964
Pittsburgh, Pa.	86,076	13,119
Jersey City, N.J.	82,546	17,665
Detroit, Mich.	79,577	6,970
Milwaukee, Wis.	71,440	3,784
Albany, N.Y.	69,422	13,276
Providence, R.I.	68,904	12,085
Rochester, N.Y.	62,386	6,078
Allegheny, Pa.	53,180	4,034
Richmond, Va.	51,038	1,239
New Haven, Conn.	50,840	9,601

The total population of the United States in 1870 was 38,558,371, of whom 1,855,827 were born in Ireland. One-half of the Irish-born population resided in the three states of New York, Pennsylvania, and Massachusetts. These three, plus New Jersey and the other five New England states, accounted for two-thirds of all Irish-born residents.

the bewildered cries of orphaned children when they heard they had no father.

What then? Is there no hope? Will ye drag on a wretched existence, degraded in the eyes of Europe—making Ireland a by-word among the nations? Will ye suffer these things so that your children may rise up in after years and say—Was it thus and thus when ye were young men, and ye never lifted your right arms to prevent it? Did ye sell not only the lives of your brothers but the honour of your country? Have ye left nothing but a heritage of shame?

No! God has not utterly forsaken us. He has left us *one* path, but one. That path is broad and clear, and open to us *now*. There *is no other*. You

Mrs. Martin and her daughters stand in front of their shop. This grocery, which also dealt in supplies for ships, stood on Water Street in late-nineteenth-century Philadelphia.

The origin of these riots lies much deeper than whiskey. They come from ignorance and prejudice, with superstitious adherence to unholy combinations, and accustomed resorts to force in their own land.

Niles' Weekly
Register (1834)

must march on it, or the ruin of your country, the death of the living, and the vengeance of the unavenged dead will lie upon your soul. . . . Rise then, men of Ireland, since Providence so wills it. Rise in your cities and your fields, on your hills, in your valleys, by your dark mountain passes, by your rivers and lakes and ocean-washed shores. Rise as a *nation*. England has dissevered the bond of allegiance. Rise, not now to demand justice from a foreign kingdom, but to make Ireland an independent kingdom forever. . . .

You look round upon a land—it is your land—trodden down and trampled and devastated, and on a persecuted, despairing people. It is your right arm must raise up that land—must make her again beautiful and stately and rich in blessings. Elevate that despairing people, and make them free and happy, but teach them to be majestic in their force, generous in their clemency, noble in their triumph.

It is a holy mission. Holy must be your motives and your acts if you would fulfill it. Act as if your soul's salvation hung on each deed, it will; for we stand already within the shadows of eternity. For us is the combat, but not for us, perhaps, the triumph. Many a noble heart will lie cold, many a throbbing pulse will be stilled ere the day of Victory will come. It is a solemn thought that now is the hour of destiny, when the fetters of seven centuries may at last be broken, and by you, men of this generation—by you, men of Ireland. You are God's instruments; many of you must be freedom's martyrs. Oh! Be worthy of the name, and as you act as men, as patriots, and as Christians, so will the blessing rest upon your head when you lay it down, a sacrifice for Ireland, upon the red battlefield. ◆

espite the textbooks' tendency to talk about "waves" of immigration, the coming of the Irish may better be described as an alternation of waves and trickles. This is particularly true when we look at the wide dispersal of the Irish over the country's many regions. An early-nineteenth-century journalist exhorted his fellow Hibernians to make their way "to every corner of this vast continent," and although they heeded his call, the pattern and volume of their diaspora varied considerably.

THE EAST

The original thirteen colonies were full of Irish settlers. During the early national period, the accelerated rate of economic growth in the New England and Middle Atlantic states offered the greatest opportunities for "making one's fortune," and attracted the majority of immigrants. Thousands of Irish clustered in and around their ports of entry (New York, Boston, Philadelphia) during the 1820s and 1930s, while others moved inland to work in the textile mills of Massachusetts, the canal- and road-building projects of upstate New York, or (somewhat later) the mining enterprises of Pennsylvania. The "big wave" of the 1840s and 1850s (the famine immigration) swept into those same Eastern centers, reinforcing the Irish presence there. While some of these newcomers "trickled" away into other regions, the majority remained near their point of arrival. This pattern repeated itself during subsequent generations: newcomers found relatives and friends, enclaves of Irishness, and (perhaps) jobs in the New York, Boston, or Philadelphia metropolitan areas, or in the subregions focused on those cities.

THE SOUTH

The Irish trickled into the South through a number of passageways. Some arrived in Colonial times, and their presence is commemorated in eighteenth-century Irish fraternal societies, like that of Charleston, and in the large "Scotch-Irish" population of the Appalachian hill country. Others arrived in the early 1800s at Southern ports, like Baltimore or New Orleans, rather than the more heavily trafficked New York and

PITY HIM WHO
MAKES HIS OPINION
A CERTAINTY.
*Traditional Irish
Proverb*

113

Boston. These pioneers were followed by an equally small percentage of the famine immigrants. By the time of the Civil War, there were substantial communities of these "new" Irish in Baltimore (whence some migrated to Washington, D.C.) and New Orleans (where the Irish were a distinctive element in the labor force), as well as smaller settlements in Charleston, Savannah, Richmond, and elsewhere. After the war, Irish immigration to the South virtually ceased. While the Southern Irish certainly did not wither on the vine, one commentator of the 1930s was not too far wrong when he spoke of the "lost Irish tribes of the South."

THE MIDWEST

The trickle of canal and road builders into the Great Lakes area during the early 1800s grew steadily in volume as the more adventurous of the Eastern Seaboard Irish ventured into the interior of the continent. By midcentury, there was already a sizable Irish population in Ohio and Indiana, while the still raw settlements at Chicago, Detroit, and Milwaukee had a solid complement of immigrants from the Emerald Isle. Even in the midst of Scandinavian Minnesota, the Irish established a presence at St. Paul. But these bolder spirits were not content to follow urban trades. Many of them took up farming, for the land was cheaper and more available than back East. The Irish farmers, dairymen, and lumbermen of the Midwest assimilated more rapidly than their city cousins, but the Irish identity remained strong in "America's Heartland," even though the flow of immigrants into the region had pretty well ceased by the 1890s.

THE FAR WEST

The Irish presence in the Far West has complex origins. They include the settlements at San Patricio and Refugio dating back to the period when Texas was still a Mexican province, as well as the gold rush of the 1840s that brought Irish fortune seekers into San Francisco. Later, there were the railroad construction gangs thrusting into the Rockies during the 1860s and the miners in Colorado and Montana during the 1870s. The Irish were also to be found among the cowboys and cavalrymen (to say nothing of the outlaws) who added to the color and violence of the frontier. And at the end of the century, Irishmen were among the prospectors who pursued golden dreams in the Klondike. As each successive opening to adventure and enrichment (or disaster) presented itself during the great era of Western expansion, the Irish were sure to be found among the pioneers and risk takers. These trailblazers included both those who had grown up in the long-established communities of the East and those who came directly from Ireland, determined to settle for nothing less than the most exciting and enriching opportunitites that America had to offer.

The Irish immigrants who left the "Irish towns" of the Eastern Seaboard for perils and opportunities of the Far West, found employment as everything from soldiers to gold miners. These men are teamsters, hauling wood to Fort Verde, Arizona, about 1874.

• • •

Thus, by many routes, and over many decades, the Irish found their way into every corner of this vast new land. From the O'Connor drowsing on a back pew of some Baptist church in Georgia to a Murphy skippering an iron ore boat on Lake Superior, from a McCarthy still firmly ensconced in South Boston to a McGovern selling computers in Honolulu, they have peopled America and left their mark on the nation. ◆

Heading West:
Good Scouts

In the opening of the American West to exploration and settlement a surprising number of Irish trailblazers led the way. In contrast to the image of the Irish as dwellers in the urban East, these far-wandering Gaels revived a tradition that stretched all the way back to the days of Brendan the Navigator. Three of them became famous in their day.

Thomas Fitzpatrick, born in County Cavan about 1799, came to the United States as a youth. Drifting westward, he made a life for himself in the Rockies as a trapper, trader, and scout during the 1820s and 1830s. He became one of those fabled "Mountain Men" who served as intermediaries between the expanding United States and the Indian nations along the frontier. He served as guide for the first wagon train bound for the Pacific through northern Montana in 1841. He aided John Charles Frémont in his great expedition of 1843–1844. Stephen Kearny's probes into California in 1845 and 1846 were also guided by Fitzpatrick. Following the American annexation of the western lands in the aftermath of the Mexican War, the Irish frontiersman served as federal Indian agent until his death in 1854.

John Mullan, born in Virginia in 1830, was a West Point graduate, commissioned in the topographical engineers. In 1853 he accompanied a party surveying a railroad route from St. Paul, Minnesota, to the mouth of the Columbia River. During this two-year expedition, he explored unknown ranges of the Bitterroot and Rocky Mountains, making daring winter journeys among the high peaks; the information he gained was vital to the further opening of the region. After service in Florida against the Seminoles, he returned to the Northwest in 1858. There he directed construction of a military wagon road from the headwaters of the Missouri River into the heart of what is now Washington State. Finally completed in 1862, the Mullan Trail was the only route through the Bitterroot range and played a major part in opening the interior of the Northwest to miners and settlers. After leaving the army, Mullan published a widely used *Miners' and Travelers' Guide to Oregon, Washington, Idaho, Montana, Wyoming and Colorado*. Once he had tried his hand in ranching and running an express service, Mullan turned to the practice of law, and continued his new career until his death in 1909.

A fifteen-year-old boy named Kelly, with the rather un-Irish given name of Luther, falsified his age and enlisted in the army in 1865, during the last months of the Civil War. Born in upstate New York, he was carried by his military service to the Dakota territory. After his discharge in 1868 this transplanted Easterner began turning himself into one of the greatest Western trappers, hunters, and scouts of the era. He earned a formidable reputation among the wild Sioux, who failed in several attempts to ambush him while he was carrying army dispatches through their territory. He served as guide to many expeditions through the Wyoming and Montana regions, where his unrivaled knowledge of the trails won him the nickname of "Yellowstone" Kelly. He was chief scout to General Miles during the Sioux campaigns of 1876–1878. Later he shifted his activities northward and guided exploring expeditions in Alaska. In 1900 Kelly, who had served the army for many years as a civilian employee, was commissioned captain for service in the Philippine insurrection. In this totally new environment, he distinguished himself in a number of campaigns, and was for a time governor of a province. By 1904 he was back "home" as an Indian agent in Arizona, and later operated a gold mine in Nevada. Finally, in 1915 he settled down on a ranch in California, where he died in 1928.

These adventurous men who scouted the way west were merely the more visible among the thousands of Irish Americans who helped the United States achieve its "Manifest Destiny." ◆

MAY THE ROOF ABOVE US NEVER FALL IN, AND MAY WE FRIENDS GATHERED BELOW NEVER FALL OUT.
Traditional Irish Toast

Letters
to the
Homeland

LETTER FROM JAMES MURRAY,
AN IMMIGRANT RESIDING IN NEW YORK CITY,
TO REV. BAPTIST BOYD, MINISTER OF AUGHELOW,
COUNTY TYRONE, NOVEMBER 7, 1737

Read this letter, and look, and tell aw the poor Folk of your Place, that God has opened a Door for their Deliverance; for here is ne scant of Bread, and if your Sons Samuel and James Boyd wad but come here, they wad get more Money in ane year for teechin a Lettin Skulle, nor ye yer sell wad get for Three Years Preechin whar ye are. . . . The Young Foke in Ereland are but a Pack of Couards, for I will tell ye in short, this is a bonny Country, and aw things grows here that ever I did see grow in Ereland; and wee hea Cows and Sheep and Horses plenty here, and Goats, and Deers, and Raccoons, and Moles, and Bevers, and Fish, and Fouls of aw Sorts. Trades are ow gud here, a Wabster gets 12 Pence a Yeard, a Labourer gets 4 Shillings and 5 Pence a Day, a Lass gets 4 Shillings and 6 Pence a week for spinning . . . a Carpenter gets 6 Shillings a Day, and a Tailor gets 20 Shillings for making a Suit of Cleaths. . . . Indian corn, a Man wull get a Bushell for it for his Day's Work here; Rye grows here, and Oats and Wheet, and Winter Barley, and Summer Barley; Buck Wheet grows here, na every Thing grows here. . . .

Now I beg of ye aw to come out here, and bring out wee ye aw the Cleaths ye can of every Sort . . . and Guns, and Pooder, and Shot, and aw Sorts of Weers that is made of Iron and Steel, and Tradesmen that come here let them bring their Tools wee them . . . fetch whapsaws here, and Hatchets and Augurs and Axes and Spades, and Shoy els . . . and aw Sorts of Garden Seeds. . . . Potatoes grows here very big . . . ye may clear as muckle Grund to plant Indian Corn in ane Month, as will maintain Ten Folk for a Year. . . .

I have been 120 Miles in the Wolderness, and there I saw a Plain of Grund 120 Miles lang, and 15 Bred, and where never gree nor Tree upon it, and I hea see as gud Meedow upon it, as ever I see in Ereland. . . . Ye may get Lan here for 10 Pund a Hundred Acres for ever, and Ten Years

THE PIG DOES NOT LOOK UP TO SEE WHERE THE ACORNS ARE FALLING FROM.
Traditional Irish Proverb

Tell ye get the Money before they wull ask ye for it;
and it is within 40 Miles of this York upon a River
Side that this Lan lies, so that ye may carry aw the
Guds in Boat to this York to sell, if ony of you comes
here. . . . Desire my Fether and Mether too, and my
Three Sisters to come here, and ye may acquaint
them, there are Lads enough here . . . and I will pay
their passage . . . for here aw that a man works for is
his ane, there are ne Revenus Hunds to rive it from
us here . . . there is ne yen to take awa yer Corn, yer
Potatoes . . . or Eggs. . . .

I bless the Lord for my safe Journey here . . . this
York is as big as twa of Armagh. . . . There is servants
comes here out of Ereland, and have served there
time here, wha are now Justices of the Piece. . . .

LETTER FROM JOHN DOYLE, IRISH IMMIGRANT IN NEW YORK CITY, TO HIS WIFE IN IRELAND, JANUARY 25, 1818

*O*h, how long the days, how cheerless and fatiguing the nights since
I parted with my Fanny and my little angel. Sea sickness, nor the
toils of the ocean, nor the starvation which I suffered, nor the constant
apprehension of our crazy old vessel going to the bottom, for ten tedious
weeks, could ever wear me to the pitch it has if my mind was easy
about you. But when the recollection of you and of my little Ned rushes
on my mind with a force irresistible, I am amazed and confounded to
think of the coolness with which I used to calculate on parting with my
little family even for a day, to come to this *strange* country, which is the
grave of the reputations, the morals, and of the lives of so many of our
countrymen and countrywomen. . . .

We were safely landed in Philadelphia on the 7th of October and I
had not so much as would pay my passage in a boat to take me ashore.
. . . I, however, contrived to get over, and . . . it was not long until I
made out my father, whom I instantly knew, and no one could describe
our feelings when I made myself known to him, and received his
embraces, after an absence of seventeen years. [The father was a United
Irish refugee of 1798]. . . . The morning after landing I went to work to
the printing. . . . I think a journeyman printer's wages might be
averaged at 7½ dollars a week all the year round. . . . I worked in
Philadelphia five and one-half weeks and saved 6 pounds, that is
counting four dollars to the pound; in the currency of the United States

the dollar is worth five shillings Irish. . . . I found the printing and bookbinding overpowered with hands in New York. I remained idle for twelve days in consequence; when finding there was many out of employment like myself I determined to turn myself to something else, seeing that there was nothing to be got by idleness. . . . I was engaged by a bookseller to hawk maps for him at 7 dollars a week. . . . I now had about 60 dollars of my own saved . . . these I laid out in the purchase of pictures on New Year's Day, which I sell ever since. I am doing astonishingly well, thanks be to God, and was able on the 16th of this month to make a deposit of 100 dollars in the bank of the United States.

As yet it's only natural I should feel lonesome in this country, ninety-nine out of every hundred who come to it are at first disappointed. . . . Still, it's a fine country and a much better place for a poor man than Ireland . . . and much as they grumble at first, after a while they never think of leaving it. . . . One thing I think is certain, that if emigrants knew beforehand what they have to suffer for about the first six months after leaving home in every respect, they would never come here. However, an enterprising man, desirous of advancing himself in the world, will despise everything for coming to this free country, where a man is allowed to thrive and flourish without having a penny taken out of his pocket by government; no visits from tax gatherers, constables or soldiers, every one at liberty to act and speak as he likes, provided he does not hurt another, to slander and damn government, abuse public men in their office to their faces, wear your hat in court and smoke a cigar while speaking to the judge as familiarly as if he was a common mechanic, hundreds go unpunished for crimes for which they would be surely hung in Ireland; in fact they are so tender of life in this country that a person should have a very great interest to get himself hanged for anything.

LETTER FROM JEREMIAH O'SULLIVAN, VIRGINIA CITY, NEVADA, TO HIS BROTHER IN IRELAND, JULY 29, 1859

*M*y dear Dan,
You will all have been wondering what has become of us since we sailed from New York. Mary will describe our long and arduous voyage to the coast of California. You know that she writes a better letter than I do and is already composing a grand narrative of our

adventures. I shall only say here that our voyage from Ireland last year was as nothing when compared to this latest voyage.

I will get on at once to the great news. We were not long arrived in this place when Owen and I found the treasure we had come to seek, yes, my doubtful brother, we have indeed struck a vein of purest silver, and are in prospect of becoming very rich men. The settlement here is full of Irish, along with what seems to be at least one of every nation in the world. But we are among the few who have had the good fortune to "strike it rich" as they say here. It will be some while yet before we can draw off sufficient ore from our mine to repay our costs, but in a year's time, our fortunes will be made.

Now, Dan, why don't you come out here and join us? I know that you were not a mere scoffer, like those others who said Owen, Mary and I were fools to go to America at all and, bigger fools to head West. You were always one to stay home because you loved the land, and it will still hold you, I know. But you can make your fortune here too. It is not just a dream. If you will write to me here and say that you are coming, I shall send you all the particulars about how you may reach this place.

Enough for now. Mary will write and give all the news to our friends and kin. Be asured that Owen also sends you his dearest affection, though as you remember, he is an even worse pen-man than I.

We hope and pray you will come and join us in this great new land. Believe me, dear Dan, your ever affectionate brother,

JEREMIAH O'SULLIVAN

LETTER FROM PATRICK MURPHY,
NEW YORK, TO HIS MOTHER IN IRELAND,
SEPTEMBER 15, 1885

*M*y dear Mother,

I hope that you are very well, as I am. This letter is written for me by Tom Rooney, for I am no scholar. You remember how much more time I spent in the hills than in the schoolroom. As I told you in my last, I am stopping with Tom and his wife, Sally, who are fine people, so you should not worry about me. I am very comfortable and eat well. Now that I am here a while, I like it better than ever. New York is a grand handsome city. But you would hardly know you had left Ireland, there are so many Irish people here. Some of them are become rich. Some of them are big men in government. For most of us it is hard work, but there is plenty of it and the pay is all right. They are always building things here. Tom worked on the great bridge they made over the river to Brooklyn a year or two ago. Now he has got me a job working with him on the new streets they are making in this city. There is always something going on if a man wants work. Soon I will be sending you some money I have saved. I know that will help you and you will not feel so bad about how I had to leave you. Well, Mother, I must end now. I hope God has you in his keeping and gives you good health. There are plenty of good Catholic people here, and no fear of losing our way, as Father Dwyer said. Give my dearest love to John, Mary and Nora, and greetings to all my friends. I will write again soon.

> Your son,
> PAT

'TIS THE FOOL HAS LUCK.
Traditional Irish Proverb

LETTER FROM THOMAS QUINN, BOSTON, TO HIS SISTER IN IRELAND, OCTOBER 22, 1925

*D*ear Kate,

Well, here I am in the "New World." I suppose you thought I'd fall off the boat. Far from it, I was too busy dancing with all the lovely ladies.

Our cousins here have been very decent to me, but I don't want to stay very long. If I had wanted a town full of Irish, I'd have stayed home. Everybody here is either a "Mick" or a "Yank" and unless you're a "Mick" with money, which I am not (yet), it's no fun.

As soon as I can, I'm off to sunny California. No, I don't expect to become a film actor, but I want to see the rest of the country. Two lads I met here are game to do a bit of exploring with me, and our plan is to work our way out to the Pacific Coast and look around as we go.

I know you used to laugh at all that talk about America being the "land of opportunity," but I still think it is, now that I am an American for all of two weeks. Anyway, Ireland is a dead loss for anyone with spirit these days. They may talk about "independence" over there, but the new crowd running things is just as bad as the other lot. I want you to think seriously again about coming out here. You would not be alone now if you made the trip.

The next letter you receive may not be from Hollywood, but it will certainly not be from "Bean Town." Westward Ho! says Mr. Quinn.

> Love,
> TOM

The Magee family of Ashmead Street, Philadelphia, about 1895.

The Molly
Maguires
Vindicated
(Assuming
They Existed)

*L*ike so many other negative images of the Irish American, the Molly
Maguires have received a great deal of publicity. From a novel by
Conan Doyle *(The Valley of Fear)* to a Hollywood melodrama starring
Sean Connery and Richard Harris, they have entered the popular imagination as a ruthless band of criminals, carrying out a reign of terror in
the Pennsylvania coalfields. Few are aware, however, of their exonera-
tion a century after their downfall. And some still insist that there never
was such an organization.

According to standard encyclopedia accounts, the Molly Maguires
were an antilandlord secret society formed in Ireland during the early
nineteenth century and imported to America by the 1850s. The origin of
the name is variously ascribed. According to some, Molly Maguire was a
heroic woman who resisted oppressive landlords during the eighteenth
century. Other accounts maintain that the members wore female clothes
during their terrorist attacks to disguise their identity. The organization
is said to have developed among coal miners in Pennsylvania as an off-
shoot of the Ancient Order of Hibernians. The Mollies expanded rapidly
after the Civil War and carried out acts of violence, arson, and sabotage
against mine owners, supervisors, and informers. A massive strike in the
Pennsylvania coalfields in 1875 was attributed to them. A detective, the
Irish-born James McParlan, infiltrated the society, won the confidence of
its leaders, and handed them over to the authorities. Twenty of the Mollies were convicted of murder and executed, and by 1878 the society was
no more.

But some deny that it ever existed. Certain labor historians contend
that the Molly Maguires were invented out of thin air by the mine bosses
who wanted to destroy the workers' leadership and their will to resist.
The men who were executed, these historians declare, were "framed" by
perjured testimony and convicted by juries that systematically excluded
Irishmen. In this view, the men who died as "Molly Maguire murderers"
were martyrs of the American labor movement, the precursors of the
United Mine Workers Union that came into existence some years later.

Historians of the Ancient Order of Hibernians, while sometimes casting doubt on the very existence of the Mollies, are chiefly concerned to

show that it was not synonymous with the AOH. One writer held that the Mollies were wolves in sheep's clothing who joined the AOH to cover up their criminal activities. Another suggests that the men who were hanged were simply the victims of anti-Irish prejudice and that their membership in the AOH—an innocent organization—singled them out for persecution. Such commentators reject McParlan's testimony that the AOH and the Molly Maguires were one and the same. Whatever the truth, John Kehoe, the alleged leader of the Mollies, was a senior official of the AOH, and four others of those hanged were AOH divisional officers or county delegates.

In December 1978, just a few days after the one hundredth anniversary of John Kehoe's death, his great-grandson petitioned the Pennsylvania Board of Pardons to "remove the stigma that hangs over my family." His argument for reversal of sentence was buttressed with ample testimony by historians and lawyers. A month later, the governor of Pennsylvania signed a posthumous pardon for Jack Kehoe. Speaking to reporters, the governor declared: "We can be proud of the men known as the Molly Maguires because they defiantly faced allegations that made trade unionism a criminal conspiracy. These men gave their lives on behalf of the labor struggle."

Thus the Molly Maguires have been vindicated—even if they never existed. ◆

At clandestine meetings like this one, Irish immigrant miners in the coalfields in western Pennsylvania plotted resistance to oppression by owner and managers. The ironically named "Molly Maguires" carried on their campaign of violent resistance between 1874 and 1876.

The Irishness
of Billy
the Kid

Billy the Kid is the ultimate American outlaw. With the possible exception of Jesse James, no other desperado of the Old West is so widely known. He has been the subject of countless books, magazine articles, stage productions, and no fewer than forty motion pictures. He has been portrayed as everything from a pathological killer to a misunderstood young rebel.

What is rarely noted about this famous frontier figure is his Irishness. The facts of his biography bristle with Irish names and contacts. At an uncertain date and place, he was born to a "jolly Irishwoman" named Catherine McCarty. Many reference works assert that he was the product of the Irish slums of New York's Lower East Side. Nothing is known for certain about his father, whose name may have been McCarty, since Catherine is usually referred to as Mrs. McCarty. At any event, her child, known as Henry McCarty and presumably born around 1860, was raised in various Midwestern towns. After the marriage of his mother to William Antrim (presumably also of Irish origin), the boy was sometimes known as Billy Antrim, Jr.

FALLING IS EASIER
THAN RISING.
*Traditional Irish
Proverb*

The legends surrounding the early boyhood of Billy the Kid, as he came to be known, suggest everything from a bright, amiable lad to an incipient juvenile delinquent. Whatever the truth of the matter, he was scarcely into his teens before trouble started. After killing a man named Frank Cahill, he stole a horse from a neighbor named Murphy and fled into the mountains. Following many adventures with bandits and Indians, he ended up in Lincoln County, New Mexico. There his associates were men like O'Keefe, O'Folliard, and McCloskey. By this time he was using the name William Bonney.

Billy found himself in the midst of a power struggle between rival landowning and business factions, a struggle that came to be known as the Lincoln County War. He and his friends attached themselves to one Tunstall, a rancher who had befriended the young fugitive and become a father figure to him. Tunstall was the archenemy of an "Irish mafia" headed by Laurence Murphy, a native of Wexford, and the Galway-born James Dolan. These men, who had come west as soldiers during the Civil

War, controlled the sheriff, William Brady, and a gang of deputized thugs—Riley, Boyle, etc.

The quarrel between these parties led to the assassination of Tunstall by a posse, and the reprisal killing of Sheriff Brady by Billy. The conflict raged on between 1878 and 1880, finally requiring the intervention of the army. Billy and his comrades gradually passed from revenge-taking into banditry, although regarded by many as being in the Robin Hood tradition of resisting oppression. Finally, in 1881, Billy was trapped and killed by the new sheriff, Patrick Garrett.

Beyond all of these Hibernian surnames, there is something very Irish about the whole epic of Billy the Kid. The story of the warrior youth who comes out of the wilderness to take part in a struggle between battling clans is reminiscent of ancient Irish tales. So too is his implacable quest for revenge against those who killed his "father," including the slaying of the slayer. The band of comrades, with a price on their heads, defying all odds and enjoying the support of the countryfolk, raises echoes of the Irish experience. And, at the end, there is the martyrdom of the young hero, who goes to his death unarmed (Billy was not carrying a gun) as if welcoming his doom. Whatever the prosaic reality of Henry McCarty's life and death, the story of Billy the Kid, romanticized over the generations, has attained a sagalike quality that gives it a peculiarly Irish aura. ◆

Billy the Kid, posing here with his personal arsenal, combined an ancestral Irish commitment to clan loyalty and revenge-seeking with the gun-slinging mentality that prevailed on the American frontier.

The Chess
Wizard

The game of chess has a long history in Ireland. It was popular among the Gaels of ancient times, and continued to be played in the homes of chiefs and nobles down through the medieval and early modern periods. The warrior class of old Irish society alternated between the real combat of the battlefield and the stylized warfare of the chessboard.

One of the greatest chess players of the modern era was an American of Irish origin, Paul Morphy. His great-grandfather, Michael Morphy, left Ireland in the early eighteenth century to pursue a military career in Spain. The family migrated to Louisiana during the time when it was under Spanish rule, and Paul Morphy was born in New Orleans in 1837. A studious, withdrawn child, he acquired an early interest in chess from his uncle, Ernest Morphy, one of the ablest players in the South. By the time he was ten, Paul was defeating the best adult players of New Orleans.

Young Morphy's brilliance came to the attention of the wider world when he was thirteen: a visiting master whom he had defeated began proclaiming that he had discovered the future champion of the world. Morphy did not welcome this notoriety. He pursued his studies for a career in the law, and resisted invitations to travel to the major chess centers until 1857. In that year he dazzled New York by winning 97 out of 100 games in a Chess Congress and capturing the trophy. The press was full of stories about his great mental endowment, his photographic memory, and his ability to reconstruct at will any given situation of a past game. Chess enthusiasts in New York persuaded a reluctant Morphy to take up the challenge from England as a matter of national honor. Arriving in London in 1858, he played all comers and rapidly demonstrated that he had no peer among British masters.

Fresh from his victories in England, Morphy went on to defeat Harrwitz, the Prussian champion. In Paris he repeated the feat he had performed in other cities of playing eight matches simultaneously while blindfolded, winning every game. The defeat of these lesser players was merely the preliminary to his confrontation with the grand master Andressen, who had just won an international tournament that was the

MAY EVERY HAIR ON YOUR HEAD TURN INTO A CANDLE TO LIGHT YOUR WAY TO HEAVEN, AND MAY GOD AND HIS HOLY MOTHER TAKE THE HARM OF THE YEARS AWAY FROM YOU.
Traditional Irish Toast

equivalent of the world championship. The match between Morphy and Andressen began on December 14, 1858, and ended two weeks later with Morphy as undisputed winner.

Morphy's reception on his return to the United States was, in its way, comparable to that accorded to Lindbergh some seventy years later. As the world's champion of chess he had demonstrated the achievements of American intellect to a skeptical world; he was a national hero. At a banquet for Morphy in Boston, Oliver Wendell Holmes presided and read a poem composed in his honor. At another gala dinner in New York the champion was presented with a silver wreath and a silver plate inscribed with a tribute from fourteen other chess masters.

Morphy was now at the climax of his career. Extremely sensitive, with no business instincts, he hated the constant talk about money among the chess players who sought to make chess a professional sport. Morphy's attitude toward the game was consistent with the old spirit of the Irish chieftains and bards. In a speech before the Union Chess Club at Boston in 1859 he declared, "Chess never has been and never can be aught but a recreation. It should not absorb or engross the thoughts of those who worship at its shrine. Unlike other games in which lucre is the end and aim of the contestants, it commends itself to the wise by the fact that its mimic battles are fought for no prize or honor. It is eminently and emphatically the philosopher's game. Let the chessboard supersede the card table and a great improvement will be visible in the morals of the community."

Evidently the tension between the commercial pressures that were brought upon him as world champion and his own view of the proper role of chess proved too much for Morphy's sensitive temperament. He became moody and abandoned his chess-playing friends. He became tormented by phobias and delusions of persecution. Upset and angry when pointed out as the chess champion of the world, he gave up the game entirely. As one contemporary put it, "He was a gentle creature and the sharp edges of the money-mad world bruised his soul." During the long twilight of his life, he lived quietly in his native city, taking comfort in religion and flowers. He died in New Orleans in 1884. ◆

YOU'D BE A GOOD MESSENGER TO SEND FOR DEATH (SAID OF A SLOW PERSON).
Traditional Irish Proverb

John Philip Holland and the "Fenian Ram"

$\mathcal{E}$arly in this century a curious myth arose that has only in recent years begun to be dissipated. Historians have done a great deal to propagate it. According to this myth, the Irish people were supposed to have no maritime tradition. Proof to the contrary would fill volumes, but there is no more powerful evidence than the extraordinary fact that two engineers who revolutionized naval concepts in the later years of the last century and the early years of this one were Irishmen. These were John Philip Holland, son of a poor County Clare coast guard, and Charles Algernon Parsons, son of the earl of Rosse from Birr, County Offaly. Holland was a submarine designer of genius from whose plans have developed the frighteningly formidable nuclear-armed submarines of the U.S. and British navies of today. Parsons, by his pioneer work on marine steam turbines, made possible the construction of the powerful battle fleets that made history in this century's two world wars. Both men ran up against the opposition of bureaucracy entrenched in outmoded ideas, opposition that both overcame by rare tenacity fortified with the compelling sense of humor we like to consider typically Irish. There the similarity ends. Parsons, the son of a wealthy and gifted father, was educated at Trinity College, Dublin, went later to Cambridge, and was able to finance his own epoch-opening experiments. Holland's father died when the future inventor was twelve, leaving a badly off widow and two other children. Most of Holland's pioneer submarine construction work was carried out in the face of very considerable financial difficulties.

John Philip Holland was born in Liscannor in 1841. A younger brother died of cholera during the famine. He was educated at St. Macreehy's National School there, where he learned English; Gaelic had been his home tongue. He went later to the Christian Brothers' school at Ennistymon and to Monastery School in Sexton Street, Limerick, showing at once an unusual aptitude for scientific studies. To continue his education and earn a living after his father's death he took the initial vows as a Christian Brother in Limerick, and went on to teach at North Monastery School in Cork and at schools of his Order in Portlaoise, Enniscorthy, Drogheda, and Dundalk. By all accounts he was an enthusias-

tic, popular, and successful teacher. He also became an accomplished musician.

Holland had always wanted to go to sea, and had studied elementary navigation before taking up teaching but bad eyesight and poor health thwarted his ambition. He read, however, with absorbed attention the story of the new concepts of naval warfare being evolved in the Civil War in North America between 1861 and 1865 and no doubt knew better than we do today how many talented seamen of Irish birth or descent were engaged on both sides. One of the most outstanding naval events of the conflict was the first sinking of a warship ever accomplished by a submarine, when the Confederate *Hunley*, designed by the Irishman John McClintock, with another Irishman in her crew, sank the U.S. steam frigate *Housatonic* off Charleston.

It was in Dundalk that Holland began seriously to study the problems of submarine navigation and built a successful model of a submarine with which he experimented in a bath. His studies took him past McClintock's efforts, the Frenchman Paul Bourgois's *Plongeur* of 1863, the achievements between 1832 and 1861 of the *bateaux poissons* of Villeroi, another Frenchman, the fifty-four successful dives of the Spaniard Narciso Monturiol in his fish-shaped *Ictileo*, the experiments of the Russian Bauer with his *Marine Devil* of 1855, the theories propounded by the English scientist Nasmyth in the Crimean War of 1853–1856, the submarine designs of the North American inventor Robert Fulton during the Napoleonic War and David Bushnell a generation before, to the very earliest pathfinders in this then most esoteric field, the seventeenth-century Dutchman Cornelis Van Drebbel and two scientific geniuses of the same period, the Minim fathers, Mersenne (friend of Descartes) and Fournier.

When Holland, continually suffering from ill health, obtained leave from the Christian Brothers to depart to the United States without having taken his final vows, he already probably knew more than any living man about the history to date of submarine navigation—a subject of which the ordinary citizen of that time had never heard or dreamed. He arrived in Boston in November 1873 to stay with his elder brother, a Fenian exile. Twenty-seven years later, by then famous, he recalled in an interview in the *Washington Post* that, though he had never taken part in politics, he did not want his inventive genius, in which he had supreme faith, "to serve John Bull." Ironically, very soon after the interview, the British navy began commissioning submarines built to his designs.

In 1875 Holland offered his plan of a submarine boat to the U.S. Navy, but the secretary of the navy dismissed it as a "fantastic scheme of a civilian landsman." In the same year he built what Henry Fyfe, the authoritative early historian of submarine warfare, was to call in 1902 "an underwater canoe," 16' x 1'8" x 2' propelled by a screw activated by a pedal. Soon after, the Trinity College Dublin graduate, the Reverend G. W. Garrett, tried out his manually operated *Resurgam*, with compressed-air tanks and stores of chemicals to purify its air after use, which so interested the Swedish gun inventor Thorsten Nordenfelt that he began to invest part of his fortune in submarine construction.

Meanwhile, the Fenian movement in the United States had begun to realize that the power of the British Empire depended on its maritime supremacy. Among numerous plans concocted by Devoy, Breslin, Dr. Carroll, and their picturesque associates was one for the use of Holland's ideas to build an instrument that would be a genuine threat to the British navy. They financed the construction of the inaptly christened *Fenian Ram*, laid down just a century ago at the foot of West Thirteenth Street in New York City by the Delamater Iron Company.

The *Fenian Ram* was 31' x 6' x 6', displaced nineteen tons, and was driven by a 15 hp petrol engine and armed with an underwater cannon fired by compressed air. Of this submarine, U.S. expert Admiral Philip Hichborn wrote:

"She was the first submarine since Bushnell's time employing water-ballast and always retaining buoyancy, in which provision was made to secure fixed centre of gravity and a fixed absolute weight. Moreover, she was the first buoyant submarine to be steered down and up inclines in the vertical plane by horizontal rudder action, as she was pushed forward by her motor, instead of being pushed up and down by vertically-acting mechanism. Her petroleum engine . . . was inefficient, and the boat therefore failed as a practical craft, but in her were demonstrated all the chief principles of successful brain-directed submarine navigation." And of Holland, Hichborn said: "After the completion of this boat, Holland led the world far and away in the solution of submarine problems." The *Gymnote* designed by the Frenchman Gustave Zédé was a bigger vessel than the *Ram*. Completed in 1886, she was the first really

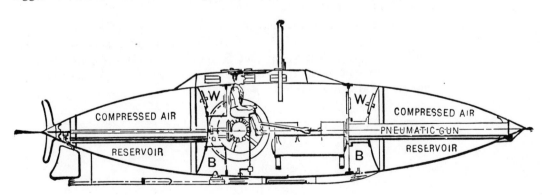

successful motor-powered submarine, but meanwhile Holland had built his number four, and had the mortification of seeing it destroyed by accident during launching.

In 1888, 1889, and 1893, Holland won competitions for submarine designs launched by the U.S. government, only to see his successful plans then turned down. Navy Secretary Theodore Roosevelt backed his number six, which underwent trials in 1898. However, there were still interminable delays before, in April 1900, spurred on by news of the successful trials by the French navy of their designer Laubeuf's *Narval*, at last the U.S. Navy bought Holland's submarine. Thus began the long and triumphantly successful story of the United States submarine service.

Splits in the Fenian movement had meanwhile disillusioned Holland with his political-minded fellow exiles, the extremists whom he accused of wanting "10 cents' worth of revolution every week." There were squabbles about the ownership of the *Ram*, which spent many years stored in a lumber shed. But she was brought out in 1916 and exhibited to raise funds for dependents of victims of the repression that followed the Rising. She is permanently on view now in West Side Park, by the Passaic River, in Paterson, New Jersey.

As for Holland, his name was made by 1900. But submarine construction now became big business. The small company he had run, financed by friends and acquaintances, disappeared; and by 1907, outmaneuvered by smart lawyers and financiers, he retired from business and public life. Moreover, he was now convinced that his brilliant invention had monstrous potentialities that he had not foreseen. He frequently expressed the hope in his last years, during which he studied aeronautics, played music, and taught Gaelic to children of Irish descent in Trenton, New Jersey, that submarines would be used only for peaceful purposes. He died shortly before the 1914 war proved how justified his fears were. In that war, German submarines alone destroyed no fewer than 12,192,000 tons of enemy shipping; in the 1939 war they sank 14.5 million tons of merchant shipping. In the two conflicts, no fewer than 959 German U-boats were lost.

However, in recent decades the experiments of Piccard, Willm, Houot, the French naval officer O'Byrne, and many others in a score of different countries, have justified Holland's vision of the great contribution submarine navigation can make to peaceful use of the ocean depths for the good of humankind. ◆

DON'T SAY EVERYTHING YOU WANT TO LEST YOU HEAR SOMETHING YOU WOULD NOT LIKE TO HEAR.
Traditional Irish Proverb

The following statement is drawn from the Report in Favor of the
Abolition of Capital Punishment Made in the Legislature of the
State of New York *(Albany, 1841). John Louis O'Sullivan, the
prominent Irish-American editor, at this time a Democratic member of
the legislature, was chairman of the committee on capital punishment
and wrote its report.*

The committee concluded this topic, therefore, by the reassertion,
with a fearless challenge of disproof, of the conviction already
above stated, that *the executioner is the indirect cause of more murders
and more deaths, than he ever punishes or avenges.* In relation to the powerful bearing of this solemn truth upon the question under discussion,
they feel that it cannot be necessary for the many more fully to enlarge.

Nor is it an untried experiment on which it is here proposed to enter.
Other communities, when in a stage of civilization, and of general moral
culture, far inferior to that which invites us now no longer to delay in
following their example, have abolished the punishment of death—and
with such a success as amply to justify us in the great reform proposed
by the committee. If it can be shown that a single community has ever
existed, which has been able to sustain itself against the dangers appre-
hended by the opponents of this reform—whose statute-books have been
kept pure from the hideous stain of blood which it is our object now to
erase from ours, and where the life of the citizen and the general order
and security of the society have yet been not less safe than they are ever
made by the presumed protection of the penalty of death—the sole
ground will be swept away on which the great public crime of its contin-
uance can be even attempted to be palliated, this ground of a supposed
"social necessity." . . .

The history of all human progress is but a record of the slow and
successive conquests of reason over error. The strongest resistance which
the latter makes is always derived from a similar appeal to the authority
of venerable antiquity. All civilizations have had their birth in barba-

THE PIG IN THE STY
DOESN'T KNOW THE
PIG GOING ALONG
THE ROAD.
*Traditional Irish
Proverb*

rism; and hence the long and obstinate retention by the former of many of the habits and ideas which were a disgrace even to the latter. It is not in this country—happily for us in a thousand ways—that such an argument as this will avail much, to turn back our hand from any good work of reform to which we are prompted. . . .

We have gone on gradually restricting more and more the application of the punishment of death, which in the country from which we derived the main bulk of our law embraced at the commencement of the present century not less than 300 offences, and still includes a large number to which we should be shocked at the thought of again extending it. These successive ameliorations of our penal law have been attended with such good effect, that no proposition has ever been advanced to retrace any one of these steps. What reason can we have to doubt that the completion of this holy reform, by abolishing the punishment of death from the last few applications at which it still lingers, will be attended with equally satisfactory results—especially with all the encouragement afforded us in the practice of the experiment wherever it has hitherto been tried? Let us, at least for consistency's sake, either restore it to the other offences for which we have abolished it, if it be indeed an efficacious restraint upon their perpetration; or if such is not the case—if the punishment of death has been found to be not only useless, but worse than useless, for that purpose, in its application to those offences—let us carry out the same progressive reform to its legitimate consummation, and erase from our statute-book the last vestige of a policy worthy only of the barbarism in which it had its origin. . . .

The committee repeat in conclusion, that they are satisfied that the time is now ripe, full ripe, for the consummation of the great and noble reform in the practice of our penal justice, which they have endeavored to discuss in the preceding pages. . . . A very large majority of the people of this State are at heart decidedly opposed to capital punishment—that the number would be exceedingly small who would not hail with high gratification at least the trial of the proposed reform as an experiment, an experiment that may be with perfect ease abandoned by the next or any succeeding Legislature—and that after the attention which has been drawn to the subject at the present session, a very profound dissatisfaction and disappointment would pervade the public mind, if any causes were allowed by this body to frustrate or delay a definite action upon it. It behooves and will well become the State of New York to take the initiative in this wise and sacred philanthropy. . . .

In accordance with the views herein above expressed, the committee ask leave to introduce a bill and a concurrent resolution.

All which is respectfully submitted, by the unanimous direction of the committee. ◆

My Country

It is, in fact, unquestionable that the Irishman looks upon America as the refuge of his race, the home of his kindred, the heritage of his children and their children. The Atlantic is, in his mind, less a barrier of separation between land and land than is St. George's Channel. The shores of England are farther off, in his heart's geography, than those of New York or Massachusetts. Degrees of latitude are not taken into account in the measurements of his enthusiasm. Ireland—old as she is, and fond as he is of calling her so—seems to him but a part and parcel of that great continent which it sounds, to his notions, unnatural to designate as the *new* world. He has no feeling towards America but that of love and loyalty. To live on her soil, to work for the public good, and die in the country's service, are genuine aspirations of the son of Erin, when he quits the place of his birth for that of his adoption.

—Thomas Colley Grattan, *Civilized America* (1859)

Irish Americans and the Draft Riots in New York, 1863

NEW YORK POST, JULY 17, 1863

*A*rchbishop Hughes has called a meeting of what he styles "the men of New York who are now called in many of the papers rioters." They are to meet near his house at two o'clock to-day. We have satisfied ourselves that the call is genuine, and that the Archbishop means to speak to the rioters, though he declined to give to the reporter, sent from this office to see him, any idea of the nature of the address he proposes to make to these persons.

We hope none others than the rioters will attend the meeting. The call is addressed to these alone; the advice they will receive can be read by peaceable and honest citizens in the journals, and it is highly desirable that in the present state of the city no crowd should collect anywhere.

We think it especially desirable that those Irish citizens who have taken no part in these riots shall stay away from this meeting. The character of the Irish has suffered greatly in the public esteem in the last few days. There is already a disposition—unjust, but not unnatural under the circumstances—to confound and condemn in a body all people of Irish birth or parentage. This is wrong. We know of many instances in which Irishmen have been warm and efficient supporters of the law. In the First Ward of this city the Irish porters and laborers have been formed into a guarding force, and have dispersed incipient riots, arrested a countryman of their own who was attempting to create a disturbance, and rescued one poor negro from the clutches of a mob. We are assured that there are other similar instances. It is highly important that the public should be enabled to distinguish between these two classes—the riotous, and the orderly and industrious. The meeting called by the Archbishop affords an excellent occasion for drawing the line; and we hope to see the peaceable and industrious Irish availing themselves of it. Their shepherd has summoned the wolves; let not the sheep attend also; let them stay at home, mind their usual business, and leave the wolves to be dealt with.

In the meantime the Archbishop's call, if it is generally obeyed, will draw together a crowd of such miscreants, assassins, robbers, house burners and thieves, such a congregation of vicious and abandoned wretches, as is not often got together. The police should be on the lookout there; they may catch many an incendiary, many a murderer, many a highway robber; and we cannot conceive that the Archbishop's safeguard could extend or that he would lend his protection to such malefactors.

Of course a strong force of the military, both cavalry and artillery, will be stationed near by, ready to act promptly and with the utmost vigor. This experiment of raising the devil is a new one. It is not easy to tell what he will do when he is raised. ◆

MAY THE GRASS GROW LONG ON THE ROAD TO HELL FOR WANT OF USE.
Traditional Irish Toast

The "Irish Vote"

EDITORIAL IN *THE IRISH CITIZEN*, NEW YORK, JUNE 12, 1869

There can be no doubt that the vote of at least half a million Irish-born citizens would be at the service of the party . . . which should really and *bona fide* press on and bring to pass a war against England. And Irish citizens, as citizens of the United States, would be quite well justified in so disposing of their votes as to bring about that most just and needful war; because it would be a strength and a blessing to their adopted country. It would operate as the best and promptest reconstruction, or rather, reconciliation, of the South. It would leave the United States in full possession of all their own continent. It would give profitable employment to hundreds of thousands of men who are now idle. It would carry off a vast mass of the floating and loafing population of our cities. It would abolish the monopoly of British shipowners, a monopoly secured to them during our war by the ravages of the Confederate cruisers. It would destroy and *cordon* off English maritime fortresses which affront and threaten our shores, from Halifax all the way round, by the Bermudas and Bahamas, to Jamaica. Lastly, such a war would settle our financial difficulties, in the only way they ever will be settled, namely, by repudiation.

We do not say, that by breaking up the British empire, it would also free Ireland, because this is not the point. It is with reference to America, and in our capacity as American citizens (as if there were no Ireland in the world) that we would give our heartiest support to that party in the United States which bases itself on war with England. But what party does so? Let there be no humbug; no party, no statesman of any party having the slightest pretension to give a direction to our foreign policy, has the slightest intention or idea of bringing on that war. Sumner, whose famous speech in the Senate has at least disgruntled the English, is perhaps the one man in America most hostile to the Irish, most thoroughly servile to England. His speech was not intended to bring on war, has no tendency whatsoever to a warlike policy; but his party, which is the predominant one now, has no objection to use the Irish national feeling in this country as a kind of threat to England. . . . It is easy for

Yankee politicians to give us cheap talk of this sort; but any Irishman who gives his vote or his support to the Radical party, *or any other party*, with the idea that he is thereby promoting a war against the enemy of his native country, will be . . . much deluded. . . .

On the whole, it would be safer and wiser for the Irish adopted citizens of this republic to abandon altogether the idea of the "Irish vote." It does no good, either to the country they have left, or to the one they have found. It exposes them to be cheated by lying politicians and to be sold and delivered by intriguing contractors for votes. They should exercise their privileges as American citizens, according to their best judgement of the interests and honor of their adopted country.

In the meantime, let them be assured that there will be no war with England. ◆

WHAT CANNOT BE HAD IS JUST WHAT SUITS.
Traditional Irish Proverb

Irish Americans marching outside the British Consulate-General in New York. Their signs bear allusions to Britain's repressive policy in Northern Ireland, and typify an ongoing effort to raise the consciousness of other Americans about injustice in the "six-county" area of Ulster. Three-quarters of a century after the events of 1916–1917, many Irish Americans regard the question of Ireland's freedom as unfinished business.

The following resolution was passed by an "Irish-American Convention" in New York City on May 14, 1917. It reflects the hope of many American supporters of Irish nationalism that the United States' entrance into the First World War would further the cause of independence for their ancestral homeland.

Whereas, the United States, according to the declaration of our honored President himself, has entered the European War to promote the cause of democracy and civilization, and

Whereas, the Allies have repeatedly proclaimed that they, too, are fighting for the same cause, and for the freedom of small nations, and

Whereas, the British Premier stated under date of April 27, 1917, that "the settlement of the Irish Question is essential to the peace of the world and essential to speedy victory in the war." . . . Now, therefore, be it

Resolved, that this assemblage of American citizens of Irish blood, loyal to the United States, and ready to defend her honor and interests, and recognizing that our Government is entitled to the best advice that Irishmen who understand the situation can give, urgently request the President and Congress to demand that England make good her promises in the only way possible in regard to Ireland, namely by according to the Irish people their indubitable right to be regarded as a sovereign people, and by granting to Ireland full national independence . . . and be it

Resolved, that we therefore submit to the President and Congress that America's entry into the war for democracy and civilization gives our Government the right, and imposes upon it the duty, to demand from England that she settle the Irish Question permanently and finally. . . . Such a settlement would be of untold benefit to the preservation of the future peace of the world, and its accomplishment would be another glorious achievement by the United States. ◆

An Irish-American demonstrator expresses her support for the Irish Republican Army and its goal of expelling British forces from Northern Ireland. The IRA is regarded by many present-day Irish Americans as continuing the liberation struggle begun during the 1916 Easter Rebellion and left unfinished when the Irish Free State was born in 1922.

*T*he Irish have always had a strong sense of history, and this remained true among those of them who settled in America. Early
immigrants and their children, however, tended to concentrate their attention on the history of Ireland rather than on the record of their own
experience in the New World. The first Irish-American newspapers and
magazines, for example, had much to say about the glories of ancient
Ireland and the sorrows of her more recent past, but almost nothing
about the Irish role in American history. It was only at the end of the
nineteenth century that an Irish-American historical consciousness
began to emerge. This awakening desire to explore the contribution of
the Irish to the building of the United States, and to make that contribution better known to the general public, would have both positive and
negative results.

The centennial celebrations of 1876 aroused a great deal of interest
in American history, and among the activities generated by this interest
were the creation of a number of societies and the publication under
their auspices of many volumes dedicated to the history of particular
ethnic groups. The American Irish were somewhat slow to join this
movement. To be sure, various books purporting to trace the "history of
the Irish Race" at home and abroad had appeared since midcentury, but
these usually concentrated on Irish rather than American affairs, were of
dubious historical value, and obviously resulted from individual initiative.

Not until James B. Cullen published his *Story of the Irish in Boston*
in 1889 was there a proposal for an Irish historical society. Cullen, who
was both the author and printer of this folio volume celebrating Boston's
Irish worthies "from colonial times to the present day," urged the creation of a historical society to show the good accomplished by the Irish
and to "awaken an appreciation of their worth as citizens." It is significant that sixteen of those who were hailed as "distinguished representative men" among the Boston Irish in the deluxe 1893 edition of Cullen's
book became charter members of the society that was, in fact, formed
three years later.

The immediate origins of the first Irish-American historical organi-

THERE IS PAIN IN
PROHIBITION.
*Traditional Irish
Proverb*

They come here ignorant and poor, without a knowledge of our institutions that should make them prize them, and without any of that self-respect that might restrain an indulgence in vicious courses. However honest their purposes, they are proverbially creatures of passion, and with the habits of dependence in which they have been educated, with their poverty and their propensity to drink to excess, they become a most dangerous engine in the hands of designing and bad men, to overawe and control our native citizens.

New England
Magazine (1834)

zation, however, lay not in Cullen's exhortation, but in a controversy that raged through newspaper columns and a riot that raged through Boston streets.

During the spring and summer of 1895, readers of letters-to-the-editor pages were treated to a protracted debate between Samuel S. Green, an eminent antiquarian, and Thomas Hamilton Murray, a well-known Irish-American journalist. The source of the argument was Green's widely circulated paper, *The Scotch-Irish in America*, in which he drew marked distinctions in "racial characteristics" between the Irish and the Scotch-Irish, claiming for the latter a "powerful and beneficent influence" in the early history of America. Murray, who had already acquired a reputation as having "done much toward elevating the Irish chapter in American history," denounced the concept of Scotch-Irish as distinguished from Irish nationality, and complained of Green's tendency to claim all non-Catholic Irish as Scotch. He was joined in this war of words by James Jeffrey Roche, editor of the *Boston Pilot*, John C. Linehan, insurance commissioner of New Hampshire, and Massachusetts police official Joseph Smith, who was described as "an Irish Protestant who also objects to the Scotch-Irish rubbish." Green's attempts to distinguish between the Scotch-Irish and what he termed the "Celtic Irish" were denounced by these antagonists as "the invention of a new Race" meant to divide and deride the Irish in America.

While these exchanges were stimulating debate in New England Irish circles, attention was shifted from the letters column to the headlines by a pitched battle in the streets of downtown Boston between Irish workingmen and participants in an anti-Catholic parade. The riot on July 4 climaxed a series of incidents growing out of the activities of the American Protective Association, a group avowedly dedicated to the defense of "the American way of life" against the menace of Catholicism, which, in the context of the time, meant the Irish menace. Much had been made in the APA's propaganda of the Irish American's supposed commitment to an alien religion and an alien national identity. He was accused of being a parasitical latecomer who merely subsisted on America's bounty without contributing to it.

Although the riot was deplored by moderates of all faiths and political alignments, and, in fact, contributed to the decline of the APA, it evidently encouraged Murray and his fellow letter writers to consult together on the best means of refuting anti-Irish slights and slurs. During the autumn of 1896, a further dispute in print between President Charles W. Eliot of Harvard and D. J. O'Connell, a federal government statistician, over the Irish population of Colonial America reinforced their decision to form an organization dedicated to vindicating the Irish role in American history.

In December 1896, Murray, Roche, Linehan, Smith, and O'Connell mailed to prominent men throughout the country a "call for the organization of an historical society whose special line of research shall be the history of the Irish element in the composition of the American people." This element, the writers complained, had received "but scant attention from chroniclers of American history." It would be the task of the projected society to investigate the achievements of all the Irish in the country without regard to distinctions of religion or origin, "to record the story of their settlement, to state the extent of their participation in the civil, military, and political activities of the land." They sought men who had "the patience to search, the knowledge and wisdom to sift and discriminate, and the ability to place the results in acceptable literary form," men whose character would command the respect and attention of the community.

Among those who appended their signatures to this invitation were two senators, two generals, an admiral, two Catholic and two Protestant clergymen, a number of political leaders, including Theodore Roosevelt, then New York's police commissioner, several descendants of seventeenth- and eighteenth-century Irish immigrants, as well as Dr. Thomas Addis Emmet, representative of a family renowned both in Ireland and in America.

The fifty men who met on January 20, 1897, resolved to establish the American Irish Historical Society, with Murray as secretary, Linehan as treasurer, and Admiral Richard W. Meade as president. This presidential choice emphasized at its very outset the society's concern with early American history and the Irish role in it. Descended from eighteenth-century Irish-Catholic immigrants, Meade was the great-grandson of a Revolutionary War patriot, nephew of the victor of the Battle of Gettysburg, and himself recently retired after a distinguished seagoing career.

Mary Harris Jones, a native of Cork, became the "elder stateswoman" of the American labor movement. "Mother Jones" died in 1930 at the age of one hundred.

The society grew in numbers and prosperity. It enrolled hundreds of members throughout the United States. It held frequent meetings at which papers were read and patriotic speeches were made. It published a journal, a newsletter, pamphlets, and monographs. It sponsored field days at historical sites, put up plaques, and laid wreaths. "A great awakening is taking place," one of the founders wrote, and "the American Irish race is becoming conscious of its history, and of that race's part in the making of this country."

Yet all this awareness and activity sprang from a motive that had very little to do with the quest for historical truth. "The true status of the Irish in America," declared a speaker at one of the society's meetings, "has never been appreciated, by reason of the prejudices associated with anything that bore an Irish name. . . . An impartial history of the deeds of Irishmen in America would effectively serve to displace any prejudice. . . . What patriotic American can fail to be moved by emotions of gratitude when he learns, among other facts, that the Irish in Ireland assisted with food and provisions for the struggling settlers of Boston in time of dire distress; that Irishmen of Philadelphia contributed large sums of money to the famished Revolutionary heroes at Valley Forge; that George Washington considered himself honored in being a member of an Irish society; that nine signers of the Declaration of Independence were men of Irish blood . . . ?"

Here are familiar themes that would be repeated endlessly in the meetings and writings of the society over the next three decades: The Irish are the victims of discrimination as foreigners. In order to end that discrimination we must show that the Irish are good Americans with a long history of service to the country. There can be no better way of doing this than by recounting the deeds of the Irish in the Revolutionary era.

The Revolution, and the Colonial period in general, constituted a golden age of antiquity for the late-nineteenth-century American imagination. In the country's relatively brief history, it was sufficiently remote to be viewed through an aura of romance and could scarcely yet cling to themes so recent and mundane as the Civil War, the great surge of immigration and industrialization, or even the winning of the West. Peopled with military heroes and paragons of civic virtue, the Revolution was the inevitable keynote of patriotic orations and the central element of major narrative histories, such as George Bancroft's.

It is scarcely surprising then that Irish immigrants and their sons, seeking acceptance into the American "mainstream," should seize upon the Revolution as a focal point of their efforts to establish a presence in their country's history. America's preoccupation with its Colonial origins and the respectful gratitude accorded to any individual or group that had shared in the nation's birth struggle, made the Revolution an obvious choice for those seeking by historical evidence to legitimize their status as Americans.

Thus it was that, as the American Irish Historical Society became a rallying place for upwardly mobile and socially ambitious Irishmen, it devoted itself almost exclusively to the study and commemoration of the Irish presence in Colonial and Revolutionary America. More than 80 percent of the articles published in its journals and nearly all of the monographs it sponsored were concerned with the period before 1800. Such excursions into the nineteenth century as it did make were usually aimed at proving the respectability and public services of eminent Irish Americans in the decades before the famine immigration.

This preoccupation with the Revolutionary era was by no means a

MAY PEACE AND PLENTY BE THE FIRST TO LIFT THE LATCH ON YOUR DOOR, AND HAPPINESS BE GUIDED TO YOUR HOME BY THE CANDLE OF CHRISTMAS. (*NOTE:* THIS TOAST REFERS TO THE TRADITIONAL CUSTOM OF LEAVING THE DOOR UNLATCHED, AND A LIGHTED CANDLE IN THE WINDOW, ON CHRISTMAS EVE.)
Traditional Irish Toast

uniquely Irish-American phenomenon. Many of the ethnic historical associations and most of the local antiquarian societies that multiplied in the last years of the nineteenth century followed the same pattern, and there are those that follow it still. Like them, the Irish organization clung to the fading tradition of the gentleman-amateur, dabbling in research with varying degrees of seriousness and success. Like them, it accumulated a substantial library, collected manuscripts, and gathered artifacts without acquiring the trained historians who could interpret these materials critically. To history as an art and as a vehicle for confounding one's enemies and enhancing one's prestige, a great deal of attention was paid; to history as a science, very little.

An exception—albeit a partial one—to this generalization is provided by the work of Michael J. O'Brien. Born in Fermoy, County Cork, in 1869, and educated at St. Colman's College, he served as a clerk in the office of the crown prosecutor for a time before coming to America, where he arrived, appropriately enough, on the Fourth of July 1889. Although his sympathy for Irish nationalism had led to the termination of his civil service career and his emigration, his inclinations were scholarly rather than activist. Shortly after his arrival he joined the Western Union telegraph company and spent the next forty-six years in its employ, traveling as an accountant to its offices throughout what had been the original thirteen colonies. Reading in early American history led to research in the records of the many places he visited and convinced him that "the Irish were in America in substantial numbers before the American Revolution," and that they were represented in equally large proportion in the Continental army, the militia, and in special levies. Unlike the founders of the American Irish Historical Society, O'Brien was prepared to spend long hours over muster rolls, court, tax, and church records, council minutes, census registers, and newspaper files to gather evidence. Like them, however, he was a man with a grievance.

As O'Brien began to publish the results of his research, the *Journal* of the society offered a natural outlet for his articles, and in due course he was elected historiographer. During the years preceding and immediately following the First World War, O'Brien's historical labors became virtually synonymous with those of the society, for as his investigations and publications increased, those of the other members of the group decreased. Scores of articles, and a dozen books, with titles like *Pioneer Irish in New England, Irish Pioneers in Maryland*, and *The Irish at Bunker Hill*, testify to his industry and to his preoccupations. His magnum opus, *A Hidden Phase of American History*, published in 1919, typifies the strengths and weaknesses of his approach. Subtitled *"Ireland's Part in America's Struggle for Liberty*, the book is specifically aimed at correcting the misstatements about a negligible Irish contribution to the Revolution made in George Bancroft's *History of the United States* and Lodge's *Story of the Revolution*. O'Brien undoubtedly marshals a

●This is an AOH parade. It is our parade. It is up to us to preserve it, protect it, and turn it over to the next generation, the way it was turned over to us since 1762— big, strong, Irish, Catholic, beautiful, and united, all marching to one tune of unity, honoring St. Patrick, the glorious Apostle of Ireland. . . .●

Francis Beirne, chairman of the New York St. Patrick's Day parade, quoted in *Irish America* (1986)

great array of data, statistical and biographical, to sustain his thesis that Irishmen were present and active during the fight for independence. His tone, however, is polemical and defensive, his belaboring of the "Scotch-Irish myth," as he and his colleagues always called it, tedious, and his assumptions based upon surnames alone, overbold. As one perceptive commentator observed, while praising O'Brien's wide-ranging research, his work would be more convincing if he had sifted his evidence with greater discrimination and claimed less for the Irish.

Given the particular concerns of its historiographer and the tendency of the other members to subordinate their own interest to this safely patriotic and fashionable theme, the researches of the society had little chance of expanding into additional aspects of the Irish-American experience. Had there been other groups prepared to venture beyond this historical province, such an obsession with early American history might have been harmless, if increasingly sterile. No such initiatives were taken, however. Irish Americans, to the extent that they exhibited a historical self-consciousness at all, seemed content to accept the society as the authoritative voice on what was worth knowing about their community's past.

The *Journal* for 1928 marks both the culmination of Michael O'Brien's historical activities and the passing of an era in the history of the Irish in America. Contained in a solid volume of five hundred pages, two-thirds of its articles are by O'Brien himself and range over records of Irish settlers in half-a-dozen colonies as well as touching upon various aspects of the Revolutionary War. The activities of the society show that the task of preparing the annual *Journal* had by now fallen entirely upon the historiographer's shoulders, with the other four members of the editorial committee all finding plausible excuses for their absence. There is, in fact, ample indication in the minutes of the 1928 annual meeting that few members were really concerned at all about what went into the *Journal*.

Much had changed in the thirty years since the founding of the society. Its headquarters had been moved to New York City. Its "fathers" had died or retired. The amateur historians who had once shared O'Brien's zeal, if not his exhaustive inquiries, were gone, and their successors were neither gentlemen-amateurs nor trained professionals, but simply passive participants in meetings that had become social rituals. Most important of all, the Irish had crossed the barrier that still kept back the hordes of later arrivals from southern and eastern Europe, and were rapidly becoming accepted and assimilated. The postwar decline in the flow of Irish immigration and the establishment of the Irish Free State had weakened the emotional tie of personal and political concern that had kept them alive to their heritage. The sense of a distinct identity —proudly acknowledged or grudgingly admitted by their fathers—was fading for the new generation of Irish Americans. With no further need

The Irish are the crybabies of the Western world. Even the mildest quip will set them off in resolutions and protests.

Heywood Broun, *It Seems to Me* (1933)

to legitimize themselves by integration into the structure of American history, they were no longer much interested in the Irish role in that history. Ironically, even the American Revolution that had long been the quintessential embodiment of Americanism for the Irish was beginning to lose its luster. There had been an Irish Day during the sesquicentennial celebrations at Philadelphia in 1926, and O'Brien had orated eloquently on his favorite theme. Still, most Americans had found other matters to excite them, and a new school of debunkers was already busy tearing down the reputations of George Washington and his fellow heroes.

GOD NEVER CLOSES ONE DOOR BUT HE OPENS ANOTHER. *Traditional Irish Proverb*

Michael O'Brien's concluding words at the thirtieth annual meeting of the society on January 28, 1928, thus amounted not merely to a personal valedictory but to a lament for a vanishing epoch. "I feel the day is coming very soon," he said, "perhaps within the limits of this year, when I shall have to quit entirely because I have done all that it is possible for one man to do, and more should not be required of me. I confess to being disappointed because I get such little assistance, cooperation, or encouragement. . . ."

Michael O'Brien and the American Irish Historical Society had come to a parting of the ways. His retirement, ostensibly due to poor health (actually, he lived another thirty years and died at the age of ninety-two), was the result of a belated realization that the Irish-American historical consciousness he had done so much to serve had faded with the circumstances that inspired it. The *Journal* ceased publication a few years later, and the society entered a long period of suspended animation, accumulating books and memorabilia in its handsome mansion on New York's Fifth Avenue, supplying reference material to an occasional student or journalist, but taking no active part in "making better known the Irish chapter in American history." Such work as was done in Irish-American history during the next thirty years was, once again, the result of individual initiative—sometimes meeting modern standards of scholarship, but random and often repetitive, leaving whole areas of the Irish experience in America still unexplored.

Since 1970, however, there has been a "second spring" of Irish-American historical consciousness. The general surge of ethnic awareness and the quest for identity and origins, especially among younger people, has combined with the renewed issue of Irish national unity to stimulate interest and enthusiasm. Locally organized groups, academic scholars, and serious amateurs have all contributed to a valuable flow of research and publication. Most hopeful of all are the abundant signs that Irish Americans, secure now in the American nation, are ready to look honestly at all dimensions of their role in making that nation. Their historical consciousness seems to have matured to the point where they are interested in facts rather than self-justification. They are ready to learn about the villains as well as the heroes. ◆

The
Transatlantic
Tuber

No other country in the world is identified with a single item of food the way Ireland is with the potato. To put it another way, in a game of word association, "Potato" always brings the response, "Ireland." Many people think of this unglamorous but nutritious tuber as native to the soil of Hibernia. In fact, the potato is an American immigrant to Ireland.

Although wild varieties probably grew as far north as what is now Colorado, the cultivation of potatoes began in South America, at least 2,000 years ago. Spanish conquerors found it to be a staple in the diet of the Inca people in the Peruvian highlands when they arrived there in the 1530s. Within a few decades, samples of this new tuber had been brought back to Spain, and the European chapter in the potato's story had begun.

According to tradition, the first potatoes in Ireland were grown in the garden of Sir Walter Raleigh's house in Youghal, County Cork. Some scholars dispute this; others say that it may possibly be true. In any case, whether or not the potato had such a celebrity for its godfather, it does appear to have arrived in Ireland by about 1588.

If ever there was a case of love at first sight, this is it. Although other countries, especially the Netherlands and Germany, gradually adopted this American import as a feature of their national diet, the process stretched out over many generations. Ireland, on the other hand, quickly accepted the potato as its own. Why? Perhaps because during a time of political change, accompanied by social and economic disruption, an easily grown, easily distributed food for the masses was just what was needed. At any rate, the soil of Ireland, both literally and figuratively, proved hospitable during the seventeenth century. By the 1690s, writers were referring to the "Irish potato" as if the two words were inseparable.

The potato returned in triumph to the Western Hemisphere during the 1720s, when Irish settlers from Ulster began its cultivation in Pennsylvania. Throughout the Colonial period, Americans customarily referred to this new vegetable in their midst as the "Irish potato," oblivious to its American origin. In the meantime, the Irish population at home was becoming increasingly dependent on a "one-crop" cultiva-

> ●The Irish forgot completely where they came from. Like everything they went through never happened.●
>
> Jimmy Breslin, G.Q. magazine (1987)

tion. When blight fell upon the potatoes, as it did at frequent intervals during the 1700s, the people went hungry. But still the population of Ireland thrived and grew on this nutritious root. If cotton was king in the American South, then the potato was king in Ireland.

The rest, as they say, is history: a piece of history all too well known to the Irish. The repeated destruction of the annual potato crop by blight during the 1840s killed or drove into exile millions of Irish men and women. The famine that resulted from the failure of the country's basic foodstuff transformed Ireland and Irish America. Whatever the future hardships of the Irish people, they would never again be totally dependent upon any single object as they had been upon the potato during the centuries preceding the famine.

In the United States, the labeling of the Irish as "spuds" has long since given way to less vivid nicknames, just as the descendants of the famine refugees have long since adopted the varied diet of their new homeland. But whether the potato is seen as a cute cliché on St. Patrick's day cards, or in the sinister character of a fodder imported by the English to feed the peasant masses, it can never lose its identification with Ireland. In its migration back and forth across the Atlantic, it is powerfully symbolic of the interaction between the Old Country and the New World. ◆

Many fled Ireland for reasons other than the famine. The First Lady of the Confederacy, Varina Howell Davis, was the daughter of a "fugitive from justice" who fled from Ireland to New York to Virginia.

COUNTIES THAT COUNT

Ireland has only 32 counties. Irish America has nearly 100. The following list includes counties in the United States named after Americans of Irish descent (some nationally prominent, others of purely local significance) and places in Ireland. Michigan takes the prize for nostalgia, with four of her counties named after counties in Ireland.

ALABAMA Butler, Calhoun, Cleburne, Cullinan, Houston, Jackson

ARKANSAS Boone, Calhoun, Carroll, Cleburne, Conway, Fulton, Jackson

COLORADO Crowley, Jackson

FLORIDA Calhoun, Jackson

GEORGIA Burke, Calhoun, Carroll, Dooly, Dougherty, Fulton, Glynn, Grady, Hart, Houston, Jackson, McDuffie, Talbot

IDAHO Power

ILLINOIS Calhoun, Carroll, Clinton, Fulton, Jackson, McDonough, McHenry

INDIANA Boone, Carroll, Fulton, Jackson, Sullivan

IOWA Boone, Butler, Calhoun, Carroll, Emmet, O'Brien

KANSAS Butler, Coffey, Doniphan, Ford, Geary, Jackson, Kearny, Riley, Sheridan

KENTUCKY Boone, Boyle, Bracken, Butler, Carroll, Casey, Clinton, Fulton, Harlan, Hart, Jackson, Lyon, McCracken, McCreary, Rowan

LOUISIANA East Carroll, West Carroll, Jackson

MARYLAND Carroll, Garrett, Talbot, Baltimore (city and county)

MICHIGAN Antrim, Barry, Calhoun, Clare, Clinton, Emmet, Jackson, Roscommon, Wexford

MINNESOTA Houston, Jackson

MISSISSIPPI Calhoun, Carroll, Jackson, Sharkey

MISSOURI Barry, Boone, Butler, Carroll, Clinton, Jackson

MONTANA Fallon, Fergus, McCone, Meagher, Sheridan, Toole

NEBRASKA Boone, Butler, Harlan, Kearney, Sheridan

NEW HAMPSHIRE Carroll, Sullivan

NEW YORK Clinton, Fulton, Montgomery, Sullivan

NORTH CAROLINA Jackson, McDowell, Rowan

NORTH DAKOTA Burke, Dunn, McHenry, Sheridan, Walsh

OHIO Butler, Carroll, Clinton, Fulton

OKLAHOMA Gavin, Grady, Jackson, McClain, McCurtain

OREGON Jackson

PENNSYLVANIA Butler, Clinton, Fulton, Sullivan

SOUTH CAROLINA Calhoun, Dillon, McCormick

SOUTH DAKOTA Jackson, Shannon

TENNESSEE Carroll, Crockett, Houston, Jackson, McNairy, Sullivan

TEXAS Calhoun, Callahan, Crockett, Crosby, Devitt, Donley, Houston, Jackson, Kenedy, Kinney, McMullen, Moore, Nolan, Reagan

VIRGINIA Carroll

WEST VIRGINIA Boone, Calhoun, Jackson, McDowell

WISCONSIN Dunn

WYOMING Sheridan

In addition, several states have a Green (or Greene) County. Others, including California, have an Orange County. New York has both.

The
New Wave

*A*fter decades of decline, Irish immigration to the United States has taken a dramatic upturn in the 1980s. Spurred by a depressed economy at home, young Irish men and women have overcome the problem of low quotas by illegally overstaying their visa time. Thus a small but significant Irish element has been added to the huge number of illegal aliens now residing in this country. The following figures, based on federal government records, show the number of tourist and business visas issued to citizens of the Republic of Ireland. While exact figures on the number of visitors who overstay their allotted time period is not available, estimates range from 10 to 20 percent of each year's total, and some observers contend that it is even higher. By contrast, the number of Irish people who entered the United States as legal permanent residents ranged from 902 in 1981 to 1,839 in 1986.

An Irish lady's maid has the privilege of riding in an oxcart with her employer during a holiday jaunt.

EMIGRANTS FROM IRELAND TO THE UNITED STATES DURING THE TWENTIETH CENTURY

Year	Number	Year	Number
1901	35,535	1936	444
1902	29,138	1937	531
1903	35,310	1938	1,085
1904	36,142	1939	1,189
1905	52,945	1940	839
1906	34,995	1941	272
1907	34,530	1942	83
1908	30,556	1943	165
1909	25,033	1944	112
1910	29,855	1945	427
1911	29,112	1946	1,816
1912	25,879	1947	2,574
1913	27,876	1948	7,534
1914	24,688	1949	8,678
1915	14,185	1950	5,842
1916	8,639	1951	3,144
1917	5,406	1952	3,526
1918	331	1953	4,304
1919	474	1954	4,655
1920	9,591	1955	5,222
1921	28,435	1956	5,607
1922	10,579	1957	8,227
1923	15,740	1958	9,134
1924	17,111	1959	6,595
1925	26,650	1960	6,918
1926	24,897	1961	5,738
1927	28,545	1962	5,118
1928	25,268	1963	5,000
1929	19,921	1964	5,200
1930	23,445	1965	5,463
1931	7,305	1966	4,700
1932	539	1967	1,901
1933	338	1968	2,268
1934	443	1969	1,989
1935	454	1970	1,562
		1971–1980	**11,600**

	TOURIST VISAS	BUSINESS VISAS
1977	31,938	4,297
1978	42,592	5,491
1979 (nine months)	31,779	4,830
1980 (not available)	—	—
1981	87,627	8,088
1982	82,268	9,368
1983	51,711	10,883
1984	57,936	12,348
1985	62,206	13,155
1986	85,090	15,273

THE IRISH SHARE OF AMERICAN IMMIGRATION

DECADE	ALL IMMIGRANTS	IRISH
1820–1830	151,824	54,338
1831–1840	599,125	207,381
1841–1850	1,713,251	780,719
1851–1860	2,598,214	914,119
1861–1870	2,314,824	435,778
1871–1880	2,812,191	436,871
1881–1890	5,246,613	655,482
1891–1900	3,687,564	390,179
1901–1910	8,795,386	339,065
1911–1920	5,735,811	146,181
1921–1930	4,107,209	220,591
1931–1940	528,431	13,167
1941–1950	1,035,039	25,377
1951–1960	2,515,479	57,332
1961–1970	3,321,777	37,461
TOTAL 1820–1970	**45,162,638**	**4,713,868 (10.4%)**

The Irish constituted 42.3 percent of all immigrants between 1820 and 1850, and 35.2 percent of those coming between 1851 and 1860. Thereafter, the percentage declined steadily, to 18.8 percent in 1861–1870, 15.5 percent in 1871–1880, 12.5 percent in 1881–1890, and 10.6 percent in 1891–1900. During 1961–1970, the Irish accounted for only 1.1 percent of all immigrants, and during 1971–1980, only .3 percent (11,600).

The McGovern family, immigrants from County Cavan, pose proudly in front of their new country's flag at their home in Philadelphia, about 1904.

DECLINE IN THE POPULATION OF IRELAND DURING THE PERIOD OF HEAVIEST EMIGRATION

YEAR	POPULATION	RATE OF DECREASE IN DECADE
1841	8,196,597	
1851	6,574,278	19.80%
1861	5,888,564	10.43%
1871	5,412,377	8.08%
1881	5,174,836	4.39%
1891	4,704,750	9.08%
1901	4,456,546	5.27%

As of 1984, the estimated population of Ireland (Republic and Northern Ireland) was 5,075,000.

NUMBER OF PERSONS IN EACH STATE CLAIMING IRISH ORIGIN (CENSUS OF 1980)

STATE	NUMBER	STATE	NUMBER
Alabama	633,036	Montana	158,575
Alaska	59,179	Nebraska	312,363
Arizona	462,777	Nevada	158,199
Arkansas	475,161	New Hampshire	192,718
California	3,727,925	New Jersey	1,444,308
Colorado	573,991	New Mexico	172,128
Connecticut	613,684	New York	2,977,518
Delaware	126,854	North Carolina	871,721
District of Columbia	37,667	North Dakota	64,547
Florida	1,617,433	Ohio	2,031,751
Georgia	848,853	Oklahoma	706,407
Hawaii	68,041	Oregon	546,512
Idaho	152,904	Pennsylvania	2,449,110
Illinois	2,027,692	Rhode Island	210,950
Indiana	1,017,944	South Carolina	484,817
Iowa	630,020	South Dakota	93,922
Kansas	489,228	Tennessee	850,949
Kentucky	672,791	Texas	2,420,367
Louisiana	588,258	Utah	137,479
Maine	201,299	Vermont	99,977
Maryland	765,871	Virginia	849,069
Massachusetts	1,564,100	Washington	824,994
Michigan	1,521,796	West Virginia	382,272
Minnesota	606,688	Wisconsin	647,653
Mississippi	408,346	Wyoming	88,714
Missouri	1,129,149		

THE IRISH ELEMENT IN THE POPULATION
OF THE UNITED STATES

YEAR	TOTAL POPULATION	IRISH-BORN POPULATION
1850	23,191,876	961,719 (4.15%)
1860	31,443,321	1,611,304 (5.12%)
1870	38,558,371	1,855,827 (4.81%)
1880	50,155,783	1,854,571 (3.70%)
1890	62,622,250	1,871,509 (2.99%)
1900	75,568,686	1,615,459 (2.13%)
1910	91,972,266	1,352,155 (1.47%)
1920	105,710,620	1,037,233
1930	122,775,646	923,642
1940	131,669,275	678,447
1950	150,697,361	520,359
1960	179,323,175	406,433
1970	203,184,772	277,000

NATIVE-BORN AMERICANS WITH ONE OR
BOTH PARENTS IRISH-BORN

1910	3,304,015	1950	1,921,385
1920	3,122,013	1960	1,619,446
1930	2,858,897	1970	1,300,000 (est.)
1940	2,109,740		

COMFORT IS NOT KNOWN IF POVERTY DOES NOT COME BEFORE IT.
Traditional Irish Proverb

IRISH LANDMARKS IN NEW YORK CITY

STATE STREET

1 State Street, renamed Whitehall by Richard Nicolls, the first English governor; later (c. 1810) home of Robert Fulton

6 State Street, residence of Christopher Colles, Dublin-born designer of New York City water system (c. 1800)

7 State Street, Mission of Our Lady of the Rosary, shelter for immigrants

Site of Castle Garden, which in 1855 became an immigration station

THE WATERFRONT

129 Front Street, birthplace of Charles O'Conor, first Catholic to be nominated for U.S. presidency (1872)

151–174 South Street, boyhood home of Al Smith

218 Pearl Street, residence of Irish-born American Revolutionary hero Hercules Mulligan

BROADWAY AREA

Corner of Cortland and West streets, the Northern Hotel, run by Fenian advocate Jeremiah O'Donovan Rossa

36 Broadway, home of Dominick Lynch, Galway-born civic and social leader of 1780s

Between Thames and Cedar streets, Cape's Tavern, first home of Friendly Sons of St. Patrick

ST. PAUL'S CHAPEL AREA

Broadway and Fulton streets, St. Paul's Chapel, noted for memorials to famous Irish Americans, including Thomas Addis Emmet, W. J. MacNeven, and General Richard Montgomery

Barclay and Church streets, St. Peter's Church, oldest Catholic parish in New York City

Brooklyn Bridge, built by William C. Kingsley, a native of Kilkenny

CITY HALL AREA

City Hall, which was built at the urging of Irish-American mayor DeWitt Clinton, who was the driving force behind the Erie Canal. City Hall was dedicated in 1812.

Cardinal Hayes Place, formerly City Hall Place, birthplace of Patrick Cardinal Hayes

Duane Street, named for James Duane, first mayor of New York after the Revolution. His father was a native of Galway.

51 Chambers Street, Emigrant Savings Bank, which was founded in 1817 by William J. MacNeven for the assistance of Irish immigrants. It was originally known as the Irish Emigrant Society.

LOWER MANHATTAN

Between Mott and Mulberry streets, Old St. Patrick's Cathedral, dedicated in 1815. St. Patrick's Free School, the first in the city, was opened here in 1817.

Five Points, large Irish-American community as early as 1820s

Greenwich Village, once the estate of Irish-born Sir Peter Warren, a wealthy New York merchant of Colonial days

Sullivan Street, in Greenwich Village, named for Revolutionary hero Brigadier General John Sullivan

480 Canal Street, offices of the *Irish World*, Irish-American newspaper founded by Patrick Ford

220 Clinton Street, birthplace of composer Edward MacDowell in 1861

Fourth Avenue and Seventh Street, Cooper Union Institute, statue of Peter Cooper by Dublin-born sculptor Augustus Saint-Gaudens.

Union Square (southeast corner of Seventeenth Street) was headquarters of the Tammany Society.

Chelsea, noted for large settlement of Irish

Madison Square, Twenty-third street and Broadway, statue of Admiral Farragut by Saint-Gaudens

(continued)

IRISH LANDMARKS IN NEW YORK CITY

MIDTOWN MANHATTAN

Murray Hill section, once the farm of Irish-born Robert Murray. At 16 Park Avenue (Thirty-fifth Street), plaque marks the geographic center of the estate. When General Howe arrived in New York on September 15, 1776, Mrs. Murray entertained him, delaying his advance on the retreating American army.

Fifth Avenue and Forty-second Street, the New York Public Library, which has a large collection of Irish and Irish-American materials

Forty-third Street and Broadway, Duffy Square, named for Reverend Francis Duffy, chaplain of the Fighting Sixty-ninth during the First World War. His statue stands here.

Forty-sixth Street and Broadway, statue in honor of composer George N. Cohan

Fiftieth Street and Fifth Avenue, "new" St. Patrick's Cathedral, designed by architect James Renwick, built between 1858 and 1910.

Fifth Avenue (Forty-second Street to Eighty-sixth Street), parade route of St. Patrick's Day parade.

Sixty-eighth Street and Park Avenue, Hunter College, named in honor of Thomas Hunter, a schoolmaster from County Down. He was first president of the teacher training college that has become Hunter.

UPPER MANHATTAN

Central Park near Seventy-second Street, the Victor Herbert Pond, named for the Dublin-born composer.

Eighty-sixth Street, Yorkville neighborhood, was the center of a large Irish population.

Central Park near 107th Street, McGowan's Pass, named for Daniel McGowan, who was involved in Revolutionary politics and whose farm was located here.

Moylan Place, 125th Street between Broadway and Amsterdam Avenue, named for Stephen Moylan, Revolutionary general who was an aide to General Washington. He was born in Cork in 1737.

Claremont Avenue, named in honor of Michael Hogan, whose birthplace was County Clare. Hogan was a leading businessman in New York after the Revolution. His mansion was also called Claremont.

287 Convent Avenue, near 141st Street, Hamilton Grange, the last home of Alexander Hamilton, designed by John McComb

McComb's Dam Bridge, Harlem River at 155th Street, named for Alexander McComb, whose father came from Antrim in 1755. McComb constructed the first dam across the Harlem River at this point. He was also an early president of the Friendly Sons of St. Patrick.

High Bridge (the Aqueduct Bridge across the Harlem River at 174th Street), designed by Reverend Thomas Levins from Drogheda, a scientist, architect, and engineer who was a pastor of old St. Patrick's Cathedral. The bridge was erected in 1842 to carry the first Croton Aqueduct.

183rd Street on the west side of Fort Washington Avenue, tablet to commemorate Margaret Corbin, an Irish American whose husband was a gunner at Fort Tryon. During the British assault on Fort Tryon, Corbin was killed and Margaret took his place until she was shot and captured by the British. ◆

Family, Neighborhood, and Jobs

(Almost) Every
Man a King

*N*o, it is not true that *all* Irishmen are descended from kings. But don't give up hope just yet. Considering the number of monarchs in Old Ireland, your chances of royal descent are still fairly good.

At various times in its ancient history, Ireland was divided into anywhere from four to nine kingdoms. These in turn incorporated several dozen subordinate kingdoms. Finally, there were the territories of individual clans, well over a hundred in number. All of these miniature realms were governed by persons variously designated a chief, lord, prince, or *ri*, the Irish word for king. Clearly, all of these potentates had to have subjects, and you may be the heir of fifty generations of ditchdiggers, but if you feel royal, you probably are.

Some, of course, will not be satisfied with this generous distribution of blue blood. When everybody's somebody, then nobody's anybody. The answer is to link up with the king of kings—the *ard ri*, or high king of Ireland. This lofty personage claims the allegiance of all the lesser kings and received tribute from all parts of the island. Here, obviously, is a dynasty worth belonging to. Unfortunately, Ireland produced three such clans: O'Neill, O'Brien, and O'Connor. But before bearers of those surnames assume lofty airs, a little more information is in order.

HOWEVER LONG
THE ROAD THERE
COMES A TURNING.
*Traditional Irish
Proverb*

If you are an O'Neill, you have to be the right kind of O'Neill. There are at least four distinct O'Neill families in Ireland that are in no way connected with one another. Those in Clare and Cork, Carlow and Wicklow, Waterford and Tipperary, and their American descendants, are out of luck. The royal house was centered in the northern province of Ulster and traced its descent from King Conn of the Hundred Battles, who ruled all Ireland in the second century A.D., and from King Niall (Neill) of the Nine Hostages (A.D. 379–405). In the fourteenth century, the dynasty (which by then no longer ruled Ireland) split into two branches, the O'Neills of Clanaboy (in Antrim and Down) and the O'Neills of Tyrone. The latter, although the junior, are the more famous of the royal lines. They include Shane the Proud (1530–1567), earl of Tyrone and leader of the Gaelic resistance to Queen Elizabeth; his nephew Hugh, "the Great O'Neill" (1546–1616), earl of Tyrone and organizer of the great revolt against English domination at the beginning of the seventeenth century;

and Hugh's nephew Owen Roe (1590–1649), commander of the rebel forces in the so-called Confederate War of the 1640s.

The direct royal line of the O'Neills, however, ran through the Clanaboy branch, "kings of Ulster and rightful successors of those of all Ireland." What was left of their estates by the nineteenth century passed by marriage to the Chichester family, which adopted the O'Neill name and in 1868 received a peerage as Baron O'Neill of Shane's Castle. Some regard the current Lord O'Neill as the heir to the family claims on the Irish kingship. Most genealogists, however, award that title to an overseas descendant of the ancient kings. The chief herald of Ireland recognizes Hugo (Hugh) O'Neill of Lisbon, Portugal, as The O'Neill and head of the House of O'Neill.

Hugh O'Neill (1546–1616) was hereditary leader of one of the great Irish clans. Queen Elizabeth recognized him as earl of Tyrone, hoping to use him as a collaborator in the task of subduing Ireland. Instead, he led a rebellion that threatened the survival of English rule.

The lineage of the O'Briens is both less complicated and less antique. They take their name from Brian Boru—Brian of the Tributes—high king of Ireland, who was killed in 1014 at the Battle of Clontarf, in his hour of triumph over the Viking invaders. Although his ancestors had been only minor chieftains in Clare, his descendants held the high kingship for several generations and remained kings of Thomond until 1540, when they surrendered it to Henry VIII, becoming earls of Thomond. Later chiefs of the O'Briens generally supported English rule in Ireland. On the other hand, William Smith O'Brien, leader of the Young Ireland Rebellion in 1848, was a member of the royal line—a descendant of Irish kings who proclaimed his country's independence. The present head of the clan is Lord Inchiquin, whose family seat, Dromoland Castle, was transformed into a hotel several years ago. If this sounds fairly straightforward, keep in mind that Brian Boru's descendants are estimated to number 100,000 worldwide.

The name O'Connor is borne by at least six distinct clans in Ireland. The royal house is that of the O'Connors of Connaught. The kings of Connaught supplanted the O'Briens in the eleventh century, and the last high king of Ireland, forced off his throne by the English invaders eight hundred years ago, was Rory O'Connor.

THE HIGH KINGS OF IRELAND

I Niall Nóigiallach mac Eochaid Mugmedóin

II Nath Í mac Fiachrach

III Lóeguire mac Néill (died c. 463)

IV Ailill Molt mac Nath Í (died c. 482)

V Lugaid mac Lóeguiri (died c. 507)

VI Muirchertach mac Ercae mac Eógain (died c. 536)

VII Tuathal Máelgarb mac Cormaic Caích maic Coirpri (died c. 544)

VIII Diarmait mac Cerbaill (died c. 565)

IX Forggus mac Muirchertaig (died c. 566)

Dommall mac Muirchertaig (died c. 566)

X Ainmuire mac Sétnai (died c. 569)

XI Báetán mac Muirchertaig (died c. 572)

Eochaid mac Domnaill (died c. 572)

XII Báetán mac Ninnedo (died c. 586)

XIII Áed mac Ainmuirech (died c. 598)

XIV Áed Sláine mac Diasmato (died 604)

XV Áed Allán (alias Áed Uaridnach) mac Domnaill (died 612)

XVI Máel Cobo mac Áedo (died 614)

XVII Suibne Menn mac Fiachnai (died 628)

XVIII Domnall mac Áedo (died 642)

XIX Cellach mac Máele Cobo (died 658)

Conall Cáel mac Máele Cobo (died 654)

XX Diarmait mac Áedo Sláine (died 665)

Blathmac mac Áedo Sláine (died 665)

XXI Sechnussach mac Blathmaic (died 671)

XXII Cenn Fáelad mac Blathmaic (died 674)

XXIII Fínsnechta Fledach mac Dúnchado (died 695)

XXIV Loingsech mac Óengusso (died 704)

XXV Congal Cennmagair (died 710)

XXVI Fergal mac Máele Dúin (died 772)

XXVII Fogartach mac Néill (died 724)

XXVIII Cináed mac Írgalaig (died 728)

XXIX Flaithbertach mac Loingsig (died 734)

XXX Áed Allán mac Fergaile (died 743)

XXXI Domnall Midi mac Murchado (died 763)

XXXII Niall Frossach mac Fergaile (died 770)

XXXIII Donnchad Midi mac Domnaill (died 797)

XXXIV Áed Oirdnide mac Néill (died 819)

XXXV Conchobar mac Donnchada (died 833)

XXXVI Niall Caille mac Áeda (died 846)

XXXVII Máelsechnaill mac Máele Ruanaid (died 862)

XXXVIII Áed Findliath mac Néill (died 879)

XXXIX Flann Sinna mac Máelsechnaill (died 916)

XL Niall Glúndub mac Áeda (died 919)

XLI Donnchad Donn mac Flainn (died 944)

XLII Congalach Cnogba mac Máelmithig (died 956)

XLIII Domnall ua Néill (died 980)

XLIV Máelsechnaill mac Domnaill (died 1022)

XLV Brian Bóruma mac Cennétic (died 1014)

XLVI Tairrdelbach ua Briain (died 1086)

XLVII Muirchertach Ua Briain (died 1119)

Domnall Ua Lochlainn (died 1121)

XLVIII Tairrdelbach Ua Conchobair (died 1156)

XLIX Muirchertach Mac Lochlainn (died 1166)

L Ruaidrí Ua Conchobair (died 1198)

Most of the more spectacular O'Connors have been from other lines, such as Arthur O'Connor, United Irish revolutionary leader and subsequently French general under Napoleon, or Feargus O'Connor, the "Lion of Liberty" who became a hero of the nineteenth-century political reform movement in—of all places—England. The royal line of descent, however, runs through the successive holders of the ancient title, the O'Connor Don—most of whom have kept out of the limelight. Until a few years ago this designation was held by the Reverend Charles O'Connor, a Jesuit priest. Since his death, there has been some dispute among genealogists as to the proper succession to the title. The question is of more than passing interest, for the O'Connors, as the most recent holders of the high kingship, probably have the best claim to it.

No doubt this seems all fantasy in an age of republicanism and nuclear families (to say nothing of nuclear wars). But surely fantasy is part of the Irish heritage and the Irish temperament. So, if you want to imagine that you are the descendant of kings, dream on. ◆

WHAT'S IN A NAME?

The following are the most frequently occurring Irish surnames in the United States, with their root derivations.

1. Murphy   O Murchadha, descendant of a *murchadh* ("sea warrior")
2. Kelly   O Ceallaigh, descendant of Ceallaigh (*ceallach*, "strife")
3. Sullivan   O Suileabhain, descendant of Suileabhain (*suil*, "eye"; Levan, a Celtic deity)
4. Brennan   O Braonain, descendant of Braonain (*braon*, "sorrow")
5. Walsh   a person of Welsh origin
6. Ryan   O Mavilriain descendant of Mavilriain (derivation of name uncertain)
7. Lynch   from the Norman French surname de Lench.
8. Dunne   O Duinn, descendant of Duinn (*donn*, "brown," hence "brown-haired")
9. Byrne   O Broin, descendant of Broin (*bran*, "raven")
10. Flynn   O Floinn, descendant of Floinn (*flann*, "ruddy")
11. O'Brien   O Briain, descendant of Briain (Brian Boru)
12. Quinn   O Cuinn, descendant of Conn
13. Reilly   O Ragailligh, descendant of Ragaillach

14. O'Connor   O Conchobhair, descendant of Conchobhair
15. Daly   O Dalaigh, descendant of Dalaigh (*dalach*, "assemblyman")
16. Kennedy   O Cinneide, descendant of Cinneide (*ceann*, "head"; *eidigh*, "ugly")
17. O'Donnell   O Domhnaill, descendant of Domhnaill
18. McCarthy   Mac Carthaigh, descendant of Carthaigh (*carthach*, "loving")
19. Fitzgerald   son of Gerald (Norman-French derivation)
20. O'Neill   O Neill, descendant of Neill ("Neill of the Nine Hostages")
21. Regan   O Riagain, descendant of Riagain
22. Burke   from the Norman French surname de Burgh or de Bourg
23. Donohue   O Donnchadha, descendant of Donnchadha (*donn*, "brown-haired")
24. Barry   from the Norman French surname de Barri
25. Casey   O Cathasaigh, descendant of Cathasaigh (*cathasach*, "watchful")

The
Big Three

*A*ccording to a turn-of-the-century census, the three most common names in Ireland were Murphy, Kelly, and Sullivan. As this was the heyday of Irish immigration to the United States, one may presume that these were the "big three" names among Irish Americans as well. For the present-day representatives of those prolific clans, in particular, it should be gratifying to review some of the more notable contributors to the American experience who have borne their names. Drawn from standard biographical listings, the rosters are by no means exhaustive.

For those not fortunate enough to be Murphys, Kellys, or Sullivans, perusal of these lists may stimulate them to catch up.

MURPHY
AUDIE war hero
CHARLES F. leader of Tammany Hall
EDGAR Episcopalian clergyman and social reformer
FRANK governor of Michigan, U.S. attorney general, Supreme Court justice
FRANKLIN governor of New Jersey, industrialist
HENRY journalist, editor
HERMAN painter
JOHN B. surgeon, medical inventor
JOHN F. painter
LAMBERT operatic tenor
MICHAEL athletic trainer, manager of U.S. Olympic teams
RICHARD assistant secretary of state
ROBERT diplomat
TIMOTHY war hero
WALTER industrialist, philanthropist
WILLIAM medical researcher, winner of Nobel Prize in medicine (1934)

KELLY
COLIN war hero
ELLSWORTH painter
EMMETT clown

ERIC   author (Newbery award, 1928)
GEORGE   playwright (Pulitzer Prize, 1925)
GRACE   actress (Academy Award, 1954)
HOWARD   surgeon, author of medical textbooks
JAMES   "the sculptor of American history"
JOHN   leader of Tammany Hall
MYRA   author, educator
WALT   cartoonist
WILLIAM   inventor (process for making steel)

KELLEY
CLARENCE   director, Federal Bureau of Investigation
EDGAR   musician, composer
FLORENCE   social worker
OLIVER   organizer of the Grange movement (1867)

SULLIVAN
ED   journalist, television producer
FRANCIS ("Fred Allen")   humorist
FRANK   essayist
GEORGE   politician, U.S. attorney in the Dartmouth College case (1817)
JAMES   governor of Massachusetts
JAMES EDWARD   sports promoter, organizer of the Amateur Athletic
    Union (1888)
JOHN   Revolutionary War general, governor of New Hampshire
JOHN LAWRENCE   heavyweight boxing champion (1882–1892)
LOUIS   architect, "father of the skyscraper"
MARK   journalist, historian
WILLIAM   historian, biographer of Jefferson

O'SULLIVAN
JOHN LOUIS   editor, politician, diplomat
TIMOTHY   photographer of the Far West
VINCENT   poet, playwright   ◆

ONE BIT OF A
RABBIT IS WORTH
TWO OF A CAT.
*Traditional Irish
Proverb*

Big Macs and
Big O's

The "original" Irish—those who were there before the English invasion of the twelfth century—are often referred to as the Macs and the O's. Names like MacDermot and O'Sullivan seem somehow more authentic than others. But what do those indubitably Irish prefixes actually mean? How many Irish Americans know the significance of these ethnic identity tags?

Both are references to ancestry. *Mac* is the Gaelic word for "son." It is sometimes written *Mc*, but this is simply a contraction. The widely held notion that *Mac* is Irish and *Mc* is Scottish is erroneous: the two versions are found in both Gaelic national traditions.

O is really a word all by itself, signifying "grandson." The apostrophe that now usually appears after it is simply the result of a misunderstanding by English-speaking clerks in Elizabethan times, who took it to be a form of the word "of," as in "light o' day."

In ancient Ireland, there were no fixed surnames. A man was known as, for example, "Cormac Mac Art" (Cormac son of Art), while his son might be called "Owen Mac Cormac." Sometimes, when a grandfather was a particularly notable figure, his name would be used, with the *O* prefix. By the twelfth century, an increasing population had led to the adoption (as elsewhere in Europe) of permanent family names. Under this system, all descendants of some distinguished ancestor took his name as their surname. Some clans put *Mac* in front of the name, and others *O*, but neither word would henceforth have a literal meaning; it would simply signify "descendant of."

That other distinctively Irish prefix *Fitz* derives from the Normans, who first brought English rule to Ireland. Although many of them soon became more Irish than the Irish themselves, they preserved a relic of their origin in this prefix, which derives from the French word *fils*, meaning "son of." Thus, Fitz Gerald signifies "son of Gerald," Fitz Maurice, "son of Maurice"; as with the *Mac*s and the *O*'s, what was originally a reference to one's literal father evolved into a permanent surname that simply signified a descendant of some medieval Gerald or Maurice.

One Irish family tried to have it both ways. The Fitzpatricks are actually of Gaelic ancestry. Their original clan name was Mac Giolla Padraig—descendant of the Devotee of St. Patrick. During the Middle Ages, they adopted the Norman form, Fitz Patrick.

Over the centuries, many Irish families dropped these patronymic prefixes, either for convenience, or under English influence. Hence the Carties (who are really Mac Carthy) and the Sullivans and Donoghues who have lost their "O's." And when was the last time you met an O'Murphy? ◆

> *Give an Irishman lager for a month, and he's a dead man. An Irishman is lined with copper, and the beer corrodes it. But whiskey polishes the copper and is the saving of him.*
>
> Mark Twain, *Life on the Mississippi* (1883)

171

My Cousin, the Earl

During the eight hundred years since the English invasion of Ireland, millions of Irishmen have fought, emigrated, or simply endured. A few, however, have made themselves agreeable enough to the Crown to earn the royal grace and favor. The highest reward for such cooperation was a peerage, a title of nobility conferred by the king or queen. The following list includes the pre-invasion Gaelic clans that were thus rewarded. Their Irish-American kinsmen may be interested in looking them up on the next visit home.

O'NEIL   Earl of Tyrone and Baron Dungannon, and, in a more recent creation, Baron O'Neill of Antrim

O'DONNELL   Earl of Tyrconnell

MacDONNELL   Earl of Antrim

MAGUIRE   Baron of Enniskillen (Fermanagh)

MAGENNISS   Viscount of Iveagh (Down)

O'HARA   Baron of Tyrawly (Mayo)

O'DALY   Baron of Dunsandle (Galway)

O'MALONEY   Baron of Sunderlin (Westmeath)

O'CARROLL   Baron of Ely (Offaly)

KAVANAGH   Baron of Ballyane (Carlow)

MacGILLPATRICK   Baron of Gowran (Kilkenny), and later Earl of Upper Ossory (Leix)

O'DEMPSEY   Viscount of Clanmalier (Offaly)

O'BRIEN   Earl and Marquess of Thomond, Earl of Inchiquin (Limerick and Clare)

MacCARTHY   Earl of Clancarty, Viscounts of Muskerry and Mount Cashell (Cork and Kerry)

O'CALLAGHAN   Viscount Lismore (Waterford)

O'QUINN   Baron of Adare and Earl of Dunraven (Limerick)

O'GRADY   Viscounts of Guillamore (Clare) ◆

A MAN IS SHY IN ANOTHER MAN'S CORNER.
Traditional Irish Proverb

The Tale of
Your Coat

I rish Americans are "crest" crazy. Such, at least, is the opinion in Ireland, where a thriving industry in heraldic hardware caters primarily to tourists and the overseas market. A number of entrepreneurs based in the United States also advertise in Irish-American periodicals, offering everything from wall plaques to signet rings, each item emblazoned with the customer's "clan crest." No other ethnic group in this country seems to have such a passion for Old World insignia.

Leaving aside, for a moment, the reasons for this armorial enthusiasm, what (other than household knickknacks) are all these purchasers getting for their money? Are "clan crests" in fact "authentic emblems of your family's proud history"?

First of all, let's discard the word *crest*. That's a technical term in heraldry, referring specifically to an emblem placed above the shield in some instances. The proper name for the object of our concern is *coat of arms*, or, simply, *arms*. This is the basic shield, upon which are emblazoned various geometrical patterns, animals, and so forth. Therefore, one should be looking for his coat of arms, not his "crest."

Unfortunately, most of the coats of arms dispensed commercially are derived from unreliable books published in the late nineteenth century and frequently reprinted since. The authors of these publications arbitrarily assigned or "borrowed" without regard to accuracy. Edward Mac Lysaght, former chief herald of Ireland, has pointed out the consequence: "Many Americans of Irish descent are in good faith using erroneous, often English, arms derived from the spurious source in question."

Mac Lysaght's own book, *Irish Families: Their Names, Arms and Origins* (first published in 1972), would appear to be the last word on the subject, but even he cannot seem to make up his mind about coats of arms. He includes arms for 243 families, based on records preserved in the Chief Herald's Office in Dublin. That would seem to be authoritative enough, but Mac Lysaght reminds his readers that by almost universal principle, arms are granted to *particular* families, not to everyone who may happen to bear the same name. Having said that, he talks about a tradition in Ireland that runs contrary to this rule and permits, say, all Maguires to use a coat of arms assigned to a person of that name. Then, just when the matter seems settled, he warns against the impropriety of a family from one area using the arms of a family of the same name from another area. He ends by suggesting that the best way to feel secure in the use of a coat of arms is for the Heraldic Office formally to certify your right to use it (for a fee, of course). No wonder people just go on buying coat-of-arms paperweights at airport gift shops.

All of which leads back to the issue of motivation: what reason can Irish Americans have for wanting a coat of arms? Amateur psychologists suggest it is yet another manifestation of the outsider's desire to belong. The heir of the once-despised Paddy and Bridget wants to take on the trappings of the "quality," from lace curtains to heraldic insignia. By displaying a coat of arms, according to this theory, the Irish American creates for himself, at one stroke, roots, pedigree, and status.

But whether this "crest" craze results from a nagging sense of inferiority or from a mere silly snobbery, it's likely that most of these heraldic shields have no real relevance to the ancestry of the people who flaunt them. And even if they do, they are relics of an outmoded social order, reflecting the decrees of a monarchy that arbitrarily assumed a right to confer or withhold distinction in Ireland. Americans of Irish origin have more important and more impressive aspects of their heritage that they can proudly display to the world. ◆

MOST COMMON SURNAMES IN IRELAND, BY COUNTY

CONNAUGHT

Galway	Kelly
Leitrim	Kelly
Mayo	Walsh
Roscommon	Kelly
Sligo	Brennan

LEINSTER

Carlow	Murphy
Dublin	Byrne
Kildare	Kelly
Kilkenny	Brennan
Leix	Dunne
Longford	Reilly
Louth	Byrne
Meath	Reilly
Offaly	Kelly
Westmeath	Lynch
Wexford	Murphy
Wicklow	Byrne

MUNSTER

Clare	MacMahon
Cork	Sullivan
Kerry	Sullivan
Limerick	Ryan
Tipperary	Ryan
Waterford	Power

ULSTER

Antrim	Smith
Armagh	Murphy
Cavan	Reilly
Derry	Doherty
Donegal	Gallagher
Down	Thompson
Fermanagh	Maguire
Monaghan	Duffy
Tyrone	Quinn

Lend Me Your Name

*Y*ou don't have to be Irish to have an Irish name—at least, not as far as first names are concerned. Americans of all origins have in recent years been appropriating distinctively Irish given names with a blithe disregard for "roots." Time was when children received the names of parents, grandparents, or other family members in grim unimaginative succession, generation after generation. Some (including, it appears, most Irish Americans) still adhere to this practice. But more and more mothers and fathers have become eclectic, looking for names that are "different" or simply "nice" without regard to family tradition. Snowball fashion, certain names gain steadily increasing public favor until they reach the national "top ten" list of most frequently bestowed names. It helps, of course, if some idol of the crowd, with high media visibility, happens to have a distinctive given name; the movie stars of the thirties probably began the phenomenon of intruding "outside" choices into traditional family nomenclature. Of course, we are not talking here about situations in which a mother of Irish ancestry and a father of some other stock each contribute something to their child's label in life. Such names as Sean Panetta or Brendan Suwolski often as not reveal an Irish woman's determination to have her side of the family duly noted. This type of ethnic blend is becoming more common nowadays.

No, the sort of incongruity we have in mind is the choice of an Irish given name for their child by parents who have no links at all to Ireland. Undoubtedly, the prime example of this sort of thing is "Kevin." For ten or twelve centuries this perfectly respectable but not very exciting name of an early medieval monk went along without attracting particular attention or heavy use. Then, suddenly, the scholarly saint's name was in, and every Tom, Dick, and Harry in the United States (or so it seemed) had become a Kevin, a phenomenon that transcends race, religion, and national origin, and seems without rational explanation.

And why are there so many Brians about? Certainly Brian Boru was a notable enough figure to justify the whole O'Brian (or O'Brien) clan calling themselves after him. But he was an Irish king, so how to explain all the little Brian Rabinowitzes and Brian Tannenbaums—not to mention the Gundersens, Espinosas, and Hsus?

Sean appears to be gaining favor and Rory—once in vogue—losing out. The rise and fall of show-business personalities seems to be the main factor here.

The numerous Barrys and Terrys, both male and female, in our present-day population may not all owe their given names to strictly Irish inspiration, but these designations indubitably lend a certain Hibernian jauntiness to otherwise drab surnames.

Hovering on the fringe of popularity are Nial (or Neal) and Owen. They are held back, it would seem, by consumer ambivalence over the images they evoke. Nial to some Americans suggests a touch of instability, while Owen, on the other hand, has a slightly stodgy aura.

Pierce (or Pearse or Piers) could have been a strong contender for the Irish "in" list, but its fate is probably too closely linked with a certain television star. His considerable charm and high visibility offered the ingredients of a nomenclature fad, but the unfortunate career eclipse that followed may have doomed the chances of this particular Irish name to make it into the big time.

Dennis (or Denis) has a certain appeal among non–Irish Americans (and it is, after all, originally French), but it has been around for a long time, in terms of celebrity visibility, without ever becoming a major choice. One suspects that (Dennis Morgan and Dennis Day notwithstanding) it strikes potential users as a trifle dull.

Seamus (Shamus), except as a nickname for a detective—perhaps now obsolete—is clearly *too* Irish to have any future on the general market. Indeed, is *anybody* actually christened Seamus anymore?

What about those classic Irish labels Pat and Mike? Patrick, to judge by its limited use outside Irish-American circles, is just too closely identified with snakes, shamrocks, raucous parades, and other stereotypes in the American mind to stand on its own. Even the Italian-surnamed Pats and Patsys usually turn out to be Pasquales.

Michael, however, is the great American success story in the name game. During the 1980s it soared to the top as the most popular name for male children. Michael, admittedly, is not an exclusively Irish name. Hebrew in origin, it has had a great revival in popularity among Jewish American families, and virtually every other ethnic group in the country has a variation of this name in its traditional reservoir of male designations. The real reason for the Michael revival, however, is probably the emergence of screen personalities such as Michael Jackson and Michael J. Fox, who made it possible for parents to give their sons a name that was both current and culture-based.

Nevertheless, the ghost of the Irish "Mike" or "Mickey" who was for so long the only Michael on the American scene hovers behind all these trendy new bearers of the name.

Irish names among American girls and women are less frequent than among males, but where they have caught on they, too, seem to have become "de-ethnicized." The "eens," for instance, have ceased to be diminutives of Irish names and become American names in their own right. Maureen and Eileen, in particular, are just as likely to be borne by women of Jewish or Italian ancestry as Irish. Cathleen (Kathleen) has some appeal to a general audience, though Noreen is almost exclusively used by Irish families.

Sheila is the "Kevin" of women's names, having an inexplicable appeal to families of virtually every origin. It has been around for a while, though, and while Kevin is clearly a phenomenon of the eighties, Sheila may be fading. Without some entertainment personality to give it a boost, it may recede into an exclusively Irish setting.

Deirdre has gained ground in recent years, for reasons hard to pin down. At first found almost entirely among those with at least an Irish grandparent or two, it now turns up in all segments of the population in all parts of the country. Often, however, it is altered to Deidre, or some other variation that omits the hard-to-say first *r*.

Among those who favor the exotic, Shevaun seems to be catching on, though not in its proper form, Siobhan. Another oddity is the use of Shaun (or Shawn), the phonetic rendering of Sean, as a girl's name.

Like its male equivalent, Patrick ("Paddy"), the name Bridget ("Bridie") is probably too deeply embedded in ethnic stereotypes to ever have a general American appeal. By contrast the name Kelly, while not an Irish given name, is certainly an Irish surname and has had a tremendous vogue in recent years. Many parents like its "pleasant, feminine sound"—a view that would doubtless surprise the warriors of the ancient O'Kelly clan.

Finally, there are a number of popular American given names derived from Irish place names. Kerry has attracted a following, although it may be derived from the name Ciara rather than the county, Ciarrigh (a distinction doubtless lost upon most Americans).

As far as other Irish counties are concerned, Galway is occasionally found as a male given name, though one must assume that Clare usually derives from other sources. The real puzzle, though, is Tyrone. Is its popularity as a given name in the United States entirely the result of Tyrone Power's fame? And if so, why is Tyrone so popular among blacks in particular? What, indeed, is in a name? ◆

Irish Americans are no more Irish than black Americans are Africans.

Bob Geldof, musician, quoted in *Irish Echo* (1987)

IRISH GIVEN NAMES, WITH THEIR MEANINGS AND ENGLISH EQUIVALENTS—NAMES OF MEN

AILBHE ("gentle one") Alby, Albert

AILIN ("of gentle birth") Allen, Alan

AMHLAOIBH (Norse, "ancestral relic") Olaf, Humphrey

AODH ("fire") Hugh, Egan

AONGHUS ("the chosen one") Angus, Niece

ART ("stone" or "bear") Arthur

BRIAN Bryan, Bernard

BUADHACH ("conqueror") Victor

CAOIMHIN ("sweet offspring") Kevin

CATHAL ("strong in battle") Cahal, Charles

CIAN ("ancient") Kean, Cain

COLM ("dove") Colum, Colman, Columba

CONALL ("tall and strong") Connell

CONCHUR ("high desire") Connor, Cornelius

CONN ("intelligence") Constantine

CORMAC ("charioteer") Charles

CRÍOSTÓIR (Greek, "Christ-bearing") Christopher

DEASÚN ("of south Munster") Desmond

DIARMAID ("a freeman") Dermot, Jeremiah

DÓNALL ("power of the deep") Donald, Daniel

DONNCHADH ("brown warrior") Donogh, Denis, Duncan

ÉAMONN (Anglo-Saxon, "blessed protection") Edmund

ÉANNA Enda

EOIN (Hebrew, "gift of God") John

EOGHAN ("well-born") Owen, Eugene

FEARGHAL ("bravest of the brave") Fergal, Virgil

FEARGHUS ("the choicest one") Fergus, Ferdinand

FIONN ("bright," an attribute of the sun god) Finn

FLANN ("bloodred") Florence

GIOLLA CHRÍOST ("servant of Christ") Christopher

LIAM (Germanic, "strong protector") William

LORCÁN (diminutive of Lorc, "fierce") Laurence

MAGHNUS (Norse, from Latin, "great") Manus

NIALL ("champion") Neil

OISÍN ("the little deer") Ossian

OSCAR (Norse, "spear of God") Oscar

PADRAIG (Latin, "noble") Patrick

PEADAR (Greek, "rock") Peter

PIARAS (Norman form of Peter) Piers, Pierce, Pearse

RUAIRÍ (Norse, "famous ruler") Rory, Roger, Roderick

SÉAMUS (Spanish Jaime, from Hebrew, "supplanter") James

SEÁN (Norman French, from Hebrew, "gift of God") John

TADHG ("poet") Teague, Timothy, Thady

TRAOLACH ("incarnation of the thunder") Tarlach, Turlogh, Terence

IRISH GIVEN NAMES, WITH THEIR MEANINGS AND ENGLISH EQUIVALENTS—NAMES OF WOMEN

ÁINE ("beauty," an attribute of the moon) Anne

AISLING ("an epiphany," "a manifestation of the divine") Esther

AOIBHEANN ("lovely shape") Eavan

BLÁTHNAID ("little flower") Florence

BRIGHID ("strength") Brigid, Bridie

CAITRÍN, CAIT, CAITILÍN (Greek, "pure") Katherine, Kate, Kathleen, Catriona

CIARA ("the dark one") Keary

DAMHNAIT ("little poet") Devnet, Dymphna

EIBHLÍN (Greek, "sunlight") Eileen, Evelyn, Helen

EILÍS (Hebrew, "word of God") Elizabeth

EITHNE ("kernel") Ethna, Edna

FIONNUALA ("bright shoulder," an attribute of the moon) Finola, Nuala

GOBNAIT ("small mouth") Abigail, Deborah

GORMFHLAITH ("the stranger lady") Barbara

GRAINNE ("perfect," "virginal," attributes of the moon) Grania, Grace, Gertrude

ÍDE ("thirst") Ida, Ita

MÁIRÉAD (Greek, "a pearl") Margaret, Marjorie

MUIRE, MÁIRE (Hebrew "of the sea," "bitterness") Mary, Maria, Miriam, Maura, Moya, May

NÓRA (Latin, "honourable") Norah, Honor

ÓRFHLAITH ("the golden lady") Orla

PROINNSEAS (Latin, "French," "frank") Frances, Fanny

SADHBH ("goodness") Sive, Sophia

SÍLE (Latin, "blind") Sheila, Cecily, Julia

SIOBHÁN, SIÚN (feminine of Sean) Joan, Johanna, Jeanne, Hannah

SORCHA ("bright") Sarah

ÚNA ("the white one," attribute of the moon) Agnes, Winifred, Freda, Inéz

AMAZE YOUR FRIENDS! (BY PRONOUNCING IRISH NAMES AND WORDS CORRECTLY)

Adomnán [a-dhov-nān]
Áed [aidh; ēdh; ē]
Airgialla [ar-yīala]
aitire [a-di-re]

Báetán [bai-dān; bē-dān]
bóruma [bō-ru-wa; bō-rū]
Brigit [bro-yid; brīd]

Cathal [ka-thal; ka-hal]
Cenél Conaill [Ke-nēl go-nil]
Cenél nEógain [ke-nēl nō-ghin]
Cerball [ker-val; ka-rūl]
Ciarán mac int saír [kīa-rān mak in tīr]
Ciarraige [kā-ra-ye; kīa-ri]
Cóemgen [koiv-yen; kī-vīn]
cóiced, cúigeadh [kō-gedth; kūi-ge]
Coirpre, Cairpre [kor-bre; kar-i-bre]
comarba [kō-war-ba]
Conchobar [kon-cho-var; kon-a-chūr; kro-chūr]
Corcu Baiscind [kor-ku vash-kin]
Corcu Duibne [kor-ku dhuv-ne; kor-ka ghī-ni]

Dál Cais [dāl gash]
Dál Fiatach [dāl vīa-tach]
Dál Riata [dāl rīa-da]
derbfhine [der-vi-ne]
Diarmait [dīar-mid]
dindshenchas [din-hen-chas; din-hyan-a-chas]
Domnall [dov-nal; dō-anl]

Eochaid [ech-idh; o-chī]
Emain [e-vin; au-in]
Eógancht [ō-gha-nacht; ō-nacht]
Étain [ē-dīn]

Feidlimid mac Crimthainn [fedh-li-midh mak kriv-thin; fēi-li-mī mak ri-fin]
frithfholaid [frith-ol-idh]

geilfhine [gel-i-ne]

Iarmumu [īar-wu-wu]

Labraid Loingsech [lav-ridh long-shech; lau-ri]
Laidcenn [ladh-gen]
Laigin [la-yin; lain]

Lebor Gabála [le-vor ga-vā-la; laur ga-wā-la]
Lóeguire, Láegaire [loi-ghu-re; lē-ghi-re; lī-re]
Lugaid [lu-ghidh; lū-ī]

Máedóc [mai-dhōg; mē-ōg]
Máel Sechnaill [mail shech-nil; mēl hyach-nil]
Mathgamain mac Cennétig [math-gha-win mak ke-ne-diy; ma-hūn]
Medb [medhv; mēv]
Muirchertach [mur-cher-tach; mwir-hyar-tach]

nemed [nevedh]
Niall Noígiallach [nīal noi-yīal-ach]

Óengus [oin-ghus; ēn-īas]
ollam [ol-av]
Osraige [os-ra-ye; os-a-rī]

rí tuaithe [rī tūe-the]
rígdamnae [rīgh-dhav-ne; rī-ghau-na]
Ruaidrí [rūedh-rī; rū-ri]

Samain [sa-vin; sau-in]
senchaid [shen-chidh; shan-a-chi]
Sétnae [shēd-ne; shēa-na]
Síl nÁedo Sláine [shil nai-dho slā-ne]
Suibne [suv-ne; swī-ni]

Tadc mac Céin [tadhg mak kēn; taig]
Tairrdelbach [tar-dhel-vach; ter-yal-ach; trē-lach]
Temair [te-vir; tau-ir]
Tethbae [teth-ve; te-fa]
toísech, taoiseach [toi-shech; ti-shach]
Tuadmumu [tūadh-wu-wu; tūa-wūa]

Ua Cellaig [ua-kel-iy; ō kal-ī]
Ua Flaithbertaig [ūa flath-ver-tiy; ō fla-har-ta]
Ua Máelshechlainn [ūa mēl-hyach-lin]
Uí Briúin [ī vriūn]
Uí Failge [ī al-ye; ī fal-ye]
Uí Máil [ī wāl]
Uí Maine [i wa-ne]
Uí Néill [ī nēl]
Ulaid [ul-idh; ul-i]

Tracing Your Irish Ancestry: Where to Dig

*A*mericans searching for their Irish roots should first collect as much accurate information as possible about names and dates and places of birth of their Irish ancestors. With the results of this preliminary research in hand, they might then profitably visit the following institutions in Ireland:

Office of the Register General   Grand Canal Street, Dublin 2. Records of all births, marriages, and deaths from 1864 onward. Useful for filling in gaps on background of ancestors who emigrated within the last hundred years or so.

Register of Deeds   Henrietta Street, Dublin 1. Records of property transactions since 1708, listed under the name of the person who sold or let out the property, and under the name of the property (farm, etc.). Unfortunately for the descendants of tenant farmers, there is no index to the names of purchasers or lease holders, so that a search for those names is extremely time-consuming.

Genealogical Office   2 Kildare Street, Dublin 2. (Formerly the Office of the Chief Herald, located in Dublin Castle.) Abstracts of all deeds and wills to the year 1800; abstracts of marriage licenses, 1630–1859; funeral certificates (for members of the property-owning classes), 1588–1729.

Public Records Office   Four Courts, Dublin 7. Wills, convert rolls (documents relating to Catholics who became Protestants); marriage records (Church of Ireland); land ownership records; census returns.

National Library   Kildare Street, Dublin 2. Various documents relating to occupiers and lessors of property.

Public Record Office of Northern Ireland   Belfast, N.I. A major repository of documents relating to all nine counties of the old province of Ulster, and, more especially, the six counties of Northern Ireland. ◆

IN THE NEW YEAR, MAY YOUR RIGHT HAND ALWAYS BE STRETCHED OUT IN FRIENDSHIP AND NEVER IN WANT.
Traditional Irish Toast

Roots Research, Presidential Style

Between the highly publicized "homecomings" of John Kennedy in the 1960s and Ronald Reagan in the 1980s, another president of the United States paid a visit to his ancestral homeland. Though now almost forgotten, the brief sojourn of Richard Nixon, October 3–5, 1970, created a minor diplomatic crisis.

United States embassy officials scoured the Irish countryside for distant cousins to meet Mr. and Mrs. Nixon—the former Patricia Ryan—but faced two problems: an excess of Ryans and not a single Milhous.

The quest for Ryans and Milhouses took embassy officials to Kildare, Tipperary, Clare, and Mayo. They had some success in trying to trace Ryan relatives in Ballinrobe, County Mayo, where Mrs. Nixon's paternal grandfather was born and lived before emigrating to the United States. The abundance of Ryans in Tipperary and Clare, where other relatives were believed to live, created major difficulties in identification among claimants to the honor.

Still more vexing was the Milhous question. The ambassador, John Moore, and several of his staff, made a number of trips to Timahoe, a hamlet about twenty miles northwest of Dublin, in county Kildare, where the president's great-great-great-great-grandfather, Thomas Milhous, lived.

This ancestor of the president was supposed to have been born in Carrickfergus, County Amtrin, in 1699, and to have moved to Timahoe with his parents when a small boy. Thomas's father, John, who died in 1710, was reportedly buried in a Quaker graveyard at Timahoe that the president was scheduled to visit. Thomas emigrated to America with his wife and children in 1729, settling in Pennsylvania.

Mr. Nixon had traced his family tree long before entering the White House. Indeed, the successor to his famous dog Checkers was an Irish setter called Timahoe.

But satisfying the chief executive's desire to meet a long-lost cousin in Ireland proved too much for the embassy. "We've been unable to find a Milhous throughout all of Ireland" was their sad conclusion. The best they could do, they concluded, was to escort Mr. Nixon around his ancestral hometown. The hundred-or-so inhabitants of the tiny hamlet did

It was sinful that Ronald Reagan ever became president. Most of the time he was an actor reading his own lines, who didn't understand his own programs. . . . But let me give him his due. He would have made a hell of a king.

Thomas ("Tip") O'Neill, former Speaker of the House of Representatives, quoted in *Irish America* (1987)

their best to tidy up the neighborhood and its disused Quaker burial ground, last used about the turn of the century, when the Quaker community broke up.

Unfortunately, there were no individual grave markers; a large stone slab contained the names of all those interred. Efforts to excavate the foundations of the Quaker meetinghouse, to trace broken fragments of the slab, and to reconstruct names and dates got nowhere.

Yet, as the two dozen regular staff members were reinforced by more than a hundred people flown in from embassies all over Europe, the problems seemed to dissolve. At any rate, Mrs. Nixon met Ryans who were duly certified as being her cousins. And, while no Milhouses were forthcoming, the president was shown various markers and artifacts allegedly linked with his ancestors. Cynics at the time (and ex-officials since) have said that the entire affair was a sham, improvised to cover the absence of authentic people, places, or things.

Perhaps, given the Irish love of a good story as opposed to a hard fact, and the American commitment to "can do," at any cost, such a result was inevitable. ◆

A contingent of the Ancient Order of Hibernians, including the uniformed Ladies' Auxiliary, keep the Irish roots strong.

Neighborhoods

ENGLEWOOD (CHICAGO): THE IRISH MOVE IN

uring the 1880s, Chicago's Irish Catholics began leaving the congested inner-city neighborhoods where they had first settled to make their homes in outlying areas. In Holy Family and Annunciation parishes they were being displaced by new immigrants, Italians and Jews on the West Side, and Poles on the Northwest Side. In St. John's on the Near South Side, Father Woldron "watched in sorrow as hundreds and hundreds of his beloved poor families surrendered their humble homes and moved in affluence to help build up and be the first families in many South Side parishes."

St. Bernard's was one of these parishes formed by upwardly mobile Irish who moved into fashionable residential districts. In July 1887, Archbishop Feehan assigned the Reverend B. P. Murray to establish a parish in Englewood, a community located eight miles south of the downtown business district. Inhabited by the descendants of New England Yankees, Englewood was "100 percent Protestant territory."

Father Murray did not attempt a backdoor entry. Protestants were horrified to learn that he had purchased a choice piece of land on Stewart Avenue, the finest thoroughfare in the area. A group of them offered to repurchase the church property "at a goodly advance in price," but the priest refused to sell. Householders talked grimly about the imminence of "an Irish invasion." With the establishment of a Catholic parish and the subsequent influx of the clannish Celts, Irish political control of the district would be sure to follow. All of the corruption, crime, and vice of the big city would pour into Englewood.

Even if these worst fears did not materialize, the Irish invasion did, and within a few years, more than six hundred families resided in St. Bernard's parish. The Irish of Englewood, who at first worshiped in temporary quarters, were determined to have a magnificent church that would compare favorably with those of their inhospitable Protestant

Out of these narrow lanes, blind courts, dirty streets, damp cellars, and suffocating garrets will come forth some of the noblest sons of our country, whom she will delight to own and honor.

Orestes Brownson,
Quarterly Review
(1843)

neighbors. Father Murray spared no expense in the construction of a grand marble edifice that would be a fitting symbol of the Irish presence. To emphasize his point, he scheduled the cornerstone-laying for the same day—September 12, 1896—and the same hour as an identical ceremony planned for a nearby Presbyterian church.

On the great day, more than 5,000 Catholics, from parishes all over the South Side, turned out to march through Englewood. Also in the parade were Irish-American police units and militia organizations like the Seventh Regiment of the Illinois National Guard and the Clan-na-Gael Guards. The Protestants, completely upstaged, carried on with their own rather glum celebrations, down the road. The good old days in Englewood were over: the Irish had, quite clearly, come to stay.

THE "IRISH CHANNEL" (NEW ORLEANS): IN THE AMERICAN QUARTER

*A*lthough travel books and popular surveys often refer to an "Irish Channel" in nineteenth-century New Orleans as though the city's Irish were segregated in some sort of ghetto, official records and newspapers contradict the image. But if the "Channel," in this sense, was something of a myth, the Irish of New Orleans were certainly a visible and vital part of the urban scene.

As early as the 1830s, three separate Irish colonies were located in the so-called American Quarter, which lay to the north of Canal Street, beyond the French Quarter. One settlement clustered around the site where the City Hall would later rise, on St. Charles Avenue. A second colony was closer to the river, around the intersection of Tchoupitoulas and Canal streets. The third straddled the New Basin Canal, and there lived the men who had dug this "navigational ditch." Evidently the term "Irish Channel" was first applied to the canal, and then, carelessly, to the Irish neighborhoods in general.

By the 1850s, the American Quarter—now known as the Second Municipality—had acquired an "Irish" church (called, of course, St. Patrick's) on Camp Street, and an elite social group (what would later be called "lace curtain") that dominated the Irish community. Numerous charitable and patriotic organizations had sprung up, along with gaudily uniformed Irish militia companies.

The 1850 census shows a strong Irish presence in each ward of the Second Municipality. It was the Third Ward, however, that came the closest to being an "Irishtown." The sections bordering on Delord and

IT'S THE FIRST DROP THAT DESTROYED ME; THERE'S NO HARM AT ALL IN THE LAST.
Traditional Irish Proverb

Tivoli streets were characterized by local newspapers as "completely Irish." The *Picayune* invited its readers to "come down to Girod Street and the precincts thereunto adjacent and you hear on every side 'illigant Irish' in the mother toungue, and with as graceful a brogue as if you stood on the banks of the Shannon or at the Lakes of Killarney."

A characteristic of New Orleans that impeded the growth of ghettos was the way in which elite housing and tenements often shared the same neighborhood. On Julia Street, for instance, on the blocks between Camp and St. Charles, stood aristocratic townhouses, while the stretch of the same street that dipped down toward the river was lined with dingy boardinghouses that catered to Irish immigrants. A group of these run-down edifices, between Magazine and Tchoupitoulas streets, was known as "Connaught Yard." The life-style at this end of Julia Street is suggested by a police report of October 27, 1860: "John Kelly was dangerously wounded by being beaten on the head by bottles and thrown downstairs from the second floor in a house at Connaught Yard on Julia Street. . . . It appears that Kelly got into some noisy altercation with a woman . . . and that she throttled and beat him over the head with a couple of whisky bottles, and then pitched him downstairs."

The Irish may not have monopolized the neighborhood, but, clearly, they could make their presence felt.

WOODSIDE (NEW YORK): BOTH SIDES OF THE TRACK

*J*ust as nineteenth-century settlers had followed the railroad line westward across the great plains, the 1920s Irish followed the elevated line eastward into Queens. In the decades following World War I, thousands of families abandoned Hell's Kitchen and other old Manhattan neighborhoods for the urban wide-open spaces across the East River. While they were to be found all the way out to the terminus of the El at Flushing, the Irish made Woodside particularly their own.

Although there were the inevitable morbid jokes about "life beyond the graves," burial grounds did provide Woodside with more recognizable boundaries than many other Queens districts could claim. The neighborhood constituted a ragged triangle bounded on the south by Mt. Zion Cemetery and on the west by New Calvary Cemetery. The right-of-way of the old New York Connecting Railroad, angling up toward Astoria, formed its eastern frontier. The vital main artery ran high above Roosevelt Avenue, on the elevated tracks of the Flushing IRT.

The semidetached houses and walkup apartment buildings that proliferated during the twenties and thirties stretched away on both sides of Roosevelt Avenue, and it was a matter of debate whether living farther away from the clatter of the trains outweighed the inconvenience of a longer walk to and from the El. Almost everyone in the neighborhood worked in Manhattan ("the city," they called it, as though Woodside were suburbia), and the big stores were there, too. For more modest shopping, a long line of stores stretched along Roosevelt Avenue, beneath the shadow of the elevated tracks. Here was one of the few places in New York where you could find an Irish (rather than German) delicatessen, or an Irish (rather than Italian) barbershop. Later on, there were Irish record stores and gift shops, bookstores and newspaper vendors, and even Irish travel agencies. Companies with names like Shamrock or Liffey announced their willingness to paint your house and move your furniture. Saloons, inevitably, multiplied rapidly, and dance halls were almost as numerous on both sides of the tracks.

For more family-oriented recreation, the El was also vital. Woodside had no public parks—aside from a few concrete-with-wooden-bench "sitting areas" near certain stations. But off to the east, near the end of the line, lay the open land that blossomed into the World's Fair grounds in 1939 (and even more spectacularly in 1964). Shea Stadium, the Flushing Marina, and other sources of innocent merriment also sprang up in later years, all readily accessible by the El. St. Sebastian's Church, with its attendant school, convent, and community facilities, soon rose just to the north of the tracks, providing a solid nucleus for the Irish Catholic community.

Some sixty years after its emergence, Woodside survives as one of New York's few remaining Irish enclaves. The older generation has died off but, instead of moving away, their children and grandchildren have stayed on because of the neighborhood's low rents and easy access to Manhattan. There has been some penetration by other ethnic groups, but this has been counterbalanced by the 1980s influx of new, young immigrants who find here a "home away from home." As the train continues its endless clatter overhead, Woodside seems as Irish as ever.

There wasn't a girl in New York who didn't want to marry Ted and go back to Ireland with him. We met on a boat ride, and he sang songs out of tune and he didn't mind, and he read his poems. Can you imagine an American doing that?

An American wife living in Ireland, quoted in the *Irish Times* (1985)

"SOUTHIE" (BOSTON): THE SAME OLD STORY

The Boston Irish never quite caught the knack of "upward social mobility." With a few—occasionally spectacular—exceptions, they have remained pretty much what they were, and where they were, a century ago. Sociologists have offered reasons for this, ranging from Yankee hostility to the "civil service mentality," but whatever the cause, things in South Boston, their residential stronghold, tend to remain the same. "Southie," as the locals call it, is still a working-class community, "blue collar and proud of it." A recent visitor described the old Irish neighborhood as a "run-down district, badly in need of renovation."

But if "Southie" looks much the same as ever, there are new voices and new faces in the bars and shops along Dorchester Avenue and the neighborhood's other principal thoroughfares. In the establishments labeled "Shannon," "Emerald," "Blarney," one hears accents fresh from the old country rising pleasantly above the flattened vowels of New England. On the sidewalks one encounters young men and women whose complexions, hairstyles, clothing, and general air of expectancy (or is it apprehension?) do not quite blend in with the crowd. They look more "Irish" than the Irish Americans around them. These are the new immigrants—most of them undocumented—who have flooded into South Boston (and nearby communities, such as Cambridge, Charlestown, and Allston) during the past few years.

No one knows for sure how many of these new Irish have settled in Boston, although most estimates suggest about 25,000. That's only a third of the number of "illegals" rumored to be living in the New York area, but in a much smaller city, the number bulks proportionally larger. The immigrants seem to prefer this area to New York. Southie, they say, is more comfortable and convivial, its residents less "uptight," readier with sympathy and support. Both the municipal authorities (many of whom are of Irish origin) and the local Irish consular officials seem more willing to protect them against the perils of deportation. Jobs are plentiful, especially in the construction industry, with cooperative unions "arranging" the necessary papers. Women usually find jobs as barmaids, domestics, or "mother's helpers," though some have secured secretarial positions. Although women earn, generally, only about a third of what their male contemporaries make, immigrants of both sexes have usually been "networked" into jobs a few days after their arrival on tourist visas.

ONE PERSON WITH A PLAN HELPS AS MUCH AS TWO PEOPLE CAN.
Traditional Irish Proverb

Most of those who are trying to blend into the scenery in Southie have fled the bleak economy of Ireland with its stagnant industries and massive unemployment. But finding a job in America does not always bring joy. Often well educated, the new immigrants might perform menial tasks because their undocumented status demands a low profile. Furthermore, they are at the mercy of employers, who can cut their wages or overwork them, knowing that they cannot leave or complain.

South Boston is full of new voices and new faces, then. But they are the voices and faces of men and women who are often exhausted by long hours of labor and tormented by emotional stress. Many of these new immigrants live in crowded, marginal housing, confined to shadowy, peripheral existence in American society. Confined to an Irish ghetto not by discrimination but by the need to "hide out" there, they sometimes succumb to destructive opportunities of the saloon culture. In Southie, it may well turn out to be the same old story, after all. ◆

The comic strip, like other manifestations of twentieth-century American culture, tells as much—or more—about the prevailing attitudes and assumptions of contemporary society as many a learned treatise. Unlike the cartoon, which is our isolated image, the comic strip conveys a narrative through a series of pictures, with a continuing cast of characters from one sequence to the next and the inclusion of dialogue and/or text within the pictures. Comic strips both reflected and catered to the way mainstream America thought about various groups—economic, social, and ethnic. In the case of the Irish, they demonstrate an evolving perception during the course of the last hundred years, from rejection to acceptance (or, perhaps, indifference).

During the late nineteenth century the Irish were still outsiders. Despite all the gains they had made since the era of the Know-Nothings and the famine immigration, most Americans, particularly those living in Midwestern or Southern small towns, regarded them as grotesque aliens. Uncouth slum dwellers, speaking in a barbarous brogue, and addicted to activities that ranged from criminal to the merely outlandish, the Irish were fair game for scorn and derision. Prevailing racial theories held that the "Celt" was a breed inferior to the "Anglo-Saxon," with a distorted simian physique that corresponded to his mental and moral shortcomings.

Appropriately enough, the first real comic strip, dating from 1895, was set in the inherently bizarre milieu of an Irish-American slum. The setting of R. F. Outcault's drawings in the *New York World* was "Hogan's Alley." Varying locales appeared in subsequent strips, always preserving the Irish context: Reilly's Pond, Casey's Alley, Shantytown, etc. In these, and the strips he drew after moving to Hearst's *New York Journal*, the artist peopled this Hibernian environment with swarms of monkeylike urchins and hags bawling from tenement windows, with their "wit" displayed through wildly distorted spelling and grammar. One figure in these scenes soon caught the public imagination: a large-headed, jug-eared boy of five or six, dressed in a smudged yellow nightshirt; although nameless, he came to be known as the Yellow Kid.

The "better sort" of New Yorker considered the squalid doings of the

THE RACING SEASON OPENS IN HOGAN'S ALLEY.

Hogan's Alley characters to be a public disgrace, and borrowed the name of the Yellow Kid to denounce Hearst for "yellow journalism." Thus the grotesque Irish-American comic strip figure came to symbolize newspaper sensationalism. For ordinary readers, he possessed a perverse charm that generated statuettes, games, and a joke book. One spinoff publication, *The Yellow Kid in MacFodden's Flats*, is generally considered to have been the first real "comic book."

In 1900, Fred Opper launched another "Irish" comic strip in the Hearst papers. "The Doings of Happy Hooligan" chronicled the misadventures of a red-nosed tramp, whose shabby wardrobe was topped off by a tin can for a hat. An eternally optimistic buffoon, Happy was forever acting on impulse and running afoul of the law as a consequence. Like the denizens of Hogan's Alley, he is more laughable than malicious, but his life-style is clearly that of a social deviant. The name Hooligan, which had already passed into British slang as a synonym for ruffian, was no doubt selected with this implication in mind. (It was apparently from a family of Irish roughnecks in Victorian London, rather than from this amiable cartoon character, that the term "hooliganism," so beloved of Soviet polemicists, was derived.) Unlike the Yellow Kid, who disappeared shortly after the turn of the century, Happy Hooligan lingered on until 1932, and the strip gradually built up a cast of disreputable characters, including the hero's two brothers, also professional tramps.

By the time of the First World War, a more benign image of the Irish in America was emerging. Compared with the exotic beings from southern and eastern Europe who had followed them into the United States since the turn of the century, the Irish now appeared a familiar and even reassuring element of stability. The considerable social and economic advances many of them had made were acknowledged. If familiarity continued to breed contempt, the emotion was now expressed in a more amiable fashion. This changing relationship between the Irish and mainstream society is mirrored in a number of comic strips that appeared during the period.

Although George McManus began drawing "Bringing Up Father" for the Hearst papers in 1913, it did not become a regular, established feature until 1916. The strip's protagonists are Jiggs, an ex-stonemason (or bricklayer) and his wife, Maggie, a former washerwoman, who have struck it rich in the Irish Sweepstakes. They live in a grand mansion, filled with ornate furniture and even more ornate servants. Maggie, the

"The Yellow Kid," America's first successful comic strip (1896), combined political satire with a slice-of-life view of Irish tenement dwellers.

The War Scare in Hogan's Alley.

It is difficult to think of more incongruous elements than the jolly, reckless, good-natured, passionate, priest-ridden, whiskey-loving shiftless Paddy, and the cold, shrewd, frugal, correct, meeting-going Yankee.

Letter from a journalist (1859)

ultimate snob, wants to move in "exclusive" society, while Jiggs, far from being embarrassed by his humble origin, wants only to slip away to Dinty Moore's Saloon to join his old cronies for corned beef and cabbage and a game of pinochle. These two distinctly homely individuals have produced an incongruously beautiful and elegant daughter, Nora, who acts as umpire in the never-ending struggles of Jiggs to escape for a night out with the boys and Maggie to "civilize" him.

The artist, himself an Irish American, is a shrewd observer of types, and understands the conflict between "shanty" and "lace curtain" impulses. But his mockery of nouveau-riche pretensions and his mobilization of a multitude of zany characters give the strip a more universal appeal. Maggie and Jiggs may have been distinctively Irish to start with, but they gradually became universal types.

"Bringing Up Father" became tremendously popular. On the strip's twenty-fifth anniversary, McManus was honored at a congressional dinner in Washington. By the time of his death in 1954, his comic creation had been translated into many languages, published in book form, adapted as a stage play, and made the basis of a movie. Perhaps the ultimate tribute came during the Second World War, when Jiggs became the insignia of the Army Air Corps Eleventh Bomber Squadron.

Another strip of this transitional period was Frank Willard's "Moon Mullins," which made its debut in 1923. Moon (full name, Moonshine) Mullins was a derby-hatted, cigar-smoking urban type (an image associated at this time with Alfred E. Smith) who first appears as a prizefight manager. (Jack Dempsey is actually portrayed in the first installment.) Although he, his kid brother, Kayo—a definite Hogan's Alley type—and certain of their friends (such as the street-wise Katy Higgins) are clearly in the Irish tradition, they made a fairly rapid shift into the mainstream, and in the later stages of their long comic strip career Moon Mullins and company shed their distinctive ethnicity.

Perhaps the clearest example of the "acceptance" of Irish Americans by the end of the Second World War can be found in "Mickey Finn." The McNaught Syndicate introduced this strip by Lank Leonard in 1936. It started as a "seriocomic melodrama" with Michael Aloysius Finn, the hardworking son of a kindly widow gaining appointment to the police force after an act of heroism and setting out on his career as a cop. The atmosphere was distinctively Irish, with characters like Mickey's partner, Tom Collins, his girlfriend Kitty Kelly, Clancy the bartender, Sergeant Halligan, and Mr. Houlihan. Eventually, however, the purely comic element prevailed and the real star of the strip became Mickey's uncle, Philip Finn, a tavern boaster, blundering ladies' man, and promoter of schemes doomed to farcical failure. Phil Finn with his derby, his bumptious air, and his saloon-smart pomposity is very definitely in the tradition of the Irish buffoon, but most of his misadventures are the familiar stuff of mainstream comedy. Although the strip continued on into the 1970s, "Mickey Finn" is essentially an amusing depiction of Irish urban life in the 1930s. As such, it reflects a much more tolerant, accepting attitude toward the perceived foibles of the Hibernian in our midst.

Comic strips of the 1940s and thereafter reveal the final stage in the migration of the Irish American from outsider to insider. Even "Dan Dunn," which began as far back as 1933 (and continued for some twenty-five years) virtually ignored ethnicity. Although U.S. Secret Service agent Dunn is Irish-surnamed (he was launched as a rival to the also vaguely Irish "Dick Tracy"), his activities and environment are unrelated to this fact. The same is true of "Invisible Scarlett O'Neil" (1940)—whose name obviously owed more to contemporary visibility of Scarlett O'Hara than to Irish identity. And so it has remained, whether career girl ("Dixie Dugan," 1942) or jockey ("Rusty Riley," 1948), or fighting man ("Combat Kelly," 1968), characters with Irish names are just that and no more. The Irish were no longer distinctive enough to be mocked, patronized, or even told apart from everybody else.

During the first half of the century comic strips competed successfully with films as the principal shaper of American popular culture. Day by day, year by year, they subtly passed on the stereotypes of adults to children, who repeated the process. For the mass of the people they were a form of instruction as well as entertainment. In these little boxes we may trace the public perception of the Irish American as he moves from despised alien to still-distinctive, but accepted, neighbor—to unhyphenated American. For better or for worse, the Irishman has vanished from the comic strips. ◆

A NEW BROOM SWEEPS CLEAN, BUT THE OLD BRUSH KNOWS ALL THE CORNERS.
Traditional Irish Proverb

From "The Old Neighborhood" to "The Suburbs"

"I was always very conscious of being Irish," H. says. "A large part of my early life was spent in an overwhelmingly Irish neighborhood in the Bronx, around Fulton Avenue and Third Avenue. It was always said that the neighborhood was 99 and 44/100 percent pure Irish.

"From the time that I was eighteen until we got married, I palled around with guys from my wife's neighborhood and almost every one of them had Irish-born parents," he says. "Often the kids themselves were born there. I can remember that during the first years of World War Two in my wife's neighborhood, it was so strongly Irish that when the Germans bombed London, there were celebrations."

H. regrets the passing of Irish New York. "Of course," he adds, "some things are better, but some things are worse. I would much rather live in the New York of that earlier world than in the one today."

Why?

"The family then was a more closely knit unit," H. says. "You got your memories from your family, a sense of tradition. Which made society itself far more stable. There was respect for authority."

H. did not want to move from the Bronx. "We loved it," he recalls.

But after World War II, apartments large enough to accommodate his growing family were expensive and hard to find. So the family moved to Rockland County.

"When we came here," he says, "Rockland County was WASP." There was a residue of anti-Catholicism and anti-Irish sentiment. There were Masonic and other influences. Irish-American friends used to say that they were discriminated against; they were even verbally and openly insulted.

"Of course," H. adds, "the influx of Irish Americans was so strong in the fifties that now Pearl River is overwhelmingly Irish."

They now live on a quiet, tree-lined street. All the children have left home. The oldest is a cardiologist with a flourishing practice in Rhode Island. The youngest attends American University in Washington, D.C., where he studies politics.

"Their break with Ireland is almost total," H. says, "and I think our family is typical of Irish Americans in general." ◆

LET HIM COOL IN THE SKIN HE WARMED IN.
Traditional Irish Proverb

Between the dark, dismal saloons of the Five Points, where famine-era immigrants drank themselves into a stupor, and the cutely named night spots of the East Side, where yuppies now play at being Irish, there is a middle ground. Here we find the sort of neighborhood pubs described by Jim Lowney in the following essay (originally published in the New York Irish Echo, *November 1, 1980). It is a social center, designed as much for talking as for drinking, and it serves both to maintain ties with Ireland and to keep a distinctive Irish-American identity alive.*

❝*It's as natural for a Hibernian to tipple as for a pig to grunt.*❞
George Templeton Strong, *Diary* (1847)

That is probably the last traditional neighborhood Irish pub in the old Colonial town of Morristown, New Jersey, has a history dating to the American Revolution.

Although the Washington Bar, now known as Hennessey's, was established in the 1920s, it is housed in a building that was once the Washington Hotel. The hotel was operating when General George Washington encamped his troops nearby during the last battles of the Revolutionary War, according to Jim Hennessey, the current publican.

"Washington's men, about two-thirds of them Irish, spent two winters near here and Washington established his headquarters just a quarter of a mile away," noted Hennessey as he pointed out a picture of the general on a white charger.

Hennessey took over the place three years ago after more than twenty years as a teacher, juvenile probation officer, and youth shelter director.

"I had worked here part-time for the previous owner, Vincent Keyes. When he decided to retire, I bought the place," he said.

The career switch was mainly economic, he confided.

"I have four children to raise and educate. I'll be working the rest of my life, so I figured it might as well be here," said the affable Hennessey.

While there are other restaurants with an Irish identity in town, Hennessey says his place is the last of the old local gathering spots.

"We can still sit here and have the best discussions anywhere, including sports, religion, and politics," he related with a grin.

The pub is located at 140 Morris Street, which is just across from the town's railroad station and just a short walk from the Morristown Green. Irish and American flags prominently displayed in a window, a green awning, and a Shamrock sign bearing the owner's name draw the visitor to the meeting place.

Inside there are scores of interesting old photographs with an Irish, historic, or sporting theme. They range from a portrait of Robert Emmet, to turn-of-the-century scenes of the old Bayley School, to pictures of Johnny Lujack and 1940-era Notre Dame football teams. In one corner there's an autographed picture of Morris County sheriff's officer Joe Walsh, who is listed in the *Guinness Book of Records* as "The Fastest Revolver Shooter."

On a day during the recent baseball playoff games a Guinness blackboard listed the simple fare as "Mets and Sausage."

On the wall Hennessey has encased a number of mementos of his opening day, February 24, 1983. Included in good luck money are Irish notes left by two Irish-born friends, Sean Powers and Marty Flanagan.

The heavy crowds usually arrive at Hennessey's during the lunch period and in the evening, so there is no live nighttime entertainment. The Irish musical atmosphere is produced by a big jukebox, which has a healthy representation of Irish tunes, both old and new. Included are songs by such performers as the Clancy Brothers, Eileen Donaghy, Brendan Shine, Brian Anthony, Johnny McEvoy, and the McCartys.

For those who want to settle down for long conversations in the back of Hennessey's, they might consider a long bench that was made from pews that were once in the old Assumption Church in Morristown.

"They're more than one hundred years old," noted the owner.

Not far from the church pews is a stately old portrait of John T. Murphy, Hennessey's maternal grandfather. He was born in Morristown in 1850 and was the son of Patrick Murphy, who hailed from Tipperary, and Elizabeth Hanley Murphy, who was born in Sligo.

Recently Jim acquired a new item from Ireland for his pub. It was brought by Kathleen Ginty Hyland, who along with her sister, Mary Agnes, runs two Irish gift shops. She presented Hennessey with a large towel with a poetic verse saluting the "Man Behind the Bar."

As customers arrive and leave Hennessey's they give and receive personalized greetings. It seems Hennessey likes people, and Helen Hall, a waitress there five years, says they like him.

"He's a wonderful man, an all-around good person, and everyone loves him," she related.

He's concerned about his friends, too. As we were about to leave he showed off an Irish handmade St. Bridget Cross.

"It helps people get home safe," said the man behind the bar. ◆

Years ago, before what was called the regular organization, politicians would go to the corner saloon, and the saloonkeeper was the doctor, lawyer, banker—and that's where a candidate would go on Sunday to meet the people of the community. . . .

Old timers would borrow money, come in for advice. The bank was at 63rd and Halsted. People wouldn't go there on the average—they'd borrow money from the saloonkeeper. A fellow running for office would visit ten or twenty of these spots. It was his way of campaigning!

"A Chicago ward politician," quoted in *The New York Times* (1920)

Stylish
Stout

The traditional symbols of Ireland—shamrock, wolfhound, and so forth—have been joined in recent years by a large glass of dark liquid. Americans, including many Irish Americans (who should have a more skeptical view about clichés), are convinced that a pint of Guinness is quintessentially Irish. The advertising barrage of assurances that "Guinness is good for you" makes it sound healthy. The frequent citations of the *Guinness Book of World Records* lend it a kind of ultimate authority. Ordering Guinness in a New York Irish pub seems both patriotic and trendy.

How did this proletarian potion become the yuppies' beverage of choice? In order to consider this question, a few basic facts are in order. The first of these, which some may find a trifle embarrassing, is that the drink (though not the actual formula) originated in England. In London, at the beginning of the eighteenth century, drinking men favored a variety of exceptionally strong beers (including one with the Irish-sounding name of "Knockdown"). Such potent brews were described as "stout." The brew was originally produced by mixing beer and ale from separate casks, but by 1722 a technique of combining the flavor and quality of the separate components in a single dark brown brew had been developed. The technique involved employing a considerable proportion of highly dried brown malt in the mixture of malts used for brewing. This "stout" drink was often called porter because many of its consumers were porters or manual laborers. The two words became virtual synonyms for a very strong and very dark beer.

The brewing industry had grown very slowly in Ireland, through a combination of economic and cultural factors, which included the rural Irish preference for homemade whiskey. By the mid-eighteenth century, however, breweries had been opened in several cities, most notably in Dublin, and the English invention called stout had already made its appearance there. It was at this moment that Arthur Guinness made his appearance. His father had been a land agent in County Kildare for an archbishop of the Church of Ireland. When that worthy died, he left young Arthur £100 in his will. This legacy started Arthur on his career. Why he became a brewer we do not know, but by 1759 he had leased a disused brewery at James's Gate in Dublin and launched the business that bears his name today, at the same location.

According to tradition, Arthur Guinness acquired a secret formula as part of his legacy from the archbishop. It would be interesting indeed if we could establish that Guinness's stout had an ecclesiastical origin, but it is more likely that the particular brew is the result of Arthur's own experiments. In any case, by the time of his death in 1803 he had attained a commanding position among Dublin brewers, and was one of the leading merchants of the city.

Over the succeeding generations, his heirs continued to combine a sound business sense with a shrewd instinct for public relations. Their employees, generally speaking, remained loyal and dedicated, and the company flourished while other breweries fell by the wayside. Attention to quality was combined with skill in merchandising. Such touches as the label bearing the image of Brian Boru's harp reinforced the concept of Guinness as a national institution. Although members of the family were elevated to the British peerage, and the corporation developed British affiliates and business involvements outside of the brewing industry, it remained strongly identified with Ireland, even after independence. The bicentennial of the brewery was marked by the Irish government with postage stamps bearing the founder's portrait, thereby acknowledging him as a virtual national hero.

There is no doubt that the Guinness story is an Irish success story, and that the brewery has been, and continues to be, deeply involved in Irish life. Thus the Guinness consumer whom we encountered a bit earlier can demonstrate his Irishness in a manner that is authentic as well as fashionable. But is Guinness really good for you? And, more important, is it really good? The answers are: maybe. Cynics will say that it has become more of a status symbol or stock image among a certain class of Irish American than it is a drinking man's drink. Less verbal Irishmen (and there are some) will simply keep quiet and down their Irish whiskey. ◆

The American may drink from morning to night without injury to his country; the German may snore himself into insensibility in a deluge of lager beer, without doing dishonour to Fatherland; but the Irishman, more impulsive, more mercurial, more excitable, will publish his indiscretion on the highway, and will himself identify his nationality with his folly.

John F. Maguire, *The Irish in America* (1868)

Still
Life

*P*atriotic claims to the contrary, whiskey was not invented in Ireland. It seems that the art/science of distilling spirits was discovered on the shores of the Mediterranean in about the eleventh century. The anonymous discoverers were unimaginative enough to use the spirits primarily for curative purposes. However, as the technique was transmitted to the colder lands of the north, the warming qualities of spirits were employed to more immediate advantage.

We have no authentic account to document the first making of whiskey in Ireland. According to some writers, the Anglo-Norman invaders of 1169 found the Irish already drinking what was described in Latin as *aqua vitae* and in Gaelic as *usquebagh*—the water of life. It is probable that Irish monks returning from pilgrimages brought distilling knowledge from the southern countries and made spirits in their monasteries for medicinal reasons. If so, the secret did not stay locked away for very long. The drinking of what we now know as whiskey became common during the Middle Ages, and the *Annals of the Four Masters* report a chieftain dying in 1405 from a "surfeit of *aqua vitae*." He may have been the most prominent, but certainly not the first, overindulger of the era.

By the sixteenth century spirit drinking had become so widespread that the English administrators in Ireland were trying to curb it because of the social evils it produced. A statute of 1556 declares that *"aqua vitae, a drink nothing profitable to be daily drunken and used, is now universal throughout the realm of Ireland."* It was stipulated that spirits could not be made without a license from the chief governor of Ireland and that those who tried to evade this requirement would be punished with fines and imprisonment. The class-based nature of this rule is shown by the clause that waived the license for peers and property-owning gentlemen. The idea was that the better sort of people might manufacture spirits for their own use, while the lower orders needed to be denied free access to intoxicants.

English government was no more successful in curbing whiskey production among the Irish population than it was with the other laws passed to ensure "the greater civility of the Irish." During the later years of Queen Elizabeth's reign it was decreed that martial law was to be

A BLESSING DOES
NOT FILL THE
BELLY.
*Traditional Irish
Proverb*

applied to "idle persons ... aiders of rebels ... and makers of *aqua vitae*." Even the death penalty, however, failed to restrain the production and consumption of *usquebagh*, which continued to "set the Irishry a mading, and breed much mischiefs."

During the tumultuous 1600s, further efforts to restrain the Irish by prohibition, licensing, fees, and fines, all failed to alter habits or raise revenue. In the more tranquil eighteenth century, when Irish militancy seemed to give way to morose apathy, the English concern shifted from the maintenance of order to the ordering of trade. By this time, a number of fairly substantial distilleries had been established in Dublin, Cork, and other cities. The production of whiskey for domestic sale and export gradually became a respectable and significant business operation, supervised and taxed by revenue officials. Throughout Ireland, however, thousands of illicit private stills had emerged from the earlier generations of harassment and continued to serve the needs of the rural masses. Government's purpose now became the elimination of unlicensed, non-tax-paying stills, rather than the elimination of whiskey drinking. The rate of success was scarcely better than it had been in earlier, wilder times. The making of whiskey from grain or potatoes continued to be a flourishing activity among Irish countryfolk down to the era of the Famine. In the meantime, such captains of industry as James Murphy of the Midleton Distillery, James Power of John Power and Son, and most notably John Jameson, made Irish whiskey a force to be reckoned with on the international market.

The Irish who came to America after the Famine came from a whiskey-drinking environment and often brought their tradition with them. American disapproval never entirely tamed this proclivity, but the saloon culture of the Irish urban ghettos placed it under certain restraints. In the United States, Irish drinking became more orderly and more varied. Above all, the saloonkeeper controlled distribution, and the consumer lost all contact with production. In the meantime, the private still was disappearing from the Irish scene, the victim of social and economic changes that included temperance crusades by the Church and more effective interference by the revenue authorities.

In the twentieth century, Irish whiskey distilling has become almost entirely an organized and regulated business. Unfortunately for the Irish economy, it has not been a particularly well-managed business, with the result that many firms have shut down or merged for survival. The American market, which was quite substantial in the nineteenth century, has to a very large degree been lost to Scottish distilleries, who have been more successful in promotional activities, even if not in the arts of production. Despite all, though, there remain a goodly number of Irish Americans who, when they ask for whiskey, specify "Irish." In so doing, they are perhaps inspired less by taste than by a dim fantasy image of some remote ancestor sitting patiently by his still waiting for his *usquebagh* to emerge. ◆

●The secret motto of the St. Patrick's Day parade is: all glory and honor to cheap politicians! Paddies to the back of the line! And that is why a big shot with an important-sounding job and an Irish-sounding last name always leads the parade.●

Jim Dwyer, *Newsday* (1987)

Irish May Apply

Everyone has heard of the sign that used to be posted at various job sites in nineteenth-century America: NO IRISH NEED APPLY. That's all gone now. Aside from anything else, such notices would be illegal. But there is a kind of reverse situation evident to anyone who looks at Irish-American newspapers. The Classified section is full of ads offering jobs to Irish men and women, and of other items in which people identifying themselves as Irish offer their services. Clearly, for some Irish in America, what you are and what you do are still connected.

The ads aimed at men seek to recruit construction workers, carpenters, and bartenders. For the ladies, there is a choice between office work and domestic employment. Nannies are particularly in demand, whether they are called that or dressed up as "mother's helpers." Quite a few of these child tenders are also expected to do housework. Instead of "no Irish" the prospective nannies are all warned these days that smokers need not apply. No one seems to care whether or not the male employees smoke. About the only variation from this pattern of employment opportunities is an occasional notice for someone to work in an Irish import store or to help out in some Irish government office in this country.

There is nothing wrong with these jobs as such, but don't they seem rather familiar? They're the standard jobs performed by generations of Irish people in America. No one specifies in his ad that the employee must be Irish, yet, obviously, he would not advertise in an Irish-oriented paper unless he thought that the Irish were the appropriate people to recruit for these posts. Is there a lingering tendency to stereotype? Before answering, let's look at the "Positions Wanted" section of the Classifieds.

People listing themselves as Irish say that they are looking for work as construction hands, bartenders, housekeepers, and mother's helpers. A "mature Irish girl" offers to be a companion to an elderly lady. A mother who lives next to St. Patrick's Church offers to take care of schoolchildren after class hours. "Seamus," young and willing, is prepared to go anywhere and do anything. Except, perhaps, for Seamus, all of these people put themselves in the Irish mold, asking to do exactly what is expected of "the Irish." It seems as if the job givers and the job seekers need only to be lined up to make a perfect match. Another part

My toughness comes from my mother's side. It's the Irish in me.

Tom Brokaw, NBC news anchorman, in *People* magazine (1986)

of the Classified ads also suggests that some Irish Americans, at least, are fairly clannish. There are offers of apartments, furnished rooms, and shared quarters, in which "mature Irish gentlemen" are encouraged to take up lodging with Irish households, and Irish "working girls" look for more of the same to share the rent. The ads are almost all for "Irish" neighborhoods, and many of them specify the parish location. The words "quiet," "sober," and "working" appear regularly. It seems that those who have space to offer have very definite ideas about the kind of people they want in that space.

The Irish in America have come out of the occupational and residential ghetto, but, like other former ghetto dwellers, some of them have yet to adjust. ◆

A middle-class neighborhood in Bethlehem, Pennsylvania. By the end of the nineteenth century a number of the Irish who had settled in mill towns could afford to live in houses such as these.

What Flaherty
Was

The following essay, by Patrick Fenton, appeared on the Op-Ed page of The New York Times *on December 3, 1983.*

*I*n the late 1940s, when I was growing up in the tenements of Seventeenth Street in the Park Slope section of Brooklyn, the death of Joe Flaherty's father was always spoken about in whispers. It would be winter, and on the kitchen table there would be jelly jars filled with rye whiskey. I would hear my father talk about how they found the body of Joe Flaherty's father, who was a union president on the Red Hook docks, floating in the Gowanus Canal. When I was older and started to hitch rides on the back of fruit trucks to the public swimming pool down in Red Hook, I always thought about the story as the trucks went by the canal.

When Joe Flaherty died six weeks ago, the obituaries praised him as a writer. That he was, but his death also summoned in me memories of a special time and place in New York when immigrants worked the docks and factories and their children dreamed of ways to escape the neighborhood.

Joe Flaherty dropped out of high school when he was sixteen, and eventually joined Local 1266 of the Grain Handlers Association, his father's old union. He took the toughest job on the docks, humping bags of grain out of the holds of ships. He grew up just a few blocks from me, down near the Park Circle section of Brooklyn. My mother, who was born in Ireland, used to take long walks with his mother through Park Slope. If life wasn't full of turns and twists, this story would have ended there. As it turned out, we both became writers.

The odds of growing up in that section of Brooklyn then and becoming a writer were very slim. The Park Slope of that time had no resemblance to the Park Slope of today. Seventeenth Street was once the hub of one of the greatest Irish working-class neighborhoods in Brooklyn. It was filled with large immigrant families, some with as many as thirteen

A BLIND MAN CAN
SEE HIS MOUTH.
*Traditional Irish
Proverb*

kids. The fathers drove trolley cars for a living, worked behind the stick of Irish bars and labored in the factories of Industry City, a line of gray factory buildings that went on for miles on the Brooklyn waterfront.

If it weren't for a weekly newspaper, *The Park Slope News*, Joe Flaherty might have simply made his peace with the old neighborhood and settled down to a life of cold mornings on the docks or midnight shifts down in Quaker Maid, one of the factories of Industry City. The paper was unique in that it encouraged some of the talent buried in that lower-class Irish neighborhood. Although I too quit high school, I spent three years writing for *The Park Slope News* about bar fights and Saturday nights in the tenements of Seventeenth Street.

Joe Flaherty wrote for *The Park Slope News* before I came there, and eventually had a piece published in the *Village Voice*. *The News* was one of those great places that you hated to leave, but once you got published outside the paper it was time to go. After a few years, I managed to get published in *New York Magazine*, and like Flaherty I moved on.

I knew who Joe Flaherty was when I was growing up in Park Slope, but I didn't meet him until I was about thirty. He was living up in Greenwich Village at the time and he invited me to his apartment to talk. He showed me a scrapbook with all the stuff he had published. On the front of it was an old picture of him when he worked down on the docks. "If you really want to find out about this city," he told me, "go out in the streets and talk to some of the guys who cut meat for a living. Talk to a guy who makes a living behind the stick. Go talk to a guy who drives a cab. They'll tell you what's really wrong with this city. They know more about it than any politician."

A few years after that, I talked to someone about doing a radio show on some of the Irish writers who came from that working-class section of Park Slope. (Pete Hamill grew up in the same area.) I wondered what it would be like to get myself, Joe Flaherty, Pete Hamill, and even Jack Deacy (who came from Bay Ridge, but who also wrote for *The Park Slope News*) to talk about writers with talent being encouraged to write even though they have no formal education. Was that chance being offered to writers from the South Bronx or to writers from whatever neighborhood is left down in Red Hook? I didn't think so.

The radio people liked the idea and asked me to put it on paper. After reading the obituaries of Joe Flaherty, I was sorry I never did that. He was probably one of the last writers to come out of the world of tenements and factories and to make it in this computer age as a newspaperman. He came from "the guys who cut meat for a living," "the guys who work behind the stick." Like Walt Whitman, he was one of "the roughs." Had he lived a little longer, he would have written a novel about our old neighborhood that would have stood up against the works of James T. Farrell. ◆

On my mother's side, my grandfather came from County Cavan and my grandmother from Cork. In fact, I belonged to the Corkmen's Association. When they read off the members' names and came to mine, somebody was sure to ask, 'How'd that Dutchman get in here?'

Robert F. Wagner, former mayor of New York, in New York *Daily News* (1987)

The Shandon Bells

With deep affection, and recollection
I often think of those Shandon bells,
Whose sound so wild would, in the days of my childhood,
Fling round my cradle their magic spells.
On this I ponder, where'er I wander,
And thus grow fonder, sweet Cork, of thee,
With thy bells of Shandon, that sound so grand on
The pleasant waters of the River lee.

I've heard bells chiming, full many a clime in,
Tolling sublime in Cathedral shrine,
While at a glib rate, brass tongues would vibrate—
But all their music spoke naught like thine;
For memory dwelling, on each proud swelling,
Of the belfry knelling, its bold notes free,
Made the bells of Shandon, sound far more grand on,
The pleasant waters of the River Lee.

I've heard bells tolling, Old "Adrian's Mole" in,
Their thunder rolling from the Vatican,
And cymbals glorious, swinging uproarious,
In the gorgeous turrets of Notre Dame;
But their sounds were sweeter, than the dome of Peter,
Flings o'er the Tiber, pealing solemnly;—
Oh! the bells of Shandon sound far more grand on,
The pleasant waters of the River Lee.

There's a bell in Moscow, while a tower and kosk o!
In Saint Sophia the Turkman gets,
And loud in air, calls men to prayer,
From the tapering summit, of tall minarets.
Such empty phantom, I freely grant them;
But there is an anthem, more dear to me,—
Tis the bells of Shandon, that sound so grand on,
The pleasant waters of the River Lee. ◆

The Harp That Once Through Tara's Halls

The harp that once through Tara's halls
The soul of music shed,
Now hangs as mute on Tara's walls
As if that soul were fled.
So sleeps the pride of former days
So glory's trill is o'er,
And hearts, that once beat high for praise
Now feel that pulse no more.

No more to chiefs and ladies bright
The harp of Tara swells,
The chord alone, that breaks at night
Its tale of ruin tells.
Thus freedom now so seldom wakes
The only throb she gives,
Is when some heart indignant breaks
To show that she still lives. ◆

Young Irish choir
boys during the
early 1900s.

Believe Me,
If All Those
Endearing
Young Charms

Believe me, if all those endearing young charms
Which I gaze on so fondly today,
Were to change by tomorrow and fleet in my arms
Like the fairy gifts fading away,
Thou would'st still be adored as this moment thou art,
Let thy loveliness fade as it will,
And around the dear ruin each wish of my heart
Would entwine itself verdantly still!

It is not while beauty and youth are thine own
And thy cheeks unprofaned by a tear,
That the fervor and faith of a soul can be known
To which time will but make thee more dear!
No, the heart that has truly lov'd never forgets,
But as truly loves on to the close;
As the sunflower turns on her god, when he sets,
The same look which she turn'd when he rose! ◆

**THE HEALTH OF THE
SALMON TO YOU: A
LONG LIFE, A FULL
HEART AND A WET
MOUTH!**
Traditional Irish Toast

At Clancy's Wake

The following dramatic sketch appeared in Truth (an illustrated humor magazine published in New York and edited by James T. Ford) on June 3, 1893. It typifies the stock American image of an Irish wake.

SCENE: Room in the house of the lamented CLANCY. The curtains are pulled down. A perfume of old roses and whiskey hangs in the air. A weeping woman in black is seated at a table in the center. A group of wide-eyed children are sobbing in a corner. Down the side of the room is a row of mourning friends of the family. Through an open door can be seen, half-hidden in shadows, the silver and black of a coffin.

WIDOW: Oh, wirra, wirra, wirra!

CHILDREN: B-b-boo-hoo-hoo!

FRIENDS (conversing in low tones): Yis, Moike Clancy was a foine mahn.— Sure—None betther!—No, I don't t'ink so!—Did he? Sure, in all th' elictions!—He was th' bist in the warrud!—He licked 'im widin an inch of his life, aisy, an' th' other wan a big shtrappin' buck of a mahn, an' him jest free of th' penumonial—Yis, he did!—They carried th' warrud by six hunder!—Yis, he was a foine mahn!—None betther, Gawd sav' 'im.

(Enter MR. SLICK, of the Daily Blanket, shown in by a maid-servant whose hair has become disarranged through much tear-shedding. He is attired in a suit of gray check, and wears a red rose in his buttonhole.)

MR. SLICK: Good-afternoon, Mrs. Clancy. This is a sad misfortune for you, isn't it?

WIDOW: Oh, indade, indade, young mahn, me poor heart is bruk!

MR. SLICK: Very sad, Mrs. Clancy. A great misfortune, I'm sure. Now, Mrs. Clancy, I've called to—

WIDOW: Little did I t'ink, young mahn, win they brought poor Moike in, that it was th' lasht.

MR. SLICK (with conviction): True! Very true, indeed! It was a great grief to you. Mrs. Clancy. I've called this morning. Mrs. Clancy, to see if I could get from you a short obituary notice for the Blanket—

WIDOW: An' his hid was done upin a rag, an' he was cursin' frightful. A dommed Oytalian lit fall th' hod as Moike was walkin' pasht as dacint as you plaze. Win they carried 'im in, him all bloody, an' ravin' tur'ble 'bout Oytalians, me heart was near bruk, but I niver tawt—I niver tawt—I—I niver—*(Breaks forth into a long, forlorn cry. The children join in, and the chorus echoes wailfully through the rooms.)*

MR. SLICK *(as the yell, in a measure, ceases):* Yes, indeed, a sad, sad affair. A terrible misfortune! Now, Mrs. Clancy—

WIDOW *(turning suddenly):* Mary Ann! Where's thot lazy divil of a Mary Ann? *(As the servant appears)* Mary Ann, bring th' bottle. Give th' gintlemin a dhrink. . . . Here's to Hiven savin' yez, young mahn! *(Drinks.)*

MR. SLICK *(drinks):* A noble whiskey, Mrs. Clancy. Many thanks. Now, Mrs. Clancy—

WIDOW: Take anodder wan! Take anodder wan! *(Fills his glass.)*

MR. SLICK *(impatiently):* Yes, certainly, Mrs. Clancy, certainly. *(He drinks.)* Now, could you tell me, Mrs. Clancy, where your late husband was—

WIDOW: Who—Moike? Oh, young mahn, yez can just say thot he was th' foinest mahn livin' an' breathin', an' niver a wan in th' warrud was bether. Oh, but he had th' tindther heart for 'is fambly, he did! Don't I remember win he clipped little Patsey wid th' bottle, an' didn't he buy th' big rickin'-horse th' minit he got sober? Sure he did. Pass th' bottle, Mary Ann. *(Pours a beer glass about half-full for her guest.)*

MR. SLICK *(taking a seat):* True, Mr. Clancy was a fine man, Mrs. Clancy— a very fine man. Now, I—

WIDOW *(plaintively):* An' don't yez loike th' rum? Dhrink th' rum, mahn. It was me own Moike's fav'rite bran'. Well I remember win he fotched it home, an' half th' demijohn gone a'ready, an' him a'cursin up th' stairs as dhrunk as Gawd plazed. It was a—Dhrink th' rum, young mahn, dhrink th' rum. If he cud see yez now, Moike Clancy wud git up from 'is—

MR. SLICK *(desperately):* Very well, very well, Mrs. Clancy! Here's your good health! Now, can you tell me, Mrs. Clancy, when was Mr. Clancy born?

WIDOW: Win was he borrun? Sure, divil a bit do I care win he was borrun. He was th' good mahn to me an' his childher, an' Gawd knows I don't care win he was borrun. Mary Ann, pass th' bottle. Wud yez kepe th' gintlemin shtarvin' for a dhrink here in Moike Clancy's own house? Gawd save yez!

(When the bottle appears she pours a huge quantity out for her guest.)

MR. SLICK: Well, then, Mrs. Clancy, where was he born?

WIDOW *(staring):* In Oirland, mahn, in Oirland! Where did yez t'ink? *(Then, in sudden wheedling tones)* An' ain't yez goin' to dhrink th'

MAY THE FROST NEVER AFFLICT YOUR SPUDS. MAY THE OUTSIDE LEAVES OF YOUR CABBAGE ALWAYS BE FREE FROM WORMS. MAY THE CROWS NEVER PICK YOUR HAYSTACK, AND MAY YOUR DONKEY ALWAYS BE IN FOAL.
Traditional Irish Toast

rum? Are yez goin' to shirt th' good whiskey what was th' pride of Moike's loife, an' him gettin' full on it an' breakin' the' furniter t'ree nights a week hand-runnin'? Shame on yez, an' Gawd save yer sowl! Dhrink it oop now, there's a dear, dhrink it oop now, an' say: "Moike Clancy, be all th' powers in th' shky Hiven sind yez rist!"

MR. SLICK *(to himself):* Holy smoke! *(He drinks, then regards the glass for a long time.)* . . . Well, now, Mrs. Clancy, give me your attention for a moment, please. When did—

WIDOW: An' oh, but he was a power in th' warrud! Divil a mahn cud vote right widout Moike Clancy at 's elbow. An' in the calkus, sure didn't Mulrooney git th' nominashun jes' by raison of Moike's atthackin' th' opposashun wid th' shtove-poler Mulrooney got it as aisy as dhirt, wid Moike rowlin' under th' tayble wid th' other candeedate. He was a good cit'zen, was Moike—divil a wan betther.

(MR. SLICK spends some minutes in collecting his faculties.)

MR. SLICK *(after he decides that he has them collected):* Yes, yes, Mrs. Clancy, your husband's h-highly successful pol-pol-politic political career was w-well known to the public; but what I want to know is —what I want to know is—What I want to know—*(Pauses to consider.)*

WIDOW) *(finally):* Pass th' glasses, Mary Ann, yez lazy divil, give th' gintlemin a dhrink. Here *(tendering him a glass),* take anodder wan to Moike Clancy, an' Gawd save yez for yer koindness to a poor widee woman!

MR. SLICK *(after solemnly regarding the glass):* Certainly, I-I'll take a drink. Certainly, M-Mish Clanshy. Yes, certainly, Mish Clanshy. Now, Mish Clanshy, w-w-wash was Mr. Clanshy's n-name before he married you, Mish Clanshy?

WIDOW *(astonished):* Why, divil a bit else but Clancy!

MR. SLICK *(after reflection):* Well, but I am mean—I mean, Mish Clanshy, I mean—what was date of birth? Did marry you 'fore then, or d-did marry you when 'e was born in N' York, Mish Clanshy?

WIDOW: Phwat th' divil—

MR. SLICK *(with dignity):* Ansher my queshuns, pleash, Mish Clanshy. Did'e bring chil'en withum f'm Irelan', or was you, after married in N' York, mother those chil'en brought f'm Irelan'?

WIDOW: Be th' powers above, I—

MR. SLICK *(with gentle patience):* I don't shink y' unnerstan' m' queshuns, Mish Clanshy. What I wanna fin' out is, what was 'e born in N' York for when he, before zat, came f'm Irelan'? Dash what puzzles me. I-I'm completely puzzled. An' alsho, I wanna fin' out—I wanna fin' out, if poshble—zat is, if it's poshble shing, I wanna fin' out—I wanna fin' out—if poshble—I wanna—shay, who the blazesh is dead here, anyhow? ◆

He was only forty-four years old and a real Irishman. I buried him in a green coffin, in a dark green suit and a green carnation.

Christine Cox, "Miss Liberty 1986," speaking of her father in the *New York Post* (1986)

Slum
Dwellers

In Maggie: A Girl of the Streets *(1893), Stephen Crane paints a grim picture of life among the Irish-American slumdwellers of New York. A pioneer in fictional realism, Crane rejects the romanticized, sentimentalized, or comic Irish types who formed the stock company from which earlier writers selected their characters. Instead, he depicts the morally degraded, culturally deprived proletariat of urban, industrial America.*

Crane's central character, Maggie (she is too lightly sketched to be called a heroine), grows to adolescence somehow untouched by the brutal and brutalized environment of the slum. Seduced by the flashy crony of her good-for-nothing brother, she is rejected by her grotesquely self-righteous, drunken mother. After a pathetic attempt to support herself by streetwalking, she commits suicide.

The following selections from this short novel illustrate the life-style and speech patterns of the "lower orders," accurately reproduced by a writer who had covered the urban scene for a local newspaper. While the word "Irish" never appears in the narrative, there is no doubt who and what these characters represent. "Pioneers of the American ghetto," as one historian has called them, the Irish were still, in those days, the principal inhabitants of the slums.

Members of the Short-Tail Gang, a band of Irish-American criminals that terrorized the Lower East Side in the 1880s, are shown under a bridge. The photograph was taken from a police boat.

*E*ventually they entered a dark region where, from a careening building, a dozen gruesome doorways gave up loads of babies to the street and the gutter. A wind of early autumn raised yellow dust from cobbles and swirled it against a hundred windows. Long streamers of garments fluttered from fire-escapes. In all unhandy places there were buckets, brooms, rags, and bottles. In the street infants played or fought with other infants or sat stupidly in the way of vehicles. Formidable women, with uncombed hair and disordered dress, gossiped while leaning on railings, or screamed in frantic quarrels. Withered persons, in curious postures of submission to something, sat smoking pipes in obscure corners. A thousand odors of cooking food came forth to the street. The building quivered and creaked from the weight of humanity stamping about in its bowels.

A small ragged girl dragged a red, bawling infant along the crowded ways. He was hanging back, babylike, bracing his wrinkled bare legs.

The little girl cried out: "Ah, Tommie, come ahn. Dere's Jimmie and fader. Don't be a-pullin' me back."

She jerked the baby's arm impatiently. He fell on his face, roaring. With a second jerk she pulled him to his feet, and they went on. With the obstinacy of his order, he protested against being dragged in a chosen direction. He made heroic endeavors to keep on his legs, denounced his sister, and consumed a bit of orange peeling which he chewed between the times of his infantile orations.

As the sullen-eyed man, followed by the blood-covered boy, drew near, the little girl burst into reproachful cries. "Ah, Jimmie, youse bin fightin' agin."

The urchin swelled disdainfully.

"Ah, what d'hell, Mag. See?"

The little girl upbraided him. "Youse allus fightin', Jimmie, an' yeh knows it puts mudder out when yehs come home half dead, an' it's like we'll all get a poundin'."

She began to weep. The babe threw back his head and roared at his prospects.

"Ah," cried Jimmie, "shut up er I'll smack yer mout'. See?"

As his sister continued her lamentations, he suddenly struck her. The little girl reeled and, recovering herself, burst into tears and quaveringly cursed him. As she slowly retreated, her brother advanced, dealing her cuffs. The father heard, and turned about.

"Stop that, Jim, d'yeh hear? Leave yer sister alone on the street. It's like I can never beat any sense into yer wooden head."

The urchin raised his voice in defiance to his parent and continued his attacks. The babe bawled tremendously, protesting with great violence. During his sister's hasty manoeuvres he was dragged by the arm.

Finally the procession plunged into one of the gruesome doorways. They crawled up dark stairways and along cold, gloomy halls. At last the father pushed open a door and they entered a lighted room in which a large woman was rampant.

She stopped in a career from a seething stove to a pan-covered table. As the father and children filed in she peered at them.

"Eh, what? Been fightin' agin!" She threw herself upon Jimmie. The urchin tried to dart behind the others, and in the scuffle the babe, Tommie, was knocked down. He protested with his usual vehemence, because they had bruised his tender shins against a table leg.

The mother's massive shoulders heaved with anger. Grasping the urchin by the neck and shoulder she shook him until he rattled. She dragged him to an unholy sink, and, soaking a rag in water, began to scrub his lacerated face with it. Jimmie screamed in pain and tried to twist his shoulders out of the clasp of the huge arms.

The babe sat on the floor watching the scene, his face in contortions like that of a woman at a tragedy. The father, with a newly ladened pipe in his mouth, sat in a backless chair near the stove; Jimmie's cries annoyed him. He turned about and bellowed at his wife:

"Let the kid alone for a minute, will yeh, Mary? Yer allus poundin' 'im. When I come home nights I can't git no rest 'cause yer allus poundin' a kid. Let up, d'yeh hear? Don't be allus poundin' a kid."

The woman's operations on the urchin instantly increased in violence. At last she tossed him to a corner where he limply lay weeping.

The wife put her immense hands on her hips, and with a chieftainlike stride approached her husband.

"Ho!" she said, with a great grunt of contempt. "An' what in the devil are you stickin' your nose for?"

The babe crawled under the table and, turning, peered out cautiously. The ragged girl retreated, and the urchin in the corner drew his legs carefully beneath him.

The man puffed his pipe calmly and put his great muddied boots on the back part of the stove.

"Go t' hell," he said tranquilly.

The woman screamed and shook her fists before her husband's eyes. The rough yellow of her face and neck flared suddenly crimson. She began to howl.

He puffed imperturbably at his pipe for a time but finally arose and went to look out of the window into the darkening chaos of back yards.

"You've been drinkin', Mary," he said. "You'd better let up on the bot', ol' woman, or you'll git done."

"You're a liar. I ain't had a drop," she roared. They had a lurid altercation.

The babe was staring out from under the table, his small face working in his excitement. The ragged girl went stealthily over to the corner where the urchin lay.

"Are yeh hurted much, Jimmie?" she whispered timidly.

"Not a little bit. See?" growled the little boy.

"Will I wash d'blood?"

"Naw!"

"Will I—"

"When I catch dat Riley kid I'll break 'is face! Dat's right! See?"

He turned his face to the wall as if resolved grimly to bide his time.

In the quarrel between husband and wife the woman was victor. The man seized his hat and rushed from the room, apparently determined upon a vengeful drunk. She followed to the door and thundered at him as he made his way downstairs.

She returned and stirred up the room until her children were bobbing about like bubbles.

"Git outa d'way," she bawled persistently, waving feet with their dishevelled shoes near the heads of her children. She shrouded herself, puffing and snorting, in a cloud of steam at the stove, and eventually extracted a frying-pan full of potatoes that hissed.

She flourished it. "Come t' yer suppers, now," she cried with sudden exasperation. "Hurry up, now, er I'll help yeh!"

The children scrambled hastily. With prodigious clatter they arranged themselves at table. The babe sat with his feet dangling high from a precarious infant's chair and gorged his small stomach. Jimmie forced, with feverish rapidity, the grease-enveloped pieces between his wounded lips. Maggie, with side glances of fear of interruption, ate like a small pursued tigress.

The mother sat blinking at them. She

delivered reproaches, swallowed potatoes, and drank from a yellow-brown bottle. After a time her mood changed and she wept as she carried little Tommie into another room and laid him to sleep, with his fists doubled, in an old quilt of faded red and green grandeur. Then she came and moaned by the stove. She rocked to and fro upon a chair, shedding tears and crooning miserably to the two children about their "poor mother" and "yer fader, damn 'is soul."

The little girl plodded between the table and the chair with a dish pan on it. She tottered on her small legs beneath burdens of dishes.

Jimmie sat nursing his various wounds. He cast furtive glances at his mother. His practised eye perceived her gradually emerge from a mist of muddled sentiment until her brain burned in drunken heat. He sat breathless.

Maggie broke a plate.

The mother started to her feet as if propelled.

"Good Gawd!" she howled. Her glittering eyes fastened on her child with sudden hatred. The fervent red of her face turned almost to purple. The little boy ran to the halls, shrieking like a monk in an earthquake.

He floundered about in darkness until he found the stairs. He stumbled, panic-stricken, to the next floor. An old woman opened a door. A light behind her threw a flare on the urchin's face.

"Eh, child, what is it dis time? Is yer fader beatin' yer mudder, or yer mudder beatin' yer fader?"

. . .

Jimmie had an idea it wasn't common courtesy for a friend to come to one's home and ruin one's sister. But he was not sure how much Pete knew about politeness.

The following night he returned home from work at a rather late hour in the evening. In passing through the halls he came upon the gnarled and leathery old woman who possessed the music box. She was grinning in the dim light that drifted through dust-stained panes. She beckoned to him with a smudged forefinger.

"Ah, Jimmie, what do yehs tink I tumbled, to, las' night! It was deh funnies' t'ing I ever saw," she cried, coming close to him and leering. She was trembling with eagerness to tell her tale. "I was by me door las' night when yer sister and her jude feller came in late, oh, very late. An' she, the dear, she was a-cryin' as if her heart would break, she was. It was deh funnies' t'ing I ever saw. An' right out here by me door she asked him did he love her, did he. An' she was a-crying as if her heart would break, poor t'ing. An' him, I could see by deh way what he said it dat she had been askin' orften; he says, 'Oh, gee, yes,' he says, says he. 'Oh gee, yes.' "

Storm-clouds swept over Jimmie's face, but he turned from the leathery old woman and plodded on upstairs.

" 'Oh, gee, yes,' " she called after him. She laughed a laugh that was like a prophetic croak.

There was no one in at home. The rooms showed that attempts had been made at tidying them. Parts of the wreckage of the day before had been repaired by an unskillful hand. A chair or two and the table stood uncertainly upon legs. The floor had been newly swept. The blue ribbons had been restored to the curtains, and the lambrequin, with its immense sheaves of yellow wheat and red roses of equal size, had been returned, in a worn and sorry state, to its place at the mantel. Maggie's jacket and hat were gone from the nail behind the door.

Jimmie walked to the window and began to look through the blurred glass. It occurred to him to wonder vaguely, for an instant, if some of the women of his acquaintance had brothers.

Suddenly, however, he began to swear.

"But he was me frien'! I brought 'im here! Dat's d' devil of it!"

He fumed about the room, his anger gradually rising to the furious pitch.

"I'll kill deh jay! Dat's what I'll do! I'll kill deh jay!"

He clutched his hat and sprang toward the door. But it opened, and his mother's great form blocked the passage. "What's d' matter wid yeh?" exclaimed she, coming into the room.

Jimmie gave vent to a sardonic curse and then laughed heavily.

"Well, Maggie's gone teh d' devil! Dat's what! See?"

"Eh?" said his mother.

"Maggie's gone teh d' devil! Are yehs deaf?" roared Jimmie, impatiently.

"Aw, git out!" murmured the mother, astounded.

Jimmie grunted, and then began to stare out the window. His mother sat down in a chair, but a moment later sprang erect and delivered a maddened whirl of oaths. Her son turned to look at her as she reeled and swayed in the middle of the room, her fierce face convulsed with passion, her blotched arms raised high in imprecation.

"May she be cursed for ever!" she shrieked. "May she eat nothin' but stones and deh dirt in deh street. May she sleep in deh gutter an' never see deh sun shine again. D'bloomin'—"

"Here now," said her son. "Go fall on yerself an' quit dat."

The mother raised lamenting eyes to the ceiling.

"She's d' devil's own chil', Jimmie," she whispered. "Ah, who would t'ink such a bad girl could grow up in our fambly, Jimmie, me son. Many d'hour I've spent in talk wid dat girl an' tol' her if she ever went on d'streets I'd see her damned. An' after all her bringin' up, an' what I tol' her and talked wid her, she goes teh d' bad, like a duck teh water."

The tears rolled down her furrowed face. Her hands trembled.

"An' den when dat Saide MacMallister next door to us was sent teh d' devil by dat feller what worked in d' soap factory, didn't I tell our Mag dat if she—"

"Ah, dat's anudder story," interrupted the brother.

"Of course, dat Sadie was nice an' all dat—but—see—it ain't dessame if—well, Maggie was diff'ent—see—she was diff'ent."

He was trying to formulate a theory that he had always unconsciously held, that all sisters excepting his own could, advisedly, be ruined.

He suddenly broke out again. "I'll go t'ump d' mug what done her d' harm. I'll kill 'im! He t'inks he kin scrap, but when he gits me a-chasin' 'im he'll fin' out where he's wrong, d' big stiff! I'll wipe up d' street wid 'im."

In a fury he plunged out the doorway. As he vanished the mother raised her head and lifted both hands, entreating.

"May she be cursed for ever!" she cried.

In the darkness of the hallway Jimmie discerned a knot of women talking volubly. When he strode by they paid no attention to him.

"She allus was a bold thing," he heard one of them cry in an eager voice. "Dere wasn't a feller come teh deh house but she'd try teh mash 'im. My Annie says deh shameless t'ing tried teh ketch her feller, her own feller, what we useter know his fader."

"I could' a tol' yehs dis two years ago," said a woman, in a key of triumph. "Yes, sir, it was over two years ago dat I says teh my ol' man, I says, 'Dat Johnson girl ain't straight,' I says. 'Oh, rats!' he says. 'Oh, Hell!' 'Dat's all right,' I says, 'but I know what I knows,' I says, 'an' it'll come out later. You wait an' see,' I says, 'you see.' "

"Anybody what had eyes could see dat dere was somethin' wrong wid dat girl. I didn't like her actions."

On the street Jimmie met a friend. "What's wrong?" asked the latter.

Jimmie explained. "An' I'll t'ump 'im till he can't stand."

"Oh, go ahn!" said the friend. "What's deh use! Yeh'll git pulled in! Everybody'ill be on to it! An' ten plunks! Gee!"

Jimmie was determined. "He t'inks he kin scrap, but he'll fin' out diff'ent."

"Gee," remonstrated the friend, "what's d' use?"

. . .

In a room a woman sat at a table eating like a fat monk in a picture.

A soiled, unshaven man pushed open the door and entered.

"Well," said he, "Mag's dead."

"What?" said the woman, her mouth filled with bread.

"Mag's dead," repeated the man.

"Deh blazes she is!" said the woman. She continued her meal.

When she finished her coffee she began to weep. "I kin remember when her two feet was no bigger dan yer t'umb, and she weared worsted boots," moaned she.

"Well, what a' dat?" said the man.

"I kin remember when she weared worsted boots," she cried.

The neighbors began to gather in the hall, staring in at the weeping woman as if watching the contortions of a dying dog. A dozen women entered and lamented with her. Under their busy hands the room took on that appalling appearance of neatness and order with which death is greeted.

Suddenly the door opened and a woman in a black gown rushed in with outstretched arms. "Ah, poor Mary!" she cried, and tenderly embraced the moaning one.

"Ah, what te'ble affliction is dis!" continued she. Her vocabulary was derived from mission churches. "Me poor Mary, how I feel fer yehs! Ah, what a ter'ble affliction is a disobed'ent chile."

Her good, motherly face was wet with tears. She trembled in eagerness to express her sympathy. The mourner sat with bowed head, rocking her body heavily to and fro, and crying out in a high strained voice that sounded like a dirge on some forlorn pipe.

"I kin remember when she weared worsted boots, an' her two feets was no bigger dan yer t'umb, an' she weared worsted boots, Miss Smith," she cried, raising her streaming eyes.

"Ah, me poor Mary!" sobbed the woman in black. With low cries, she sank on her knees by the mourner's chair, and put her arms about her. The other women began to groan in different keys.

"Yer poor misguided chil' is gone now, Mary, an' let us hope it's fer deh bes'. Yeh'll fergive her now, Mary, won't yehs, dear, all her disobed'ence? All her t'ankless behavior to her mudder an' all her badness? She's gone where her ter'ble sins will be judged."

The woman in black raised her face and paused. The inevitable sunlight came streaming in at the window and shed a ghastly cheerfulness upon the faded hues of the room. Two or three of the spectators were sniffing, and one was weeping loudly. The mourner arose and staggered into the other room. In a moment she emerged with a pair of faded baby shoes held in the hollow of her hand.

"I kin remember when she used to wear dem!" cried she. The women burst anew into cries as if they had all been stabbed. The mourner turned to the soiled and unshaven man.

"Jimmie, boy, go git yer sister! Go git yer sister an' we'll put deh boots on her feets!"

"Dey won't fit her now, yeh fool," said the man.

"Go git yer sister, Jimmie!" shrieked the woman, confronting him fiercely.

The man swore sullenly. He went over to a corner and slowly began to put on his coat. He took his hat and went out, with a dragging, reluctant step.

The woman in black came forward and again besought the mourner.

"Yeh'll fergive her, Mary! Yeh'll fergive yer bad, bad chil'! Her life was a curse an' her days were black, an' yeh'll fergive yer bad girl? She's gone where her sins will be judged."

"She's gone where her sins will be judged!" cried the other women, like a choir at a funeral.

"Deh Lord gives and deh Lord takes away," said the woman in black, raising her eyes to the sunbeams.

"Deh Lord gives and deh Lord takes away," responded the others.

"Yeh'll fergive her, Mary?" pleaded the woman in black. The mourner essayed to speak, but her voice gave way. She shook her great shoulders frantically, in an agony of grief. The tears seemed to scald her face. Finally her voice came and arose in a scream of pain.

"Oh, yes, I'll fergive her! I'll fergive her!" ◆

Mobility

James Shields (1806–1879) was a native of Tyrone who had a remarkable career in America, serving as a general in two wars and as a senator from three different states.

*T*hose Irish Americans who were prepared to move out quickly from the traditional immigrant environment often gained striking material rewards for their display of initiative. James Shields, born in Tyrone in 1806, came to the United States in his teens. He moved to the frontier region of Illinois, soon gained a leadership position there and became a successful lawyer. During the Mexican War he distinguished himself as a militia commander and was brevetted major general for gallantry. He was appointed governor of the Oregon territory, then elected senator from Illinois (1849–1855). Still restless, he moved to Minnesota and was elected as one of the first senators from that new state (1858–1859). The prospect of new opportunities then drew him to California. At the outbreak of the Civil War he was commissioned as a general of volunteers. After the war he moved once again, to Missouri, and at the time of his death (1879) was serving as senator from that state. Shields still holds the record of being the only man who ever represented three different states in the United States Senate.

Less spectacular, but still instructive, is the story of Patrick J. Hurley. His father, Pierce O'Neil Hurley, preferred the Texas frontier to the Irish centers of the East Coast, then moved restlessly northward into Indian territory (now Oklahoma), where his son Patrick was born in 1883. Like his father, the younger Hurley tried his hand both at coal mining and ranching, but went on to become a lawyer, representing the Choctaw Nation at Washington. As an administrator, general, cabinet officer, and diplomat he was a highly visible and controversial national figure for some forty years. Although an outspoken Republican who served as President Hoover's secretary of war, he was prepared to work with the New Deal of Franklin Roosevelt. During World War II he represented Roosevelt in Australia and New Zealand, and later the Middle East; after the war he was President Truman's ambassador to China. Although always consciously Irish, he broke free of the regional, religious, political, and social environment with which most Irish Americans were identified, and this, as much as his force of personality, aided his rise. ◆

A Constructive Contribution

"The Irish came to America," one nineteenth-century immigrant ruefully observed, "thinking that the streets were paved with gold. When we got here we found that not only were they not paved with gold —they were not paved at all. And *we* were supposed to pave them."

One Irish American who undertook these constructive labors on a grand scale was John Daniel Crimmins. His immigrant father had worked his way up from hod carrier to head of his own construction firm in New York City. From this beginning, the younger Crimmins transformed himself into a major contractor and capitalist. He erected over four hundred buildings, laid down miles of streets, viaducts, and gas lines, and "gave his regards to Broadway" by repaving the "Great White Way." He also built the greater part of New York's elevated railway network and did the tunneling for underground electrical cables. He also served on the board that oversaw the completion and preservation of Central Park.

When he was not building skyscrapers, Crimmins was busy preserving Irish history and culture. He was an ardent collector of Irish books and manuscripts, and promoter of Irish causes, ranging from home rule to the American Irish Historical Society (of which he was president in 1905). Furthermore, he was a pioneer in serious research into the Irish-American past, authoring two useful books, *Irish American Historical Miscellany,* and *St. Patrick's Day—Its Celebration . . . 1737–1845.*

Both in the enduring marks he left on the urban infrastructure and skyline and in his commitment to his Irish heritage, John Crimmins is a fitting symbol of the hundreds of thousands of humbler Irish laborers who literally built modern America. ◆

The sin of the Irishman is ignorance—the cure is Liberty.

Thomas Orne White, *Harvard College Commencement Address* (1840)

Drill, Ye Tarriers, Drill

Oh, every morn at seven o'clock
There are twenty tarriers on the rock.
The boss comes along and says, "Be still
And put all your power in the cast steel drill."

CHORUS:

Then drill, ye tarriers, drill.
Drill, ye tarriers, drill.
Oh, it's work all day
Without sugar in your tay
When ye work beyant on the railway,
And drill, ye tarriers, drill.

WHILE THE CAT IS
OUT THE MOUSE
WILL DANCE.
*Traditional Irish
Proverb*

The boss was a fine man all around
But he married a great, big, fat Far Down.
She baked good bread and baked it well,
And baked it hard as the hobs of hell.

CHORUS

The new foreman is Dan McCann.
I'll tell you sure he's a damn mean man.
Last week a premature blast went off,
And a mile in the air went big Jim Goff.

CHORUS

When pay day next it came around,
Poor Jim's pay a dollar short he found.
"What for?" says he, then came this reply:
"You were docked for the time you were up in the sky." ◆

The Irish Underground

*T*he next time you're sitting (or, more likely, standing) in the subway, you might want to pass the time by reflecting on the Irish role in introducing this unique system of mass transportation to the world.

According to ancient tradition, the Danaans, defeated by the invading Gaels, retreated into the depths of the earth. From their subterranean tunnels, these sinister original inhabitants of Ireland would henceforth pop up here and there to work mischief. This is certainly the origin of the leprechaun legend. It also suggests that the Irish invented the subway system. Moving from myth to fact, however, there is no doubt that the Irish were, in every sense, deeply involved in building, maintaining, and operating four of the world's first six subways.

In 1860, when the British Parliament authorized a three-and-a-quarter mile "underground railway" in London, connecting Paddington Station with Farringdon Road, Irish labor was mobilized on a large scale. The old "cut and cover" method of construction required thousands of pick-and-shovel men—exactly the sort of work for which Irish migrants were recruited. Thus, when the line was opened in 1863, it was not only the first subway (the British have never used that term, though), it was also a product of Irish sweat and strain.

It was nearly three decades until the advance of technology made possible the replacement of steam-driven engines, which filled the underground with steam and soot, by electrically powered trains. At about the same time, the technique of constructing a subterranean tube to provide the necessary tunnel stimulated new projects on both sides of the Atlantic. During the 1890s London expanded its own network, while Glasgow and Boston built their first subway lines. All three cities confided much of the work involved in creating and running these electrical rail systems to their Irish residents. Completed in 1897, the Boston line initially ran one and a half miles under Tremont Street using trolley cars on the subway tracks.

New York had long relied upon its elevated railways. The first El had opened on Manhattan's Ninth Avenue in 1867, with a cable-drive mechanism. Four years later, steam locomotives were introduced. Although electricity was not introduced until the end of the century (the

HE KNOWS MORE THAN HIS "OUR FATHER."
Traditional Irish Proverb

223

6I never hear an Irishman called Paddy, a colored person called nigger, or the contemptuous epithet 'old beggar man,' without a pang at my heart, for I know that such epithets, inadvertently used, are doing more to form the moral sentiments of the nation than all the teachings of the schools.9

Lydia M. Child, *National Anti-Slavery Standard* (1841)

Chicago El had its first, in 1895), most New Yorkers seemed satisfied with their elevated railways. "Preposterous!" scoffed one prominent citizen, "the people of New York will never go into a hole in the ground to ride." Not the least among the opponents of change were the Irishmen employed as drivers and maintenance workers on the Els and trolleys, who feared the creation of a competing form of transportation.

Progress could not be halted, though, and the New York subway opened for business in October 1904, the world's sixth (Budapest and Paris had also preceded it), and ultimately to be the biggest and best known. The first line ran north from City Hall to the Grand Central Terminal, then west to Times Square, then north again to the entrance of Central Park. A great network of additional lines would spread across the city during the next four decades.

Despite their initial opposition, the New York Irish not only found plenty of jobs in the construction of the subway, they found many more in running it. The subway became a supplement to, rather than a replacement for, the surface transit, and the Irish soon established a monopoly in the transportation system. Motormen, conductors, change-booth attendants on the subway were likely to have an Irish accent down to and through the 1940s, when New York's underground expansion came to an end. The Transit Workers' Union, under Irish-born leaders like the picturesque Mike Quill, preserved a Celtic image long after the ethnic composition of the rank and file reflected the city's population shifts.

Even though present-day subway systems in the United States may not always inspire admiration and appreciation, their initial construction, their expansion, and their operation may still serve as a historical monument in which the Irish can take pride. ◆

The building of the Union Pacific Railroad opened up the Far West to trade and settlement during the post–Civil War years. Irish workmen, like those shown here, formed a large proportion of the labor force and frequently had to double as Indian fighters.

LETTER TO THE EDITOR IN *THE TRUTH TELLER* (NEW YORK), NOVEMBER 24, 1832

We the subscribers, natives of Ireland—and adopted citizens of the United States—have been in the employment of Hance and Brooks, carpenters, in the Sixth Ward for some time, and consider ourselves justifiable in stating that from the time we were in their employment— and the usage received from them—there could be no objection to our abilities as workmen or our conduct as men, until the . . . late election.

It is well known by a respectable portion of our fellow-citizens of both the Sixth and Fourteenth Wards, that the above carpenters were very active in the cause of the opposition in the late election in the said wards, and, for their over-reaching the bounds of prudence and discretion, got very roughly handled the second day of the election. Mr. T. C. Colt, foreman to the above firm, presented to the subscribers a set of opposition tickets each, and said to us, if we would go to the polls and vote these tickets, that each one should receive his wages for any time lost on that occasion; and we believe that such order could or would not originate with the foreman. The above tickets were indignantly refused by every man, as well as the proffer of wages, and our reply was that we should go to the polls and vote according to our consciences, and any time spent there we were willing to lose; for we would vote for "Old Hickory"—the Man of the People!!!

The conduct of the above employers was most materially altered towards us on the following morning, and language very unbecoming and unusual was resorted to by one of them particularly, who said that Irishmen should not be encouraged in this country, and that he would not have one of them about his premises—that he would sooner have inferior workmen, if any others could not be obtained, than have an Irishman employed in future. The aforesaid Hance and Brooks were determined to be consistent, and they kept their word, for the next day they discharged from their employment every Irishman in the concern!

JAMES PURCELL   THOMAS HUSTON
JOHN KEENAN   MICHAEL FORRESTAL
MICHAEL DONOGHUE

Paddy on the Railway

In eighteen hundred and forty-one
I put me corduroy breeches on
I put me corduroy breeches on
To work upon the railway.

CHORUS:
Filli-me-cori-oori-ay
Filli-me-cori-oori-ay
Filli-me-cori-oori-ay
To work upon the railway.

In eighteen hundred and forty-two
I left the Old World for the New,
Bad cess to the luck that brough me through
To work upon the railway.

CHORUS

In eighteen hundred and forty-three
'Twas then that I met sweet Biddy McGee.
An elegant wife she's been to me
While working on the railway.

CHORUS

In eighteen hundred and forty-four
I traveled the land from shore to shore,
I traveled the land from shore to shore
To work upon the railway.

CHORUS

In eighteen hundred and forty-five
I found myself more dead than alive.
I found myself more dead than alive
from working on the railway.

A clash between strikers and militia during the Baltimore and Ohio railroad strike of 1877. Irish workers took a leading role in the labor-management struggles that spanned the closing decades of the nineteenth century.

CHORUS

It's "Pat do this" and "Pat do that,"
Without a stocking or cravat,
Nothing but an old straw hat
While I worked on the railway.

CHORUS

In eighteen hundred and forty-seven
Sweet Biddy McGee, she went to heaven;
If she left one kid she left eleven,
To work upon the railway.   ◆

Changing
Jobs

*I*rish immigrants of the mid-nineteenth century were confined to a few occupations. The average, unskilled man worked as a casual laborer, picking up jobs here and there whenever he could. Those with a bit more polish might be found as porters, bartenders, or soldiers, while those who had skills (and could overcome local prejudice) might find employment as carpenters or blacksmiths. Those with a bit of capital usually put it into a saloon or boardinghouse. The white-collar Irish might be found as clerks, schoolteachers, and, of course, clergymen.

Irish-born women, at the same period, were concentrated in even fewer occupations than their male counterparts. In 1850 about 75 percent of employed immigrant women worked as domestics, with the remainder (mostly in New England) in textile mills.

By the beginning of the twentieth century, the Irish had made their way into a wider variety of employment. The old cliché of the Irish hod carrier or ditchdigger now applied to only one in five newcomers, and even the unskilled were more likely to be working steadily as the railroad or factory hands. By the turn of the century, the Irish made up 18 percent of America's coachmen and drivers, and 11 percent of its longshoremen and policemen. Six percent of the Irish then owned their own business, which was more than six times the percentage in 1850. Educated Irishmen were still most often found as teachers or priests, although more of them were going into politics. Also notable by 1900 was the emergence of the Irish farmer, widely scattered throughout the United States, but more frequently found in the Midwest than in the East. Many of these had moved out into "the wide open spaces" initially as railroad workers, miners, or soldiers. For women, there was little change on occupationaal prospects by 1900, although by that time some 2 percent had gained enough training to work as teachers.

By 1920, when the great era of immigration was at an end, Irish-born men were to be found in virtually the whole range of occupations that industrial America had to offer. Women immigrants, however, still lagged behind; indeed, the percentage of employed Irish-born women who worked as domestic servants had risen to 81 by 1920.

The children of Irish immigrants had far greater success in job mo-

●*That's why all Irishmen are cops. They love it. Alone they're nothing. When they put on the uniform and get a little power they start destroying everything.* ●

Jerry Anguilo, reputed Mafia leader, quoted in the *Boston Herald* (1985)

bility than their parents. By 1900 some 5 percent had entered the professional ranks. By the turn of the century daughters of Irish-born parents
had obtained a notable position in the teaching field and were more
numerous in that profession than women of any other immigrant group.

By the 1980s, the descendants of Irish immigrants had made a massive move into the white-collar ranks. Irish Americans were heavily represented in law, medicine, and the sciences, and moving up in the
business world. Clearly the occupational straitjacket that had bound
their ancestors had been cast aside. For the Irish, the "land of opportunity" had finally lived up to its name. ◆

A young viewer of
the St. Patrick's
Day parade,
wearied by all the
crowds and noise,
is given a boost by
an Irish-American
cop.

Laying Down
the Law

$\mathcal{T}$he legal profession has always held a strong appeal for Irish Americans, confirming, as it does, social and educational status at the same time that it offers professional rewards. Until fairly recently the pattern of recruitment at prestigious law firms and corporate headquarters denied opportunity to most Irish Catholics, however, and turned them toward careers in public service and politics. The resultant proliferation of Irish-American judges at local, state, and federal levels has produced many distinguished jurists.

At the highest level, John Rutledge of South Carolina was a member of the first Supreme Court in 1789, though rejected by the Senate for the chief justiceship in 1795. Roger B. Taney of Maryland, who won fame with the Dred Scott decision, was a member of the Supreme Court from 1835 to 1864, and chief justice for much of that period. Edward D. White of Louisiana, appointed to the court in 1894, served as chief justice from 1910 to 1921. Other justices of Irish origin included Joseph McKenna (1898–1925), Frank Murphy (1940–1949), and James F. Byrnes (1941–1942). William J. Brennan, appointed in 1956, and Sandra Day O'Connor (the first woman member), appointed in 1981, representing widely differing perspectives on the law, maintained an Irish-American presence on the Supreme Court through the 1980s. ◆

Supreme Court Justice Sandra Day O'Connor, the first woman member of the Court.

Return of the
Green Ghost

*P*erhaps presidential speech writers shouldn't really be called ghost writers. After all, they're on the federal payroll, and their names are well known. But Americans like to preserve their illusions, including the one that when the president speaks he is talking from his own head and heart. And surely, they thought, the wit and eloquence of Ronald Reagan were the spontaneous product of his Irish heritage.

The Irish heritage was certainly a factor in whatever virtue the speeches may have possessed, but while the voice was the voice of Reagan, the words were the words of Noonan. Peggy Noonan, White House speech writer, was responsible for some of President Reagan's most moving moments, such as his 1984 address at the D-Day anniversary ceremonies and his response to the 1986 *Challenger* space shuttle disaster. Her ability to coin emotion-packed phrases earned her the nickname among her fellow writers of "La Pasionaria."

Peggy Noonan was the product of an Irish-working-class family in New Jersey who began her career as a premium adjuster at an insurance company, then moved on to writing radio commentaries for CBS News. Despite her achievements after joining the White House staff, which made her the most visible of the presidential "ghosts," she resigned shortly before the end of the Reagan presidency to stay home with her infant son and work on a book about Washington politics and life-styles. But when she heard candidate George Bush on the radio using "recycled" material, she decided to return to the battlefield.

After arranging with her husband and mother to look after the baby, she reported for duty with George Bush. In a sense, she reinvented the Republican nominee. She gave him a simpler, self-deprecating style, which she felt would make best use of his accessibility, the feeling of approachability that she found he projected in personal contacts. Nevertheless, she realized the neccessity of "hitting a home run" in the acceptance speech that Bush made at the Republican National Convention. For writer and nominee alike this was the most important speech of all. By the time Bush had finished, to the cheers and applause of the delegates, and the scarcely less admiring response of the TV commentators, Noonan knew she had won the game.

●The mere fact of being an Irishman is considered to be a crime in American belief.●

Francis Wyse,
America: Its Realities and Resources (1846)

I spent 90 percent of my salary on good Irish whiskey and women. The rest I wasted.

Tug McGraw, baseball player, quoted in *Irish America* (1988)

Through constant repetition during the subsequent campaign such phrases as "warts and all," "a quiet man," "kinder and gentler," and, of course, "read my lips" entered the permanent national vocabulary of political catchwords. Nor was Noonan simply the recorder of Bush's own preferred notions. According to insiders, some of his staff asked her to take the word "gentler" out of the acceptance speech on the ground that it would perpetuate the "wimp" image. The writer insisted on keeping it, arguing that "only a man utterly confident of his own strength can talk like this."

Nor did Peggy Noonan's services end at the convention. She continued to transfigure Bush's vocabulary with her own eloquence. As one reporter put it, the pre-Noonan Bush talking about drugs would speak of "a narced-up terrorist kind of guy," instead of what Noonan called "a deadly scourge." And instead of being virtually tongue-tied when asked why he was in politics, Bush could respond with the Noonanesque declaration that he wanted to help his country "celebrate the quieter, deeper successes that are made not of gold and silk."

The return of Peggy Noonan reached its climax on Inauguration Day, 1989, as the newly sworn President Bush told the American people that "a new breeze is blowing, and a nation refreshed by freedom stands ready to push on." In the words of a *New York Times* correspondent, "Ms. Noonan was one of a handful of people . . . who were pivotal in helping the new President win the prize he had sought so long and hard."

After this brief moment in the public spotlight, the White House's green ghost returned to her interrupted chores as mother and author. Having put words in the mouth of a charming but sometimes confused Irish-American movie actor and a less-than-articulate WASP politician, Peggy Noonan remained proud of her work. In a parting comment on the importance of a political speech, she declared: "It makes people less lonely. It connects strangers with simple truths." ◆

The Irish in Outer Space

A new generation of Irish Americans seeking heroes and heroines need look no farther than the ranks of the astronauts. These skilled, courageous men and women combine the daring of explorers with a principled commitment to public service. Among those of Irish origin who have served in the U.S. space program, several names stand out.

James McDivitt was one of the trailblazing astronauts with *Gemini* and early *Apollo* space missions, 1965–69. Michael Collins piloted the *Apollo 11* space craft during the mission (July 16–24, 1969) that included the first landing on the Moon. Later, Collins became director of the National Aeronautics and Space Museum in Washington, D.C. During the October 1984 flight of the space shuttle *Challenger*, Kathryn Sullivan became the first American woman to walk in space. On the *Challenger*'s last flight, January 28, 1986, Christa Corrigan McAuliffe, the first teacher in space, perished with her fellow crew members in the explosion of the shuttle.

The setback to America's space program that resulted from the *Challenger* disaster delayed but will not prevent the exploration of outer space. In that renewed adventure, young Irish Americans will draw inspiration from their gallant predecessors. ◆

I HAVE KNOWN MANY, LIKED NOT A FEW, LOVED ONLY ONE. I DRINK TO YOU.
Traditional Irish Toast

The Gold
Miner's
Daughter

Evalyn Walsh was the daughter of an immigrant miner who struck it rich in the gold fields of Colorado and moved his family to Washington, D.C., in an effort to buy social advancement. Her marriage in 1909 to Edward B. McLean, heir of a Cincinnati publishing family, was a lavish event, followed by an even more lavish honeymoon. During their two-month tour abroad, the new Mrs. McLean acquired the famous 92.5 carat diamond called the Star of the East. This was merely a prelude to her purchase, a few years later, of the famous Hope Diamond. Evalyn Walsh McLean's insatiable greed for gaudy trinkets was not diminished by the sinister reputation of this gem, which had gone from the forehead of an Indian idol to the possession of the ill-fated Marie Antoinette to a series of unlucky owners. McLean herself remained unfazed by the tragedies that overtook her family. Her husband died mad, her daughter committed suicide, one son died in an accident at the age of eight, and another boy expired after a lengthy confinement in a sanitarium.

Evalyn Walsh McLean swept aside all misfortunes and obstacles to become the grandest of Washington's hostesses. She frequently wore the Hope Diamond, along with the Star of the East and six diamond bracelets, as personal jewelry at her parties. Although she had squandered most of her fortune by the time of her death in 1947, she had fulfilled her immigrant father's ambition to live in the grand style. As for the unlucky Irish-American diamond, no one cared to purchase it, and it was ultimately donated to the Smithsonian Institution. ◆

The
Unsinkable
Upstart

*M*argaret Tobin was born in 1867 in Hannibal, Missouri. Her father, John, was a ditchdigger for the municipal gasworks and lived in the "shanty Irish" section of town. After working in a tobacco factory and as a waitress, Maggie followed her sister and brother-in-law west to Colorado, where she became a clerk in a Leadville dry-goods store. Before long she met and married James Brown, who had great dreams of "striking it rich" in the mines. His dreams were fullfilled in the 1890s when he found gold and suddenly became a wealthy man. The Browns moved to Denver and set up housekeeping in grand style. Margaret Tobin Brown (or "Molly" Brown, as she preferred to be called) had social ambitions, but was snubbed by the leading families of Denver, who despised her lowly origins and her husband's pushy ways.

Molly found consolation for her social frustrations at home through frequent trips abroad, where her ornate costumes and display of gems were taken as typically American. She had the additional satisfaction of marrying off her sister to a German nobleman. The rough, tough manner she retained from her youth was accepted as picturesque among her European acquaintances.

In 1912 Molly Brown chose to return from a visit abroad on the great new British liner *Titanic*. When the ship struck an iceberg and lifeboats were launched, she took charge of one of them. Her dynamic, forceful personality, resilient spirit, and fierce self-confidence helped the survivors endure the shock and sorrow of that terrible night. The *Titanic* might be going down, she told the others, but she was "unsinkable." The image of the "unsinkable Molly Brown" was one of the brighter elements in the gloom surrounding the *Titanic* tragedy. Molly was hailed as a heroine by fellow survivors and became an instant celebrity.

MAY YOU LIVE AS LONG AS YOU WANT, AND NEVER WANT AS LONG AS YOU LIVE!
Traditional Irish Toast

Fame and fortune both diminished over the next twenty years. Extravagance and generosity had brought Molly near to poverty by the time of her death in 1932. A newspaper reported that "Mrs. Brown was formerly Miss Margaret Tobin, daughter of an Irish peer," thus perpetuating what was perhaps one of her own "tall tales." For a later generation, the stage and screen versions of the "Unsinkable's" career would provide yet another version of Molly's rise from the ditchdigger's shanty. ◆

Funny,
You Don't
Look Irish

BY VIVIAN CRISTOL, in *The New York Times*

For one bright year of my childhood I was pure, unadulterated Irish. Later I was to discover that the American-born Currys, Devlins, and McGoverns of my small-town Pennsylvania neighborhood qualified as more Irish than I, though I was born in Dublin, because I was Jewish, too. Evidently one diluted the other, and neither was a state of grace in that time or place. But for that shining year I was five and back with my mother in Ireland, where I belonged. I wanted to stay forever.

To an apartment-bred child, my grandparents' farm in Tullow, County Carlow, was a free, green, magical world. Never before had I tasted warm, bubbling milk or smelled sweet hay in a barn. Never had I gathered newly laid eggs or become friends with cows and a donkey.

Indoors, the big house rang with rich brogue and the girlish giggles of six aunts. Mother bloomed anew in this loving circle and I felt part of a real family at last. They taught me Irish songs and poems, gave me piano lessons, pampered and spoiled me; so did the nuns at the Brigidine Convent just down the road. The girls had all attended convent school, but Mother was the first of them to marry and I, the first exhibit. All the way from America!

I was unaware of how atypical were the music and books, or even the high German sometimes spoken in the house. Nor how instrumental this tiny flame of "Kultur" had been in drawing the parish priest and local vicar to my grandparents' table and winning them acceptance. Forgotten, now, the initial shock of actually meeting and conversing with a Jew.

NEVER TAKE A WIFE THAT HAS NO FAULTS.
Traditional Irish Proverb

Though I was loath to leave the countryside at all, mother had friends and errands in Dublin. She would show me the Georgian house on Rathmines Road where I was born. We would look for American funny-papers and pretzels, which I missed. And my paternal grandmother was waiting to meet me. I was neither her first nor only grandchild, but my father was her favorite and across the sea.

The gulf between us was palpable that day, and part of me still envies the strong ties of heritage that bound a whole community together and left us alone on the other side. This commonality was their bulwark against such apartness. It made my father feel his Jewishness all his life. But that bond of Jew to Jew had vanished for Mother and me in the Irish countryside. Vulnerable to the psychological inroads of an Ireland we loved, we fled home to Tullow.

Over the years, when I have looked back to Tullow with longing, I have wondered what prompted my grandfather to detach himself from this huddle of Jews in Dublin and solo into the hinterlands. He loved animals, they said, especially horses, and yearned for the land, but that hardly seems to tell it. There must have been other factors—educational perhaps—that differentiated him from the other Dublin "poor cousins" even then. All of them had found refuge there from Russian pogroms, or threats of pogroms, but he had bold dreams. And the enterprise to pursue them. He took himself a cultivated, Frankfurt-bred wife, brought her back, and headed south. They thrived in Tullow.

So did I. Inevitably I became increasingly, then aggressively Irish. The year was 1922, that bloody year of civil war after the treaty with England had been signed. As Irishman fought Irishman from Kilkenny, Templemore, Abbeyleix, and round to Arklow, the village of Baltinglass fell, then Tullow. For a few traumatic nights we were routed from our beds and whisked downstairs to comparative safety. Wet blankets were hung to stop stray bullets from the street. Ours was the only house in Tullow big enough to be commandeered by the Nationalists, the girls whispered excitedly among themselves. But Grandpa was too much the realist to find romance in war. In his mind's eye he envisioned his seven comely daughters amid a roistering band of soldiers, and the Jewish father in him surfaced. Within a month the family exodus to London had begun. For all of us, the idyll in Ireland was ended. ◆

"Typhoid Mary," the first typhoid carrier recognized in the United States (1906), is usually listed as Mary Mallon, a native of Ireland. It appears from later research that she was actually born in Germany.

Kennedy
Quips

Whether or not the Irish reputation for wit and charm is entirely deserved, John Fitzgerald Kennedy certainly lived up to the public's expectations. The following is a random sampling of his graceful and humorous touch in addressing mass audiences.

Presidential candidate John F. Kennedy, at a political rally in Muskegon, Michigan, September 1960: "I want to express my appreciation to the governor for introducing me as the potentially greatest president in the history of this country. I think he is overstating it by a degree or two. George Washington wasn't a bad president and I do want to say a word for Thomas Jefferson. But, otherwise, I accept the compliment."

In Salem, Oregon, September 1960, Kennedy explains why Jacqueline, his wife, who was expecting a child, has not accompanied him: "Ladies and gentlemen, I would like to introduce my sister, who is representing my wife, who is otherwise committed."

Addressing a youth rally in which many children were present, in Girard, Ohio, October 1960: "If we could only lower the voting age to nine, we'd sweep the state."

San Diego, California, November 1960, referring to the Republican "truth squad" that dogged his footsteps everywhere he went: "I see where the 'truth squad' has been ditched. They told the truth once and now they are not allowed to travel around anymore."

Speaking to the Democratic Women's Club, Queens, New York, November 1960: "I have come here to ask your help. There's an old Irish saying,

The young J.F.K. Returning home as a war hero after his dramatic experience in the Pacific, U.S. Navy Lieutenant John F. Kennedy almost immediately launched his political career. By 1946 he was a member of Congress. Soon elected to the Senate, he went on to become the youngest man ever to be elected president.

'Never send a boy to do a man's job—send a lady!' "

At the National Press Club, Washington, D.C., December 1960: "A few Catholics have criticized me because of my assurances that, as president, I would not be influenced by the Vatican. Now I can understand why Henry the Eighth set up his own church."

Addressing a farmers' cooperative meeting in Grand View, Missouri, December 1960: "How can you possibly vote Republican? I know one farmer who planted corn last year, and then said to his neighbor, 'I hope I break even this time—I really need the money.' "

Presidential comment at a White House function, January 1961, honoring his new administration appointees: "The reason for this reception is my desire to see some of the names I have been reading about in the newspapers."

Kennedy, joking at a dinner given by Jacqueline at the White House, May 27, 1961, in honor of his forty-fourth birthday: "When we got into office, the one thing that surprised me most was to find that things were just as bad as we'd been saying they were."

When Arthur Hays Sulzberger, chairman of the board of *The New York Times,* purchased a new rocking chair, he received this note from President Kennedy, dated May 1, 1961: "You will recall what Senator Dirksen said about the rocking chair—it gives you a sense of motion without any sense of danger."

At a private dinner among friends at the White House, January 1962: "There is no city in the United States in which I get a warmer reception and less votes than Columbus, Ohio."

Replying to the suggestion that his brother, Attorney General Robert Kennedy, would make a fine president: "I have consulted Bobby about it and, to my dismay, the idea appeals to him."

Shortly after his election as president of the United States, Kennedy sent his education bill to Congress without mention of federal aid to parochial schools. Alluding to Catholic criticism, he joked: "As you all know, some circles invented the myth that after Al Smith's defeat in 1928, he sent a one-word telegram to the Pope: 'Unpack!' After my press conference on the school bill, I received a one-word wire from the Pope: 'Pack!' "

BEAUTY WON'T MAKE THE POT BOIL. *Traditional Irish Proverb*

Addressing the faculty and student body at the University of California at Berkeley, March 1962: "This has been a week of momentous events around the world. The long and painful struggle in Algeria came to an end. Both nuclear powers and neutrals labored in Geneva for a solution to the problem of a spiraling arms race, and also to the problems that so

vex our relations with the Soviet Union. The Congress opened hearings on a trade bill, which is far more than a trade bill, but an opportunity to build a stronger and closer Atlantic community. And my wife had her first and last ride on an elephant."

In April 1962, having just been named an honorary chief of an Indian tribe in Wisconsin, President Kennedy donned the feather headdress and proclaimed to his Indian audience: "The next time I see cowboys and Indians at the movies, I'll be with us!"

At the famous White House dinner honoring Nobel Prize winners: "I think this is the most extraordinary collection of talent, of human knowledge, that has ever been gathered together at the White House—with the possible exception of when Thomas Jefferson dined alone."

'TIS ON HER OWN
ACCOUNT THE CAT
PURRS.
*Traditional Irish
Proverb*

Speaking at a fund-raising banquet at the Mayflower Hotel in Washington, D.C., June 1962, in honor of Matthew McCloskey, who had just been appointed ambassador to Ireland: "I commend this idea of a $250 dinner. This is like the story of the award of prizes by the Moscow Cultural Center, the first prize being one week in Kiev and the second prize being two weeks. For $100 you get speeches; for $250 you don't get any speeches. You can't get bargains like that anymore!"

To Press Secretary Pierre Salinger, November 1962: "Karl Marx wrote for the *Herald Tribune,* but that is not why I canceled my subscription."

Referring to the thin-skinned sensitivity of his vice president, Lyndon B. Johnson, during a White House staff meeting, December 1962:

"Writing a birthday note to Lyndon is like drafting a state document."

President Kennedy, while visiting Cork, Ireland, in June 1963, introduced his friend and traveling companion: "And now I would like to introduce to you the pastor at the church I go to. He comes from right here in Cork—Monsignor O'Mohoney. He is the pastor of a poor, humble flock in Palm Beach, Florida."

In Galway, Ireland, June 1963, the president invited his audience to the White House: "If you ever come to America, come to Washington and tell them, at the gate, that you come from Galway. The word will be out —it will be *Cead mille failte*" ["a hundred thousand welcomes," in Gaelic].

New Ross, Ireland, June 1963: "Some years ago, an Irishman from New Ross traveled to Washington. In order to let his neighbors know how well he was doing, he had his picture taken in front of the White House. On the back of the picture, he wrote, 'This is my summer home. Come and see it.'"

In Duganstown, Ireland, June 1963, at an elegant buffet prepared in President Kennedy's honor by his third cousin, Mary Ryan: "I want to thank all of those who prepared this. It was a great effort on their part. We can promise that we will come only once every ten years."

Wexford, Ireland, June 1963: "Ladies and gentlemen, I don't want to give the impression that every member of my administration in Washington is Irish. It just seems that way. But now let me introduce the head of the American Labor movement, whose mother and father were born

President John F. Kennedy confers with Attorney General Robert F. Kennedy. The lives and deaths of these two brothers constituted a story of triumph and tragedy that had a special poignancy for Irish Americans.

241

Joseph P. Kennedy, Sr., the patriarch of the Kennedy clan, celebrates his birthday amid his grandchildren. During the 1980s several of these youngsters carried on the family tradition by launching their own political careers.

right here in Ireland—George Meany, who is traveling with us. And I would like you to meet the only man with us who doesn't have a drop of Irish blood in his veins, but who is dying to—the head of protocol of the United States, Angier Biddle Duke."

Dublin, Ireland, June 1963: "When my great-grandfather left here to become a cooper in East Boston, he carried nothing with him except two things: a strong religious faith and a strong desire for liberty. And I am glad to say that all of his great-grandchildren have valued that inheritance. If he hadn't left, I'd be working over here at the Albatross Company." ◆

*T*he Boston Irish pride themselves on remaining true to their traditions. Not surprisingly, the two most promising political figures to
emerge from their ranks in the 1980s have blended the rhetoric of change
with the assurance of continuity.

Joseph P. Kennedy II conveys continuity in his very name and face.
He is a member of the dynasty: grandson of the political patriarch who
orchestrated his family's rise to power, nephew of the martyred president and son of the martyred senator, nephew of Massachusetts's current
senior senator. Almost foreordained to a political career, he laid the
groundwork during his twenties by establishing and directing a successful "citizen's energy" enterprise in the Boston area, and then, in 1986,
announced his candidacy in the Eighth Congressional District. This was
the seat formerly occupied by his uncle John Fitzgerald Kennedy, and
subsequently by House Speaker Thomas "Tip" O'Neill. To many loyalists, it seemed almost indecent to deny the aspirations of the new Kennedy, and—despite a hotly contested Democratic primary—he won the
seat handily in November.

Yet "Young Joe" knew it was not enough to rely on the magic of his
name. Running in Maryland, where she had no political roots, his sister
Kathleen was defeated in that November 1986 Congressional election. It
was in presumably "safe" Charlestown that his uncle Edward Kennedy
had been bombarded with tomatoes and rotten eggs by a predominantly
Irish crowd when he spoke in favor of school busing a few years earlier.
Joe understood that his constituents feared radical change and resented
interference with their accustomed patterns of life. The candidate
pledged to fight for "the poor, the elderly, and ordinary working-class
families" while criticizing programs that "maintained people in poverty," denouncing abortion, and supporting the death penalty. Clearly,
the rampant liberalism associated with his uncle Ted would not serve
Joe's interests in neighborhoods like Allston, Brighton, and—above all—
Charlestown, and tailored his campaign to fit the conservative tastes of
working-class Irish voters.

Raymond Flynn was elected mayor of Boston in 1983, latest in a long
line of Irish occupants of City Hall that included John "Honey Fitz"

Fitzgerald (Joe Kennedy's great-grandfather), the picturesque James Michael Curley, and the sorely tried Kevin White, whose tenure had been marked by fiscal woes and racial violence. Within a short while Flynn began to achieve national recognition as a constructive and healing administrator and polls showed an unprecedented 75 percent approval rate of his performance. Here, surely, was a new type of mayor, with new ideas about how to handle the needs of the city. It might be so, but Flynn, too, was aware of the need to emphasize his roots, to appeal to the Boston Irish love of tradition.

"My grandparents were born in Galway and Cork, my parents were born here," he told an interviewer. As he was growing up in the same house as his grandparents, "the Irish heritage and culture were a major part" of his upbringing, particularly as related to traditions and family values." More specifically, Flynn continued, "I learned, at a very early age, the great traditions of the Irish people, the values of hard work, and a deep sense of commitment to Church, family, community, and country. Those values have had a profound meaning and impact on me through the years. Those values have helped me in my job as mayor of a major American city."

Flynn has also laid great emphasis on his South Boston working-class background, one which he shares with his wife. Both their fathers were longshoremen; his mother was a cleaning woman; the work ethic that they imparted to their children, he insists, is one that must be passed on to the next generation. He assured his interviewer, too, of his intense Catholicism, stressing his admiration for the Church's post-Vatican advocacy of tolerance and social justice.

Flynn cannot claim the dynastic ties that benefit Joseph Kennedy in his political career. Instead, he identifies himself with the icons and self-congratulations. The indubitably corrupt James Michael Curley has been praised by his successor as a misunderstood and persecuted figure. The late Richard Cardinal Cushing was, for Flynn, "one of the greatest religious leaders who ever walked the face of this earth." The late Speaker of the House John W. McCormack is honored by Flynn as a champion of the oppressed. The Irish of South Boston, far from being the racists that their anti-integration violence might suggest, are, Flynn has insisted, friends of the underprivileged because they knew discrimination in their own past.

Keeping alive the tradition of Boston Irish support for the national cause in the Old Country, Flynn has spoken out and written (far more frequently and vigorously than Kennedy) on the troubles of Northern Ireland. Indeed, he has won that badge of distinction for a Boston politician, a personal denunciation from the British government.

Both Joseph Kennedy and Raymond Flynn have been astute enough in the launching of their political careers to maintain that balance of change and continuity in their public discourse that is still essential to success in Boston. Among the Irish there, a generalized liberalism and a localized conservatism is still the winning combination. The setting remains the familiar one established generations ago. But the urban revolution that has come to such strongholds of Irish power as New York and Chicago seems destined to come to Boston in its turn. The Irish may cling to South Boston, refusing to retreat to the suburbs, but can they cling much longer to City Hall? And what of the future of these two Boston-based Irishmen?

Flynn and Kennedy are very different types, both personally and in terms of their origin within the Irish-American social structure. The mayor speaks politely of the Kennedys and says that working-class Irish people admire rather than resent the success of such superachievers. Nonetheless, there is an inevitable tension between proletarian and lace-curtain aristocrat that may someday emerge in a direct rivalry. Both men have been suggested as future candidates for the governorship or for the U.S. Senate. It will be interesting to see how their respective links to the Boston Irish survive such a competition. Boston is the essential base for any expansion of Flynn's activities. For Kennedy, the Eighth District is merely the most convenient starting point for a potential bid for the White House. If Kennedy neglects his local supporters once he establishes himself in Washington, he may find his plans thwarted. If Flynn, on the other hand, remains too parochial in his allegiances, he may never progress beyond the mayoralty.

In the meantime, it is worth remembering that the dynamic black politician Mel King, after losing to Flynn in 1983, returned to the fray in 1986 to challenge Kennedy in the Democratic primary. Although he was again defeated, his campaign and his voter support were even more impressive than they had been three years earlier. The wave of the future may be one that completely alters the familiar setting of Boston politics and introduces new faces of a very different kind. ◆

NEAREST THE HEART COMES FIRST OUT.
Traditional Irish Proverb

A Ford in
Their Future

When Henry Ford, Sr., visited the city of Cork in the early 1920s, he was coming home. His father, William, had emigrated from a nearby village seventy years earlier. His visit coincided with the opening there of the first Ford Motor Company plant outside of the United States.

A delegation from the Hospital Building Fund called on him at his hotel, and he pledged £5,000. The next morning, the local paper headlined: HENRY FORD GIVES £10,000 TO HOSPITAL. The delegates soon returned with profuse apologies for the "error." They offered to have a new headline inserted: HENRY FORD DID NOT GIVE £10,000 TO HOSPITAL. Ford smiled wryly and said that he would make it £10,000 after all, if he could specify a biblical quotation to be inscribed on the hospital.

"Certainly," said the delegate. "What is it?" He responded: "I came among mine own—and they took me in." ◆

THE IRISH-AMERICAN RICH
(IN APPROXIMATE ORDER OF WEALTH)

Ford family, Detroit, Michigan—Ford Motor Co. and Ford Foundation

Mellon family, original base, Pittsburgh, Pennsylvania—oil, banking, aluminum, industrial equipment

Kennedy family, Boston, Massachusetts and New York, New York—real estate, diversified stock and bond holdings

Scully family, Lincoln, Illinois—farming and real estate in Illinois, Nebraska, and Kansas

O'Connor family, Victoria, Texas—ranching, oil, banking

Brady family, Far Hills, New Jersey—investment banking and family holding company

Leo Corrigan, Jr., Dallas, Texas—real estate, hotels, and shopping centers

Edwin L. Cox, Dallas, Texas—oil production

Edward J. Daly, Oakland, California—airline industry

Edward M. Carey, New York, New York—energy resources

John F. Connelly, Philadelphia, Pennsylvania—packaging products

Thomas J. Flatley, Boston, Massachusetts—real estate development

Patrick E. Haggerty, Dallas, Texas—industrial technology

John H. McConnell, Worthington, Ohio—steel processing

Bernard P. McDonough, Parkersburg, West Virginia—merchandising

Patrick McGovern, Waltham, Massachusetts—computer technology

C. H. Murphy, Jr., El Dorado, Arkansas—oil production

William O'Donnell, Chicago, Illinois—game machine manufacturing, real estate

GENTLEMEN OUR COUNTRY.

HENRY FORD. AND HIS FIRST CAR.

Henry Ford, shown here in his first automobile, was the father of America's greatest industry and founder of what is still one of its "Big Three" companies. His father left County Cork during the Famine Era, and the company opened a branch factory in that part of Ireland some seventy years later.

Alfred E. Smith, wearing his famous brown derby, sets off on a holiday outing, amid family and friends.

CONEY ISLAND
EXPRESS

6

Culture

U.S. PRESIDENTS OF IRISH ORIGIN (DIRECT PATERNAL LINE)

Andrew Jackson, son of Andrew Jackson, who emigrated from County Antrim to South Carolina in 1765.

James Polk, great-great-grandson of William Polk, who emigrated from County Donegal to Maryland in 1690.

James Buchanan, son of James Buchanan, who emigrated from County Donegal to Pennsylvania in 1783.

Chester Arthur, son of William Arthur, who emigrated from County Antrim to New York in 1815.

William McKinley, grandson of James McKinley, who emigrated from County Antrim to Pennsylvania in 1800.

Thomas Woodrow Wilson, grandson of James Wilson, who emigrated from County Antrim (via Scotland) to Virginia in 1807.

John Fitzgerald Kennedy, great-grandson of Patrick Kennedy, who emigrated from County Wexford to Massachusetts in 1848.

Richard Nixon, great-great-great-great-grandson of James Nixon, who emigrated from County Kildare to Delaware in 1705.

Ronald Reagan, great-grandson of Michael Reagan, who emigrated from County Tipperary (via England) to New York in 1853.

This certificate of membership in the Hibernian Society of Philadelphia demonstrates that President Andrew Jackson was proud to acknowledge his Irish parentage. He was also aware that, by the 1830s, the "Irish vote" was worth cultivating.

Foreigners
No More

To call the members of the Hibernian race foreigners would be an anomaly, as they are an integral part of Americanism. The Irish have become an integral part of us, and even those of us who may be descended from the passengers of the *Mayflower* can hardly look upon them as foreigners. Once here, the Irish have bound us so closely to that little isle whence they came that we can no longer look upon Ireland as a foreign country. . . . Everyone in the United States knows that the "Old Country" can refer only to the Emerald Isle, and every American audience of non-Hibernian extraction is familiar with Irish songs and allusions to Ireland. It has become a very part of us. We feel that, after the United States, Ireland is the country in which we take the most interest. This very remarkable psychological state is due entirely to the Irishman's wonderfully passionate patriotism. . . . But the Irishman's love for his old home has never made him relegate America to a second place.

—editorial in the Brooklyn *Eagle*
(1916)

◆

The Fenian Congress in session at Philadelphia, in November 1865. With the end of the Civil War in the United States, the Fenians were preparing to form their thousands of members among the Union Army veterans into an army for the invasion of Canada.

Resolution
Passed by
Fenian
Congress at
Chicago,
November
1863

*W*hereas, it has been proved to the Fenian Brotherhood, not alone through the authorized reports of the Head Centre, but also through the forced acknowledgements conveyed in certain recent denunciations emanating from the enemies of the Irish race, that there exists among the men of Ireland a numerous and widely extended national organization, which was heretofore named The Irish Revolutionary Brotherhood, but which, having grown in numbers and power, in subordination to its constituent authorities, and in discipline under the wise and able directions of its central executive, is now known as the Irish Republic, be it resolved—

That we, the centres and delegates of the Fenian Brotherhood, assembled in this convention, do hereby proclaim the Republic of Ireland to be virtually established, and moreover that we pledge ourselves to use all in our influence, and every legitimate privilege within our reach, to promote the full acknowledgement of its independence by every free government in the world. ◆

Three military leaders of the Fenian Brotherhood, photographed on the eve of their invasion of Canada in 1866. General William Sweeny, the "minister of the war" of the Irish republic that had been proclaimed in exile a few years earlier, is accompanied by General Spear and Colonel Mechan.

An Editorial Statement

FROM *THE SHAMROCK,*
NEW YORK, DECEMBER 15, 1810

*O*ur paper, freed from party bickerings and partial details, shall, on the whole, be a general recorder of noteworthy news, and, particularly as it respects Ireland, a literary and historical panorama of passing events. . . .

It is our wish, and shall be our editorial study, to unite Americans and Irishmen by a bond of friendly intercourse and political amity, having for its object the general good. Gratitude, the first of all moral virtues, will always trace the conduct to be pursued by the Irishman and convince him how conscientiously he should discharge the debt he owes to the nation which, throwing open to him all the advantages of being free in the midst of freedom, offers the greatest encouragement and reward for any employment of art or essay of genius.

As to native Americans, we shall endeavour to impress the political strength and general advantages derivable to them from the residence of a people who, instilled with a love of liberty triumphing even over their constitutional love of country, would separate themselves from their green fields, their health-bestowing climate, and their best friends, to seek an association and residence with a people whom they knew but by character, and in a country of which they knew still less. The characteristic hospitality of the Irishman receives, in his own country, an additional impulse when exercised towards the visiting American. A corresponding sentiment should ever warm the heart of the American at home . . . from this reciprocation of friendship and good offices, we confidently anticipate the happy result of harmony and cooperation. . . .

On the general subject of national allegiance, it is not our province to descant further than to say that every inhabitant owes allegiance to the government by which he is protected during his residence under the same. If he is a sojourner or an alien, every political interference not warranted or required by the Law is presumptuous and improper; if naturalized, the country of his adoption, by conferring a new favour, acquires a new and indispensable right to every aid that his talent or enterprise, his head, his hand, and his heart can contribute to the protection of his adopted country. . . . ◆

WHERE THE TONGUE SLIPS, IT SPEAKS THE TRUTH.
Traditional Irish Proverb

*J*ohn Louis O'Sullivan (1813–1895) was descended from three generations of Irish soldiers of fortune and adventurers, and in his own life exhibited the restless energy of his heritage in a highly volatile environment—Jacksonian America. As editor of the *United States Magazine and Democratic Review* (1837–1845) he championed the optimistic and expansionistic causes of the era, and coined the famous term *manifest destiny* to describe the God-given mission of the United States to rule all of North America—or perhaps the whole Western Hemisphere. He later put his theories into practice by taking part in an unsuccessful expedition to conquer Cuba. As a New York State assemblyman in the 1840s he championed liberal (and often unpopular) causes such as public welfare programs and abolition of the death penalty. As minister to Portugal from 1854 to 1858 (he was the first Irish American to hold a major diplomatic post), he drew the United States into a number of international disputes through his activism. Although less involved in public affairs after the Civil War, he reentered the limelight in 1886 when, nearly eighty years old, he made a lengthy oration in French at the dedication of the Statue of Liberty to thank France for its gift. By then O'Sullivan had become a relic of a more flamboyant era when Americans, including immigrants, had believed all things were possible in this brave new world. ◆

MAY YOU DIE IN BED AT NINETY-FIVE YEARS, SHOT BY A JEALOUS HUSBAND (OR WIFE).
Traditional Irish Toast

Three Cheers for Democracy!

The Irish were long regarded as the most committed adherents of the Democratic party. In the party's formative years, some of their number lent ideological brainpower as well as practical muscle power to the Jacksonian cause. The following extracts on "The Democratic Principle" are from the first issue of the United States Magazine and Democratic Review *(October 1837). They are from the pen of its editor, John L. O'Sullivan, who shared the radicalism of many educated Irish immigrants. Men like O'Sullivan hoped to preserve America from the aristocratic system that had stifled the common people in the Old World.*

We believe, then, in the principle of democratic republicanism, in its strongest and purest sense. We have an abiding confidence in the virtue, intelligence, and full capacity for self-government, of the great mass of our people—our industrious, honest, manly, intelligent millions of freemen.

. . . For Democracy is the cause of Humanity. It has faith in human nature. It believes in its essential equality and fundamental goodness. It respects, with a solemn reverence to which the proudest artificial institutions and distinctions of society have no claim, the human soul. It is the cause of philanthropy. Its object is to emancipate the mind of the mass of men from the degrading and disheartening fetters of social distinction and advantages; to bid it walk abroad through the free creation "in its own majesty"; to war against all fraud, oppression, and violence; by striking at their root, to reform all the infinitely varied human misery which has grown out of the old and false ideas by which the world has been so long misgoverned; to dismiss the hireling soldier; to spike the cannon, and bury the bayonet; to burn the gibbet, and open the debtor's dungeon; to substitute harmony and mutual respect for the jealousies and discord now subsisting between different classes of society, as the

HE WHO IS BAD AT
GIVING LODGINGS
IS GOOD AT
SHOWING THE WAY.
*Traditional Irish
Proverb*

consequence of their artificial classification. It is the cause of Christianity, to which a slight allusion has been already made. . . . And that portion of the peculiar friends and ministers of religion who now, we regret to say, cast the weight of their social influence against the cause of democracy, under the false prejudice of an affinity between it and infidelity (no longer, in this century, the case, and which, in the last, was but a consequence of the overgrown abuses of religion found, by the reforming spirit that then awakened in Europe, in league with despotism), understand but little either its true spirit, or that of their own faith.

It is, moreover, a cheerful creed, a creed of high hope and universal love, noble and ennobling; while all others, which imply a distrust of mankind and of the natural moral principles infused into it by its Creator, for its own self-development and self-regulation, are as gloomy and selfish, in the tone of moral sentiment which pervades them, as they are degrading in their practical tendency, and absurd in theory, when examined by the light of original principles. . . . ◆

I implore you to discard forever those foolish —those insensate quarrels —those factious broils (too often, alas, the fruits of intemperance) in which our country is disgraced, the peace and order of society violated, and the laws of heaven trampled and outraged.

Father Theobald Mathew, quoted in the *New York Tribune* (1851)

When the Irish
Vote Counted

During the New York mayoral election of 1867, Horace Greeley's Republican newspaper, the Tribune, *attempted to shake the Irish commitment to the Democrats with editorial rhetoric.*

The nomination of Fernando Wood and Mr. Hoffman, neither of whom has a drop of Irish blood in his veins, for Mayor of a city, three fourths of whose Democratic voters are Irish, is an insult to the honor of the Old Sod which every true Irish Democrat will avenge, if he is not lost to all sense of the glory of the land that bore him. . . . Awake, slumbering sons of old Ireland, and give such a demonstration of your affection for the Irish name and blood as will command the reverence of those miscreants. . . . Why not elect an Irish Mayor, on an exclusively Irish ticket? Irishmen, stand up for your rights and the Mayoralty is yours. Nominate an Irishman, elect an Irishman, and then, when you call upon him in the City Hall, you've got an Irish Mayor as sure as there's never a snake or toad in Ireland. ◆

"THE EDITOR'S EASY CHAIR,"
HARPER'S NEW MONTHLY MAGAZINE, JULY 1872

Is there any nationality which has become so entirely a passionate romantic sentiment as the Irish? The largest halls will be crowded by the most rapt and enthusiastic audience to hear a fervid orator denounce the invader and despoiler, and prophesy that from her ruins and her desolation Erin will rise again triumphant. It is a faith even more actual and intense than that of the Israelites in their restoration. Traditionally they wait with their hearts turned toward Zion and the Holy City. One day, they say, all the tribes will be gathered again, and the chosen people shall be supreme. But they make no raids upon Palestine. They throw no banners to the breeze at the Hebrew headquarters in foreign cities. They do not march annually in solemn procession and shake metaphorical fists at abstract tyrants, and kindle with tearful enthusiasm as the legends of Tara and the Druidical hill, of Patrick and the monasteries, are fondly repeated.

That story of the royal residence upon the hill of Tara; the pavilion here, the summer palace there; the proud coronation of Brian Boru as king of united Ireland; the coming of Patrick, saint of the sunny life; the declaration of the Druids that he spake truth; the prostration of the queen in recognition of his Divine mission—all this imposing tale, recited a hundred times in every form of rhetoric, is as familiar to every Irishman as the news of the morning to the diligent reader. There is no spectacle more interesting than that of the Irish throng hanging upon the words of an Irish orator as he tells the old tale. They are all sure that Ireland was once the calm seat of a lofty civilization, the chosen land of religion, the mother of arts and learning. Soft and fair were the fields of their native land; stately and beautiful the temples that a pure faith builded; peaceful, frugal, and industrious the people that tilled the fertile soil, and whose voices filled the air with the sound of prayers and hymns of adoration.

As the impassioned orator proceeds, the picture becomes more vivid and alluring. The sympathetic crowd behold with fascination. If the speaker be a priest, still more a friar in the garb of his order, most of all if he be a Dominican or a Franciscan, whose ministry first combined in theory the virtues of the cloister with those of society, how profound is the attention! All lands dwindle before the historic reality of Ireland, which they hear described, and what nation to-day rivals that ideal nation which was old when Rome was new—the nation to which they belong!

"It is my land," fervently exclaims the orator, "my native land! I am born of that race, so intensely peculiar—one of the master races of the world! My fathers, your fathers, were the spiritual children of Saint Patrick. It is our faith that has maintained our nationality. Often all has perished but that; but while that remains Irish nationality is indestructible. Of all nations the most Christian at its first conversion, the most Christian still. For what were the three chief characteristics of the founder of our religion but poverty, chastity, and obedience? These were the vows of the monastic orders. By these the Christian character was most fully developed. And these are the characteristics of my countrymen to-day!"

WHERE THERE'S
LOVE, THERE'S
ENOUGH.
*Traditional Irish
Proverb*

Not the sanctity of the temple restrains the applause. That eager multitude, hard-working men and women, of little education, sit or unconsciously rise as they listen, and revenge themselves upon the cruelty of fact by delight in that illimitable fancy. Yet the orator has few charms, and little real eloquence. His voice, indeed, is full and manly, but it has little music, nor is his action graceful, nor is his oration lit with imagination. But he certainly gives you a fresh impression of the intensity of the Irish national feeling. "The Danish invaders found as they landed on Irish soil what I wish every other invader had found—a grave." They are not startling words from an Irishman to Irishmen; but they are strange to hear from one calling himself a Christian minister standing before a Christian altar. Yet they are spoken with a feeling which seems the more sincere when he adds, "I preach no rebellion, nor do I pretend to hate Englishmen, among whom I have true and beloved friends."

That remark showed how purely a sentiment the Irish nationality has become. It has virtually ceased to be a cause. For the raids which they make are of small proportions and upon a distant soil, and the headquarters from which banners are flung to the breeze are far, very far, from the hill of Tara. The splendors of a civilization all traces of which have perished, the docile innocence of primitive people which the ardent imagination can readily picture, a universal goodness and power and supremacy and happiness which nobody can disprove more than he can prove, all lift the argument into the realm of twilight and shadows and romance. If there were a great civilization here, did it not perish in conflict with a greater? In the course of history do the more powerful influences succumb to the weaker? If, as the orator declares, it is his Church which has maintained the nationality of Ireland, how has it maintained it? Has it made the people intelligent and prosperous? Has it freed them from superstition, and broken all spiritual shackles? Has it taught them the arts of industry, and preached peace and good-will? It has been wickedly persecuted, no student will deny; but did it never persecute? The power of its priesthood has been almost absolute. But responsibility is commensurate with power. How has it discharged that responsibility in elevating its people?

These are the questions that follow in the mind on many a hearer the sad words of the orator. "The greatness of my country is seen in her ruins," he says, with a feeling to which the sensitive heart of the audience thrills in response. But what are those ruins? Are they buildings only? Are they only the round towers, the cromlechs, and the mossy stones of fallen monasteries? What constitutes a state, O fervent father? And what is that which, while it remains, may smile at all other ruins? If you ask us to see Ireland in its ruins, we may look and discover warmth of feeling, generosity, genius, the qualities of a historic race; but we shall look for them elsewhere than on the hill of the druids or among the foundations of Armagh.

As he ends, the orator turns toward the altar for a moment; then, putting his hand under his Dominican robe, he descends the steps and disappears from the church. The organ fills the air with the pathetic melody which Moore's song has made familiar:

> "The Harp that once through Tara's halls
> The soul of music shed."

The audience, delighted for an hour and a half, rises and pours out at the doors, every one prouder that he comes of a nation which built the round towers, and which furnished the most learned scholars of the Middle Ages. It has not been a discourse which rooted them faster in the land which they have chosen for a home and for their children's country. Its moral is twofold: First, that the English invaded Ireland, sought to obliterate its nationality by every monstrous means, and are the authors of its long misery, and second, that the nationality will endure only so long as the dominant form of religious faith in Ireland remains unchanged. But the cultivation of an aimless traditional hatred is certainly worse than useless, and mere sentimental passion is fatal to vigorous character.

It would be well if orators who come to us from abroad would remember that any appeal to any part of the population of this country which tends to destroy its homogeneity is a little impertinent. The condition of the true power and permanence of the American nation is assimilation, not aggregation. A great nationality will spring from intimate union and transfusion, not from patching and confederating. The instinct of union is not partisan or local, it points to the necessary law of national existence and development. Real union is delayed and a genuine nationality is impossible so long as we rally in different clans with no common

In our personal experience we are familiar with the most ignorant and unfortunate of the Irish nation. We see, in servile employments, those who have been exposed to all the debasing influences that degrade mankind. Is it fair to draw from these a standard by which to judge a whole people?

Samuel G. Goodrich, *Ireland and the Irish* (1841)

261

*The Irish
working man:
we do not know
what we should
do without him;
we do not know
what we shall do
with him.*

Notes of a New
Englander (1855)

slogan. In other days, when an American traveler entered his name upon the book of a hotel by some Italian lake, or far up a Swiss valley, as from Virginia or Texas, the little fact had a significance which really involved civil war. Akin to the feeling which made that entry is the division of American citizens by the name of other countries, and the appeal sometimes made in politics to this vote or to that vote. How will the Germans go? How will the Irish vote? are questions which really imply that they are not Americans, and therefore ought not to vote at all.

The audience which the fervid orator of whom we have been speaking addressed was an American audience. It was, indeed, largely composed of citizens who were born in Ireland, or who were descended from an Irish ancestor. But if the hearer waited to hear them exhorted to reproduce in their chosen new country the virtues which the orator described as distinguishing their ancestors in the old, he listened in vain. They were told of the isle of saints, of the scholars, of the seats of learning full of men devoted to temperance and all the virtues. But let the hearer remember what the orator forgot to say—that the same virtues and the same education and intelligence would make their new country greater than their old. They were told that their form of religious faith had preserved their nationality. But let them not forget that they have changed their nationality, and that here all forms of religious faith are equal. Messieurs, the orators may cry *resurgam*, and prophesy the restoration of the grandeur and the glory of Tara and of Armagh. But what then? We are Americans.   ◆

*O*atrick Jerome Gleason (1844–1901) was born in Tipperary and emigrated to America at the age of eighteen. Much of the next ten years were spent in Brooklyn as a distillery worker, saloonkeeper, and dabbler in local politics. After an unsuccessful run for the assembly, he decided to try his luck in California. By 1874 he had done so well in business and stock speculation on the West Coast that he was able to return home and purchase a trolley line in Long Island City.

Encompassing the northwest corner of Long Island, the newly incorporated municipality was a major point of commuter and commercial contact between New York and its still largely rural hinterland. As Gleason gradually expanded and improved his network of horse-drawn trolleys, he became a wealthy and influential member of the community. In 1881 he was elected, as a Democrat, to the Board of Aldermen, representing the predominantly Irish First Ward. His colleagues soon elected him board president. By 1886 he had become mayor of Long Island City.

A muscular six-foot-three, sporting a huge handlebar mustache and a leonine head of hair, Gleason was a striking figure, and he soon earned the attention of the New York press for the pugnacity that matched his formidable appearance. The mayor's short temper led him to use his fists, at various times, on rival politicians, trolley-line employees, and even ordinary citizens. Only his assault on a reporter (a fellow Celt named Crowley) got him in trouble, however: he spent five days in jail for it in 1890, during his second term.

It was his clashes with big business, though, that won Gleason his greatest notoriety, as well as the nickname "Battle Ax." His principal target was the Long Island Rail Road, whose encroachments upon residential areas had aroused much resentment among "the lower orders." On several occasions, Gleason and his supporters used axes to knock down fences and smash sheds belonging to the railroad, and the delighted New York newspapers promptly dubbed the picturesque Irishman "Battle Ax" and printed frequent accounts of his exploits. The mayor also led police raids on slaughterhouses and factories that were polluting the environment and even clashed with the Catholic hierarchy over the expansion of Calvary Cemetery at the expense of open fields.

THE JEWEL MOST RARE IS THE JEWEL MOST FAIR.
Traditional Irish Proverb

Gleason's campaign for a second three-year term was carried on with characteristic bravado: preceded by a bugler, he drove about the city behind his "matched pair," Gladstone and Parnell, scattering pennies to children. But those same children, in school, had been given campaign posters to put up, and their teachers had been threatened with dismissal if they (mostly union franchised women) did not "deliver" the votes of their male relatives. Gleason won by a majority of 331 out of 5,441 ballots cast.

Between 1889 and 1892, Gleason created his most durable monument, the First Ward School. No doubt his faithful Irish-American supporters deserved better facilities for their children, who were attending classes in warehouse, converted tenements, and abandoned buildings. But the massive structure, built at an estimated cost of $300,000 (then an astronomical sum) raised charges of graft and corruption. Gleason was accused of running a political machine and abusing public funds. Denounced for selling his own land to the city for an undisclosed sum, he was also accused of purchasing a used fire engine for $20 and selling it to the municipality for $2,200. The files recording these and other transactions were carried off by Gleason when he left office.

Indeed, the mayor himself was carried out of City Hall in 1892. Defeated for reelection in a close race, he refused to concede and actually had the city clerk certify that he had won. A state court ruled otherwise, however, and Gleason, whose girth had grown to match his height, was carried down the front steps, still protesting, by a squad of policemen, amid the jeers and groans of his loyal Irish constituents.

Running as an independent in 1895, Gleason split the Irish vote and defeated the regular Democrat, John Madden, though he won by only 30 votes. This last tenure of office was marked by new charges of fraud from his disgruntled opponents and a bitter court case over whether Gleason had ever actually been naturalized. The most dramatic development, however, was the decision by Queens County's citizens to merge with New York City. Far from being disconcerted by this prospect, Battle Ax announced in the summer of 1897 that he would be a candidate for mayor of the new, "Greater" New York. He launched his campaign by hosting a huge picnic for 14,000 constituents. They were carried on a fleet of ten excursion boats to Yonkers, where they feasted on 600 gallons of ice cream, 3,600 bottles of soda, and other goodies in proportion, while brass bands serenaded them with his marching song, "Battle Ax," and other rousing tunes. It was all in vain. The election went to Robert Van Wyck, the annexation of Long Island City proceeded on schedule, and on January 1, 1898, Patrick Gleason was once again a private citizen.

This time there would be no comeback for Battle Ax. His financial affairs (perhaps overstrained by campaign expenditures) were in disarray; in 1899 he filed a petition for bankruptcy. Beset by political and business reverses, he died of a heart attack at the age fifty-seven. ◆

When New York's Tammany regime was in full fever, at the turn of the century, Chicago Irish politics was still in the Dark Ages. As one commentator put it, instead of a centralized monarchy, the Chicagoans had a collection of clans, each one jealously guarding its own domain. But this late blooming was a result of the city's relative newness. Once the Irish got their act together, they put on quite a show—a show that ran long after Irish rule in New York was only a memory.

The Irish were a numerous and influential element in the Windy City's politics by the early 1900s, when powerful aldermen like Michael "Hinky Dink" Kenna and Johnny Powers ran their wards like personal fiefdoms (Powers controlled his district for more than thirty years). But it was not until the election of a distinctly non-Irish mayor, Anton J. Cermak, in 1931, that a structure began to emerge in Chicago. Cermak built an elaborate patronage system that linked the wards to City Hall as they had never been linked before. His successors built a full-fledged "machine" upon this foundation after Cermak was assassinated while riding at President Roosevelt's side in 1933. Mayors Edward J. Kelly and Martin J. Kennelly superimposed the Irish political tradition upon this new organizational structure, to create the apparatus inherited and perfected by Richard J. Daley.

Daley grew up in the Irish working-class neighborhood of Bridgeport on Chicago's South Side, and derived both his hard-core political support and his personal emotional strength from his roots in this Irish community. As he rose to the mayoralty in the 1950s, Daley maintained an ethnic focus that continued throughout the twenty years of his dominance. He interwove the city and county machine with the state, and even the national functioning of the Democratic party, so that, of necessity, he had to maintain ties with Poles, Italians, and even—"in their place"—blacks. But the nucleus of his regime throughout was Irish. Indeed, the common saying was that "Chicago is owned by the Jews, lived in by the blacks, and run by the Irish."

To be sure, the system of patronage through which Daley's Chicago was run rested upon certain principles of universal validity that transcended parochial bounds. As quoted by the political analyst Milton Ra-

It is not surprising that the Irish are ignorant, and, as a consequence thereof, are idle, shiftless, poor, intemperate, and barbarian. Of course they would violate our laws, these wild bison, leaping over the fences which easily restrain the civilized domestic cattle, will commit great crimes of violence, even capital offences, which certainly have increased rapidly of late.

Theodore Parker, *A Sermon on the Moral Condition of Boston* (1850)

kove in his studies of the machine, these principles included "Don't make no waves," "Don't back no losers," and, above all, the rule in filling jobs: "We don't want nobody nobody sent." Still, there was clearly a pecking order—determined by the zeal their leaders had shown in delivering the neighborhood's vote—both in the allocation of municipal employment and in the delivery of municipal services. That pecking order was: Irish, other white ethnic groups, blacks; Hispanics—predominantly Chicanos—were the last to arrive in the area and, inevitably, were the last to receive any consideration from the regime.

By the early 1970s, Daley was being described as an anachronism, at least outside of Chicago—and out of range of the mayor's own hearing, for "Dick" did not take kindly to criticism. The triumph, and death, of the Kennedys seemed to have led Irish America into an era of final assimilation. The urban machine, in all its varieties, seemed to have been superseded by new political modes. Reporters began referring to Daley as "the last of the bosses." The harsh tactics of his police during the antiwar demonstrations and racial upheavals of 1968 added to an unsavory reputation throughout the country and throughout the world.

Daley remained unshaken and unrepentant, however, during the last years of his rule. Regularly reelected without serious challenge, he appeared invulnerable until struck down by a fatal heart attack in 1976.

During the caretaker administration of Michael Bilandic that followed Daley's death, cracks began appearing in the machine. Those on the outer fringes of patronage and municipal service were becoming openly rebellious. While most of the City Council members occupied themselves in squabbling over spoils, one of Daley's followers, Jane Byrne, identified the sources of discontent. By presenting herself as the redresser of grievances and the champion of a "new politics," she managed to throw the old guard into disarray and win an upset victory over Bilandic in the 1979 mayoral election.

Despite the novelty of having a woman in City Hall, Jane Byrne was indisputably Irish, and she might have been able to hold the old Daley constituency together while fulfilling her reform promises had she been less belligerent and abrasive. Understandable, perhaps, as a form of overcompensation by a woman fighting for power in a male-dominated profession, this characteristic toughness was unfortunately combined with a reckless determination to grab publicity at any price. During the campaign, for example, she had run an audio tape of Mayor Daley praising her work as his consumer affairs commissioner. This "endorsement from the dead" may have marked her, as she claimed, as his anointed heiress, but it deeply offended the Daley family and many of their friends. Furthermore, her fiscal irresponsibility—and her defensiveness about it—antagonized almost everyone.

By the time of the 1983 election, Byrne was in deep trouble. The unreconstructed old guardists in the City Council had never really accepted her leadership of the Cook County and municipal Democratic apparatus, while Richard Daley, Jr., the old boss's son, made an open bid to oust her. Though utterly lacking in his father's political skills, the younger Daley succeeded in disrupting the party and opening the way for Harold Washington. As the candidate of Chicago's large black population who felt that the time had come for a candidate of their own, Washington was able to turn the old ethnic politics of the Irish machine upside down. At the same time he was able to attract the vote of white liberals who had been disillusioned by the failure of Byrne to deliver the promised reforms. After an acrimonious primary and a bitter general election, Byrne was out, and Chicago had its first black mayor.

The usually warring factions of the Chicago Democrats gathered in the City Council chamber in December 1986 to mark the tenth anniversary of Richard Daley's death. Mayor Washington was there, speaking nothing but good of the deceased—who had been, at various times, both patron and nemesis of the city's blacks. The mayor's sworn enemy, Council President Edward Vrdolyak, was there, too. He and Washington had spent most of the last three and a half years feuding, and now the hero of Chicago's Slavs was preparing to run against the incumbent in the upcoming Democratic primary. But Jane Byrne was nowhere to be seen.

Within a few weeks, the former mayor was very much in evidence. This was a new Jane Byrne—much more subdued, much more restrained in her rhetoric, even when criticizing the man who had replaced her. Her campaign was organized with the help of nationally renowned public-relations and media consultants.

But all was for naught. When the smoke cleared, in the spring of 1987, Harold Washington had won another term. Jane Byrne had lost— and so, for good measure, had another Irish-American mayoral candidate, the assessor, Thomas Hynes.

THE THING THAT OFTEN OCCURS IS NEVER MUCH APPRECIATED. *Traditional Irish Proverb*

But the era of dramatic changes was not over yet. Following the sudden death of Harold Washington, several black candidates competed against one another to succeed him. Jane Byrne made a new bid for the mayoral nomination and was swept aside. And the Cook County state's attorney announced his candidacy. He was none other than Richard M. Daley, the son of the former "boss." When the smoke of battle cleared, the name of Daley once again appeared on the door of the mayor's office.

Was it the old days all over again? That remains to be seen, but it would not be on the basis of an Irish political machine, which has ceased to function. The old Tenth Ward once gave the lead to Chicago. Now, belatedly, the Irish of the Windy City are following their compatriots in other parts of America into the suburbs, and only 15 percent of the urban population can wear the green with any authenticity on St. Patrick's Day. Chicago's Irish politicians no longer have a natural constituency, and the new electorate may turn back upon them the old dismissal: "We don't want nobody nobody sent." ◆

An Attack on "Boss Kelly" of Tammany Hall, 1880

EDITORIAL IN THE *NEW YORK HERALD,* OCTOBER 24, 1880

But this Kelly will find that American opinion is not to be put down in that way. Irishmen who, like Kelly, are without the tact and sense that is the natural endowment of Irishmen with brains, but who have all the faith in bellowing and roaring and vindictive speeches that is equally an endowment of the more brutal of the breed, may imagine that what resists them in its characteristically still and temperate way yields before them, but if they do, they indulge in a vain fancy and since this champion of Irish and Catholic dictation seems to wish this issue to be made—since he wants it understood that his way must be supreme, and that whoever objects shall be overwhelmed, if possible, by a deluge of vile names raked from the cesspools of his imagination or the yet fouler recesses of his memory—he can have the issue made just as distinctly and clearly as the case may require. For when a Catholic Irishman, the leader of the Irish Catholic party, announces and boasts that he will decide political conflicts in this neighborhood as suits his good pleasure by means of the suffrages of thirty thousand Irish Catholic voters upon whom he can count, the people have an opportunity to see just what sort of an institution the Catholic church is in politics and to understand what a farce it would be to pretend that free government can continue where it is permitted to touch its hand to politics, or, indeed, to exist, for where it exists, it will not leave politics alone. This is a Protestant country and the American people are a Protestant people.

◆

Honest John Kelly was the first Irish American to head Tammany Hall. The headquarters of the New York Democrats had long depended on Irish votes to dominate the city, but it was not until the corrupt Tweed Ring was ousted in 1871 that an Irishman actually became Boss.

*A*lthough Ronald Reagan was the first president of Irish descent to go from California to the White House, a number of West Coast Irishmen were to be found in the next-highest office in the land, that of United States senator, during the last century. Although George Murphy may have been the first Irish-American movie actor to become a senator from California, the careers of his predecessors were even more remarkable.

David Broderick was born in Washington, D.C., in 1820, the son of an immigrant stonecutter, a trade that David himself followed in early youth. In 1849 he moved to California and became involved in smelting and assaying gold. Entering politics, he became a delegate to the state's constitutional convention, a member of the state's senate in 1850, and president of that body in 1851. He was elected United States senator in 1857. His term was cut short two years later by an episode all too typical of those early days in the Far West, when he was mortally wounded in a duel with Chief Justice David S. Terry of the California Supreme Court.

Eugene Casserly, also born in 1820, emigrated from West Meath as a child. His family ensured a good education for him, and after graduation from Georgetown he studied law and started a practice in New York in 1844. He moved to San Francisco in 1850 and divided his time between law and journalism until elected to the United States Senate in 1869. After his term in Washington, he again practiced law and aided in the revision of the state constitution; he died in 1883.

John Conness was born in Galway in 1821, arrived in the United States in 1833 and learned the trade of piano maker in New York City. He, too, fol-

David Broderick

James Fair

Eugene Casserly

lowed the gold rush to California in 1849, eventually shifting from mining to mercantile activities. He was repeatedly elected to the state assembly from 1853 to 1861. He served in the United States Senate from 1863 to 1869. Having apparently satisfied both his political and business ambitions, he retired from both fields, and spent the last forty years of his life in Boston.

James Fair was born in Tyrone in 1831; in 1843 his parents brought him to Illinois, where he received his early training in business. Although based in California, and actively engaged in mining there between 1849 and 1860, not until he acquired the Bonanza property in Nevada did he make his fortune. In partnership with three other Irish-American entrepreneurs—John Mackay, J. C. Flood, and William O'Brien—he transformed the Nevada gold and silver mines into one of the most profitable enterprises in the world. While he represented Nevada in the U.S. Senate from 1881 to 1886, Fair continued to expand his real estate holdings in San Francisco and to develop manufacturing in other cities of the Pacific Coast; he died in San Francisco in 1894. ◆

KEEP A THING FOR SEVEN YEARS AND YOU'LL FIND A USE FOR IT.
Traditional Irish Proverb

Was Al Smith Irish?

lfred E. Smith, governor of New York (1919–1929) and Democratic nominee for president of the United States in 1928, was the most famous Irish American of his day. He has long been regarded as the quintessential Irish Catholic urban politician, the product of generations of Irish mastery of Tammany techniques.

In recent years, however, his ethnic credentials have been questioned. It has even been claimed, either seriously or facetiously, that he was an Italian American. In the spirit of Smith's own dictum, "Let's look at the record," an examination of the record ought to set the matter straight.

The future governor's father died in 1886, aged fifty-one. His death certificate lists his name as Alfred Emanuel Smith, and his birthplace as New York City; it also shows that his father, named Emanuel, was born in Italy and that his mother, Magdalena, was born in Germany. Research in New York State census records has established that the aforementioned Emanuel Smith was born in Genoa in 1813 and was naturalized in the United States in 1825. Thus, Al Smith's father was half Italian and half German.

The governor's mother, Catherine Mulvehill, was Irish on her paternal side, although, by some accounts, her maternal stock was English.

Presumably, the governor's Genoese grandfather adopted an American name when he emigrated, for Smith is not a name one is likely to encounter in Italy. His original name does not appear in any surviving records.

Does this mean that Al Smith was really Italian? Or, for that matter, German? It would seem that anyone (especially an American) with two, three, or even four nationalities among his ancestry is free to identify with whichever of them he prefers, and it is clear that Alfred E. Smith (the younger) identified with his maternal background. Raised in an Irish-American neighborhood, conditioned by a social, religious, educational, and political environment that was overwhelmingly Irish American, he perceived himself, and was perceived by others, as an Irishman. In the last analysis, this famous Irish-American politician remains Irish because he himself chose to be Irish. ◆

The Irish are a very fair people—they never speak well of one another.

James Boswell, *The Life of Samuel Johnson* (1790)

Senator Joe

ew Irish Americans have had a more enduring impact upon the public consciousness of the United States than Joseph R. McCarthy. His very name has been transformed into a new word in the national language—McCarthyism. Yet, more than three decades after his death, the simple facts of who he was and what he did have become somewhat blurred. Americans are fond of historical references but not particularly adept at retaining the historical facts. Rather than reargue the symbolic significance of McCarthy, which will always remain controversial, it may be more useful to disentangle the main events of his career from the emotional overgrowth that obscures the individual.

Joseph Raymond McCarthy was born in 1908 at Grand Chute, Wisconsin, in a farming area known as the "Irish settlement." His mother, Bridget Tierney, was a native of Ireland, while his father, Timothy McCarthy, was of mixed Irish and German ancestry. After attending country schools, young Joe worked his way through the college and law curriculum at Marquette University. He practiced law in Wisconsin until 1939, when he was elected judge of the Tenth Judicial Circuit Court. In 1942, during World War II, he resigned from this post and obtained a commission as a first lieutenant in the U.S. Marine Corps. He attained the rank of captain during service in the Pacific theater of operations. Following the war, in 1945, he campaigned successfully for his former post in the Circuit Court. The next year he was elected on the Republican ticket to a six-year term in the U.S. Senate.

McCarthy first attracted national attention in February 1950, with the charge that fifty-seven employees of the Department of State were Communists. The accusation, which was never substantiated, marked the beginning of a bitter feud between the senator and the Truman administration. During the next three years he repeatedly accused various high-ranking officials in the State Department of subversive activities. He made many political enemies and won a wide popular following by his methods, which became known as McCarthyism. In 1953 President Truman defined McCarthyism as "the corruption of truth, the abandonment of . . . fair play and 'due process' of law . . . the use of the 'big lie' and the unfounded accusation . . . in the name of Americanism and se-

curity." The senator's supporters defined McCarthyism as relentless determination to expose Communist conspiracy, particularly in the government.

Reelected to the Senate in 1952, McCarthy was named chairman of the Committee on Government Operations in January 1953. As head of its Permanent Subcommittee on Investigations, he broadened the scope of his inquiries, successively probing alleged Communist activities in the U.S. Information Agency, the Central Intelligence Agency, the Government Printing Office, the United Nations, and the U.S. Army. The army investigation culminated in accusations by the secretary of the army that McCarthy and members of the subcommittee staff had threatened army officials in efforts to obtain preferential treatment for a former unpaid consultant of the subcommittee who had been drafted. Claiming "blackmail," McCarthy countercharged that the army had used the draftee as a "hostage" in an attempt to halt the subcommittee's investigation. The subcommittee, with McCarthy temporarily relinquishing his membership, conducted open hearings on the conflicting claims from April 22 to June 17, 1954. Widely publicized in the press and given nationwide radio

SICKNESS IS THE
PHYSICIAN'S FEAST.
*Traditional Irish
Proverb*

CABINET OFFICERS OF IRISH ORIGIN

SECRETARY OF STATE

Louis McLane, 1833–1834
John C. Calhoun, 1844–1845
James Buchanan, 1845–1849
James G. Blaine, 1881, 1889–1892
William J. Bryan, 1913–1915
Bainbridge Colby, 1920
Alexander M. Haig, 1981–1982

SECRETARY OF THE TREASURY

Louis McLane, 1831–1833
Roger B. Taney, 1833–1834
Hugh Mc Culloch, 1865–1869, 1884
Daniel Manning, 1885
Franklin MacVeagh, 1909–1913
William G. McAdoo, 1913–1918
Andrew Mellon, 1921–1922
David M. Kennedy, 1969–1971
John B. Connally, 1971–1972
Donald T. Regan, 1981–1985

SECRETARY OF THE INTERIOR

Thomas Mc Kennan, 1850
William P. Clarke, 1983–1985

SECRETARY OF LABOR

Maurice J. Tobin, 1949–1953
Martin P. Durkin, 1953
James P. Mitchell, 1953–1961
Peter J. Brennan, 1973–1975
Raymond J. Donovan, 1981–1985

SECRETARY OF WAR

Henry Knox, 1789–1795
James McHenry, 1796–1800
John C. Calhoun, 1817–1825
George W. McCrary, 1877–1879
Patrick J. Hurley, 1929–1933

SECRETARY OF DEFENSE

James V. Forrestal, 1947–1949
Neil H. McElroy, 1957–1959
Robert McNamara, 1963–1968

ATTORNEY GENERAL

Roger B. Taney, 1831–1833
Wayne MacVeagh, 1881
Joseph McKenna, 1897–1898
Harry M. Daugherty, 1921–1924
Frank Murphy, 1939–1940
J. Howard Mc Grath, 1949–1952
J. P. McGranery, 1952–1953
Robert F. Kennedy, 1961–1964
John N. Mitchell, 1969–1972

SECRETARY OF COMMERCE

John T. Connor, 1965–1967

SECRETARY OF HEALTH AND HUMAN SERVICES

Margaret (O'Shaughnessy) Heckler, 1983–1985

The Cabinet of President Jefferson Davis of the Confederate States of America (1861–1865) included John Regan (Texas) as secretary of the treasury and Stephen Mallory (Florida) as secretary of the navy.

WHAT'S GOT BADLY, GOES BADLY.
Traditional Irish Proverb

and television coverage, the investigation produced many sensational developments. Each side under scrutiny offered convincing testimony, but little substantiation, in support of its accusations. In August, the subcommittee, failing to agree on the controversy, issued majority and minority reports. In the Republican report McCarthy, his aides, and the army officials involved were mildly criticized; the Democratic report was sharply critical of McCarthy and his aides, mildly critical of the army officials. Meanwhile, the Senate voted to establish a special committee to consider a proposal censuring McCarthy for conduct unbecoming a senator. On the basis of the committee's findings, the Senate voted (on December 2) to condemn him for his conduct toward two senatorial committees. His influence both in the Senate and on the national political scene diminished steadily thereafter. By the time of his death in 1957, McCarthy had lost all his influence. ◆

here are plenty of other churches bearing the name, including a cathedral in Dublin (a Protestant edifice since the Reformation). But for millions of people throughout the country and, indeed, throughout the world—Catholic and non-Catholic alike—St. Patrick's, in New York, is *the* cathedral. It is undoubtedly the best-known religious structure in the United States, a landmark that is visited by streams of tourists.

Yet its construction began at a time when the Catholic Church was regarded with suspicion and hostility, and the Irish who made up the bulk of the Church's membership were still despised alien intruders in Anglo-Saxon America. Nativist and Know-Nothing riots were a recent memory in 1850 when Archbishop John Hughes defiantly launched his grand design. The monumental church sketched by architect James Renwick was to be built on land far above the center of town. Seemingly both impossible and irrelevant, it was dubbed "Hughes' Folly."

Overcoming all obstacles and protests, the redoubtable Tyrone-born prelate laid the cornerstone in 1858. The initial funding came not, as legend has it, from the pennies of Irish working girls, but from contributions of $1,000 each extracted from 103 of the more well-to-do members of the community. Nevertheless, both in the labor that was lavished on it over the next two decades and in the enthusiasm it gradually aroused among the faithful, it became an *Irish* church. And when it was consecrated on May 25, 1879, it bore (like the old, small cathedral downtown that it replaced) the name of Ireland's patron—and New York's—St. Patrick.

Situated on what is now the busiest stretch of the city's grand boulevard, Fifth Avenue, the massive Gothic Revival white marble building occupies an entire square block. In the traditional cruciform floor plan, its three aisles are more than 300 feet long, with side chapels, and an ambulatory around the apse at the east, from which other chapels lead. The plan and proportions of the cathedral are predominantly French Gothic in style, while the twin towers (completed in 1886) are in the German Gothic mode.

When St. Patrick's was consecrated, New York's Catholics were still

It's a very holy day at home, and since I don't go to church too often and am not too holy, I like it better here.

Michael Sullivan, immigrant, explaining why he prefers St. Patrick's Day in New York, in the *Daily News* (1986)

overwhelmingly Irish. Irish immigrants and their descendants in fact made up nearly a third of the city's population. And the vaults beneath the cathedral where the successive archbishops repose—McCloskey and Corrigan, Farley, Spellman and Cooke, reflect the persistence of this Celtic presence in the hierarchy. But the city gradually lost its Irish tone, immigrants from Eastern and Southern Europe altered the makeup of urban Catholicism, and the shifting residential patterns left the parish without parishioners, except for those who worked in or visited the business district during the day. Perhaps the last prominent Irish American to attend Mass regularly at the cathedral was the former postmaster general and Democratic national chairman, James A. Farley, who resided nearby at the Waldorf, until his death shortly before the church's centennial.

By the time it marked its hundredth anniversary, St. Patrick's had become virtually a public building, filled every day by throngs of visitors. Rabbis and Protestant clerics rubbed elbows with governors and cabinet officers at ecumenical services. Jazz Masses, African drums, exotic hymns in strange languages echoed beneath its vaulted ceiling.

Yet, for all its changes in these changing times, St. Patrick's retains its special identification with the Irish. It is an identification that goes beyond the March 17 ritual when the great parade marches past the dignitaries on the cathedral's steps. Day in and day out, this great building stands as a reminder of Irish-American faith in the religion they brought from their old home and faith in themselves as committed citizens of their new country. ◆

St. Patrick's Cathedral in the late 1880s, a decade after its formal dedication. The archbishops who have presided over New York's Catholics during the last century and a half (all of them Irish) are buried in a crypt beneath the cathedral.

New Cathedral of New York
Fifth Avenue, 50th, & 51st. Streets.

The Irish and American Catholicism

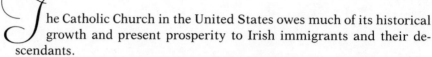 he Catholic Church in the United States owes much of its historical growth and present prosperity to Irish immigrants and their descendants.

Before their great nineteenth-century influx, the Church had few members and only a fragmentary organization. Although the first bishop, John Carroll, was of Irish origin, the clergy was largely of English or French extraction. The change began with the creation of new dioceses in 1808 and a consequent demand for English-speaking clergy that Ireland was called upon to fulfill. Irish priests, and Irish-born bishops in New York and Philadelphia, marked the beginning of a trend. Thereafter the number of Irish priests steadily increased, and with it (despite the opposition of Catholics of other origins) the number of Irish bishops. By 1850 more than a third of the priests in the United States were of Irish birth, most of them from the College of All Hallows in Dublin, which sent over 1,500 priests to America. When New York's John McCloskey was named the first cardinal of the United States in 1875, the Vatican, in effect, confirmed the ruling position of the Irish. Indeed, only four of America's first seventeen cardinals were not Irish. By the end of the nineteenth century, despite the beginning of immigration from other Catholic countries, more than half of all the clergy were of Irish background, and to most Protestants "Catholic" and "Irish" were synonymous.

The Irish made the parish the nucleus of Catholic religious life, as well as of their own social identity, in the United States. Before the great wave of Irish immigration at midcentury, Catholicism in this country had been too weak in numbers and finances to maintain a firm structure. In many areas, Mass was held in whatever building was available, and the priests were often itinerant. They had little authority over the Catholic population, whose attendance at services was irregular. The Irish clergy took an active role in ministering to the immigrants, and in helping them to adjust to their new country. A whole network of needs and services developed in the centers of Irish settlement, during the midcentury period, creating a bond between priest and people that found expression in strong parish units. The parish became a rallying place, a support unit, an educational and recreational center, and, of course, a spiritual reservoir. Through the steadily growing parish structure, their bishops were able for the first time to mobilize political pressure, build up the Church's revenues, and promote such enterprises as abstinence societies and colonization of Western lands. The parishes also provided the justification (and the funds) for schools, hospitals, asylums, and orphanages.

It was the Irish, too, who took the lead in creating the system of Catholic higher education in the United States. Their hierarchy was determined that the Catholic population should be secured in their faith at all levels of instruction. As parish schools stimulated the growth of diocesan high schools in the late nineteenth century, a growing number of students of Irish background acquired the training, as well as the financial means, to attend college. By 1900, scores of institutions had been created to meet this demand. By World War II, there were hundreds of them. A large proportion of the faculty members, lay as well as clerical, were Irish by birth or descent.

The Irish leadership of the American Catholic Church defined the official position of their denomination on all the great questions of the day, from Church-state relations and slavery to labor relations and social welfare. Irish prelates, such as Archbishop Hughes, Cardinal Gibbons, Cardinal Cushing, and Cardinal Spellman, were perceived by the general public as the embodiment of Catholic thought and principles of conduct.

The proportion of Catholics of Irish descent declined steadily after 1920: by 1980 they accounted for only about 17 percent of the total. But they continued to dominate the Church's leadership. During the 1980s over half of the bishops and a third of the priests were still men of Irish extraction. Clearly, the ethnic group that had done most to create the Church's massive presence in the United States would have to yield its long predominance in the face of changing demographics. But, just as clearly, the highest levels of power would be the last ones surrendered.

As I have been told repeatedly, women and blacks are underrepresented in major faculty posts because of discrimination, but Catholics are underrepresented because their religious commitment and their family experiences prevent them from being good scholars. A friendly economist put it well to me recently: 'How can you be a priest and work with computers?' How, indeed.

Andrew Greeley,
The New York Times
(1986)

The
HAP

$\mathcal{T}$he late 1950s were the heyday of the HAP—the Hibernian-American Princess. At hundreds of nun-run colleges all over the country, the HAP was in full flower.

The small, Catholic girls' schools were usually located in the affluent suburbs of major cities. They were Irish-dominated, of course, because in those days the Irish still dominated the Church. The bishops were Irish, as were the presidents of the colleges and most of the sisters on the faculties. The boards of trustees were made up of Irish bankers and businessmen, lawyers and politicians.

The HAPs were the most visible and powerful students in each school. Not that they were necessarily the academic stars. Their leadership was social rather than intellectual. They were the class officers, ran the dances and charity events, and were the confidantes of the mother superior.

Their fathers had put them into these colleges so that they could spend a few years in a morally secure environment before making a suitable marriage. A smattering of culture was a useful acquisition, but serious study was superfluous. After all, it was not as if they would ever have to earn a living.

Just as the class of Irish Americans from which they came strove constantly to emulate the WASPs, so the HAPs eagerly imitated all of the fads and fashions of the "Seven Sisters" schools, and eagerly sought dates with Ivy League men. Since wealthy Irish Americans had been excluded from ultimate social acceptance because of their Catholicism, they tended to make their religion a matter of ostentation—turning necessity into a virtue. The HAPs followed their parental lead by outdoing the nuns in organizing religious ceremonies and festivals. Naturally, this endeared them even more to the operators of the school, who already counted on large alumnae donations.

To be sure, not all of the students in these schools were HAPs. And just as well, for it was no fun being a princess unless you had some peasants around. There were the Irish-American girls who had gotten in on some sort of scholarship or other, and who had no pedigree or purse to their names. There were the inevitable Italo-Americans, who might have plenty of money behind them, but who were regarded with suspicion because their fathers were probably gangsters. There was likely to be a sprinkling of other Catholic ethnics, too few and too obscure to be of any account. And then there were the girls from Latin America. There were nearly always a few of these, but they presented problems. Normally no HAP would want to associate with anything so unspeakably outlandish as a Hispanic. But, on the other hand, some of these girls came from families that owned half of Nicaragua or whatever, and you might always get invited down to spend your vacation on a *hacienda* or cruising the Caribbean in a presidential yacht. Whatever their origins, these "ordinary" girls understood that they were the mere rank and file, lucky to be allowed to follow the lead of the HAPs.

Many factors have combined to eliminate the HAP. The Church has changed, the role of women in society has expanded, and the Irish-American elite has become more assimilated. Brains are more esteemed, careers are more sought after, and moral proprieties have altered. The day of the small Catholic girls' college has passed. Some may sigh for times gone by, but how many really mourn the passing of the HAP? ◆

HE COMES LIKE THE BAD WEATHER (I.E., UNINVITED). *Traditional Irish Proverb*

A Tale
to Tell

Writers of Irish origin have made major contributions to the mainstream of American literature. But there is also a distinct body of Irish-American fiction. In "Echoes from the Next Parish" (An Gael, spring 1984) Daniel J. Casey provides an introduction to the authors who have drawn upon their own ethnic experience for their subject matter.

The poet and the storyteller have, from the dawn of Gaelic civilization, occupied prominent places in the social order. The fascination for word-wielding has followed the Irish down the days. It is no accident, then, that Irish writers have contributed more than their share to English-language literature over the past two centuries. No accident that Ireland has produced a Yeats, Synge, Joyce, O'Casey, and Beckett among a score of modern heavyweights.

But what of the American Irish? Sharers in the commonweal, their contribution to American literature over the same two centuries has gone unheralded. There were, of course, a few headliners—James T. Farrell, F. Scott Fitzgerald, Mary McCarthy—but until recently, the American Irish have made their reputation in politics, religion, and the law, and had only a marginal impact on the world of letters.

The Immigrants Even before the famine, literary views of the American Irish—in the fiction of Hugh Henry Brackenridge, James Fenimore Cooper, and Sara Hale—offered broad caricatures lifted from earlier British models. They were Yankee translations of a stage-Irish stereotype. Brackenridge's *Modern Chivalry* (1792–1815), "the first distinctly American novel," introduces Teague O'Regan, a bog-trotting Irish servant, who accompanies his learned squire on a tour of Pennsylvania. O'Regan, a profligate opportunist, blunders from one sordid escapade into another and charms innocent females with an incredible brogue. Listen to Brackenridge's rendering of Teague's love-chat:

God love your shoul, my dear cratur, but you are de beauty of de world. Sleeping or waking, I could take you to my heart and ate you wid de very love of my shoul dat I have for you. De look o'd dur face, like de sun or de moon, run trugh me, and burn up like a coul o'd de fire: dat I am shick and fainting to take du in my arms, my dear cratur.

After tumbling into bed with a nonconsenting chambermaid, Teague cleverly shifts the blame for his assault to an innocuous Presbyterian minister. And, when he is at last persuaded to "fess up" to clear the preacher, he extorts a bit of "smart money" for his trouble. It's "a thankless thing to do these things free," says the rogue. So the Irishman enters the pages of American fiction as a burlesque, as the butt of Brackenridge's heavy satire on American democracy. The image of the rascally rapscallion, superstitious simpleton, and cowering lockpuller travels well.

The postfamine writers went a step further and vilified the immigrants. They were no longer comic fools; they became, after 1850, a rabblement overwhelming the American cities, draining available resources, and leaving in their wake disease, corruption, and crime. They were characterized as violent, lazy, shiftless, dirty, dishonest, and alcoholic. But, because they were illiterate and dependent, they were unable to respond to prejudicial attacks and unwilling to offend the establishment. At midcentury the Irish in America were more concerned with economic survival than they were with national pride.

Unfortunately, the earliest Irish-American novelists, writers like Mary Anne Madden Sadlier, advanced the stereotype and churned out moralistic pap exhorting the immigrants to disavow the past and emulate the Yank work ethic. As industrious laborers and steadfast domestics serving their "betters," the Irish would, they were told, earn high marks in this world and the next. Even the first serious challenge to Paddyism, Thomas D'Arcy McGee's *History of the Irish Settlers in North America* (1855), which extolled Ireland's ancient glories, accepted the emigrant's failings as consequences of his origin.

Despite the length and strength of the Irish tradition, then, Irish-American writers in the nineteenth century produced a body of second-rate prose fiction that served to underscore nativist charges of inferiority. It was a century of acculturation and adjustment, not an age of leisure and high art.

The Second Generation There were, of course, Irish immigrants like Fitz-James O'Brien, remembered for his tales of the supernatural, and John Boyle O'Reilly, editor of the Boston *Pilot*, who came to the States in their mid-twenties and who wrote fiction. But Irish-American literature properly begins with the Chicago journalist Finley Peter Dunne, who contributed hundreds of humorous dialect sketches to the national press between 1893 and 1919. Dunne's spokesman was Mr. Mar-

●Restless yet indolent, shrewd and indiscreet, impetuous, impatient, and improvident, instinctively brave, thoughtlessly generous, quick to resent and forgive offenses, to form and renounce friendships. . . .●

J. W. Croker, *A Sketch of the State of Ireland* (1808)

tin Dooley, a bartender-philosopher who provided a chronologue of Bridgeport, an Irish neighborhood on Chicago's South Side. The sketches offered political commentary and social history that added a new dimension to Irish character. Dunne was witty and well informed and, for millions of newspaper readers, his Mr. Dooley became the quintessential Irishman.

James T. Farrell was another South Side Chicagoan who, in the thirties, published an autobiographical trilogy that catalogued the short, sordid career of William "Studs" Lonigan. Farrell's fiction offered a comprehensive sociological study, albeit an uncomplimentary one, of the Chicago Irish from 1915 to the Depression. "I am a second-generation Irish American. The effects and scars of immigration are upon my life. The past was dragging through my boyhood and adolescence," Farley once confessed. *Studs Lonigan* (1932–1935) traces the tribulations of that boyhood and adolescence. And Betty Smith's *A Tree Grows in Brooklyn* (1943), set in the Williamsburg section of Brooklyn in the same time period, captures the ambience of the cold-water flats with empty larders and the Tammany-sponsored children's excursions up the Hudson River. Her heroine, Francie Nolan, was not as scarred as Studs; still, there was, in Smith's novels, a sense of desperation to "fly the nets" of her ghetto neighborhood.

F. Scott Fitzgerald, Mary McCarthy, and John O'Hara were not graduates of the street academies; they came from favored circumstances. Fitzgerald attended the Newman School and Princeton; McCarthy finished at Vassar; and O'Hara, a doctor's son, aspired to Yale, though his father's untimely death put Yale out of reach. Irish backgrounds are sublimated in the fiction of these three: "Irish" was, after all, a stigma among the nouveaux riches. Yet their fiction is also autobiographical: In *This Side of Paradise* (1920), Fitzgerald not only creates the Jazz Age, he sheds his Irish identity; in *Memories of a Catholic Girlhood* (1957), McCarthy spurns her lace-curtain origins; and in *The Doctor's Son and Other Stories* (1935), O'Hara sounds a final salvo on his birthright.

Jimmy Molloy, the young narrator of "The Doctor's Son," experiences disillusionment. It is, coincidentally, the same Jimmy Molloy who, in *Butterfield 8* (1935), says, "I want to tell you something about myself that will help to explain a lot of things about me. You might as well hear it now. First of all, I am a Mick. I wear Brooks Brothers clothes and I don't eat salad with a spoon and I probably could play five-goal polo in two years, but I am a Mick. Still a Mick." Fitzgerald, McCarthy, and O'Hara spent their professional lives coming to terms with Molloy's dilemma.

Though Dunne imbues his Dooley with native intelligence and wit and Smith adds a dash of sentiment to the character, the second-generation writers generally aspire to American respectability at the price of Irish culture. What we find in the best fiction of the period—in the works

●*Our rulers are partly American scoundrels and partly Celtic scoundrels. The Celts are predominant, however, and we submit to the rod and the sceptre of Maguires and O'Tooles and O'Shanes. . . .*●

George Templeton Strong, *Diary* (1849)

of Farrell, Fitzgerald, McCarthy, and O'Hara—is a frustration and bitterness with a transported Irishness that has restricted social movement and shackled the imagination. The Irish come off as ignorant, materialistic, and corrupt.

The Postwar Regionalists By the first half of the twentieth century the Irish had proven themselves. There was no longer the preoccupation with covering their "scars of immigration." With the Germans, they had been this country's first white ethnics, and most of them were already third- and fourth-generation Americans.

The Celtic tidal wave had crested at the Eastern Seaboard and washed across the northern half of continental America. About 60 percent of the immigrants had settled in New England and in the middle Atlantic states. Another 25 percent had pushed on with the westward migration into the north-central states. The rest had been scattered across the country, with concentrations in the major rail centers and in the port cities of Louisiana, Texas, and California.

COWS FAR FROM HOME HAVE LONG HORNS.
Traditional Irish Proverb

But after World War II, the regional differences became more pronounced. The Bostonians, heirs to the Old World values, established the genteel tradition of the Yankee Irish. A majority of New Yorkers, Philadelphians, and Chicagoans who had risen in the ranks of business and the civil service melded into the wasteland of suburbia. And, in the Midwest and the South, where the Irish were often an indistinct minority, they sought a wider sense of community by emphasizing their religion over their Irishness.

Edwin O'Connor's *The Last Hurrah* (1956), set "in a New England City" in 1948, is more than a political novel about the changing of the guard; it is an analysis of the passing of a tradition. O'Connor's Frank Skeffington calls himself "a tribal chieftain." Between wakes and dances, he liberally dispenses favors to petitioners, but he recognizes that he is the end of the line. In *The Last Hurrah*, O'Connor has fictionalized the final campaign of Mayor James Michael Curley of Boston and glossed over the corruption of his political machine, but he has also provided a memorable slice of New England Irish Americana.

Elizabeth Cullinan perfectly catches the atmosphere of New York City, where she grew up in the security of pre-Vatican II. Her fiction, particularly her prize-winning novel, *House of Gold* (1970), provides a chronicle of lower-middle-class Irish-American urban life and of the young women caught in the conflicts of tradition and modernism.

The Irish that turn up in the Midwest fiction of J. F. Powers are often clerics. Powers has, in four short-story collections and a novel, decimated scores of them. He takes on the collared golf pros, television personalities, trigger-happy exorcists, and bingo emperors, as well as the new liberals, the hippie priests promoting strobe-light Masses and drive-in confessionals.

In *Morte D'Urban* (1962) and in *Lions, Harts, Leaping Does* (1963),

Powers is the comic-satirist who balances the sacred and the profane, who makes Irish Americans laugh at their own excesses. He is one of the most skillful writers of fiction today.

Finally, among the regionalists, there is Flannery O'Connor, an important Southern writer of Irish background who was reared a Georgia Catholic. The Irish-American quality of her work is, of course, sublimated—it is *felt* rather than stated, expressed as an intellectualized Catholicism rather than an Irish consciousness. Though she produced only four major works and died in 1964 at the age of thirty-nine, O'Connor's literary reputation has grown since her death.

What may be said is that the further Irish-American literature moves from Ireland and from the Irish ghettos, the less continuity it has. Some authors, writing from the crumbling citadels of the culture, mourn its passing like the death of an old friend, while others regard it as a nightmare from which they have never quite awakened. The echoes from the next parish are, however, becoming fainter; Irish character is, in the regional fiction, evolving and producing a new hyphenate hybrid. But the personality is rooted in the New World and the idiom is now distinctly American.

The New Breed   In the last generation Irish-American writers have gained confidence. Among the New Journalists, Jimmy Breslin, the late Joe Flaherty, and Pete Hamill have produced hard-hitting news copy and realistic fiction. In three recent autobiographical novels—*World Without End, Amen* (1973), *Fogarty and Co.* (1973), and *The Gift* (1973)—the New York writers explore the tragic father-son/generation chasm in Irish-American families. Black humorists J. P. Donleavy and Tom McHale have given us two of the most outrageous comic novels in *The Ginger Man* (1955) and *Farragan's Retreat* (1971). Donleavy's dastardly antihero, Sebastian Dangerfield, romps through "dear, dirty Dublin" shattering the saints and scholars myths of the oul' sod, while McHale's Farragan clan churns up the bigotry stewing in the hearts of the Irish-American superpatriots during the Vietnam travesty. And Mark Costello has offered a wonderfully crafted collection, *The Murphy Stories* (1973), a case study of the artist gone amok in a psychic tug of war.

A SOFT WORD NEVER YET BROKE A TOOTH.
Traditional Irish Proverb

Even the last six years have yielded a number of promising titles: John Gregory Dunne's compelling character contrast cum murder mystery, *True Confessions* (1978); James Carroll's classic replay of the Irish-American saga, *Mortal Friends* (1978); and Mary Gordon's escape to reality, *Final Payments* (1978). Even more promising is William Kennedy's brilliant Albany trilogy; *Legs* (1975), *Billy Phelan's Greatest Game* (1978), and *Ironweed* (1983). Kennedy's talent for re-creating the urban microcosm, where machine politics rule, goes beyond a unique reportorial vision. Kennedy is a master storyteller and stylist.

Current Irish-American fiction still emphasizes the paralyzing grip of church and family and neighborhood on the psyche. It still stresses the need to break the soul-fetters of the past. It mocks—sometimes savagely—the narrowness of traditional values, yet it finds little or no consolation in modernism. But the current fiction totally ignores the immigrant experience; the conflicts that are played out in these novels emanate from an American subculture that is divorced from Ireland by several generations. Apart, then, from an incidental reference or a "walk-on," by the seventies, Irish-American fiction has made the transition. As the eminent Celticist John Kelleher says in his "Irishness in America," "Like it or not, we're on our own."

Over the past eighty years Irish Americans have made their mark in American letters. In addition to the litany of novelists surveyed in these pages, there have been other voices: the dramatists—Eugene O'Neill, William Gibson, and Shelagh Delaney; and the poets—Robert Kelly, Galway Kinnell, Frank O'Hara, and Robert Creeley—to name a few. It seems as though, when the Irish became literate in America, they produced and continue to produce works of imperishable quality.

The truth is that the Irish Americans, like the Irish themselves, have only lately discovered the cultural archives they are heirs to. Until recently, it was rare to find, in Irish-American fiction, a sense of pride in a shared literary tradition that dates back to early Christian times. It was rarer still to find the genuine sense of humor that has characterized Irish literature down the days. But Irish Americans are now reading Yeats and Synge and Joyce and O'Casey and Beckett with new purpose, and they are finally beginning to shake the debilitating inferiority, self-pity, and guilt of three centuries of British and American casting.

The Irish have been assimilated, and the Irish-American novelists are no longer as preoccupied with hyphenate identity as were Farrell, Fitzgerald, and O'Hara. They no longer have to prove themselves statistically as soldiers fighting in wars that were not theirs or as dray-horse builders of railroads they could not afford to use. They have graduated into the corporate structure and been admitted to the country club with an unlimited line of credit. But has the cost of cultural assimilation and abandoned ethnic identity been too high? Not exactly. What has happened in recent years is part of the grand evolutionary scheme; it is a kind of cultural trade-off that is written into the price of emigration. If the Irish-American writer draws now from non-Irish and non-ghetto experiences, his fiction will simply reflect those experiences.

The phenomenon in America is that the Irish Americans, like other ethnics, have gained access to the universities in unprecedented numbers and that the writers among them have been introduced to literary traditions that deny American stereotypes and infuse a new ethnic pride. The younger generation of Irish Americans will, of course, continue to explore American themes, but they will also feel a special kinship to Yeats and Joyce and the others because they will sense, in their Irish counterparts, a shared heritage that gives voice to the imagination. ◆

Notwithstanding the natural beauty and fertility of Ireland, poverty and misery prevail, and the spirit of industry is discouraged.

Nathaniel Huntington, *System of Modern Geography for Schools* (1836)

Seamus Heaney: The Liberating Gift of Utterance

The Irish poet Seamus Heaney has become an American poet as well, for he spends half the academic year at Harvard. His subject matter, to be sure, remains largely Irish, but his verse has found a wide audience in the United States. For Irish Americans it has a special appeal. The following article by Natalie Ganley, originally published in the Irish Echo *(New York) on March 14, 1987, portrays Heaney during a visit to Washington.*

f you want to look at the truth about a country, it is better to consult a poet than the police," said Ambassador Padraic MacKernan as he introduced Seamus Heaney to an overflowing audience at the Hirshhorn Auditorium in Washington last month. The program was jointly sponsored by the Smithsonian and the International Poetry Forum.

Direct, forceful, supple, and subtle is how the ambassador described Heaney's poetry. "Heaney offers us a shock of recognition," said MacKernan, "wherein our past and present predicaments are revealed to us."

Carrying his own carton of books through the revolving door of the Hirshhorn Gallery, Heaney looked healthier than he did two years ago when he last visited Washington. He filled out his not-so-crumply suit becomingly. Under the cropped mane the color of bleached winter grass, the boyish face seemed at ease, smiled often.

One loves Heaney not just for his colossal poetry, but for the freshness he delivers, the unaffected affability that lures the listener into his digging, his "hankering," as he calls it "for the underside of things."

Poetry should be both familiar and formal, Heaney said, then promised some of each during the evening. But even to the formal poetry Heaney lent a familiarity, and the audience sighed with equal pleasure at the music of old favorites and some challenging new poems.

He nodded first to the Harvard connection. (Heaney seems to be a somewhat permanent fixture now with the modern poetry course he teaches there each spring.) He pulled from his sheaf of papers the villanelle written as a commission for the school's 350th birthday last year. He identified with Harvard in its infancy, Heaney said, because it was found behind the cowsheds.

"The smell of the byre was one I knew well in my Derry days," he said. "Further, I think many prosper on the lair as well as in the library."

In the poem John Harvard comes back and remembers the time when "the atom lay unsplit, the west unwon" and "when frosts and tests were hard."

"It's a sly political poem." Heaney grinned and read, "John Harvard walked the yard. The books stood open, the gates unbarred."

With "Follower" Heaney jumped back to his father and his rural roots in the north of Ireland. The core of his private mythology, Heaney explains, is the pump in his village of Mossbawn. "It was even the dating system of the 1950s," he recalls. "We called that time 'before the water,' meaning before the mains and electricity were installed."

Heaney's father was a farmer "to whom any flicker of childhood activity was an affectation," says Heaney. So the poet thought the occasion of his father's flying a kite with him worthy of a poem.

"A Kite for Michael and Christopher" ends with the word "strain." Heaney pointed out its double meaning (sweetness, as in a song, and tension) as a springboard for some observations about the relationship between poetry and politics. "No one knows better than writers that poetry must be a balance of the two, the song and the tension," says Heaney. "Matthew Arnold, after his lush early lyrics, beat himself into a corner of responsibility with somber dutiful civic poetry."

Heaney sees poetry "as divination, as a restoration of the culture to itself." Anyone undertaking such a task does not do so lightly. "To forge a poem is one thing, to forge the uncreated conscience of the race, as Stephen Dedalus put it, is quite another and places daunting pressures and responsibilities on anyone who would risk the name of poet."

"*In extremis*, in times of great crisis," says Heaney, "the vision is renewed. But in the dull economics of day-to-day life, it disappears. So it has to be reimagined constantly by the poet. As poets we have analogies, myths available to us to get the story told and retold."

Recently Heaney finished another commission, this time for Amnesty International. "They are a wonderful group," he says. "They keep the guilt moving where it has to be moved." Still, he adds, he was somewhat reluctant to accept the commission because of the "embarrassment of attaching oneself to something so immaculate."

The poem is "The Republic of Conscience." The republic is a place where there are "no porters, no interpreters, no taxis," where you carry your own burden. The precious metal of the country is salt (for the sting of conscience, explains Heaney). Here seashells are held to the ear at births and funerals. It is a place "where embassies were independent and ambassadors were never relieved."

Daniel D. Emmett (1815–1904) organized the first minstrel show in the United States in 1842, in which he introduced his original composition "Dixie." The song became the "national anthem" of the American South.

"Mud Vision" is also placed somewhere in the future and was inspired, Heaney says, by moving statues and the like. He confesses he isn't sure what it all means, but labels the poem "surrealistic."

"It used to be," Heaney said jokingly, "when some poet would say, 'I didn't know what I meant by that poem,' I would think of him as pretentious. But the older I get the more tolerance I have for pretension."

The longest and perhaps most moving poem of the reading was drawn from his latest book, *Station Island*. A pilgrim, on his way to St. Patrick's Purgatory in Lough Derg, County Donegal, meets the ghost of a friend killed in a local skirmish. Here Heaney was the actor taking both parts. The already exalted art of Irish conversation he elevated to a new height.

Like the *Station Island* poems "Underground" and "Holding Course," two pieces about married life interweave myth, fairy tale, modern literature, and history. The sonnets to his mother, who died two and a half years ago, are a compelling portrait, her "white cups unchipped," a bright counterpoint to Heaney's "neolithic" father. Finally, there is "Peacock Feather."

Heaney tells the story of arriving at his sister's house in Gloucestershire and realizing he had forgotten to buy a present for his niece's christening some six days earlier.

"Oh, go upstairs and write something," his wife said to him.

"Since it came so freely I had no respect for it"—Heaney shrugged —"but over the years I think it is one of the best things I have ever done. We found a peacock feather in the yard and wrapped it with the poem."

It is Heaney at his best: crisp, compressed, wry, deeply in touch with place. Its words, as Anne Burnham says in her thoughtful program notes, are "to be savored, turned over on the tongue, and relished for their lovely heft and shape and ring."

In the last poem of *Station Island*, the ghost of Joyce prods Heaney on. "It's time to swim out on your own," Joyce tells him, "and fill the element with signatures on your own frequency, echo soundings, searches, probes, allurements, elver-gleams in the dark of the whole sea."

The pilgrim has listened well. The elver-gleams glow brighter and sharper with each visit. He should come to town more often. ◆

*H*ad her parents lived, Mary McCarthy once remarked, they would have been "a united Catholic family, rather middle class and wholesome" and she might have grown up to find herself "married to an Irish lawyer and playing golf and bridge, making occasional retreats and subscribing to a Catholic Book Club."

However tragic the loss of both mother and father at age six, there is evident relief at having escaped the prosaic presents of the Irish-American bourgeoisie. Mary McCarthy has instead attained fame as novelist, critic, journalist, and cultural historian, and none of the nineteen volumes she has produced has been selected by a Catholic Book Club.

Whatever their particular theme, McCarthy's works of fiction and nonfiction taken together constitute a chronicle of the past half-century, seen from the liberal intellectual perspective that she chose for herself. She involved herself in the "follies and preoccupations" of the New York intelligentsia who became her adopted family: "Sexual freedom in the 1930s, radicalism in the forties and fifties, Vietnam and the social upheavals of the sixties, Watergate and terrorism in the seventies." Whatever the subject, one commentator has noted, the voice is always consistent. McCarthy's "point of view is always moral (at times moralistic); the angle of vision, feminine; the tone, logical and cool." Unlike such contemporaries as Philip Rahv or Edmund Wilson (with both of whom she was romantically involved), McCarthy did not adopt a consistent set of radical attitudes in her criticism of politics and literature. The very individuality and immediacy of her writing made its mark on those who might otherwise have demanded a consistent "line." Robert Lowell spoke of her as "our Diana, brash to awkwardness, blurting out ice-clear sentences above the mundane gossip" of their colleagues. Norman Mailer hailed her as "our First Lady of Letters, our saint, our umpire, our lit arbiter . . . our Joan of Arc."

Not all her fellow members of the New York literary intelligentsia appreciated her rigor and combativeness. Alfred Kazin wrote of her "wholly destructive critical mind" and her "unerring ability to spot the hidden weakness or inconsistency in any literary effort and every person. To this weakness she instinctively leaped with cries of pleasure—sur-

Living for the most part on vegetable food and with scarcely any beverage other than water or milk, those people have a flow of animal spirits and vivacity of temper unknown in countries whose inhabitants constantly feed on flesh and strong drink.

Robert Bell, *A Description of the Peasantry of Ireland* (1804)

prised that her victim, as he lay torn and bleeding, did not applaud her perspicacity." McCarthy was famous for attacking fashionable writers or ideas and defending those that were out of favor with the intelligentsia. Her feuds with fellow critics Diana Trilling and Lillian Hellman were legendary.

All this righteous sword-wielding (Mailer's Joan of Arc image is matched by another writer's description of her as a "Valkyrie maiden") has its origin in McCarthy's fierce self-absorption and self-confidence. In her autobiographical volumes, *Memories of a Catholic Girlhood* (1957) and *How I Grew* (1987), she recalls growing up in Seattle with a commitment to "shining, starring somehow." She was determined, on graduating from Vassar, to work for "a better, more interesting course of history." Her fiction reinforced and defined her persona through a series of characters who spoke for her. "Over the years," Michiko Kakutani has pointed out, "McCarthy has written tirelessly about her own life, busily mythologizing herself in the process of inventing a gallery of alter egos . . . she is Meg in *The Company She Keeps*—the clever Vassar girl, 'a princess among the trolls.' She is also Martha, the truth-telling 'Bohemian lady' in *A Charmed Life*. She is Kay, iconoclast and scoffer in *The Group*. And she is Rosamund, the ardent and willfully noble esthete in *Birds of America.*" Some reviewers of McCarthy's novels have found them too mannered and didactic in their exposition of her point of view. She lacks the essential fictional gift, one asserted, by being unable to imagine people other than herself. Her "basilisk vision and supple, symmetrical style," it has been argued, are best employed in such works of cultural history as *The Stones of Florence*, in which her "keen intelligence and freshness of perception" are coupled with "common sense and an old-fashioned sense of responsibility." Karl Miller, editor of *The London Review of Books*, sees her in "the Voltairian enlightenment tradition."

She is a distinct personality in American literary circles, much more of an intellectual in the European style. "But at the same time," Miller adds, "she's rather thoroughly American—someone who is bright, and optimistic and practical."

Something of this rather grim practicality comes across in the following passage from *How I Grew*, in which she speaks from the perspective of old age:

"When you have committed an action that you cannot bear to think about, that causes you to writhe in retrospect, do not seek to evade the memory: make yourself relive it, confront it repeatedly over and over, till finally, you will discover, through sheer repetition it loses its power to pain you. It works, I guarantee you, this surefire guilt-eradicator, like a homeopathic medicine—like in small doses applied to like. It works, but I am not sure that it is a good thing."

In her seventies and living in Paris, McCarthy is as involved as ever in the concerns of the day while pursuing various studies that may lead to a work of nonfiction, growing out of her current interest in Gothic architecture, or that may simply expand her horizons, for she insists that no day is satisfactory unless somehow her store of knowledge is increased. Those who have known her the longest say she has mellowed, but her self-assurance and brisk judgments seem as firmly in place as ever.

Surveying Mary McCarthy's career and character, trying to place this "first lady of American letters" in some context more specific than Bohemia or Utopia, one is reminded of those Irish Catholic origins from which she sought so fiercely to distance herself. Despite the secular humanism, there is a spiritual dimension. Despite the exaltation of sexual freedom, there is a puritanical note. Despite the avowed liberalism, there is an assertive dogmatism. Whatever the Joan of Arc flourishes of her younger days, the mature McCarthy suggests nothing so much as a sharp, shrewed, rigorous mother superior, dispensing alternate reprimands and exhortations. In fleeing from her lace-curtain background, did she perhaps carry an unrealized infusion of it with her? Just as Mary McCarthy is an expatriate from the United States, so she is an expatriate from Irish America. But, as many expatriates—especially those of Irish origin— have discovered, you never really leave home. ◆

HE THAT LOSES THE GAME, LET HIM TALK AWAY.
Traditional Irish Proverb

Write Your
Way to Fame
and Fortune

The superheated world of blockbuster best-sellers acquired two new inhabitants during the 1980s—both of them Irish American, and both of them writers who emerged from unlikely backgrounds to win their way to novelistic fame and fortune.

Mary Higgins Clark, a widow with five children to support, developed a newly discovered talent for writing radio shows into a successful production company. When she ventured on a first novel, she received the not-very-princely advance of $3,000. But *Where Are the Children?* was a tremendous success, earning $100,000 for the paperback rights. All five of her subsequent thrillers were best-sellers, and in 1988 she signed a $10.1 million contract covering her next five books.

Tom Clancy, an insurance agent with "a wife, two children . . . mortgages, car payments, and related bonds of middle-class life" to hold him back, nevertheless determined to pursue his childhood dream of being a novelist. The three books he has published since 1984 (*The Hunt for Red October*, *Red Storm Rising*, and *Patriot Games*) have earned him between five and six million dollars, and he has signed a new contract that reportedly guarantees him $4 million for a novel as yet unwritten and unconceived.

Clearly, the literary luck of the Irish is still alive and well in America!

♦

A LITTLE HELP IS
BETTER THAN A
DEAL OF PITY.
*Traditional Irish
Proverb*

*W*illiam Kennedy has put Albany on the literary map of the United States. To those who know the town only as the capital of New York (which they had to memorize along with the other state capitals), or even to those who have driven through its drab streets, it may seem an unlikely venue for a distinguished writer's work. But Kennedy, as the National Book Critics Circle Award, a MacArthur Foundation Grant, and the 1984 Pulitzer Prize certify, is a fiction writer of distinction, and his fiction is set firmly in this seemingly unpromising locale. During the decade or so preceding his Pulitzer laurels, he produced the three novels of what came to be known as the Albany Trilogy. Set in the Depression era, *Legs, Billy Phelan's Greatest Game*, and *Ironweed* established their author as "an insightful interpreter of time and place."

The trilogy became a tetralogy in 1988, with the publication of Kennedy's long-promised novel, *Quinn's Book*. Although its events take place in the mid-nineteenth century, they still take place in Albany, and its characters are ancestors (literal or spiritual) of some who figure in the earlier tales.

Kennedy is more than a regional novelist, though. He has not only transformed the unpromising environment of Albany into a literary locale, he has also joined the ranks of those who have portrayed the Irish experience in America. His principal characters are the Albany Irish: Jack Diamond and his criminal cohorts in *Legs*, Billy Phelan and his wandering father, Francis (the protagonist of *Ironweed*), and Daniel Quinn of *Quinn's Book*, whose grandson and namesake appears in the 1930s stories.

William Kennedy is himself a product of the environment about which he writes. After a "typical" Irish Catholic upbringing, and a stint on a local newspaper, he took the traditional step of the Irish writer and withdrew from the parochial world of priests and politicians, in order to practice his craft. He went "about as far as I could go and still be in the United States"—to Puerto Rico. But, like other Irish exiles, he remained a prisoner to his place of origin, gradually realizing that he was "a person whose imagination has become fused with a single place. And in that place finds all that a man needs for the life of the soul."

John R. Gregg (1867–1948), a native of County Monaghan, invented the system of shorthand writing that bears his name.

Kennedy's novels are undoubtedly concerned with the specifics of the Albany Irish experience—the schools, churches, election campaigns. His image of the amiably corrupt machine run by the city's longtime boss Daniel O'Connell exhibits the skill of the historian and journalist, as well as the novelist. The doings of Famine Era immigrants and bootleg-era gangsters are redolent of time and place.

But Kennedy also addresses a dimension of the broader Irish-American experience that is not dealt with by writers such as Edwin O'Connor, who has written so memorably about the tensions between prelates and politicians. Kennedy has said that writers such as O'Connor have left some things out, either to be polite to the Church or to Irish society, or perhaps out of squeamishness. He felt that such writers did not reflect Irish-American life as he knew it. He thought he had to bring in the bawdyhouses, the gambling, and the violence. The idealized Irish life of home and church was part of the story, but the dissolute doings among the "raffish" Irishmen were also part of the story. He wanted to write about tough, dirty-minded, and foul-mouthed brawlers and bigots, who could also be generous, funny, and honest in their own way. He felt that this dimension of Irish-American life had to be presented in all its harshness—"its wit, anger, sexuality, deviousness."

Kennedy has not, however, sought to revive the realism of the early James T. Farrell. His work has too much of the romantic, even the dreamlike, about it. He has said that his writing possesses a "surreal dimension that goes with any society in which religion plays such a dominant role."

William Kennedy is, thus, a writer conscious not only of his Irishness, but also of his place in the evolution of Irish-American fiction writing. While basing himself firmly in the place he knows best, he seeks to portray the Albany Irish as reflections of the general experience of the Irish in America, which is itself a combination of universal human frailties and the particular characteristics of what used to be called "the Celtic Race." ◆

*A*mericans love to mark centennials, and it is not surprising that the one hundredth anniversary of Eugene O'Neill's birth (1988), should have inspired celebrations as far back as 1986. O'Neill was, after all, the only American playwright to win the Nobel Prize for Literature. The two-and-a-half-hour production on public television in the fall of 1986 was, if a trifle premature as centennial observance, a full and deserved tribute to an author of prodigious industry (fifty-one plays), innovative boldness, and ardent honesty. One important dimension of O'Neill was, however, strangely lacking from this production—his Irishness.

To be sure, there were a few quotations alluding to his charm, or temperament. One woman speaks of "this attractive Irish guy, as attractive as hell." His wife describes him as "a rough, tough, black Irishman," and "a tough Mick . . . who only loved his work." And, of course, his father's Irish birth and devout Catholicism are mentioned. But these are mere flourishes in the script. Of O'Neill's own profound awareness of his Irish heritage, and of its influence on his work, there was virtually nothing in this lengthy eulogy.

This type of omission was nothing new. O'Neill himself noted it (with amusement, amazement, annoyance—or perhaps all three) in a 1945 letter to his son. "The critics have missed the important thing about me and my work," he wrote, "the fact that I am Irish."

Why did the critics miss this point—and continue to miss it forty years later? Perhaps because they were not prepared, either in terms of information or of assumption, to deal with anything "Irish" beyond the stereotypes generally recognized in the United States. This Irishness of O'Neill must be approached on two levels. The first, fairly obvious, is that of Irish influences and Irish content—family background, charac-

Eugene O'Neill, the son of an immigrant actor, was profoundly imbued with a sense of Irish history and literary heritage.

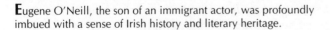

ters, plots, and themes. The second level is the more subtle, personal one of motivation and intention.

As to formative influences, O'Neill's childhood was saturated in Irish consciousness. His father, the celebrated actor James O'Neill, though largely self-educated, was full of Irish lore and history. The country that James had left as a ten-year-old famine emigrant was recollected in nostalgic glow as a fairy-tale land of beauty. The O'Neills, he told his sons, were a great and noble clan who had produced mighty warriors like Shane the Proud and Eoghan Ruadh. (It was after this Eoghan, mistakenly anglicized into Eugene, that he named his youngest son.) But the greatest and noblest of all O'Neills was surely Hugh O'Neill, the earl of Tyrone, who had led a great rebellion against English domination, outplanned and outfought Queen Elizabeth's generals, and ranked as respected statesman in the courts of Europe. A brilliant, polished Renaissance gentleman, raised at the royal court, he combined the arts of advanced civilization with the passion and power of tribal chieftainship. A charismatic leader, he had sought to reinvigorate his people's traditional culture while securing their freedom in the complex environment of early-seventeenth-century European politics. The Great Tyrone, as the Irish called him, must have made a deep impression upon young O'Neill—all the more because the name of his clan's ancestral home, Tyrone, derived from Tir Eoghan (Land of Owen), the name that his father had bestowed upon him. He would name a son of his own after Shane the Proud, but the name Tyrone would have a deeper and more pervasive implication for him.

SWEET IS WINE,
BITTER ITS
PAYMENT.
*Traditional Irish
Proverb*

Irish parental influences—from his immigrant father, who had clawed his way out of desperate poverty, and his convent-bred mother, who came of prosperous, genteel Irish stock—were reinforced by Catholic schooling in an era when the training of Catholic youth was still largely in Irish hands. And then, after a brief stay at Princeton and a period of knocking about the world as sailor, gold prospector, and drifter, he encountered a touring company from the Abbey Theatre. He was fascinated by techniques, style, rhythms that he had never dreamed could be conveyed on the stage. By 1914 he had dedicated himself to a career as a playwright, and by 1920 was making a success of it. In these early years, Irish dramatists—Synge in particular—had a great influence on him, and his plays frequently contain Irish characters and attempt to capture the Irish cadences of speech.

The catalogue of obvious Irishness can be extended throughout the remainder of O'Neill's life (illness forced him to give up writing some years before his death in 1953). It would include small but significant items like the choice of Irish names for his children (Shane, Oona) to the planning of a nine-play cycle tracing the history of America through the interwoven fortunes of two families, one Yankee, the other Irish. The only play of this projected group that he actually finished, *A Touch of* the Poet, like another late work, *A Moon for the Misbegotten*, make clear his continuing preoccupation with Irish characters and the rich rhythms of Irish speech. The posthumous productions of *Long Day's Journey into Night* in 1957 won O'Neill his fourth Pulitzer Prize. Critics were fascinated by dramatic and psychological aspects of this powerful depiction of the author's own family—whom he called the Tyrones—but again slighted the Irish dimension. Quite apart from its significance as a device for making peace with the ghosts of his father, mother, and brother, O'Neill has created here a fascinating depiction of an Irish-American family in the early years of the century. Most critics apparently felt that it was the personal conflict and revelations of hidden guilt that mattered, and that the Tyrones could just as well be Italian Americans or WASPs.

But the Irishness of Eugene O'Neill goes beyond the fact that his father was born in Kilkenny or that he occasionally used characters with names like Cornelius Melody or Josie Hogan. One must also examine that second level, of motivation and intent.

A writer's initial motivation is often as much negative as positive— his contempt for something second-rate and a conviction that he could do better himself. O'Neill was motivated by revulsion toward an American theater tradition that was, in large part, an American Irish theater tradition. Since the 1830s, Irish-born actors, writers, and managers had been remarkably prominent in both the serious and comic theater. James O'Neill was only one of many good-looking, flamboyant Irish men and women who had trod the stage from New York to San Francisco. Dion Boucicault's melodramas, such as *The Colleen Bawn* and *The Shaughraun* had fascinated both immigrant and native audiences during the Civil War period. Edward Harrigan's comic vignettes of Irish life had delighted theatergoers in the 1880s. Vaudeville was largely an Irish preserve in the 1890s. By the turn of the century George M. Cohan had established his renown as a man who wrote songs and sang them or wrote plays and acted in them, to say nothing of producing, directing, and dancing. The worst sort of "stage Irishman" was a chattering buffoon, usually drunk, ridiculously belligerent, or—when he was not hopelessly inept—a cunning rogue. The music-hall image conveyed by performers like Cohan was more positive but equally stereotypical— "genial, witty, lighthearted, sentimental" and ready to sing "My Wild Irish Rose" on cue. "Serious" actors, like James O'Neill, favored booming voices, florid gestures, exaggerated reactions in stock situations.

To be sure, the Irish were not the creators but merely the most obvious purveyors of an American approach to the theater that demanded escapist entertainment over all other considerations. O'Neill revolted against this tradition, aiming at a theater that drew upon the intuitive, poetic, mystical, tragical elements of Irish sensibility. He wished to transform the clown into the symbol of a new realism and a new seriousness in American drama.

Near Elmira, I passed the night at a tavern, where I was annoyed by the noise and ubiquity of a parcel of Irish waggoners, half-beast-half devil, from which I was relieved only by their getting too drunk to continue their revel.

Henry B. Bascom, *Diary* (1847)

Like the earl of Tyrone, Eugene O'Neill strove to unite and liberate his people. He strove to transcend the cliché of "shanty" versus "lace curtain." He confronted boldly the bondage imposed upon Irish Americans by both nativist assumptions and their own ambivalence. Like Tyrone, he claimed an aristocratic right to reproach and chastise. His unsparing portrayal of Irish faults roused cries of resentment all the way from *Straw* in the 1920s to *A Moon for the Misbegotten* in the 1950s, but in O'Neill's lordly view it was his mission to reveal the hard truth, not to approve or flatter.

O'Neill believed that the Irish had a spiritual quality and an innate feeling for language that shone forth in the work of their great literary figures. He was inspired by Synge and Yeats and encouraged by the judgment of Joyce and O'Casey that he "wrote like an Irishman." The American Irish, he felt sure, had not lost that special gift though it had been diminished by their struggle for survival in a hostile and materialistic society. They had been corrupted, and, in the theater, at least, had been corrupters themselves.

How fitting, then, that a renewed Irish sensibility should contribute to the birth of a new drama in the United States. Raising American theater art from provincial insignificance to world stature would be the greatest of all Irish contributions to America. O'Neill would play the part of Tyrone, the great leader, not as politician or soldier (roles in which many other Irish Americans had sought fame) but as a prophet.

Thus, throughout his literary career, regardless of whether or not specific plays had an "Irish" content, O'Neill was moved by his Irish consciousness. Like the earl of Tyrone, he would transform that which was debased and degraded into a proud and vital force. Like Tyrone he would seek help abroad, but rely primarily upon native resources. Like Tyrone, he would constantly search for new strategies and tactics to attain his goal. And like Tyrone he met opposition from his closest kinsmen.

A BLACK HEN LAYS A WHITE EGG (I.E., DO NOT JUDGE BY APPEARANCES).
Traditional Irish Proverb

Shortly before his death (in 1920), James O'Neill saw the premiere of Eugene's play *Beyond the Horizon*. Afterward he remarked to his son: "It's all right, if that's what you want to do, but people come to the theater to be entertained, not to be depressed. Do you want them to go home and commit suicide?" Eugene O'Neill later wrote that "the theater must give us what the Church no longer gives us—a meaning." In the cynical judgment by the patriarch of the O'Neills of Tyrone lay the failure of the American theater. In that prophetic vision by his son lay the American theater's hope. ◆

When All's Said and Dunne . . .

The critics had overlooked a key element in evaluating his work, Eugene O'Neill once remarked—the fact that he was Irish. They might do well to note the same fact about another American writer to whom they have been giving increasing attention, John Gregory Dunne. Once known chiefly as the husband of the much-praised novelist Joan Didion and her collaborator on a number of successful screenplays, Dunne has published seven books, including three novels, *True Confessions* (1977), *Dutch Shea, Jr.* (1982), and *The Red, White and Blue* (1987). Beyond the Irish-American characters and allusions that all of these books contain, but which are not really central to them, there is a consistent and recognizably Irish strain of tragicomedy.

Whether the author himself would acknowledge this pervasive sensibility is unclear. Even in the postwar New England of his youth, being the grandson of an Irish Catholic immigrant was not the key to social success. His father was a prosperous West Hartford physician, and he himself attended Princeton, but he has recorded that when his classmates asked what college the elder Dunne had attended, he had replied "Harvard," which was true enough as to medical school, but concealed the embarrassment of the Catholic undergraduate college that preceded it. Dunne would later outgrow this juvenile snobbery and draw upon his background, despite a journalistic (*Time* magazine) and Hollywood career fully in the mainstream.

The protagonists of all three of Dunne's novels are products of Irish America: the detective and his priest brother in *True Confessions*, the sleazy lawyer Dutch Shea, and the narrator of *The Red, White and Blue*, Jack Broderick, his monstrous millionaire father, Hugh, and his brother (also a priest). Whatever their present level of wealth, sophistication, or infidelity, they emerge from an environment that was, in every sense of the word, parochial. It was "the Catholicism of novenas and mite boxes and cake sales in the parish hall and diocesan tours of the Emerald Isle, and the funny thing that happened to Onions Galliher, him with the walleye in the Department of Parks who goes out to the ballgame at Candlestick with Father Edso Kiley and the Mercy nuns from over to Holy Sepulcher . . ." The ecclesiastical politicians who figure in each of

●*The originally Celtic race is less mixed. . . . The common classes are strongly marked with the national peculiarity of features, and by this they are readily recognized in other countries.* ●

A Pictorial Geography of the World (1856)

Dunne's novels display the mixture of Vatican suavity and Tammany ruthlessness that epitomized the Irish domination of the American Catholic Church through the 1960s. Nevertheless, in none of these books (even *True Confessions*, which involves the sordid circumstances surrounding the death of a monsignor, and the cover-up) is religion the central theme.

But it is neither his ancestry nor his use of Irish-American characters and elements in his novels that constitutes Dunne's "Irishness." Reviewers have spoken of his "crackling dialogue," gritty characters, and "fierce, unblinking stare at acts of brutality." These are surely features of many contemporary Irish writers, yet not so uniquely as to make Dunne stand out from other American novelists. Commentators have come closer to the mark when they spoke of a sense of *abundance* in his prose style, of "multitudes of pungent phrases strung together, rich descriptions tumbling over one another." Again and again there is a wild rush of words evoking the grotesque incongruities of life. Here, for instance, is Jack Broderick's recollection of his days as a newspaper man:

I was the perfect sidebar reporter, the kind who wrote about the deaf old woman and her fourteen cats who lived in the Haight across the street from the family of nine killed in the fire set by their son-in-law, recently released from the state mental facility in Napa. I gave the names of all fourteen cats and described the smell of the kitty litter as the deaf old woman rambled on about the son-in-law from across the street, such a nice boy, really, quiet, don't you know, we used to talk about what to feed the cats, he was partial to the 9 Lives, I like the Tender Vittles myself, the tuna chunks, that's my favorite, and the liver, that's a nice treat, too, he liked the finicky eater's menu, I guess it takes all kinds. . . .

What distinguishes Dunne's writing is a torrent of images, at once horrendous and hilarious. Jokes and comic stories seem to flood his brain, it has been said, like water overflowing a barrel. No individual, institution, or viewpoint is exempt from his mockery. But Dunne is not merely cynical. His comedy is always poised on the edge of horror, as a Central American gunman in a Mickey Mouse sweatshirt obliterates a nun's face with his bullets, or the severed head of a murdered labor leader makes a bizarre reappearance. Reality, he constantly reminds us, is ridiculous, and often ghastly as well.

Such perceptions and such images have been part of Irish literary expression from earliest times. Whether in the outlandish doings of ancient saga-men or the bizarre convolutions of Joycean fiction, a long line of Irish writers has portrayed the human tragicomedy in a glorious rush of words.

Consciously or unconsciously, Dunne is part of this tradition of the prolix, joking, shocking imagers of human folly. He is currently its leading representative among American writers. Critics of his work should, indeed, take note of the fact that he is Irish. ◆

$\mathcal{T}$o envy those whom one despises—there is enough in that shameful passion to poison one's whole life." It is tempting to apply this observation by an eminent French writer to F. Scott Fitzgerald and John O'Hara. Both men stood on the periphery of America's social "establishment," doomed to exclusion from it by their Irish Catholic background. Both men, in their novels and short stories, brought keen powers of observation to the manners and morals of an elite that both fascinated and repelled. Yet there are enough differences between these two Irish-American writers, despite their similar background and parallel subject matter, to demand care in using verbs like "envy" and "despise" as if their reactions were identical.

Certainly both men recognized a common "lace curtain" origin. In 1933 O'Hara, who had not yet published anything, wrote a "fan letter" to Fitzgerald, already famous for *This Side of Paradise* and his many short stories. He praised Fitzgerald's depiction of an Irish-American social climber in a recent piece, and complained about the "climbing" proclivities of the Irish in America. He confessed that he himself felt prouder of some old American connections on his mother's side than of his "black Irish" father who had been an eminent surgeon. "I go through some cheap shame" he added, "when the O'Hara side gets too close for comfort. If you've had the same trouble, at least you've turned it into a gift."

Fitzgerald responded that he was "half black Irish and half old American stock." The Irish half of the family, he said, had the money and looked down upon the Maryland side. The circumstances of his youth assured that no matter what great things might happen to him, "I should still be a parvenu."

Both men were conscious of the social inferiority of the Irish in America. Both were uncertain as to their own status. Avowedly contemptuous of the "climber," they nonetheless hoped to be accepted by "those who really mattered."

There were dissimilarities as well as similarities, however. While both families were financially secure (the one through professional success, the other through commerce), O'Hara was brought up in an environment (Pottsville, Pennsylvania) where even the rich Irish were kept

John O'Hara

F. Scott Fitzgerald

at arm's length by the Anglo-Saxon elite, while Fitzgerald's native town (St. Paul, Minnesota) was dominated by such Catholic gentry as Mrs. James J. Hill, the wife of the railroad magnate. O'Hara attended Catholic prep schools that were, in his eyes, innately inferior; due to his father's death and the evaporation of his estate, young John did not attain his dream of entering Yale. Fitzgerald was a graduate of Princeton.

After working as a reporter, film critic, and movie scriptwriter, O'Hara won critical recognition with *Appointment in Samarra* (1934) and *Butterfield 8* (1935). A period of short story and Hollywood writing was followed by such novels as *A Rage to Live* (1949), *Ten North Frederick* (1955), and *From the Terrace* (1958), which brought him tremendous financial success but little praise from critics. Reviewers of these later novels noted his meticulous observation and depiction of upper-class Americans: how they spoke, dressed, behaved. But these commentators deplored the emptiness of his characters, their lack of any internal vitality to match the scrupulously detailed exteriors. O'Hara, a meticulous recorder of the externals that constituted the behavior patterns of the upper class, did not seem to be able to penetrate the façade, to find their human essence.

Less obvious to critics was O'Hara's persistent denigration of the Irish. The note of resentment he had sounded in his 1933 letter to Fitzgerald continued throughout his literary career. Irish-American characters, whenever they appear in O'Hara's writings, are, at best, stereotypes and, at worst, criminals or despicable social climbers. From Harry Reilly, the crude nouveau riche of *Appointment in Samarra* to Creighton Duffy, the corrupt political manipulator of *From the Terrace*, the characters who spring from O'Hara's own Irish Catholic background are presented in contemptible contrast to the well-bred Anglo-Saxons with whom the author sought to identify himself.

Fitzgerald's novels—particularly *The Beautiful and the Damned* (1921), *The Great Gatsby* (1925), and *Tender Is the Night* (1934)—as well as his short stories, had already established him as a major American writer long before O'Hara began to publish. But during the late 1930s his career and his health declined, and in 1940 he died, at the age of forty-four. Like O'Hara he wrote about that social class to which he did not quite belong, although he came closer to gaining acceptance into it, thanks to a combination of charm and good luck. Unlike O'Hara's, however, his description of externals was accompanied by an insight and depth of sympathy that enabled him to create genuinely human characters. In its tragic sense of life his art transcends that of O'Hara, whose strength lies chiefly in accurate depiction of outward forms.

While sharing O'Hara's Irish ambivalence, Fitzgerald feels and expresses it in a markedly different way. When James Malloy, in *Butterfield 8*, proclaims "I am a Mick," and goes on to declare that, for all his Brooks Brothers clothes and his refined table manners, he will never be anything else but a "Mick" in the eyes of Protestant Americans, he is pouring out O'Hara's own anguish. Fitzgerald does not emphasize his Irishness, much less agonize over it, in his writings. There are many references, usually favorable, to "Irish" physical and personality traits, and there are a number of Irish-American characters, such as Father Darcy in *This Side of Paradise* and Rosemary Hoyt in *Tender Is the Night*, who are balanced, fully rounded human beings. But it is in his sensibility, his attitude toward his subjects that Fitzgerald most significantly reveals his Irish Catholic upbringing. Like O'Hara, he ceased to be a practicing Catholic early in adult life. But while the ex–altar boy from Pottsville made an apparently clean break, Fitzgerald continued to be influenced by the values absorbed in youth throughout his life. His preoccupation with the life-style of the rich is undercut by evident disapproval of their hedonistic conduct. His depictions of "Jazz Age" society, far from being celebrations of a heedless amorality, reflect an inbred conservatism and a strong moral sense. The "outsiders" who appear so frequently in his stories project his own fascination with the rich people who are so "different from you and me." Again and again they are destroyed or disillusioned when they come into too-close contact with this charmed circle. And yet they are driven to make that intimate contact, as is the upstart, Gatsby. As another of these projections of Fitzgerald's own point of view puts it, access to the precincts of glamour and wealth both "enchanted and repelled" him. Recognizing the spiritual emptiness that lay within

Although California sent Irish senators to Washington as soon as it was admitted to statehood, San Francisco, the "Irish Capital of the West," did not have its first Irish mayor until the election of James Phelan (1861– 1930) in 1897.

the citadels of privilege, Fitzgerald was able to create characters who suffer as well as glitter. They have far more than the single dimension of O'Hara's precisely painted pictures of establishment types.

Both Fitzgerald and O'Hara can be said to envy and to despise the American upper class about which they write. In Fitzgerald's case the tendency to despise predominated in the end, for his Irish sensibility and ingrained values enabled him to grasp the tragedy that lay at the core of so many worldly achievements. This insight into his subject matter made him a better writer at the same time that it underlined the futility of his own ambition. "Making it" was, in the end, only another route to heartbreak and failure.

With O'Hara, on the other hand, envy proved the stronger force. While he occasionally lashed out, both in his writings and in his conversations, against the hypocrisies of "society," he was consumed by a desire to "belong." Once he attained a fortune from his best-sellers, he committed himself to a standard and style of living that aped that of his fictional characters. The "Mick" who had proclaimed bitterly, through one of his characters, that the Irish could never be assimilated, continued to hope against hope that he was wrong. He allowed his craving for acceptance to blind him to the emptiness of the prize he sought. Unlike Fitzgerald, O'Hara created hollow characters, because he could not bear to look beyond the façade of Anglo-Saxon self-confidence. He abandoned the unique opportunity that his position on the periphery of the establishment gave him in the hope that his silence would be rewarded—or in fear of learning the worthlessness of his own dreams.

HONEY IS SWEET,
BUT DON'T LICK IT
OFF A BRIAR.
*Traditional Irish
Proverb*

F. Scott Fitzgerald and John O'Hara were outsiders. The circumstances of their birth and upbringing guaranteed that status, for as Irish Catholics in white Anglo-Saxon Protestant America they were automatically inferior. Not as inferior as working-class Irish Catholics, and certainly not as unacceptable as most other ethnic and racial groups, but still inferior. Only the most superficial observer will deny that it is still a fact of life. Each of them came to terms with this fundamental reality of Irish-American life on his own terms as an artist and as a human being. Fitzgerald died young and broke. O'Hara died old and rich. ◆

When James Thomas Farrell died in 1979 at the age of seventy-five, many readers of his obituary uttered that classic comment reserved for the demise of faded celebrities, "I thought he died a long time ago." Obviously they had not seen the article in *The New York Times* several years earlier that confirmed that Farrell was alive and well and writing in New York. Both the article and the rather strained phrases of the obituary made clear, however, that Farrell's writing was no longer read. Tribute was paid to the tough-minded, clear-eyed young writer from a working-class Irish district of Chicago who had conveyed that environment with such intense realism in his Studs Lonigan trilogy during the early 1930s and in his semiautobiographical tales of the O'Neills and the O'Flahertys in the late 1930s. Commentators acknowledged the influence of Farrell on writers such as James Jones and Norman Mailer. And in some cases they alluded vaguely to a less successful body of work in later years. In plain fact, the postwar period was a failure.

But the impact of Farrell's early work should not be dismissed lightly. Into an American literature that was still largely bogged down in the genteel tradition, he introduced an inspiring realism that shocked the timid and awed the perceptive among his readers. Moreover, he was the first to depict the everyday life of working-class and lower-middle-class Americans of immigrant stock. His Chicago Irish were not the slum dwellers who had been glimpsed in a few earlier novels by outsiders, such as Stephen Crane's *Maggie: A Girl of the Streets*. They were the ordinary people among whom he had grown up: people holding jobs, raising families, attending Mass, going to school. The protagonist of his trilogy, Studs Lonigan, is traced from adolescence through young manhood, as he experiences disillusionment, disintegration, and death. But Studs is not a malnourished tenement child, perishing through sheer deprivation. Farrell wants this clearly understood. "Had I written *Studs Lonigan* as a story of the slums," he pointed out, "it would then have been easy for the reader falsely to place the motivation and causation of the story directly in immediate economic roots. Such a placing of motivation would have obscured one of the most important meanings which I wanted to inculcate into my story. Here was a neighborhood several steps removed from the slums and dire economic want, and here was manifested a pervasive spiritual poverty."

There is nothing in Studs Lonigan's environment that could be called positively evil. His parents, his teachers, his Church all seek to set a conventional example of hard work and decent behavior. But they offer nothing to fulfill the dreams and romantic aspirations of youth. The neighborhood offers only a cultural vacuum, a setting in which even the clergy neglect the spirit of man, in their preoccupation with material matters. Studs must draw his spiritual sustenance from the streets, from the fellowship of the gang, where the "tough guy" is the hero, and kindlier, gentler feelings must be concealed or abandoned. His mind, offered nothing better, becomes saturated with fantasies of aggression in which he beats up other males and ruthlessly exploits all females.

Lonigan is not simply a product of Depression-era Chicago. Like all great fictional creations, Farrell's work has a wider and more lasting relevance. The cultural poverty that shaped the boy Studs has afflicted generations of young people brought up in an atmosphere where the life of the mind is ignored or despised. Long after the straitened circumstances of the 1920s had given way to an era of prosperity, working-class and lower-middle-class Irish Americans lingered in a wasteland of minimal expectations and narrow assumptions. Certain patterns of behavior, certain goals were favored, while all others were regarded with suspicion or hostility. Safe thinking, conventional slogans, discouragement of imagination characterized the communities in which whole generations of new young Lonigans grew up. Even improved opportunities of education had limited impact on thousands of boys—and now, girls as well—who passed through high school, even college, without opening their minds and hearts. Preoccupied with strictly vocational goals, they existed in a world where money and entertainment were more plentiful than in the 1920s but life proved just as barren. Violence continued to preoccupy and fascinate them, and aimless cruising about in automobiles extended the range of gang activities. Drinking and drugs fueled their fantasies and aggressions.

To be sure, not all Irish Americans remained trapped in the intellectual and spiritual dead end that Lonigan's life embodied. Moreover, with some modifications, the cultural poverty that Farrell depicted could be paralleled among other ethnic groups and even in other countries. Nonetheless, the important—and frightening—thing about Studs Lonigan and his companions is that we can still see them among us in the closing decades of the twentieth century. Not innately vicious, they are bereft of moral or emotional substance, pursuing barren, self-destructive fantasies because the values preached to them are so obviously mere empty formulas. The cynical arrogance and self-delusion of Studs Lonigan endures among those who might be his grandchildren. James T. Farrell is alive and well. ◆

DON'T LEAVE A
TAILOR'S REMNANT
BEHIND YOU.
*Traditional Irish
Proverb*

"Hunger" Pangs

When they first heard the news, Irish Americans were delighted. The Abbey Theatre, Ireland's National Theatre, would be staging a production in New York during March 1988. The cultural prestige of this famous institution was undoubted. The Abbey had an international reputation. What better alternative to the familiar inanities of the St. Patrick's Day season?

Everyone expected a classic piece by Synge, O'Casey, or one of the other great names in Irish drama. Instead, it was announced that the traveling company would offer *The Great Hunger*, a play by Tom MacIntyre, based on a poem by Patrick Kavanagh. What was that all about? Something to do with the era of the Potato Famine, presumably. No doubt an evocation of Ireland's tragic history, expressed with the poetic eloquence that characterized Ireland's playwrights, including this fellow MacIntyre, whoever he was.

Most of those who dutifully made their way to the play's opening performance were unaware the title referred not to the famine but to the sexual frustrations of the rural Irish. They were unaware, too, that the production had stirred controversy in Ireland and on a European tour (the French evidently liked it, the Russians did not) by its eccentric character. The children and senior citizens who had been brought along in a gesture of cultural patriotism might not have been baffled or upset by the sexual element; even Irish Americans have grown sophisticated in these matters by now. What confounded virtually the entire audience was the fundamental concept underlying the production.

The Abbey Theatre, founded as an outlet for the eloquence of sparkling poets and honey-voiced actors, had chosen to reject the very spoken word that had made it world-famous. Instead, it had come up with a piece of what might be called—to use the pretentious phrase lately in vogue—performance art. Gestures and visual and natural effects were substituted for text. "There are some words in the play," a reviewer noted, "but they are insistently and boringly repetitive."

The single set was a potato field, where a farmer named Maguire and various other characters alternate athletic horseplay with incomprehensible symbolic action. Those inevitable icons of Irish life, the Mother and the Priest, are in evidence, but not to any evident purpose.

Professional critics found the work not only baffling but disheartening. The primary difficulty, *The New York Times* reviewer wrote, was not "the play's dearth of poetry, but the familiarity and ingenuousness of the performance techniques. As produced by the Abbey's experimental theater lab, the play is an artifact of the 1960s." It was as if the Open Theater and other European and American innovative theaters of the past twenty years had never existed. In other words, it was just so much stale potatoes.

The Irish-American audience, if less critically informed, was more polite. Most of them actually remained for the second act. Some even said, a bit tentatively, that the piece was "interesting," or that the performers were "very energetic." There were no riots, no demonstrations, but the word gradually got about that this was not what Irish Americans had expected of "their" national institution. The production, which had hoped to remain for three weeks, closed in two.

When last heard of, the Abbey Theatre touring company was in Stamford, Connecticut, presenting Synge's *Playboy of the Western World*. End of experiment. ◆

A DIMPLE IN THE CHIN, A DEVIL WITHIN.
Traditional Irish Proverb

The Irish in America have produced undisputed "major figures of American literature," such as O'Neill and Fitzgerald, as well as writers whose chief work has been reflective of their distinctive ethnic background. But there have been others, of Irish heritage, who contributed to the general fund of our national literature without securing an unchallenged place among the greats. Some, well known in their own day, are now neglected; others are viewed primarily as exemplars of regional or contemporary values. Here are a dozen Irish-American writers whose reputations have fluctuated over time. Although victims of changing literary fashions, all of them are deserving of attention.

Fitz-James O'Brien (c. 1828–1862) A Limerick-born member of the gentry, who came to America in 1852 after gambling away his inheritance. During the next decade, his plays, poems, and particularly his short stories, in the *Atlantic* and *Harper's* made him one of New York's leading literary personalities. His work is full of the macabre and the mysterious, and "What Was It?" has been described as "a masterpiece of horror," the equal of Poe's best tales. O'Brien was killed in action while serving as an officer in the Union army.

Charles G. Halpine (1829–1868) After emigrating to the United States in 1851, he worked as a journalist in Boston, New York, and Washington. While serving with the Northern forces during the Civil War he began a series of essays and anecdotal tales under the pseudonym of Miles O'Reilly that won him a tremendous following. His books, including *The Life and Adventures of Private Miles O'Reilly* (1864) and *Baked Meats of the Funeral . . . by Private M. O'Reilly* (1866) presented a "G.I." view of too-often-romanticized military campaigns.

Abram J. Ryan (1838–1886) Born in Maryland and ordained as a Catholic priest, he served as a chaplain with the Confederate army. During two decades as a pastor in Mobile, Alabama, he won renown as a poet who drew upon patriotic as well as religious themes. His lyrics endeared him to the South and caused him to be called "the Poet of the Confederacy." Such pieces as "The Conquered Banner," "The Sword of Robert E. Lee," and "The Lost Cause" were memorized by generations of Southern schoolchildren.

Joel Chandler Harris (1848–1908)   The son of a "wandering Irishman," he was born in rural Georgia, and worked as a journalist in Savannah and Atlanta. His fame rests on his creation of Uncle Remus, the "darky" storyteller who narrates the doings of Brer Rabbit and other folk characters. Harris based more than half a dozen Uncle Remus books on the tales he heard from plantation blacks during his childhood.

Kate Chopin (1851–1904)   Born Katherine O'Flaherty, to Irish parents living in St. Louis, she moved to rural Louisiana after marrying a plantation manager. Her short stories, collected in *Bayou Folk* (1894) and *A Night in Acadie* (1897) give a vivid picture of Cajun life. It was her novel *The Awakening* (1899) that created the greatest sensation, however. Its candid treatment of racial intermarriage and adultery was extremely daring for those days.

Louise Imogen Guiney (1861–1920)   Born in Boston, the daughter of a colonel who commanded one of Massachusetts' Irish regiments in the Civil War. The poems contained in her numerous volumes of verse, particularly *The White Sail* (1887) and *Happy Ending* (1909), retained their popularity with anthologists and textbook compilers (if not with the critics) for many decades.

John Boyle O'Reilly (1844–1890)   After involvement in Fenian plots in Ireland, O'Reilly was banished to a penal colony in Australia, from which he escaped to America in 1869. Joining the staff of the *Boston Pilot*, he soon was its editor and became one of the most prominent figures in Irish America. His many volumes of poetry, ranging from patriotic odes to lyrical ballads, were favorably received by critics, who ranked him "well above the usual level of Hibernian versifiers."

James Whitcomb Riley (1849–1916)   As a native of Indiana, his verse contributions to the Indianapolis *Journal* established his reputation as "the Hoosier Poet." Riley wrote many dialect poems dealing with scenes of simple life and "marked by kindly humor, pathos, sincerity, and naturalness." He published more than a dozen collections of verse between 1883 and 1915, including those which take their titles from his best-known poems: "The Old Swimmin' Hole," "Little Orfant Annie," and "When the Frost Is on the Punkin." Riley has been called "the poet laureate of democracy."

George Kelly (1887–1960)   Member of a Philadelphia Irish family best known for producing Princess Grace of Monaco, Kelly was himself an actor before becoming a playwright. Although his dramas range from *The Torch Bearers* and *The Show Off* in the early 1920s to *Reflected Glory* in 1936, his best-remembered work is *Craig's Wife*, which was awarded the Pulitzer Prize for 1925.

Marc Connelly (1890–1980)   Born in small-town Pennsylvania, Connelly made his name on Broadway as early as 1921. As author or coauthor he was responsible for a long series of hit plays. He touched upon a wide variety of themes, culminating in his successful adaptation of a

"Negro dialect" work into the memorable *Green Pastures*, which gained him the Pulitzer Prize in 1930. He later became a professsor of drama at Yale.

Philip Barry (1896–1949)   Born in Rochester, New York, Barry was a lace-curtain, Ivy League (Yale *and* Harvard Graduate School) Irishman, who succumbed to the lure of the theater rather than the solid advantages of the law firm or the boardroom. His well-received plays began with *You and I* (1922), delighted the critics with *The Animal Kingdom* (1932), and reached their peak with *The Philadelphia Story* (1939).

Phyllis McGinley (1905–1978)   This Oregonian was a witty verse chronicler of suburban life whose poems appeared in such sophisticated periodicals as *Vogue* and *The New Yorker*. Although some considered her light verse too light, she won the 1961 Pulitzer Prize for her collection, *Three Times Three*.

Flannery O'Connor (1925–1964)   Grave illness and an early death limited the quantity of O'Connor's work, chiefly contained in two collections of short stories, *A Good Man Is Hard to Find* (1955) and *Everything That Rises Must Converge* (1965), and two novels, *Wise Blood* (1952) and *The Violent Bear It Away* (1960). The two chief influences reflected in her unconventional writings are her Southern and her Irish Catholic heritages. Whether the considerable critical esteem she enjoyed in the 1970s will endure or increase remains to be seen.   ◆

IT'S ALMOST AS GOOD AS BRINGING GOOD NEWS NOT TO BRING BAD.
Traditional Irish Proverb

The Stage
Irishman

The stage Irishman habitually bears the general name of Pat, Paddy, or Teague. He has an atrocious Irish brogue, perpetual jokes, blunders and bulls in speaking, and never fails to utter, by way of Hibernian seasoning, some wild screech, or oath of Gaelic origin, at every third word. . . . His hair is of a fiery red, he is rosy-cheeked, massive, and whiskey-loving. His face is one of simian bestiality, with an expression of diabolical archness written all over it. He wears a tall hat, with a clay pipe stuck in his face, an open shirt collar, a three-caped coat, knee-breeches, worsted stockings, and cockaded shoes. In his right hand he brandishes a stout blackthorn or sprig of shillelagh, and threatens to belabor therewith the daring person who will tread on the tail of his coat. For his main characteristics (if there is such a thing as psychology in a stage Irishman) are his swagger, his boisterousness, and his pugnacity. He is always ready with a challenge, always anxious to back a quarrel, and peerless for cracking skulls at Donnybrook Fair.

—Maurice Bourgeois, *John Millington Synge and
the Irish Theatre* (1913)

Lola

*S*he was the most celebrated (some would say "notorious") entertainer of her day. She was the "toast of three continents" and the "uncrowned queen" of a Central European kingdom. She was born in Limerick and is buried in Brooklyn.

The daughter of a British army officer, Marie Dolores Eliza Rosanna Gilbert first saw the light of day in the City of the Treaty Stone in 1818. She attended schools in Scotland and France, and was scheduled to be married to "a gouty old judge" at age nineteen. To escape this fate, she eloped to a remote corner of Ireland with a Captain Thomas James, whom she divorced a few years later. It was at this point that she made the transition from being adventuresome to being an adventuress. After only a couple of months' practice, she made her stage debut in London as "Lola Montez, Spanish Dancer."

Although the staid British were disapproving (or perhaps less accepting of frauds), the pseudo-Spaniard had a spectacular success on the Continent. In Paris and St. Petersburg, Berlin and Dresden, the glamorous and flamboyant Lola created a sensation, and her tours between 1843 and 1847 made her a European personality. Men fought (and died in) duels over the affections of the bewitching dancer.

In 1847, Lola performed at the principal theater in Munich, where she captivated the aging King Ludwig I. The doting monarch showered her with gifts, granted her an annual allowance of 20,000 florins, settled her in a magnificent mansion, and conferred upon her the title of countess of Lansfeld. Not content with merely material rewards, the strongminded, ambitious Lola meddled in Bavarian politics, seeking to become the real ruler of the country. But she was too liberal for conservatives, while liberals refused to accept the support of a royal favorite. In the revolutionary storm that swept over the German states during 1848, King Ludwig was deposed and his mistress was forced to flee.

After another brief marriage, to a mere lieutenant named Heald (presumably handsomer, and certainly younger, than Ludwig), which ended with his death, Lola set out to conquer the New World. From 1851 to 1853, she danced and acted her way across America. She and the rambunctious young republic seemed ideally suited to each other. She even

Broadway's first contribution to the American "melting pot" thesis, Abie's Irish Rose, a play about the romance between an Irish girl and a Jewish boy, ran for a record 2,327 performances in New York City during the 1920s.

found a third husband, one P. P. Hull, in San Francisco, although the marriage could not long stand the strain of her life-style. From the West Coast, the next logical step was Australia, which she toured in the mid-1850s. The exuberant frontiersmen of New South Wales and Victoria were delighted with the dashing dancer, all the more so when she delivered a public horsewhipping to a newspaper editor who had cast aspersions on her character.

Returning to the United States, Lola launched a new career, as a lecturer on such subjects as "gallantry," "the secrets of beauty," and "heroines of history." In 1859 she settled in New York City and devoted herself to works of charity, particularly care of the inmates of the Magdalen Asylum (for "fallen women"). She died in Astoria on January 17, 1861, and was buried in Brooklyn's fashionable Greenwood Cemetery. Her tomb is still pointed out to visitors among the graves of the many other famous people buried there.

As she was born in Ireland and emigrated to America, Lola Montez certainly qualifies as an Irish-American celebrity. One suspects, however, that such an ethnic designation would have seemed too prosaic to her. She would surely have preferred to be remembered as "a woman of the world." ◆

A WET MOUTH DOES NOT FEEL A DRY MOUTH (I.E., PLENTY DOES NOT UNDERSTAND WANT).
Traditional Irish Proverb

*T*he story is told that when Helen Hayes was to open in a new play in New York in 1966, she was warned that it was likely to have a hostile reception. Both the subject and structure were controversial, and the premiere was expected to provoke, at best, a mixed reaction from audience and critics. Someone remarked to the actress that the critics were going to "spit on" her. "Whoever spits on Helen Hayes," she replied, "spits on the American flag. Let's get that curtain up." It would appear that Miss Hayes's Irish was up, along with the curtain.

To be honored and esteemed by all Americans, and to retain, at the same time a sense of one's Irish roots: these are the hallmarks of a truly distinguished Irish American. Surely no one is more entitled to that designation than Helen Hayes, who has long been recognized as "the first lady of the American theater."

The actress's Irish blood is revealed not only in anecdotes that show the tough streak underlying her gentle demeanor, but also in her own account of her family background. She took her stage name, and perhaps some of her bravado, from her maternal grandfather, Patrick Hayes, who seems to have been a forceful character. He was also the nephew of Catherine Hayes, one of nineteenth-century Ireland's most honored performers. Helen Hayes proudly recalls that Catherine was hailed as the "Swan of Erin" and was beloved throughout Ireland. Her singing made her the toast of London's Albert Hall, and she was a favorite in America when she toured the country in the 1850s. The American Miss Hayes reverently preserves copies of the sheet music bearing her great-great-aunt's picture that was circulated all over the country.

Unlike the ebullient Irish emigrant Hayeses, Helen's paternal ancestors, the Browns, came to America in Colonial times and prospered as solid, dependable, middle-class, "backbone of America" folk. Helen's father, Francis VanArnum Brown, was in the meat-packing business, and evidently showed uncharacteristic originality when he married the lively Irish-American girl who became Helen's mother on October 10, 1900, in Washington, D.C. Mr. Brown was not at all enthusiastic about his wife's ambitions for young Helen, which were launched early when the girl was enrolled in a dance studio and led to her stage debut at the age of six, in

'TIS A FINE HORSE THAT NEVER STUMBLES.
Traditional Irish Proverb

a charity show where she portrayed a Gibson Girl bathing beauty. This appearance, to her mother's delight and evidently to her father's alarm, led to theatrical offers, ultimately to a 1909 musical comedy, the first of her thousands of New York stage appearances.

Thus began a career in the theater, both "legitimate" and cinematic, that has spanned eight decades. Between engagements as a child performer, she attended the Holy Cross and Sacred Heart academies in Washington, like more conventional Irish-American girls. Few of those girls would ever have had the lifetime learning experience and worldwide travels that constituted her true education.

As befits an actress who transcends ethnic roles, Helen Hayes has played American, English, Scottish, French, Italian, and Russian women. However, the great Irish-American playwright Eugene O'Neill, who always preferred actors of Irish stock to perform his Irish roles, gave her the opportunity to reach back to her roots in two notable performances. She brought particular distinction to the part of Nora Melody in *A Touch of the Poet*, and of Mrs. Tyrone in *Long Day's Journey into Night*.

It was in the latter persona, as a convent-educated girl who married an overbearing Irish-born actor, that Helen Hayes ended her stage career, in her native city, where it had begun. During the 1971 run of O'Neill's play at the Catholic University of America, she developed serious bronchial problems, brought on by an allergy to dust, that had evidently built up during sixty years of standing about in the backstages of the world. In subsequent years, however, she continued her movie and television work, and brought a mature distinction to even small, "cameo" roles. She also found time to do radio broadcasts and participate in benefit programs for the elderly, encouraging them to make the most of what she called "the best years."

Over the years, Helen Hayes has been awarded Oscars, Tonys, Emmys, and scores of other medals, trophies, and ribbons at home and abroad. In 1986 the Presidential Medal of Freedom was bestowed upon her, and she has received the Kennedy Center Honors recognition, as well as having an annual award for outstanding professional work in the theater named after her. When, in April 1989, the Players Club of New York marked its one-hundredth anniversary by admitting its first female members, she was an inevitable choice for inclusion among the handful of women to be inducted.

Only a few weeks after being honored by her fellow thespians, Helen Hayes was invited to be grand marshal of the parade up Broadway that celebrated the bicentennial of the presidency. Two years earlier, she had been grand marshal of the St. Patrick's Day parade in the nation's capital. In these two symbolic roles, Helen Hayes demonstrated that, offstage as well as on, she continues to enjoy the affection and esteem of Irish Americans and of all Americans.

STARS OF STAGE AND SCREEN

The sheer volume and variety of the Irish contribution to American popular entertainment is suggested by this following list of performers, which is by no means exhaustive. It is deliberately eclectic, including both Academy Award winners and supporting character actors, and ranging from the silent film era to contemporary television productions. Some of those listed are typecast as Irish personalities while others are scarcely thought of as Irish Americans at all; some, indeed, such as Anthony Quinn and J. Carroll Naish, are best as Latins or miscellaneous ethnics.

Brian Aherne	James Dunn	Paul Kelly	Pat O'Brien
Sara Allgood	Irene Dunne	Arthur Kennedy	Erin O'Brien-Moore
Ed Begley	Richard Egan	Edgar Kennedy	Carroll O'Connor
Mary Boyd	Mia Farrow	J. M. Kerrigan	Donald O'Connor
Peter Boyle	Barry Fitzgerald	Jack Lord	Una O'Connor
Stephen Boyd	Errol Flynn	May McAvoy	Maureen O'Hara
Alice Brady	Ava Gardner	Donald McBride	Dan O'Herlihy
Scott Brady	Edward Gargan	Darren McGavin	Dennis O'Keefe
Walter Brennan	William Gargan	Patrick McGoohan	Ryan O'Neal
George Brent	Jackie Gleason	Frank Mc Hugh	Barbara O'Neil
Edward Brophy	James Gleason	Horace MacMahon	Henry O'Neill
Pierce Brosnan	Mary Gordon	Thomas Meighan	Maureen O'Sullivan
James Burke	Alan Hale	Thomas Mitchell	Annette O'Toole
Ellen Burstyn	Jack Haley	Colleen Moore	Peter O'Toole
(Edna Gilhooley)	Richard Harris	Tom Moore	Mary Philbin
James Cagney	Helen Hayes	Victor Moore	Tyrone Power
Nancy Carroll	Susan Hayward	Jack Mulhall	Anthony Quinn
Jimmy Conlin	Anjelica Huston	George Murphy	Ronald Reagan
Dolores Costello	John Huston	J. Carrol Naish	Pat Rooney
Bing Crosby	Walter Huston	Kate Nelligan	Robert Ryan
Dennis Day	Alice Joyce	Jack Nicholson	Martin Sheen
Brian Dennehy	Buster Keaton	Lloyd Nolan	Arthur Shields
William Devane	Gene Kelly	Edmond O'Brien	Brooke Shields
Brian Donlevy	Grace Kelly	George O'Brien	Hal Skelly
Patrick Duffy	Gregory Kelly	Margaret O'Brien	Spencer Tracy

What Ever Became of Maureen O'Hara?

$\mathcal{T}$he classic screen colleen of the 1950s—that was Maureen O'Hara. For millions of American moviegoers, she became an Irish archetype: the spirited redhead, a charmer, with just a touch of the shrew. We can never forget her, even if—Heaven forbid!—we should want to, for there she is on television, in *The Quiet Man*, playing that quintessential Irishwoman, Mary Kate Danaher; the film—and the role—are destined to be seen every St. Patrick's Day, for all eternity. But where did she come from? And where has she gone?

She was Maureen Fitzsimmons for the first twenty years of her life. Born in 1921 at Milltown, County Dublin, she grew up in a family of singers and actors, taking a theatrical career as a matter of course. After training in Ireland and England, she joined the Abbey Theatre in 1939, but left almost immediately for London, to make the film *Jamaica Inn*. This, in turn led to her departure for Hollywood, to play the role of Esmeralda in *The Hunchback of Notre Dame*, with Charles Laughton (himself half Irish, incidentally; his mother was from Cork), who decreed that she must become Maureen O'Hara, insisting that no one in America would ever get "Fitzsimmons" straight.

A decade of Hollywood films followed—sometimes five a year. Many —such as *The Spanish Main* in 1945—were costume epics, in which she played everything from a Castilian grandee to a French adventuress. Probably the most memorable was *How Green Was My Valley* (1941), directed by John Ford. This picture, which won the Academy Awards for best film and best direction, brought her into contact with Hollywood's most able, most irascible, and most "Irish" film-maker.

Maureen got along well with the often terrible-tempered Ford, being a "young woman of spirit" herself. He was already envisioning the film that eventually became *The Quiet Man* and actually obtained her commitment to appear in it as early as 1944. Her loyalty to Ford and his project remained steady during the succeeding seven years, as he plotted the story, worked on a script, and tried to sell the idea to several major studios. They told him, O'Hara recalls, that this "silly little Irish story" would never make any money.

In 1951, after overcoming a multitude of financial and artistic vicissitudes, Ford was able to make *The Quiet Man* on location in Ireland. Whatever the critics might say about its sentimentality (one called it "a green-tinted Irish-American valentine to the Old Country"), the movie was a tremendous popular success, and has retained its appeal over the decades. Its most memorable component, of course, is the rugged courtship of O'Hara by John Wayne in the role of Jack (Sean) Thornton, the returned "Yank." As the object of this "quiet man" 's affections, as well as the last survivor of all the major performers in the film, O'Hara has become a kind of living icon of Irishness.

The post–*Quiet Man* years were busy ones, including several more films with Wayne and another sentimentally Irish film under Ford's direction (*The Long Gray Line*, costarring Tyrone Power). In several of these —including *Mr. Hobbs Takes a Vacation* and *The Parent Trap*—she revealed a comedic talent that had not been exploited previously. By the late 1960s, however, her desire to have more free time (especially after marrying the flier Charles Blair) and, perhaps, a changing environment in Hollywood, led her to withdraw from picture-making.

Settling in St. Croix, O'Hara aided her husband in the development of his Caribbean airline service; she has continued to make her home there since his death, although she maintains a residence at Glengariff, County Cork, as well as an apartment in Los Angeles. Although out of the public eye since the early 1970s, she kept in touch with various Irish-American organizations. In 1986, in an extensive and reminiscent interview with a writer for the magazine *Irish America*, she let it be known that she would "love to be" chosen as grand marshal of the New York St. Patrick's Day parade.

In the always-intense competition for the grand marshal's position, Maureen was a nonstarter. Several other female candidates canceled each other out, and a man—as ever—was elected. Some took her interest to be purely frivolous, while others uttered weighty denunciations of her lack of previous "involvement." What had she ever done, they demanded, for the cause of Irish freedom? Undaunted, the evergreen star set her sights on "next year." As she told the magazine, "the public hasn't seen the last of me yet, not by any means." ◆

●The excess of poverty and crime among the Irish, as compared with the natives of other countries, is a curious fact worthy of the study of the political economist and the ethnologist.●

Report of the New York Association for Improving the Condition of the Poor (1860)

Hollywood Looks at the Irish

Though the American film industry had plenty of Irish performers and even a few Irish filmmakers (ranging from Mack Sennett to John Ford) in its ranks, Hollywood usually resorted to stereotypes during its inductive period. Little that came from the major studios between 1930 and 1960 reflected knowledge of, or interest in, authentic Irish-American life. The principal categories of Irish-stereotype films were:

The Religious Movie. The image of Irish-American Catholicism presented in films like *Boys Town* (1938), *Going My Way* (1944), *The Bells of St. Mary's* (1945), and *Fighting Father Dunne* (1948) was bland and amiable. Priests, portrayed by Pat O'Brien, Barry Fitzgerald, Spencer Tracy, or Bing Crosby, were full of warmth and wisdom, but ready to fight for their parishioners or for worthy causes. No insight into the tensions and conflicts within Catholicism was to be found.

The Gangster Movie The prominence of certain Irish hoodlums during the "roaring twenties" had reinforced the concept of the Irish as America's criminal class, whatever rising role might be assigned to newer immigrant groups. James Cagney, in *Public Enemy* (1931), *Angels with Dirty Faces* (1938), and *The Roaring Twenties* (1939) became the archetype of the Irish urban thug, often with actors like Pat O'Brien, Regis Toomey, and Lloyd Nolan portraying policemen only one step removed from the criminal ghetto.

The Military Movie In a multitude of soldier, sailor, and soldier-of-fortune films including *The Fighting 69th* (1940) and *The Sullivans* (1944) the virtues of patriotism and courage accorded to the Irish were diminished by the suggestion of simple-minded pugnacity as the stereotype that explained the martial virtues.

The "Irish Family" Movie Raucous domestic scenes provided the setting from comic or melodramatic plots in films such as *The Irish in Us* (1935) and *Three Cheers for the Irish* (1940).

As the Irish moved into the mainstream by the late 1950s, they ceased to attract the attention of moviemakers and became merely Americans with Irish surnames. But the memories (and the clichés), preserved on film, linger on. ◆

IRISH-AMERICAN ACADEMY AWARD WINNERS

1931–1932 Helen Hayes, best actress *(The Sin of Madelon Claudet)*

1935 Victor McLaglen, best actor *(The Informer)*
John Ford, best director *(The Informer)*

1936 Walter Brennan, best supporting actor *(Come and Get It)*

1937 Spencer Tracy, best actor *(Captains Courageous)*
Alice Brady, best supporting actress *(In Old Chicago)*
Leo McCarey, best director *(The Awful Truth)*

1938 Spencer Tracy, best actor *(Boys Town)*
Walter Brennan, best supporting actor *(Kentucky)*

1939 Thomas Mitchell, best supporting actor *(Stagecoach)*

1940 Walter Brennan, best supporting actor *(The Westerner)*
John Ford, best director *(The Grapes of Wrath)*

1941 John Ford, best director *(How Green Was My Valley)*

1942 James Cagney, best actor *(Yankee Doodle Dandy)*
Greer Garson, best actress *(Mrs. Miniver)*

1944 Bing Crosby, best actor *(Going My Way)*
Barry Fitzgerald, best supporting actor *(Going My Way)*
Leo McCarey, best director *(Going My Way)*

1945 James Dunn, best supporting actor *(A Tree Grows in Brooklyn)*

1948 Walter Huston, best supporting actor *(The Treasure of the Sierra Madre)*
John Huston, best director *(The Treasure of the Sierra Madre)*

1949 Mercedes McCambridge, best supporting actress *(All the King's Men)*

1952 Anthony Quinn, best supporting actor *(Viva Zapata!)*

John Ford, best director *(The Quiet Man)*

1954 Grace Kelly, best actress *(The Country Girl)*
Edmond O'Brien, best supporting actor *(The Barefoot Contessa)*

1955 Jack Lemmon, best supporting actor *(Mister Roberts)*

1956 Anthony Quinn, best supporting actor *(Lust for Life)*
Dorothy Malone, best supporting actress *(Written on the Wind)*

1958 Susan Hayward, best actress *(I Want to Live)*

1960 Burt Lancaster, best actor *(Elmer Gantry)*

1962 Gregory Peck, best actor *(To Kill a Mockingbird)*
Ed Begley, best supporting actor *(Sweet Bird of Youth)*

1963 Patricia Neal, best actress *(Hud)*

1967 George Kennedy, best supporting actor *(Cool Hand Luke)*

1970 Helen Hayes, best supporting actress *(Airport)*

1973 Jack Lemmon, best actor *(Save the Tiger)*
Tatum O'Neal, best supporting actress *(Paper Moon)*

1974 Art Carney, best actor *(Harry and Tonto)*
Ellen Burstyn, best actress *(Alice Doesn't Live Here Anymore)*

1975 Jack Nicholson, best actor *(One Flew Over the Cuckoo's Nest)*

1980 Robert Redford, best director *(Ordinary People)*

1981 Maureen Stapleton, best supporting actress *(Reds)*

1983 Jack Nicholson, best supporting actor *(Terms of Endearment)*
Hal Roach, honorary award

1985 Anjelica Huston, best supporting actress *(Prizzi's Honor)*

Both Janet Gaynor and Mary Pickford, best actress in 1927–1928 and 1928–1929 respectively, had Irish connections, as did Lionel Barrymore, best actor in 1930–1931. Walt Disney, of Irish-Canadian origin, received many special academy awards, the first in 1930.

The Most Famous Fictional Irish American

The best-known character to emerge from the mind of an Irish-American writer is not one of Finley Peter Dunne's Chicago saloon-philosophers, or Jimmy Breslin's New York cops or William Kennedy's Albany losers. It is a Georgia belle named Katherine S. O'Hara. Scarlett O'Hara, to use the middle name that she usually employs, is undoubtedly famous. In the fifty years since Margaret Mitchell published her epic novel, *Gone With the Wind*, the book has sold millions of copies in two dozen languages and continues to sell at an annual rate of 250,000 paperbacks in the United States alone. The film, one of the great box-office successes of all time, continues to flourish in periodic re-releases, occasional television special showings, and endless overseas bookings. Certainly, Scarlett is a well-known lady.

But "Irish-American"? We are so used to thinking of her as a Southern archetype that we forget her origins. As her surname proclaims, she was not a member of the Anglo-Saxon mainstream, or even of the "Scotch-Irish" element so widespread in the South. Her father, Gerald O'Hara, a native of Meath, had fled to America after a violent incident had made Ireland "too hot to hold him." His adventures in the New World, his marriage to a French Creole from New Orleans, and his acquisition of the Georgia plantation he named Tara, after the stronghold of Ireland's ancient high-kings, are all described in some detail in the novel, although barely alluded to in the film. What the movie does include is two scenes that strongly reinforce the Irish background of the heroine. One is a glimpse of the O'Haras at their family rosary in the evening, with the slaves standing respectfully by and Scarlett fidgeting impatiently. More evocative still is a dialogue between Scarlett and her father as they gaze out over the fields and he speaks emotionally of the land. "Oh Pa," she teases him, "you talk like an Irishman." Gerald responds that he's proud to be Irish, and reminds "Katie Scarlett," as he always calls her, that she, too, is half Irish and that those with Irish blood always have a special bond to the land. The land, he says, is the only thing that endures. This, of course, is a central theme of the novel, and it is from the "rich, red soil of Tara" that Scarlett finds the strength to continue after the disasters of the Civil War. It is "home" to Tara that she returns, at the story's end, to renew her hope and determination. For all her "Georgia peach" attributes there is a powerful strain of Irishness in her.

Margaret Mitchell was very conscious of her own Irish roots, which stretched back through her mother's side of the family. Her Catholic links—through convent schooling, the influence of her grandmother's stories of the old days, and the image of her grandfather, Thomas Fitzgerald, a plantation owner who was the model for Gerald O'Hara—all contributed to her choice of the O'Hara family to embody her story of the decline and fall of the Old Regime. There is a charming irony in the fact that the Confederacy's downfall should be viewed through the eyes of a minority—the tiny Irish Catholic community of the mid-nineteenth-century South. ◆

WHEN THE GOAT GOES TO CHURCH, HE NEVER STOPS TILL HE GOES UP TO THE ALTAR.
Traditional Irish Proverb

Cagney and Cohan: Irish-American Symbols

When James Cagney died in 1986, one also thought of George M. Cohan, who had died forty-four years earlier. The mental connection was inevitable, for the two were perpetually linked by Cagney's portrayal of Cohan in the film biography *Yankee Doodle Dandy*. Cagney had won an Academy Award for his performance as the flag-waving showman in a year—1942—when patriotic fervor was at its highest. Cagney, who had also been a song-and-dance man in his earlier days, was an appropriate choice for the part and gave an outstanding performance. But, actually, the two men had little in common, aside from their Irish background, and their entertainment careers followed very different patterns. Indeed, the images that they projected as performers made them symbols in the public minds of two different types—perhaps the only types—of Irish Americans.

Cohan was active in show business for most of his life (1878–1942), first as a member of a family vaudeville troupe, then, from 1901, as author, director, and producer of a long string of successful Broadway musical comedies. In the characters he created—and often played— Cohan became the quintessential "Irishman" for millions of Americans —amiable, cheerful, always ready with a smile or tear, always prepared to burst into a sentimental song and raise a convivial cup. This light-hearted, if somewhat lightweight, character was proud of his origins: like "Harrigan," he was "proud of all the Irish blood that's in me." His loyalties, however, very definitely lay on this side of the Atlantic. With songs such as "Over There," "You're a Grand Old Flag," and, of course "I'm a Yankee Doodle Dandy," he emphasized the 110 percent patriotism of the Irish American. And—patriotism aside—what could be more American than "Give My Regards to Broadway"? This potentate of the popular stage ventured only once into the realm of "serious" theater then dominated by his fellow Celt, Eugene O'Neill, when he played the father in *Ah, Wilderness!* (1932).

It was during this period, when Cohan stood at the pinnacle of his career as a stage entertainer, that Cagney was beginning his, as a film performer. During the 1930s he starred in a series of gangster films, of which *Public Enemy* is the most famous. These established him in the minds of moviegoers as the street-wise Irish tough guy—cocky, self-confident, aggressive, always ready with a snarl or a blow. His role in *The Fighting 69th* (1940) took him off the streets and into uniform, but kept him in character. Even the totally different assignment he received in *Yankee Doodle Dandy* failed to permanently alter the Jimmy Cagney of popular imagination. (Cohan, who had recommended Cagney for the role, saw the film a few months before his death and was greatly impressed by the actor's talent as a song-and-dance man; Cagney called Cohan "the real leader of our clan.")

Cagney made many films during the twenty-odd years after the Cohan tribute. Although he played everything from an American agent in Occupied France to a rancher in the Old West, not to mention an Irish revolutionary in 1920s Dublin *(Shake Hands with the Devil)*, it was his *Public Enemy* persona that endured. It was fitting, therefore, that when he came out of retirement in the early 1970s to do a cameo role in *Ragtime* it was to play Inspector Thomas Byrnes. Although the part was a brief one, arranged to accommodate Cagney's age and poor health, he seemed back in character as a real-life turn-of-the-century New York police official with a reputation for ruthlessness and playing both sides of the law.

. . .

Between them, Cagney and Cohan epitomized the Irish American for most of their fellow countrymen during the first half of the twentieth century. The screen actor was the tough "Mick," the stage actor, the genial "Pat." Both images embodied favorable and unfavorable elements. The Cagney type was admirable in his brash self-assertiveness, but it helped preserve the "Irish gangster" clichés that only gradually yielded to those of the "Italian gangster." The Cohan type was convivial and charming, but it suggested the shallow emotionalism and reinforced the idea of the "drinking Irish" just as Cagney suggested the "fighting Irish."

From the birth of Cohan to the death of Cagney stretches a span of 108 years. At its beginning, the Irish were still the alien, excluded objects of contempt and hostility. By its end, they have become the most assimilated and the most successful of all immigrant groups. The images that Cagney and Cohan conveyed have now yielded to a variety of life-styles, occupations, and attitudes too varied to encompass in one or two stock characters. Were those images stereotypes? It seems better to call them symbols, marking an intermediate stage from the stereotypical Irish of the nineteenth century to the assimilated Irish of the twenty-first. ◆

George Michael Cohan was the father of the American musical comedy. In a long career as author, composer, director, and performer, he often drew upon his favorite themes: star-spangled patriotism and Irish nostalgia.

The Green
Screen

*S*ome may want to know in advance who and what they're going to
be seeing on television around March 17. Others will wish to cram
for their next game of Irish trivia. For all of these, and the merely curious
as well, the following summaries cover some of the principal movies
about the Irish and Irish Americans. The films include the good, the bad,
and the silly, but this compilation is far from comprehensive. Most of
those omitted are better forgotten entirely.

The Informer (RKO, 1935)   Directed by John Ford. Starring Victor
McLaglen. A simple-minded hanger-on betrays an IRA leader to earn a
reward that will help him emigrate. He finds that he can escape neither
the wrath of his former comrades nor the pangs of his conscience.

Beloved Enemy (United Artists, 1936)   Starring Brian Aherne,
Merle Oberon, David Niven. Amid the turmoil of the 1921 Irish rebellion,
a rebel leader steals the heart of a British officer's fiancée.

The Plough and the Stars (RKO, 1936)   Directed by John Ford. Starring Barbara Stanwyck, Preston Foster, Barry Fitzgerald, Arthur
Shields, Una O'Connor, Bonita Granville. Screen version of the Sean
O'Casey play, but not on a par with the original. In 1916 Dublin, amid
the "troubles," a man's marriage is threatened by his nationalist commitment.

Parnell (MGM, 1937)   Starring Clark Gable, Myrna Loy, Edmund
Gwenn, Donald Crisp. Charles Stewart Parnell, the champion of Irish
nationalism during the late nineteenth century, finds his career tragically destroyed when he becomes involved with a married woman.

The Fighting 69th (Warner Brothers, 1940)   Starring James Cagney,
Pat O'Brien, George Brent, Jeffrey Lynn, Alan Hale, Frank McHugh.
Serving with the famous Irish-American regiment in the muddy trenches
of World War I France, a cynical wise guy surprises his buddies with
heroism that costs him his life.

Going My Way (Paramount, 1940)   Starring Bing Crosby, Barry
Fitzgerald, Rise Stevens, Frank McHugh. Crosby plays a young priest
sent to serve in a tough New York parish under the watchful eye of its
tightfisted pastor. Academy award for Best Picture.

Hungry Hill (GFD/Two Cities, 1946)   Margaret Lockwood, Dennis

Price, Cecil Parker, Michael Denison, Siobhan McKenna, Dan O'Herlihy. Three generations of an Irish family are trapped in an ongoing feud.

Captain Boycott (GFD/Individual/Universal, 1947) Starring Stewart Granger, Kathleen Ryan, Alastair Sim, Robert Donat, Cecil Parker, Noel Purcell, Niall MacGinnis. Hard-pressed Irish farmers, threatened with eviction, organize to resist oppressive landlords and their agents.

My Wild Irish Rose (Warner Brothers, 1947) Starring Dennis Morgan, Arlene Dahl, Andrea King, Alan Hale, George Tobias. A period musical that follows Irish tenor Chauncey Olcott through an on-again-off-again romance with Lillian Russell.

The Luck of the Irish (Twentieth Century-Fox, 1948) Starring Tyrone Power, Cecil Kellaway, Anne Baxter, Lee J. Cobb, and Jayne Meadows. A New York journalist visiting Ireland meets a leprechaun, whose efforts to be helpful only complicate the journalist's love life.

Fighting Father Dunne (Warner Brothers, 1948) Starring Pat O'Brien, Darryl Hickman, Una O'Connor. A priest works to help poor boys amid the squalor and violence of an urban slum.

Top o' the Morning (Paramount, 1949) Starring Bing Crosby, Barry Fitzgerald, Anne Blyth, and Hume Cronin. The Blarney Stone disappears, and complications—with music—follow.

The Fighting O'Flynn (United Artists, 1949) Starring Douglas Fairbanks, Jr., Helena Carter, and Richard Greene. In the 1790s, a restless young adventurer foils French plans to invade Ireland. An odd perspective: keeping Ireland safe for the British!

The Quiet Man (Republic/Argosy, 1952) Starring John Wayne, Maureen O'Hara, Barry Fitzgerald, Victor McLaglen, Ward Bond. A former boxer returns from America to Ireland in search of a peaceful retirement and a wife. A boisterous comedy, full of "Irish wit and color."

Captain Lightfoot (Universal, 1955) Starring Rock Hudson, Barbara Rush, Jeff Morrow, Kathleen Ryan. Hollywood's idea of a nineteenth-century rebel's struggle against injustice and British rule.

The Search for Bridey Murphy (Paramount, 1956) Starring Teresa Wright, Louis Hayward, Kenneth Tobey, Richard Anderson. A Colorado businessman whose hobby is hypnotism persuades a neighbor to let him transport her back into her previous existence as a long-dead Irish peasant. The tension builds when she seems unable to return from her previous life.

The Last Hurrah (Columbia, 1958) Starring Spencer Tracy, Jeffrey Hunter, Diane Foster, Pat O'Brien, Basil Rathbone, Donald Crisp. As Frank Skeffington, the veteran political boss of a New England town, Tracy takes to the campaign trail in a final reelection bid. John Ford directs a fine cast of characters in his tribute to the Irish-American political style.

Darby O'Gill and the Little People (Disney, 1959) A blend of animation and live performers, starring Albert Sharpe, Janet Munro, Sean

●*The thing about Irish movies is that so few directors get the conception right.* The **Quiet Man** *is as close to Irish life as* **Star Wars** *is to contemporary American life. Blarney exists only in Americans' imagination. The idea of 'fighting Irish' is a myth that began in American pubs. I've never seen an Irishman strike a blow. That doesn't mean that they can be bullied.*●

Tony Huston, filmmaker, in the *Los Angeles Times* (1986)

Connery, and Jimmy O'Dea. An Irish caretaker on the verge of losing his job falls down a well into the realm of the little people. There he ultimately wins the right to have three wishes granted. Blarney-soaked family fare, with good special effects.

Shake Hands with the Devil (United Artists/Troy/Pennebaker, 1959)   Starring James Cagney, Glynis Johns, Don Murray, Dana Wynter, Michael Redgrave, Sybil Thorndike, Cyril Cusack, and Richard Harris. A surgeon in 1921 Dublin leads a double life as secret leader of the IRA and grows attached to violence for its own sake rather than a means to an end.

The Night Fighters (Allied Artists, 1960)   Original title: *A Terrible Beauty*. Starring Robert Mitchum, Anne Heywood, Dan O'Herlihy, Cyril Cusack, and Richard Harris. At the beginning of World War II, the IRA revives its activities in a northern Irish village.

The Girl with Green Eyes (United Artists, 1964)   Starring Rita Tushingham, Peter Finch, and Lynn Redgrave. Filmed on location in Dublin, this brief film traces the relationship between a naive shopgirl and a worldly-wise writer.

Young Cassidy (MGM/Sextant, 1965)   Starring Rod Taylor, Maggie Smith, Edith Evans, Flora Robson, Michael Redgrave, Julie Christie, Jack McGowran, Sian Phillips, T. P. McKenna. A lightly fictionalized account of the early Dublin years of Irish dramatist Sean O'Casey.

The Fighting Prince of Donegal (Disney, 1966)   Starring Peter McEnery, Susan Hampshire, Tom Adams, Gordon Jackson, and Andrew Keir. Another cinematic rearrangement of Irish history, this time purporting to tell the story of Red Hugh O'Donnell's struggle against the encroachments of Queen Elizabeth I. Anachronisms run rampant.

Ulysses (Walter Reade, 1967)   Starring Maurice Reeves, Milo O''Shea, Barbara Jefford and T. P. McKenna. Based on James Joyce's novel, this film follows a young poet and a Jewish journalist through twenty-four hours in Dublin.

Finian's Rainbow (Warner Brothers/Seven Arts, 1968)   Starring Fred Astaire, Petula Clark, Tommy Steele, and Keenan Wynn. A leprechaun attempts to find and bring back a pot of gold taken to America by an old wanderer. Based on—but not as good as—the 1947 Broadway musical hit.

The Molly Maguires (Paramount/Tamm, 1970)   Starring Richard Harris, Sean Connery, Samantha Eggar, Frank Finlay, and Anthony Zerbe. A detective infiltrates a secret society in the 1870s Pennsylvania coal mines.

Ryan's Daughter (MGM/Faraway, 1970)   Starring Sarah Miles, Robert Mitchum, John Mills, Trevor Howard, and Leo McKern. In 1916 Ireland, a rural schoolmaster's wife falls in love with a British officer. Impressive scenery, but overlong. Mitchum is miscast.   ◆

Georgia
O'Keeffe

Georgia O'Keeffe was born on a wheat farm near Sun Prairie,
Wisconsin, on November 15, 1887. Her father, Francis Calixtus
O'Keeffe, was a native of Ireland whose mother had "dabbled in art."
When O'Keeffe died, on March 6, 1986, The New York Times
recorded the event in a front-page notice by Edith Evans Asbury.

Georgia O'Keeffe, the undisputed doyenne of American painting and
a leader, with her husband, Alfred Stieglitz, of a crucial phase in
the development and dissemination of American modernism, died yesterday at St. Vincent Hospital in Santa Fe, New Mexico. She was ninety-
eight years old, and had lived in Santa Fe since 1984, when she moved
from her longtime home and studio in Abiquiu, New Mexico.

As an artist, as a reclusive but overwhelming personality, and as a
woman in what was for a long time a man's world, Georgia O'Keeffe was
a key figure in the American twentieth century. As much as anyone since
Mary Cassatt, the American Impressionist painter who worked with
Degas in France, she raised the awareness of the American public to the
fact that a woman could be the equal of any man in her chosen field.

As an interpreter and manipulator of natural forms, as a strong and
individual colorist and as the lyric poet of her beloved New Mexico landscape, she left her mark on the history of American art and made it
possible for other women to explore a new gamut of symbolic and am-
biguous imagery.

Miss O'Keeffe was strong-willed, hardworking, and whimsical. She
would wrap herself in a blanket and wait, shivering, in the cold dark for
a sunrise to paint; would climb a ladder to see the stars from a roof; and
hop around in her stockings on an enormous canvas to add final touches
before all the paint dried.

Miss O'Keeffe burst upon the art world in 1916, under auspices most
likely to attract attention at the time: in a one-woman show of her paintings at the famous "291" gallery of Alfred Stieglitz, the world-renowned
pioneer in photography and sponsor of newly emerging modern art.

A MAN OF LEARNING
UNDERSTANDS THE
HALF-WORD.
Traditional Irish
Proverb

331

From then on, Miss O'Keeffe was in the spotlight, shifting from one audacious way of presenting a subject to another, and usually succeeding with each new experiment. Her colors dazzled, her erotic implications provoked and stimulated, her subjects astonished and amused.

She painted the skull of a horse with a bright pink Mexican artificial flower stuck in the eye socket. She painted other animal skulls, horns, pelvises, and leg bones that gleamed white against brilliant skies, spanned valleys and touched mountaintops, all with serene disdain for conventional notions of perspective. She also painted New York skyscrapers, Canadian barns and crosses, and oversized flowers and rocks.

The artist painted as she pleased, and sold virtually as often as she liked for very good prices. She joined the elite, avant-garde, inner circle of modern American artists around Stieglitz, whom she married in 1924. Stieglitz took more than 500 photographs of her.

THREE WITHOUT RULE—A WIFE, A PIG, AND A MULE. Traditional Irish Proverb

"He photographed me until I was crazy," Miss O'Keeffe said in later years. Others have called the pictures Stieglitz took of her the greatest love poem in the history of photography.

Her beauty aged well to another kind—weather-beaten, leathery skin wrinkled over high cheekbones and around a firm mouth that spoke fearlessly and tolerated no bores. And long after Stieglitz had died, in 1946, after Miss O'Keeffe forsook New York for the mountains and deserts of New Mexico, she was discovered all over again and proclaimed a pioneering artist of great individuality, power, and historic significance.

Miss O'Keeffe had never stopped painting, never stopped winning critical acclaim, never stopped being written about as an interesting "character." But her paintings were so diverse, so uniquely her own, and so unrelated to trends or schools that they had not attracted much close attention from New York critics.

Then, in 1970, when she was eighty-three years old, a retrospective exhibition of her work was held at the Whitney Museum of American Art. The New York critics and collectors and a new generation of students, artists, and aficionados made an astonishing discovery. The artist who had been joyously painting as she pleased had been a step ahead of everyone, all the time.

. . .

The art critic John Russell added a further appreciation.

It would be difficult to imagine American painting in the first half of this century without the presence of Georgia O'Keeffe. The presence, as much as the work, was what impressed, and it in no way diminished with age. It was a memorable experience to see her come into a room, even when she was well over ninety. Gliding along the floor with one tiny quick step after another, she fixed the newcomer with an eye that was both penetrating and remarkably clear. No words were wasted, and

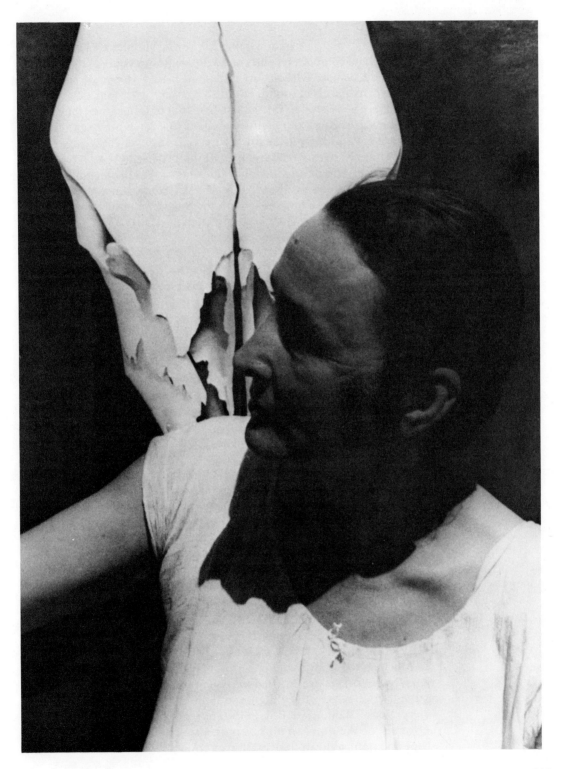

it was evident that she had no time for bores, but she spoke her say—firmly, clearly, completely, and concisely—without equivocation.

She had, as goes without saying, a longer and deeper perspective in time than anyone else around. Faced as we were with someone who had enrolled as an art student at the Art Institute of Chicago as long ago as 1904, the art world of our century seemed to stretch almost to infinity, with one small and unmistakable figure forever in view.

Undeniably, her marriage helped. (It helped her husband, too, by the way.) She and Alfred Stieglitz made one of the great partnerships. It was to his credit that he saw at once that she was an immensely gifted artist who had yet to have a fair shake with the American public. As the American public in 1916 was, to a large extent, Stieglitz's public, it was a happy day for her when he looked at her work and made his legendary comment, "At last, a woman on paper!"

But it was also a happy day for Stieglitz, in that Miss O'Keeffe released a strain of lyrical tenderness in his photography that led to the long and celebrated series of studies of her in every possible state of dress and undress and from every possible angle. She was his muse, and he her manager, and the world of art has not often seen as neat a match. Nor did she ever in any way subordinate herself to Stieglitz, formidable as he was.

In her work, she was probably best known and most influential for the reworkings of natural form that lent themselves—much against her will—to all manner of psychological and symbolic interpretations. If what seemed to her a perfectly straightforward exploration of botanical form got her interpreters tied in knots, she ignored the contortions of debate and went on exactly the same as before.

At this distance in time, however, it does sometimes seem that the voluptuous presences that she could distill from quite ordinary flowers did indeed have a transcendental quality. Admittedly, they could sometimes be read almost as scientific documents of natural growth and fulfillment, but there was something more to them than that—the kind of reworking and reshaping and intensifying that we associate with the jungles of the Douanier Rousseau and the outsize vegetation of Max Ernst. None of this had her warrant, or that of most of her admirers, but it was a tribute to a way of painting that never passed into history but remained as fresh and vital as when she first perfected it.

Her work was dominated in later years by the landscape and the architecture of New Mexico, where she lived for so long. . . .

Much as she treasured New Mexico over a period of more than fifty years, New Yorkers are entitled to remember that there was also a time, in the early heyday of the high-rise building, when she excelled as an interpreter of Manhattan. But, in the end, she is likely to be remembered above all for the quite small but immensely potent evocations of landscape and natural form that still have some of their secrets intact. ◆

AND MAY YOU BE HALF AN HOUR IN HEAVEN BEFORE THE DEVIL KNOWS YOU'RE DEAD. SLAINTE!
Traditional Irish Toast

*In the highly specialized world of art criticism and museum
management few individuals were more gifted and principled than
James Johnson Sweeney. His distinguished, and somewhat combative,
career is summed up in the following obituary notice by Grace Glueck,
published in* The New York Times *of April 15, 1986.*

James Johnson Sweeney, an art critic, historian, exhibition organizer, and museum director who served in prominent posts at the
Museum of Modern Art and the Guggenheim, died yesterday at his home
in Manhattan. He was eighty-six years old, and had suffered a stroke last
month.

A forceful spokesman for the new and the experimental, Mr. Sweeney
was a big, athletic-looking man whose ceaseless activities—writing,
traveling, organizing exhibitions, and doing administrative tasks—were
carried out with a zest that awed his associates. As a curator and director, he was demanding and innovative, and he often found himself at
odds with his employers. From 1945 to 1946, he served as director of the
department of painting and sculpture at the Modern—where he organized several shows, among them a memorial exhibition of the works of
Piet Mondrian—but resigned when a change in administrative structure
abridged his authority.

In 1952, he was appointed director of the Guggenheim Museum, and
served in that post during the construction of Frank Lloyd Wright's then
highly controversial building. He changed the museum's narrow focus
on "nonobjective" arts by presenting shows and acquiring the works of
pioneer modernists as well as younger European and American artists.
In the words of Aline Saarinen, art critic for *The New York Times* during
that period, he "symbolically as well as literally swept the place clean,"
painting the walls white, taking pictures out of what he believed were
distracting frames, and replacing the second-rate with world-class works
kept in storage at the museum.

But Mr. Sweeney was not a fan of the Wright building, which he believed had not been designed to show pictures to best advantage. He devised a method of hanging them on rods projecting from the walls, but could not overcome the feeling that the building was less a museum than a monument to the architect. When, in 1959, visitors began to pour in, and the museum's patron, Harry F. Guggenheim, asked for a more popular educational approach to the public, Mr. Sweeney resigned. He cited "the differences" between himself and the board of trustees over "the use of the museum and my ideals."

Appointed director of the Museum of Fine Arts in Houston in 1961, he stayed there for seven years. His professionalism and high standards of quality served the museum well, as he acquired works from ancient Greece and New Guinea along with sculptures by Rodin and Alexander Calder. A Sweeney exploit well remembered by Houstonians was his bringing to the museum—with great difficulty—a sixteen-ton Olmec head that he had spotted half buried in a Mexican jungle. The head arrived by ship in Houston in time to complement a show of Mexican art that he had organized. After he left Houston, in conflict over what he felt was trustee interference with his running of the museum, Mr. Sweeney served in the early 1970s as art adviser and chairman of the executive committee at the Israel Museum in Jerusalem.

Mr. Sweeney was born in Brooklyn, the son of a prosperous importer of laces and textiles whose family had come from Donegal, Ireland. During World War I, he attended officers' training school in Louisville, Kentucky, before going on to earn a B.A. degree at Georgetown University in Washington. He played guard on the football team there and, while doing graduate work in literature at Cambridge University, he joined the rugby team. He also established records as a shot-putter at both schools.

Always interested in literature, Mr. Sweeney was in his early years an editor of the Paris literary magazine *Transition*, and helped James Joyce edit the manuscript of his *Work in Progress*. He was himself the author of several books, among them *Plastic Redirections in Twentieth-Century Painting*, as well as numerous catalogue essays, articles, and reviews. At his death, he had just completed the text for a book on his friend the Spanish sculptor Eduardo Chillida, to be published in October by Harry Abrams.

Mr. Sweeney is survived by three sons—Sean, of Saudi Arabia, Siadhal, of County Mayo, Ireland, and Tadhg, of Cambridge, Massachusetts —and two daughters, Ann Baxter of Chapel Hill, North Carolina, and Ciannait Tait of Glasgow, as well as fourteen grandchildren and four great-grandchildren.

The funeral Mass will be said at noon Thursday at St. Stephen of Hungary Church, 414 East 82d Street. ◆

Irish Pioneers of American Photography

*A*lthough sometimes listed as a native of Ireland Mathew Brady (1823–1896) was probably born at Lake George, New York, the son of Irish immigrants. By the 1850s his "photographic gallery" on Broadway in New York City and his portraits of all the notables of the day had made him the best-known photographer in America. During the Civil War Brady won still greater fame as the pictorial historian of the war. He and his thirty-eight assistants traveled far and wide, under the most dangerous circumstances, to record the lives of generals and ordinary soldiers and to portray the horrors of the battlefield. Photography, still a young art, came of age under the guidance of Mathew Brady.

Among Brady's helpers were many fellow Irish Americans, including Alexander Gardner, T. C. Roche, and Timothy O'Sullivan, who played a leading role in post–Civil War photography. To these must be added the names of D. F. Barry, John Moran, T. J. Hines, W. T. McGillycuddy and Stephen Horgan. As photographers to military and scientific expeditions and chroniclers of railroad building and mining, most of these men participated in the opening up of the American West. They played a major role in raising America's consciousness of its magnificent Western landscape. O'Sullivan, in particular, has been hailed as "an explorer and a poet."

Some of Brady's followers made contributions to science as well as to art. Roche was a talented chemist who experimented successfully during the 1880s with bromide photographic papers. Horgan developed a technique by which photographs were copied on zinc and copper and then printed on paper. Horgan's discovery made possible the transition from woodcut to halftone illustrations that marks the beginning of "modern-looking" newspapers and magazines. The first halftone appeared in the New York *Daily Graphic* on March 4, 1890, and Horgan, who was a keen Irish nationalist, chose a slyly ironic subject, "A Scene in Shanty Town."

To Brady and other bold, talented pioneer photographers of Irish origin their fellow Americans owe a profound debt in fields of historical, geographical, social, and scientific knowledge. ◆

Mathew Brady

Three Irish-
American
Architects

*T*hat the Irish built America, as laborers on its roads, canals, railroads, and urban strucures, is a familiar truism. But some of them have helped design its most notable buildings. Three Irish architects, whose careers span two centuries, made a special contribution to the American scene.

Kilkenny-born James Hoban came to the newly independent nation in 1785, after training with leading architects in Ireland. Settling in Washington as it was emerging from the Potomac marshes, Hoban designed and supervised the construction of the executive mansion between 1792 and 1800. The President's House, as it was often called, was modeled upon the duke of Leinster's residence, one of the ornaments of Georgian Dublin (and now the seat of the Irish parliament). Following the British burning of the American capital in 1814, Hoban oversaw the reconstruction (1817–1829) of what henceforth would be known as the White House.

Louis Sullivan, born in Boston in 1856, was the son of an immigrant from Cork and a Swiss-born mother. During the era of great urban expansion between 1890 and 1920 his buildings graced all the major cities of the United States. He is regarded as the father of modernism in architecture, especially through the adaptation of modern materials to the needs of the city by his development of the skyscraper.

Such striking contemporary designs as the Ford Foundation Building and the CBS Tower in Manhattan and the TWA terminal at Kennedy Airport are the work of Kevin Roche. This Dublin-born architect heads a New York–based firm that plays a dominant role in shaping the cityscape. Roche, the winner of the prestigious Pritziger Prize in 1979, has been hailed as the leading architect in the United States today. ◆

The Bare-Knuckled Irish

The English introduced boxing into Ireland, and, unlike their attempts to create "civility" in that troublesome country, it was a tremendous success. The Irish rapidly developed an affection for, and a skill in, pugilism that they would later carry across the Atlantic.

Peter Corcoran was the first Irish boxer to win an "international" reputation. After defeating all heavyweight challengers in and around Dublin, he moved on to London. There he became the protégé of Colonel Dennis O'Kelly, an ex-laborer who had won fortune and social status as a gambler. O'Kelly arranged a bout with Bill Darts, the English champion, and on May 18, 1771, Corcoran knocked him out in less than one minute. Corcoran was declared champion. In this and subsequent fights, he won a great deal of money for his promoter, but he set an unhappy precedent for many of his successors by dying a pauper.

The fame of Corcoran and other early Irish boxers was far eclipsed, however, by that of Dan Donnelly, the subject of countless stories and songs. Born in Dublin, he followed his father's trade of carpentry. He gained his first reputation as a tavern brawler. After arranging a match with a leading English boxer, Hall, some Irish "sporting gentlemen" set up a training camp where Donnelly prepared for the contest away from his drinking companions. The highly publicized fight attracted 40,000 spectators, who saw Donnelly beat Hall in seventeen rounds on September 14, 1814. Donnelly spent his prize money within a week.

The English champion, George Cooper, came over a few months later to meet the Irish hero, and was soundly defeated at "Donnelly's Hollow" at the Cunagh of Kildare; an obelisk was later erected by Irish enthusiasts to mark the spot. Donnelly carried the Hibernian cause to England, where he beat yet another English champion, named Oliver, in thirty-two rounds in a match near London. This is a contemporary description of round one of the Donnelly-Oliver fight, on July 21, 1819:

The Irish champion was cool and collected, with nothing hurried in his manner. Upwards of a minute passed in sparring. . . . Donnelly made two hits with his left, which fell short, in consequence of Oliver's getting away. Long sparring. Oliver had an offer to hit, but Donnelly, on the

> ❛*I grant that Pat is a little too familiar, but he does not mean to be impertinent; he's as simple and unsophisticated as a child, and honest as he is light-hearted.*❜
>
> The Omnibus (1833)

alert, retreated. More sparring and dodging over the ground, till they got to the ropes in the corner of the ring, when Donnelly hit severely with his left. Several sharp exchanges occurred, till they both went down, grappling desperately, Oliver undermost. Five minutes had elapsed. (Loud shouts of "Bravo Donnelly" from the "boys of the sod.")

At that time a round lasted until one or the other fighter was thrown or knocked to the ground.

A STRIP OF
ANOTHER MAN'S
LEATHER IS VERY
SOFT.
*Traditional Irish
Proverb*

Another contemporary description of "Ireland's sporting god" concentrates on his physical appearance: "It may be said of Donnelly that he is all muscle. His arms are long and strong, his shoulders uncommonly fine . . . and prominently indicative of their punishing quality; . . . in height nearly six feet; in weight about thirteen stone."

Donnelly's heavy-drinking and free-spending ways sapped his health and ruined several business ventures in which he invested. When he died suddenly in 1820, at the age of thirty-two, he had little in a material way to show for his achievements. Indeed, even his grave did not remain undisturbed. The tales of his abnormally long reach led grave robbers to dig up his body to sell to medical researchers. His enormously long arms were studied as a curiosity by surgeons. One of Donnelly's arms is still on display in Ireland.

The feats of the great Dan Donnelly were an inspiration to the immigrant Irish who became the mainstay of boxing in nineteenth-century America. The Irish-born Mike McCool and Joe Coburn defeated all comers in the 1840s. James Ambrose, from Cork, was bare-knuckle heavyweight champion in the early 1850s. Fighting as "Yankee Sullivan," he maintained his domination of the American prize ring until 1853; he ended his days in a California jail, mysteriously murdered in his cell.

The man who defeated Yankee Sullivan was the Tipperary-born John Morrissey. Brought to New York as a child, he spent his teens as a "runner," steering newly landed immigrants to boardinghouses and beating up dockside rivals. From alley fighting to prizefighting was a natural transition, and, by the time he was twenty-two, this "fine broth of a boy" had knocked out the unfortunate "Yankee" and gained the heavyweight championship. That Morrissey was a battler, no one could doubt. Even his nickname, "Old Smoke," testified to that, for it alluded to a barroom fracas in which he had been knocked against a coal-stove, caught fire, but had come back, coattails smoking, to flatten his opponent. But Morrissey, unlike so many of his fellow pugilists, was a shrewd manager of his own career and his own money. Not only did he exploit his popularity to win a seat in Congress, he opened a fashionable and successful gambling establishment at Saratoga Springs, and died a millionaire.

For "respectable" Americans, however, Morrissey's story merely confirmed the disreputable character of the Irish, who thrived in the equally odious immoral spheres of boxing, gambling, and politics. The righteous could point to a prizefight in Rhode Island in 1856 between

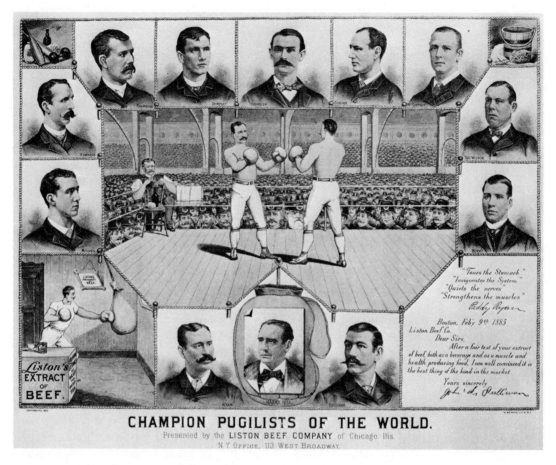

CHAMPION PUGILISTS OF THE WORLD.
Presented by the LISTON BEEF COMPANY of Chicago, Ills.
N.Y. OFFICE, 113 WEST BROADWAY.

Barney Ford and James Laverty. When Laverty lost, his manager claimed a foul. The audience split into rival factions, knives and guns were drawn, and a full-scale battle erupted. Then there was the Sayers-Heanan fight in 1860. The Irish-American John Heanan met the Englishman Tom Sayers for the world heavyweight championship in London and lost on an alleged foul. The New York and Boston Irish raged over this treachery and organized hostile demonstrations against visiting British dignitaries that embarrassed those in the United States who could not care less what happened to boxers at home or abroad.

The bare-knuckle era really came to an end in 1882, when Paddy Ryan, a native of Thirles, County Tipperary, lost the heavyweight championship to an immigrant's son, John L. Sullivan. "When Sullivan struck me," he said, "I thought a telegraph pole had been shoved against me sideways." Although bare-knuckle fighting would continue for a time, new rules, and a new acceptability in the public mind soon transformed boxing from a brutal spectacle into what might legitimately be called a sport. But the legends of clashing titans and mighty deeds would live on as a memorable part of the Irish experience. ◆

The grueling prizefight between John L. Sullivan and Paddy Ryan in 1882 is pictured here as the centerpiece of an advertisement endorsing the health-giving properties of Liston's beef.

The Great
John L.

His colors are the Stars and Stripes,
He also wears the Green,
And he's the grandest slugger that
The ring has ever seen.
No fighter in the world can beat
Our true American,
The Champion of all champions,
John L. Sullivan.

In his heyday (this popular song dates from 1890), John Lawrence Sullivan was more than a celebrity, he was a national hero, adored by millions, in a way that no prizefighter—and certainly no Irish American—had ever been esteemed before. Yet he was no better a man—and, in some ways, a worse one—than his predecessors. As a realistic commentator put it: "He was a drunkard, this god. He was a loudmouthed, vulgar, oversized bully. At least for the greater part of his life he was a spoiled, irresponsible, disagreeable roughneck. An S.O.B. of the first water . . . if he ever drank any. Yet he was a god."

Sullivan's status reflected not only the new acceptability of pugilism as a legitimate sport, but the acceptability of the Irish as Americans. For all his popularity in the immigrant community, John L. was very definitely an American. He was, in fact, typical of the blustering self-confident, vulgar "go-getter" that was taking over American society in the late nineteenth century. Although he did make a pious pilgrimage to his father's birthplace, he was less than impressed by the typical village welcome to the returning Yank. On being shown the ancestral homestead, he blurted out: "I guess the old man was a good judge, to get out of here."

Born in 1858, the "Boston Strong Boy" evaded his mother's genteel aspirations to steer him into the priesthood, and became a plumber's apprentice—a job he lost when he broke his boss's jaw in a dispute. He began earning money with his fists when he was nineteen, and soon came under the shrewd management of William Muldoon. A succession of victories over increasingly more prestigious fighters led, at last, to his famous confrontation with the reigning heavyweight champion, Paddy Ryan.

The match, on February 7, 1882, was the last championship contested under the old London Prize Ring rules—bare knuckles, the ring pitched on bare turf, the rounds marked by knockdowns. Despite the remote location of the match, in Mississippi City, Mississippi, Sullivan's growing reputation and Muldoon's adroit public relations had attracted a big crowd and national attention. After a comparatively short nine rounds, Sullivan landed the blow that gave the United States a new champion.

Although Sullivan did fight later bare-knuckle matches (notably the epic seventy-five-round battle with Jake Kilrain in New Orleans in 1889), he much preferred the new rules of boxing that had been developed in England by the marquis of Queensberry. These involved padded gloves, rounds of fixed duration, a hard-floored ring, and no wrestling, gouging, or spitting, such as the old London rules (which survived in America long after they had been dropped in London) permitted. Sullivan advocated a quick, clean contest of strength and his advocacy helped win acceptance for the marquis's rules in the United States. Thus Sullivan did much to transform the prize ring "from an animalistic slaughter house into an arena of pugilistic skill."

Sullivan traveled to the British Isles and Australia to maintain his status as not merely America's but the world's greatest boxer. A typical "brag" went as follows: "I challenge any and all of the bluffers who had been trying to make capital at my expense to fight me either the last week of August this year, or the first week in September at the Olympic Club, New Orleans, for the purse of twenty-five thousand dollars and an outside bet of ten thousand dollars, the winner of the fight to take the entire purse. First come, first served. I can beat any man in the world. . . . "

Sullivan's sayings ("The bigger they are, the harder they fall") and pronouncements were on everybody's lips. Music hall performers endlessly repeated the line: "Let me shake the hand of a man that shook the hand of John L. Sullivan!" It was reported that Sullivan called on the president whenever he was in Washington, even though his opinions and actions seemed to arouse more interest than those of the White House's occupants. A reporter portrayed the great man at the peak of his fame:

And then John L. Sullivan, raw, red-faced, big fisted, broad shouldered, drunken with gaudy waistcoat and tie, and rings and pins, set with enormous diamonds and rubies—what an impression he made! Surrounded by local sports and politicians of the most rubicund and degraded character (he was a great favourite of them), he seemed to me, sitting in his suite at the Lindell, to be the apotheosis of the humorously gross and vigorous material. Cigar boxes, champagne buckets, decanters,

BUTTER TO BUTTER IS NO RELISH (SAID WHEN TWO MEN DANCE TOGETHER OR TWO WOMEN KISS EACH OTHER). *Traditional Irish Proverb*

beer bottles, overcoats, collars and shirts littered the floor, and lolling back in the midst of it all in ease and splendour, his very great self, a sort of prizefighting J. P. Morgan.

"Aw, Haw! haw! haw!" I can hear him even now when I asked him my favourite questions about life, his plans, and the value of exercise etc. "He wants to know about exercise! You're all right, young fella, kinda slim, but you'll do. Sit down and have some champagne. Have a cigar. Give him some cigars, George. These young newspaper men are all right to me. I'm for 'em. Exercise? What I think? Haw! haw! Write any damn thing yuh please, young fella, and say that John L. Sullivan said so. That's good enough for me. If they don't believe it, bring it back here and I'll sign it for yuh. But I know it'll be all right and I won't stop to read it neither. That suit yuh? Well, all right. Now have some more champagne and don't say I didn't treat yuh all right, 'cause I did. I'm ex-champion of the world, defeated by that little dude from California, but I'm still John L. Sullivan—ain't that right? Haw! haw! They can't take that away from me, can they? Haw! haw! Have some more champagne, boy."

BETTER BE SPARING AT FIRST THAN AT LAST.
Traditional Irish Proverb

After ten years as champion of the world, an overweight and over-confident John L. Sullivan went down to defeat on September 7, 1892. Outboxed and outmaneuvered for twenty-one rounds by the younger, lighter James Corbett, the exhausted Sullivan finally collapsed under a flurry of blows to the head. An unprepared and stunned sporting world had lost its most picturesque and popular figure.

Sullivan never fought again. Taking his downfall (after 200 victories) in good spirits, he became an actor (an occupation almost as congenial to his temperament as fighting) and, after finally giving up liquor, a temperance lecturer. When he died in 1918, despite the rigors of a Boston winter and the distractions of a world war, thousands of loyal admirers gathered to pay their last respects.

Corbett, the son of a San Francisco stable hand, was also an "Irishman," but he never captured the fancy either of his fellow Celts or of the public at large as Sullivan had. Newspapermen, impressed by his sophisticated air and his stylish clothes, dubbed him "Gentleman Jim" (he had, in fact, been a bank clerk); the Boston Irish dismissed him as a "Western dude." John L. had been a link to the harsh but glorious days of Dan Donnelly, a link between Ireland and America. After his time, boxing would never be quite the same. ◆

The beginning of the fight," the commentator intoned, "was a repeat of the fight at Philadelphia the year before. Tunney was the cleverer boxer, and out-pointed Dempsey, who, however, showed more of his old fighting spirit than he had done before. In the seventh round Dempsey landed no fewer than seven blows on the point of Tunney's jaw. Tunney went down. . . . "

The scene was Chicago, 1927. Jack Dempsey was out to avenge the loss of his title to Gene Tunney the year before. It was a crucial moment for the man whom many considered the only Irish boxer worthy to form a "trinity" with Dan Donnelly and John L. Sullivan.

When Dempsey was a boy, the Irish skill dominated the boxing rings of America. William Harrison Dempsey was born in 1895 in Manassa, Colorado, just three years after Sullivan lost to Corbett. A year before that the "original" Jack Dempsey (born in Kildare) had lost his middle-weight championship to Bob Fitzsimmons; his given name would later be adopted by the young fighter from Colorado. Fitzsimmons had gone on to take Corbett's title in 1897. Men with names like O'Brien, Dillon, Ryan, and O'Dowd continued to hold the championships down through the turn of the century.

But things were changing. As early as 1905, the Ancient Order of Hibernians was questioning the degrading effect on the Irish image in America of their association with boxing. "We note with growing alarm," the AOH convention declared, "the notorious custom of crimi-nals, pugilists, and the abandoned and submerged tenth of society adopt-ing Irish names, both Christian and surnames." Despite their denunciation, many boxers without a drop of Irish blood continued to take Irish "ring names" to exploit the prominence of the Irish in the fight game. Most Italian fighters, for instance, continued to go by Irish pseud-onyms until the 1930s.

The youth from Manassa at first showed no inclination to pugilism as he drifted, more or less a hobo, around the West. Eventually, however, he fell in with a fight promoter who recognized his potential, and with good training and good management he began to attract attention in the boxing world. His powerful left hand gave him eighteen knockouts in

NO MAN EVER GAVE ADVICE BUT HIMSELF WERE THE BETTER FOR IT.
Traditional Irish Proverb

345

Jack Dempsey

1915–1916. In 1918 the veteran Jim Flynn caught him off guard and felled him in the first round, but in the following year he had his revenge on Flynn, and inflicted eighteen more knockouts. Mechan, Morris, Bill Brennan, and Gunboat Smith—all went down before him as he battled his way to the top. Finally, in 1919, on the Fourth of July, at Toledo, he defeated Jess Willard and captured the heavyweight championship.

The "Manassa Mauler," as the sportswriters called him, never gained the sort of popularity achieved by John L. Sullivan. Perhaps the mood of the 1920s was simply more cynical than that of the nineties. Or perhaps it was simply that Dempsey was by nature a much less outgoing, jovial type. In any case, he won respect, aroused enthusiasm, but did not engender worship. In 1920 he defended his title against Billy Miske and Bill Brennan, and in 1921 faced the popular Frenchman Georges Carpentier. A sports commentator contrasted the two fighters:

"Carpentier was a magnificent and fascinating figure of a man. His movements were like a panther's and his personality electric. But he was never really a heavyweight. Dempsey was unpopular with the crowd, and Carpentier received an ovation which must have made him think he was in Europe again. In the second round he landed his famous right-hand punch on the point of Dempsey's jaw. It had the weight of his body and the ambition of his life behind it. It shook Dempsey, but it broke Carpentier's thumb. Before the end of the round, Dempsey had knocked Carpentier through the ropes. In the fourth round Carpentier took a count of nine, and when he rose to continue the fight, was finally laid out with a right to the jaw, from which he did not recover for five minutes."

The Irish showed far more enthusiasm when Mike McTigue—"Bold Michael from County Clare"—won the light heavyweight championship in Dublin on St. Patrick's Day, 1923, by defeating "Battling Siki," the Senegalese who had taken the title from Carpentier the year before.

Dempsey continued to defend his title, most notably against Luis Firpo in 1923, but a successful rival was emerging in the person of James Joseph Tunney. Gene, as he was known, was a New York City boy who had enlisted in the marines during the war and won the boxing championship of the American Expeditionary Force. Back in civilian life, he had many victories and a few setbacks, but after 1923 was clearly a contender for the heavyweight championship. On September 23, 1926, he finally met Dempsey, in Philadelphia. The Manassa Mauler was not his usual self. The fight dragged on to its conclusion and the referee's decision awarded the title to Tunney.

It was to reverse this loss that Dempsey confronted Tunney again the following year at Chicago. After seven rounds, there occurred that "crucial moment" already described, when Dempsey, seeming once again like his old self, drove a series of powerful blows to Tunney's jaw. The commentator continued:

"Tunney went down . . . but the referee did not start to count. A local

THE WIFE (OR HUSBAND) OF YOUR CHOICE TO YOU.
Traditional Irish Toast

rule had been agreed upon before the fight . . . that in the event of one man going down the count should not be started till the other man had retired to a neutral corner. As soon as Dempsey had done this, the referee began to count. Tunney rose as nine was called, and for the rest of the round succeeded in eluding Dempsey. Whether Tunney would have been able to rise had the count been started, as is usual, directly he fell, will be a matter of controversy forever."

Tunney emerged fresh and clear-headed from his corner for the eighth round, and from then on was always the aggressor, with Dempsey rapidly weakening. The former champion was knocked down, and had the fight gone beyond ten rounds he would almost certainly have been knocked out. Tunney had retained the title, and the career of the Mauler was over.

WHEN THE HAND
CEASES TO
SCATTER, THE
MOUTH CEASES TO
PRAISE.
*Traditional Irish
Proverb*

Tunney retired, undefeated, in 1928. Dempsey did not officially quit the ring until 1933. The former became a distilling executive, the latter opened a restaurant. Both men received naval reserve commissions in the Second World War and aided in the sports and morale-building aspects of the war effort. Both enjoyed comfortable retirements, as virtual elder statemen. Tunney's son became a United States senator.

One sports historian has summed up Dempsey's claim to greatness: "Dempsey may certainly rank among the great heavyweights of the past. He was not so fine a boxer as Corbett, or so wily a strategist as Fitzsimmons. He had not Jeffries' immense strength, and certainly none of Johnson's defensive genius. But he had more fighting spirit than was in all four of them rolled together. He was rugged, and strong, and persistent."

Dempsey's failed comeback attempt, followed by Tunney's resignation of the title, marks the final round in the Irish dominance of professional boxing. There were random flareups of Irish pride, to be sure, as when Jimmy McLarnin won the welterweight title in 1933, or Billy Conn, a Pittsburgh Irishman, challenged the "unbeatable" Joe Louis in 1941. But, for the most part, the role of the underdog, battling with his fists for material reward and social recognition, was abandoned by the Irish. The new immigrants, such as the Italians, and later the blacks and Hispanics, struggled as the Irish had, for recognition, for "fame and fortune." In the meantime, the Irish had moved on. ◆

The Old
Ball Game

The Irish adopted the national pastime of baseball with greater immediate success than any other immigrant group. Only in later years have the sons of the newer immigration challenged the Irishman's preponderance in the national game. The reputation of Irish ball players was so great that others frequently took Irish names to help them in their baseball careers. Leopold Christopher Hoernschemeyer of Cincinnati, for example, played in the National League as Lee Magee in the second decade of the present century. Several catchers whose names are of Southern or Eastern European origin have taken the name "Mickey" in emulation of Mickey Cochrane, one of the greatest catchers in the history of the game. The All-Time Register of Players and Managers abounds with Irish names. Some were first-generation immigrants; the majority were American-born of Irish immigrant parents. Every baseball fan knows Ernest L. Thayer's "Casey at the Bat" and Grantland Rice's "Casey's Revenge."

In a region as remote as Iowa, the Irish helped establish the game before the Civil War. A box score for a six-game series between Dubuque and Davenport in 1878 indicates that almost all the players had Irish names. Charles Comiskey on that occasion caught for Dubuque. Ten years later, when the Des Moines Colts wanted to bolster their pitching staff, they brought in Bill Fagan, an old, hard-drinking Irish pitcher, from New York and paid him $225 a month. Peter J. ("Smiling") Daniels, a native of Ireland, was a big-league pitcher in the 1890s. Edward C. Duffy, born in Ireland in 1844, played shortstop for Chicago in 1871. Ferguson Malone, another native Irishman, caught and played first base for the old Athletics in the 1870s. Anthony Mullane of Cork pitched and played the infield a decade later. John Joseph ("Dirty") Doyle was a National League infielder in the 1890s. Jimmy Archer, who caught for Pittsburgh and Chicago in the first two decades of this century, was a native of Dublin. As late as 1952, of the thirty-four men on the roster of the Cleveland Indians, representing eighteen nationalities, the Irish led with fourteen.

Michael J. Kelly ("King Kelly") was the son of an Irish immigrant papermaker in Troy, New York. "King" played with several minor teams

BIG HEAD AND LITTLE SENSE.
Traditional Irish Proverb

349

and was with the Cincinnati Reds when "Pop" Anson brought him to Chicago, where he remained from 1879 to 1887. A big, convivial, hard-to-manage Irishman, and a great umpire-baiter, Kelly did equally well as a catcher, an outfielder, or a shortstop, and led the league in batting in 1886. When he was sold to Boston in 1887, he was known as the "Ten Thousand Dollar Beauty," but his real claim to baseball immortality rests upon his feats as a base runner, celebrated in the popular song "Slide, Kelly, Slide." In 1888 Kelly published *Play Ball: Stories of the Diamond.* He died in 1894. He was appearing in a Boston theater at the time, with the London Gaiety Girls, in the role of "Casey at the Bat." Legend has it that when he fell off a stretcher during his last illness, he remarked with the Irish humor that never failed him, "This is my last slide."

John Joseph ("Mugsy") McGraw came from Truxton, New York, and was the eldest in an Irish family of nine. What little education he had he received at St. Bonaventure College after he had begun his baseball career. He was a slight, little man whose aggressiveness made up for his lack of avoirdupois. McGraw played the infield for the Baltimore Orioles before he began managing the New York Giants in 1902 at the age of twenty-nine. "The Little Napoleon," a rough disciplinarian and a real master of the game, won ten National League pennants. It was he who converted Christy Mathewson from a first baseman to a pitcher. "The Old Roman," Charles A. Comiskey, was the son of an Irish immigrant who came to the United States with his family in the bleak year of 1848. The father became a politician in the Irish ward of Chicago, and here Charles was born. The boy was apprenticed to a plumber, but in 1875, at seventeen, he began to play third base for Milwaukee. During his long career as an active player, he also pitched and played first base. He helped Ben Johnson organize the American League and was the owner of the Chicago White Sox until his death in 1931.

The list of big-league managers contains such familiar Irish names as Pat Moran, Hugh Jennings, Joe McCarthy—the stocky Irishman from Buffalo who won pennants for the Yankees—Connie Mack, Joe Cronin, Steve O'Neill, and many others. In Baseball's Hall of Fame in Cooperstown, New York, there are plaques for George ("Mickey") Cochrane, one of the game's greatest catchers; Joseph Jerome ("Iron Man") McGinnity, the pitcher; James H. ("Orator Jim") O'Rourke, one of baseball's early heroes, who played behind the plate and in the outfield in twenty-one major league seasons until he was past fifty; Hugh Duffy, brilliant outfielder who batted .438 in 1894; King Kelly, who stole eighty-four bases for Boston in 1887; Cornelius McGillicuddy, great catcher, manager of the Philadelphia Athletics, and the game's "Grand Old Man"; Ed Delahanty, one of the game's greatest sluggers; and Roger Patrick Bresnahan, "the Duke of Tralee," battery mate of the great Mathewson and a manager in the National League.

America has had several Irish baseball clans, but there is none to surpass the Delahanty tribe of Cleveland. The six sons born to James Delahanty and Bridget Croke, Irish immigrants, all left their mark in the annals of the national game. Five of the boys played in the major leagues; the sixth might have done so, and already had been drafted by Brooklyn, when he was hit by a pitched ball that ended his career. Big Ed Delahanty, the eldest of the tribe, once hit four home runs in one game and was the only player who won the batting championship in both the National and American League. He batted .408 for Philadelphia in 1889 and .376 for Washington in 1902.

Though dynasties like the Delahantys are no more, and even individual Irish-American players are few, contemporary baseball has not entirely lost the Celtic touch. Among the outstanding players of later years have been Mike McCormick of the Giants and Mike Flanagan of the Orioles, both winners of the prestigious Cy Young Award, in 1967 and 1979, respectively. And how could there be a more Irish name than that of Nolan Ryan, who, with more than 5,000 strikeouts, holds the all-time major league record? ◆

Connie Mack adds his unusual touch of sartorial formality to the dugout as he plots strategy with his players.

The Mighty
Macs

When it comes to legendary figures, a few simple facts are often help-ful. The following brief summaries outline the careers of the three most famous Irish-American baseball personalities.

McGinnity, Joseph Jerome (1871–1929). Born in Rock Island, Illinois. McGinnity's baseball career as a right-handed pitcher lasted thirty-two years, beginning with 1893, when he played on the Montgomery team of the Southern Association. He was with the Baltimore team of the National League from 1897 to 1900, the Brooklyn team of the National League from 1900 to 1902, the Baltimore team of the American League in 1902, and the New York team of the National League from 1902 to 1908. From 1908 to 1925 he pitched for and managed several minor league teams. Because of his endurance McGinnity was nick-named "Iron Man." Five times in his career he pitched two games in one day; in 1903 he pitched 434 innings, still a National League record. He won 31 games and lost 19 in 1903 and won 35 and lost 8 in 1904. During his entire major league career McGinnity pitched 467 games, winning 247 and losing 142, for a lifetime percentage of .635. McGinnity was elected to the Baseball Hall of Fame in 1946.

McGraw, John J. (1873–1934). Born in Truxton, New York. He be-came a professional player at the age of sixteen; at seventeen he was third baseman for the Baltimore team (the Orioles) of the National League, which won the National League championship in 1894, 1895, and 1896. McGraw managed the team in 1899, played with the St. Louis National League team in 1900, and managed the Baltimore team of the American League in 1901 and 1902. From 1902 to 1932 he was the man-ager of the New York team (the Giants) of the National League. During this period the team won ten National League championships and three world championships, one of the best managerial records ever made in baseball. Many of the players who worked under McGraw subsequently became major league managers. McGraw introduced many tactical in-novations into the game, and in three trips abroad as manager of groups of players he introduced the game to Europe and the Orient. As a third baseman he played in 1,082 games and had a lifetime batting average of .334. He was elected to the Baseball Hall of Fame in 1937.

New York manager John McGraw before a May 1911 game.

ALL THE WORLD
WOULD NOT MAKE A
RACEHORSE OF A
JACKASS.
*Traditional Irish
Proverb*

Mack, Connie, real name Cornelius McGillicuddy (1862–1956). Born in East Brookfield, Massachusetts. He began his career in 1884 as a catcher with the Meriden team of the Southern New England League, and played with the Hartford team of the same league from 1884 to 1886, with the National League teams of Washington from 1891 to 1889, and Pittsburgh from 1891 to 1899. As a player he participated in 736 games and had a lifetime batting average of .249. He managed the Pittsburgh team from 1894 to 1897, and became the manager of the Philadelphia team (the Athletics) of the American League in 1901. Under his leadership the Athletics made one of the most remarkable records in baseball history, winning nine American League championships and five world championships. Connie Mack was elected to the Baseball Hall of Fame in 1937. He retired as the Athletics manager in 1950. He wrote *My 66 Years in the Big Leagues* (1950). ◆

A Connecticut Yankee in Ireland

Perhaps the most visible Irish American in the sporting world during the last few decades, Mike Burke was a businessman rather than a player, but a highly energetic and colorful businessman. His Irishness, moreover, was more than name-deep. The following account of his career is extracted from an obituary by John T. McQuiston published in The New York Times *on February 7, 1987.*

Michael Burke, who as president of the Yankees got the city to refurbish Yankee Stadium and kept the team from moving to the Meadowlands in New Jersey, died Thursday in Ireland. He was seventy years old.

Mr. Burke led the Yankees from 1966 to 1973, when the team was sold to George Steinbrenner by CBS.

The ebullient and articulate Mr. Burke then became president of Madison Square Garden, where he was also president of the Knicks, chairman of the Rangers, impresario of boxing, and grand master of Holiday on Ice.

Mr. Burke was born in Enfield, Connecticut, and attended high school in Hartford, where he was a star athlete.

He won a scholarship to the University of Pennsylvania, where he played football before World War II. He was offered a professional football contract and joined the Philadelphia Eagles in 1941, but left shortly thereafter to serve with the United States Office of Strategic Services, the forerunner of the Central Intelligence Agency.

His activities took him behind enemy lines in Italy. He later infiltrated into France, where he joined the Resistance to prepare for the D-Day invasion. He was awarded the Navy Cross, the Silver Star, and the French Médaille de la Résistance.

After the war, he came home and went to Hollywood, where he helped in the production of the film *Cloak and Dagger*, which was based on his life behind enemy lines and which starred Gary Cooper.

However, Mr. Burke was soon back in Europe, serving as an adviser

A TAIL IS PART OF THE CAT (I.E., A MAN RESEMBLES HIS FAMILY).
Traditional Irish Proverb

to the United States High Commissioner in Germany, John J. McCloy, from 1951 to 1954.

When he next returned to the United States, he became general manager of the Ringling Brothers and Barnum & Bailey Circus.

In 1956, Mr. Burke was hired by the Columbia Broadcasting System and soon named vice president in charge of developing new areas of business expansion.

One of his first recommendations was that CBS underwrite a new Broadway musical with an old George Bernard Shaw theme. The multi-million-dollar hit was *My Fair Lady*.

In the early 1960s, the Yankees were for sale and Mr. Burke suggested CBS buy the team, which it did in 1966 for $13.2 million.

In September of 1966, he became president of the Yankees and took on the task of rebuilding the baseball club. When he left the club in 1973, his title was general partner and chief executive.

Mr. Burke's, as well as CBS's association with the Yankees, however, was disappointing. CBS sold the team in 1973 for $10 million after suffering an operating loss of $11 million.

"The trouble was," Mr. Burke once said, "we didn't go in and feel the goods. We bought a pig in a poke."

One of the better moments in Mr. Burke's leadership of the team occurred in 1972 when he reached an accord with the administration of Mayor John V. Lindsay. In return for keeping the Yankees in New York, the city agreed to rebuild Yankee Stadium.

Mr. Burke's leverage was a threat to move the Yankees to New Jersey, an offer the football Giants did not refuse. The Giants were subsequently criticized by the news media for their move to the Meadowlands, while Mr. Burke's Yankees were grandly praised.

The refurbishing of the stadium was to have cost $24 million, but ended up costing the city more than $100 million.

Mr. Burke's tenure at Madison Square Garden was also filled with controversy and problems created by the growth and competition from the new sports complex in East Rutherford, New Jersey.

After his retirement from the Garden in 1981, he left the United States and traveled in Europe before settling in Ireland, where he owned a 500-acre farm in the village of Aughrim, 35 miles east of Galway.

He purchased the farm in 1960 after visiting the region regularly as an escape from the hectic pace of his offices in Manhattan.

In an interview at his farm in 1982, he said: "I had an immensely happy time doing the Yankees and Madison Square Garden. I loved every minute of it. And I love New York. Top to bottom.

"It's just at this stage in my life, there is this strong pull that Ireland has on me—emotional and romantic, I supose—but also because my family has been here for 800 years and there has always been a strong rush of Irish blood in my veins." ◆

I could then go to a fair, or a wake, or dance. . . . I could spend the winter nights in a neighbour's house, cracking jokes by the turf fire. If I had there but a sore head I could have a neighbour within every hundred yards that would run to see me. But here one has so much land that they calls them neighbours that live two or three miles off.

Letter from an Irishman in Missouri (1860)

The Man from
Mudville

Every summer for the last hundred years, aficionados of America's national sport have been reminded of the days when baseball was more of a sport and less of a business by "Casey at the Bat." Ernest L. Thayer's poem portrays a formidable slugger from the glory era of the Irish in baseball, the Mighty Casey, whose pride goes before his fall. The closing lines have preserved their ironic reminder of the vanity of human wishes, ever since the actor De Wolfe Hopper first recited them in June 1888:

> *And somewhere men are laughing,*
> *And somewhere children shout,*
> *But there is no joy in Mudville—*
> *Mighty Casey has struck out.*

The poem has inspired endless parodies ("Casey at the Bank" has been suggested as a suitable variant now that million-dollar contracts are the norm). It has generated more than a dozen sequels, in which Casey becomes a fully rounded character with a wife and children (in some of them, he returns to redeem his name from disgrace). Two movies got the germ of their plots from the story of Mudville's catastrophe, and William Schuman composed an opera, *Mighty Casey*, which has been staged at Cooperstown (giving the immortal batter a kind of status in Baseball's Hall of Fame).

A CAT'S MILK GIVES NO CREAM (SAID OF A STINGY PERSON).
Traditional Irish Proverb

But was there a *real* Casey? Rumor assigned the distinction of being the inspiration for the great man to a number of players, both professional and collegiate. Two actual Caseys tried to claim the fame that went with the name. Tim Casey, a shortstop for the old Boston team, was not taken very seriously: his hitting record would hardly justify anyone seeing him as the model for a renowned slugger who fails in the crunch. But Daniel Michael Casey, a pitcher for the Philadelphia Nationals, was a more plausible claimant. He had a good second career for himself during the 1890s by personal appearances at vaudeville theaters, where he would proclaim, "I am the Mighty Casey," and recite the poem to delighted audiences.

It was not until 1935 that the author, Thayer, revealed the identity of the original Casey. When he wrote the poem fifty years earlier for his paper, the *San Francisco Examiner*, he needed a name for the overconfident, overbearing batter. He remembered one Daniel Henry Casey, a classmate at Worcester Classical High School, back in 1881. This Casey was the typical "big Irishman," a six-foot-two-inch teenager weighing over 200 pounds. Thayer had mocked Casey in a school newspaper and Casey came close to beating him up. When Thayer wanted a name for his large, proud, fierce athlete, he thought of D. H. Casey.

Thus, this famous fictional Irish American had a real enough model. But the authentic Casey never became a baseball player. He became a teacher. At the time of his death in 1915, he was principal of Grafton Junior School in Worcester. If he recognized himself in the famous poem, he left no comment. ◆

HARSH IS THE POOR MAN'S VOICE—HE SPEAKS ALL OUT OF PLACE.
Traditional Irish Proverb

Billiard Ball
and Medicine
Ball

*I*rish-American giants dominated the major sports—boxing and baseball—in the late nineteenth and early twentieth centuries. Among the host of peripheral figures who added color to the era two other Irishmen, Michael Phelan and William Muldoon, are particularly notable.

Michael Phelan, an enthusiastic Irish nationalist, was America's first billiard champion. In 1851 he visited Ireland and England, ostensibly to demonstrate his skill with cue and billiard balls, but actually to establish contact with Irish revolutionaries. In 1858 Phelan won $10,000 in a billiard match in San Francisco, and the next year, he became national champion in a match in Detroit that carried a purse of $15,000. Early in 1860, Phelan made an exhibition tour of the South. With his son-in-law, Hugh W. Collender, he began manufacturing billiard tables. The new firm advertised "Phelan's Improved Billiard Tables and Combination Cushions" and published *The Billiard Cue*, a journal devoted to the game. Phelan owned "Phelan's Magnificent Billiard Rooms" in New York at Broadway and Tenth Street.

FROM IRELAND TO AMERICA TO THE OLYMPICS

John Flanagan (born in County Limerick) won the hammer throw for the United States at Paris Olympics of 1900 and again at St. Louis in 1904 and London 1908.

Martin Sheridan (born in County Mayo) won the discus event at the 1904 and 1908 Olympics.

James Mitchell (born in County Tipperary) was a runner-up in both hammer and discus events in 1904; Con Walsh (born in County Cork) won the bronze medal for the hammer throw in 1908.

John Hayes (born in County Tipperary) won the gold medal for the marathon in the London Olympics of 1908.

Pat McDonald (born in County Clare) won the gold medal for the shot-put at Stockholm in 1912.

Matt McGrath (born in County Tipperary) and Paddy Ryan (born in County Limerick) were medal winners in various categories of the hammer throw from 1912 to 1924.

WOODROW WILSON
THOMAS R. MARSHALL

PARADE OF OLYMPIC ATHLETES

William Muldoon was born in New York State, the son of Patrick Muldoon and Maria Donohue. At eighteen, he began to earn a living as a bouncer in dance halls and eating places in New York. Thereafter, he worked as a laborer, longshoreman, and cabdriver on New York's East Side. He became a policeman in 1876 and organized the Police Athletic Association. He won national fame as a wrestler and, on one occasion, wrestled Clarence Whistler for eight hours without a decision. Muldoon took a troupe of American wrestlers to Japan, and when he retired from the police force in 1900, operated a saloon in New York and became a trainer of pugilists and wrestlers. On an estate in Westchester County, the ex-policeman opened a training and health center for tired businessmen. Here he put the tycoons of Wall Street through their paces, kept them on a strict diet, forbade all alcoholic drinks, and invented "the medicine ball" for his aristocratic clientele. In 1921, the "Iron Duke" was appointed chairman of the Boxing Commission of New York.

A parade honoring American winners (several of them Irish) of the 1912 Olympics passes Democratic party headquarters, where the just-nominated Woodrow Wilson's name is displayed.

IRISH-AMERICAN OLYMPIANS

1896	Thomas Burke	Gold medals, 100-Meter and 400-Meter Dash
	James B. Connolly	Gold medal, Triple Jump
1900	John Flanagan	Gold medal, Hammer Throw
1904	John Flanagan	Gold medal, Hammer Throw
	Martin Sheridan	Gold medal, Discus
1906	Martin Sheridan	Gold medals in 16-Pound Shot-Put and Discus
1908	Martin Sheridan	Gold medals in Discus and Greek-style Discus
	John Flanagan	Gold medal, 16-Pound Hammer Throw
1912	Frederick Kelly	Gold medal, 110-Meter Hurdles
	Matt McGrath	Gold medal, 16-Pound Hammer Throw
1920	Patrick Ryan	Gold medal, 16-Pound Hammer Throw
	Jack Kelly, Sr.	Gold medal, Single Sculls
	Edward Eagan	Gold medal, Boxing (Light Heavyweight)
1924	Daniel Kinsey	Gold medal, 110-Meter Hurdles
1928	Helen Meany	Gold medal, Women's Springboard Dive
1932	Eddie Tolan	Gold medals, 100-Meter and 200-Meter Dash
	Edward Flynn	Gold medal, Boxing (Light Welterweight)
1952	Parry O'Brien	Gold medal, 16-Pound Shot-Put
	Patricia McCormick	Gold medal, Women's Springboard and Platform Dives
1956	Parry O'Brien	Gold medal, 16-Pound Shot-Put
	Patricia McCormick	Gold medal, Women's Springboard and Platform Dives
	Harold Connolly	Gold medal, 16-Pound Hammer Throw
1968	Bill Toomey	Gold medal, Decathlon
1984	Mary Meagher	Gold medal, Women's 100-Meter and 200-Meter Butterfly
	Michael O'Brien	Gold medal, 1500-Meter Freestyle Swimming
	Rick Carey	Gold medals, 100-Meter and 200-Meter Backstroke

Conan the
Hibernian

A perennially popular barbarian, Conan has enthralled heroic-fantasy enthusiasts for more than fifty years. As Gerald A. Kelly points out in the following essay (originally published in An Gael, Fall 1986), *the mighty warrior has Irish roots.*

*H*ello out there, Conan fans!

Did you know that your favorite sword-and-sorcery barbarian from Cimmeria (star of paperbacks, comic books, and two movies) is actually Irish? You didn't? You thought that the great fantasy writer Robert E. Howard just made him up? Well, *leigi agus gheobhfaidh sibh fios* (read and you will get knowledge)!

Born in Texas in 1899, Robert Howard always said that he inherited his storytelling talent from his Irish-born grandmother. The myths and legends of her homeland were his favorite entertainment when he was a boy. He put his talent to use early, and, as a teenager, he published his first stories in the action/mystery/supernatural pulp magazines of the pre-World War I period.

One of the things that first set Howard's storytelling apart was his detailed presentation of the fictitious peoples, cultures, cities, and kingdoms he wrote about. Even the supernatural aspects of his stories fit so perfectly as to make you believe that they belonged in the historical settings Howard placed them in.

By the time Howard reached his tragic thirtieth year, he was a self-educated expert on the ancient peoples of the Indo-European expansion and the cultures with which they came in contact. Howard theorized that great civilizations have risen and fallen with barely a trace, and risen again to mimic almost identically what had gone before. He believed, at least in part, that gods have been created through the accretion of legends around great ancestral heroes, and in support could have argued that the Celts believed themselves descended from their god of death, who was known by many names, one of which was Donn. "The Dark One."

O'BRIEN'S GIFT AND HIS TWO EYES AFTER IT (I.E., REGRETTING IT).
Traditional Irish Proverb

With these ideas in mind, Howard worked backward to create the "Hyborian Age," a period thirty thousand years before our own era in which he placed the ethnic and cultural "ancestors" of the Greek classical world. Howard's "Stygia" stands for Egypt, "Corinthia" for Greece, "Aesirland" and "Vanirland" for the ancestral homelands of the Nordic peoples, and "Cimmeria" for the homeland of the earliest Celts.

Howard sought the men behind the gods as well as the gods behind the men. Thoth-Amon was the great god of wisdom during late dynastic Egypt, yet Howard's Thoth-Amon is only a mortal Stygian wizard, though a great one. Because a mortal cannot rationally worship himself, Howard chose Set, the most ancient of Egyptian gods (or at least a rival for that distinction with Osiris) as Thoth-Amon's deity. After all, an ancient man needs an ancient god.

THERE'S NONE FOR
BAD SHOES LIKE
THE SHOEMAKER'S
WIFE.
*Traditional Irish
Proverb*

In choosing Cimmeria as the name for his Celtic homeland, Howard was alluding to Homer's *Odyssey*. Homer claims that far to the west, on the opposite shore of the great river Okeanos (the outer bound of the earth), "lie the community and city of the Cimmerian people, hidden in fog and cloud, nor does Helios, the radiant sun, ever break through the dark to illuminate them with his shining but always a glum night is spread over wretched mortals." (Conan fans should here recognize Howard's source for his gloomy description of Conan's homeland.) It is there that Odysseus summons the shades of the dead, who cannot speak until they have eaten earthly food again, and there that the slain Achilles laments: "Never try to console me for dying. I would rather follow the plow as slave to another man, one with no land allotted him and not much to live on, than be a king over all the perished dead" (Lattimore translation, p. 168)

Such a picture is very unlike the Celtic concept of the Otherworld (Tir n-Aill in Old Irish). Although placed in the west, and often described as an island, Tir n-Aill was imagined by the Celts as an ideal paradise. Warriors fought gloriously all day and sated themselves in feasting and lust all night. The Celts gave their underworld names like Tir na nOg (Land of Youth), Magh Mell (Plain of Delight), and Tir na mBan (Land of Women). Little wonder Celtic warriors had no fear of death.

As for Homer's location of Cimmeria, some of Howard's contemporaries construed it to be Britain, and the name Cimmeria (or Kimmeroi as Homer would have it) sounds like Cymru, the Welsh name for themselves and Wales (meaning "friends").

In point of fact, everybody in the ancient world placed the mythical Cimmerians to the east, where they were supposed to have made alliance with King Ashurbanipal of Assyria to kill King Gugu of Lydia. The latter had stolen Ashurbanipal's ring of invisibility, which was set with a dragon's eye for a gemstone (evidently the same legend referred to in Plato's Dialogues). At any rate, we can conclude that Homer's Cimmeria matches up with a Celtic Cymru only by chance.

There are two famous Conans in Irish myth. The first is the backstabbing, blustering bully of the Finn stories. The second is the Fomorian Conan. Conan, by the way, was a common early Celtic name.

The stories of Finn are pretty well known, and you can find them easily enough in Lady Gregory's *Gods and Fighting Men* as well as in other retellings.

The Fomorian Conan appears in "Orgain Tuir Chonain," which is found in the Lebor Gabala ("Book of the Conquest"). Conan is chief of half the Fomoire (the demon-gods of Irish myth, the dark side), and he levies tribute on the descendants of Nemed (the third group of people to inhabit Ireland). Each Samhain (November 1), which is the Feast of the Otherworld (and which has a vestigial survival in our Halloween), the Nemedians must pay two-thirds of their milk, corn, and children to Conan. At last they revolt: Conan is killed by the hero Fergus Leth-Derg. Victory appears complete until Morc Mac Dele, chief of the rest of the Fommoire, arrives with his host and slaughters all but thirty of the original sixty thousand Nemedians. (You can find this story retold in *Ancient Irish Tales*, edited by Cross and Slover.)

Howard's Conan began to attain popularity in the late 1920s, even as the stories became tragic, grim, and melancholy, reflecting Howard's personality problems and the imminence of his tragically early death. But the archetypal fascination of his work remained. With the resurgence of interest in literary fantasy during the 1960s, Howard's stories were rescued from the pulp heaps and became available to a new generation of readers. Conan became a popular celebrity, passing from literature into the world of comic strips and movies. Conan's appearance at a theater near you still bears witness to a young Texan's passion for his Irish heritage.

The evils . . . are not derived from the native character of these people. Give them the same advantages which are enjoyed by others, and they will stand upon a level with any of their neighbors.

Knickerbocker (1833)

U.S. COLLEGES OFFERING IRISH STUDIES COURSES

Arizona
Tempe: Arizona State University
Tucson: University of Arizona

California
Claremont: Pomona College
Los Angeles: Loyola Marymount University
    University of California at Los Angeles
San Jose: San Jose State University
Santa Barbara: University of California at Santa Barbara
Santa Cruz: University of California at Santa Cruz
Stanford: Stanford University

Colorado
Boulder: University of Colorado
Colorado Springs: Colorado College
Denver: Metropolitan College
    University of Denver

Connecticut
Bridgeport: Sacred Heart University
Danbury: Western Connecticut State
Fairfield: Fairfield University
Hamden: Quinnipiac College
New Britain: Central Connecticut State College
New Haven: Berkeley College, Yale University
New London: Connecticut College
Storrs: University of Connecticut
West Hartford: St. Joseph's College
    University of Hartford
Willimantic: Eastern Connecticut State

Florida
Coral Gables: University of Miami
Gainesville: University of Florida
Lakeland: Florida Southern College
St. Petersburg: Eckerd College
Tallahassee: Florida State University
Winter Park: Rollins College

Georgia
Athens: University of Georgia
Atlanta: Georgia State University
    Georgia Institute of Technology
Gainesville: Brenau College

Idaho
Boise: Boise State University
Moscow: University of Idaho
Pocatello: Idaho State University

Illinois
Carbondale: Southern Illinois University at Carbondale
Charleston: Eastern Ilinois University

Chicago:	University of Chicago
	Loyola University, Lewis Towers Campus
	University of Illinois at Chicago Circle
Edwardsville:	Southern Illinois University at Edwardsville
Evanston:	Northwestern University
Lake Forest:	Lake Forest College
Monmouth:	Monmouth College
Peoria:	Bradley University
River Forest:	Rosary College
Urbana:	University of Illinois

Indiana

Bloomington:	Indiana University
Fort Wayne:	Indiana-Purdue at Fort Wayne
Goshen:	Goshen College
South Bend:	St. Mary's College
Valparaiso:	Valparaiso University

Iowa

Cedar Rapids:	Coe College
Des Moines:	Drake University
Dubuque:	Loras College
Grinnell:	Grinnell College

Kansas

Atchison:	Benedictine College

Kentucky

Louisville:	University of Louisville

Louisiana

Lafayette:	University of Southwest Louisiana

Maine

Biddeford:	St. Francis College
Orono:	University of Maine
Portland:	University of Maine at Portland
Waterville:	Colby College

Maryland

Baltimore:	The Johns Hopkins University
Chestertown:	Washington College

Massachusetts

Boston:	Boston State College
	Boston University
	Emerson College
	Emmanuel College
	Northeastern University
	Simmons College
Bridgewater:	Bridgewater State
Brockton:	Massasoit Community College
Chicopee:	College of Our Lady of the Elms
Lowell:	Lowell State College
	University of Lowell
North Andover:	Merrimack College

(continued)

North Dartmouth:	Southeastern Massachusetts University
Norton:	Wheaton College
Springfield:	Springfield College
Waltham:	Brandeis University
Wellesley:	Wellesley College
Wenham:	Gordon College
Westfield:	Westfield State College
Worcester:	College of the Holy Cross

Michigan

Detroit:	Mercy College
	Wayne State University
Grand Rapids:	Aquinas College
	Calvin College
Lansing:	Lansing Community College
Marquette:	Northern Michigan University

Minnesota

Mankato:	Mankato State University
Minneapolis:	Augsburg College
	University of Minnesota
Northfield:	Carleton College
	St. Olaf College
St. Paul:	College of St. Catherine
Rochester:	Oakland University
Winona:	St. Mary's College

Missouri

Kansas City:	University of Missouri
Kirksville:	Northeast Missouri State University

Nebraska:

Omaha:	Creighton University
	University of Nebraska at Omaha

New Hampshire

Durham:	University of New Hampshire
New London:	Colby-Sawyer College

New Jersey

East Orange:	Upsala College
Jersey City:	Jersey City State College
	St. Peter's College
Lawrenceville:	Rider College
New Brunswick:	Rutgers University
Rutherford:	Fairleigh Dickinson University
South Orange:	Seton Hall University
Trenton:	Trenton State College
Union:	Kean College of New Jersey
Upper Montclair:	Montclair State College

New York

Albany:	State University at Albany
Annandale-on-Hudson:	Bard College
Aurora:	Wells College
Binghamton:	State University of New York at Binghamton

Buffalo:	Canisius College
	State University of New York at Buffalo
	State University College of New York at Buffalo
Canton:	St. Lawrence University
Clinton:	Hamilton College
Cortland:	State University College of New York at Cortland
Fredonia:	State University College of New York at Fredonia
Garden City:	Nassau Community College
Geneseo:	State University College at Geneseo
Geneva:	Hobart and William Smith Colleges
Hamilton:	Colgate University
Hempstead:	Hofstra University
Millbrook:	Bennett College
New Rochelle:	College of New Rochelle
New York	
Bronx:	Fordham University
Brooklyn:	St. Francis College
Manhattan:	City University of New York, Baruch College
	City University, John Jay College of Criminal Justice
	City University, Herbert H. Lehman College
	Columbia University
	New School for Social Research
	New York University
	Pace University
Queens:	St. John's University
Staten Island:	Wagner College
Olean:	St. Bonaventure University
Oneonta:	Hartwick College
Potsdam:	State University College of New York at Potsdam
Purchase:	Manhattanville College
Rochester:	Nazareth College
	St. John Fisher College
Rockville Centre:	Molloy College
Schenectady:	Union College
Southampton:	Long Island University—Southampton College
Stony Brook:	State University of New York at Stony Brook
Syracuse:	Onondaga Community College
	Syracuse University
Tarrytown:	Marymount College
Troy:	Rensselaer Polytechnic Institute
White Plains:	College of White Plains of Pace University
North Carolina	
Boone:	Appalachian State University
Asheville:	University of North Carolina at Asheville
Chapel Hill:	University of North Carolina
Durham:	Duke University
Greensboro:	Greensboro College
Jamestown:	Guilford Technical Institute
Wilmington:	University of North Carolina at Wilmington
Winston-Salem:	Wake Forest University

(continued)

North Dakota

Fargo:	North Dakota State University
Grand Forks:	University of North Dakota
Valley City:	Valley City State College

Ohio

Akron:	The University of Akron
Bowling Green:	Bowling Green State University
Cincinnati:	University of Cincinnati
Cleveland:	Cleveland State University
	John Carroll University
Columbus:	The Ohio State University
Dayton:	The University of Dayton
Delaware:	Ohio Wesleyan University
Hiram:	Hiram College
Kent:	Kent State University
Oxford:	Miami University
Springfield:	Wittenberg University
Toledo:	University of Toledo
Youngstown:	Youngstown State University

Oregon

Eugene:	University of Oregon

Pennsylvania

Altoona:	The Pennsylvania State University at Altoona
Bethlehem:	Lehigh University
	Moravian College
Bloomsburg:	Bloomsburg—University of Pennsylvania
Bryn Mawr:	Bryn Mawr College
Chester:	Widener University
East Stroudsburg:	East Stroudsburg—University of Pennsylvania
Edinboro:	Edinboro State College
Erie:	Gannon College
Glenside:	Beaver College
Gwynedd Valley:	Gwynedd-Mercy College
Kutztown:	Kutztown—University of Pennsylvania
Lancaster:	Franklin and Marshall College
Lewisburg:	Bucknell University
Meadville:	Allegheny College
Philadelphia:	La Salle College
	St. Joseph's College
	Temple University
	The University of Pennsylvania
Pittsburgh:	Carnegie-Mellon University
	University of Pittsburgh
Reading:	Albright College
Scranton:	University of Scranton
Swarthmore:	Swarthmore College
University Park:	Penn State University
Villanova:	Villanova University
West Chester:	West Chester State College
Wilkes-Barre:	King's College
Williamsport:	Lycoming College

Rhode Island
Kingston: University of Rhode Island
Providence: Brown University
                             Providence College
                             Rhode Island College

South Carolina
Columbia: The University of South Carolina
Hartsville: Coker College
Rock Hill: Winthrop College
Spartanburg: Converse College
                             Wofford College

South Dakota
Brookings: South Dakota State University

Tennessee
Knoxville: University of Tennessee
Memphis: Southwestern at Memphis
Nashville: Vanderbilt University

Texas
Austin: University of Texas
Arlington: University of Texas at Arlington
Irving: University of Dallas
Stephenville: Tarleton State University

Vermont
Marlboro: Marlboro College
Middlebury: Middlebury College
Winooski: St. Michael's College

Virginia
Blacksburg: Virginia Polytechnic Institute and State University
Charlottesville: University of Virginia
Fairfax: George Mason University
Harrisonburg: James Madison University
Hollins: Hollins College
Norfolk: Old Dominion University

Washington
Bellingham: Western Washington University
Seattle: University of Washington
Tacoma: University of Puget Sound

West Virginia
Bethany: Bethany College
Morgantown: West Virginia University

Wisconsin
Appleton: Lawrence University
Ashland: Northland College
Beloit: Beloit College
Eau Claire: University of Wisconsin–Eau Claire
Green Bay: University of Wisconsin–Green Bay
Madison: University of Wisconsin–Madison
Milton: Milton College

(continued)

Milwaukee:	Marquette University
River Falls:	University of Wisconsin–River Falls
Superior:	University of Wisconsin–Superior
Whitewater:	University of Wisconsin–Whitewater

Wyoming

| Laramie: | University of Wyoming |

District of Columbia

The American University
Catholic University of America
Georgetown University
George Washington University

TWO AND A HALF CENTURIES OF IRISH-AMERICAN ORGANIZATIONS

1737 Charitable Irish Society (Boston)
1767 Ancient and Most Benevolent Order of the Friendly Brothers of St. Patrick (New York)
1771 Society of the Friendly Sons of St. Patrick for the Relief of Emigrants from Ireland (Philadelphia)
1784 Friendly Sons of St. Patrick in the City of New York
1799 Hibernian Society of Charleston, South Carolina
1803 Hibernian Society of Baltimore
1816 Shamrock Friendly Association (New York)
1825 Friends of Ireland (for Catholic Emancipation)
1836 Ancient Order of Hibernians in America
1848 Hibernian Benevolent Emigrant Society (Chicago)
1856 Catholic Society for the Promotion of Actual Settlements in North America
1858 Fenian Brotherhood
1867 Clan na Gael
1869 Catholic Total Abstinence Union of America
1876 United Irish Societies of Chicago
1880 Irish National Land League of America
1890 Gaelic Athletic Association (Chicago)
1891 Irish National Federation of America
1891 American Irish Historical Society
1904 United Irish Counties Association of New York
1916 Friends of Irish Freedom
1920 American Association for the Recognition of the Irish Republic
1937 Eire Society of Boston
1940 American Friends of Irish Neutrality
1947 American League for an Undertaken Ireland
1960 American Committee for Irish Studies
1962 Irish American Cultural Institute
1963 American Irish Foundation
1967 American Irish Immigration Committee
1970 Irish Northern Aid Committee
1971 American Committee for Ulster Justice
1974 Irish National Causes
1975 Ireland Fund
1977 Ad Hoc Congressional Committee for Irish Affairs

Major
Research
Collections for
Irish Studies
in the United
States

CALIFORNIA
Berkeley

University of California, Bancroft Library. 94720

Sean O'Faolain. 3 boxes of manuscripts including drafts and revisions of
short stories.

Los Angeles

University of California, William Andrews Clark Memorial Library, 2520
Cimarron Street. 90018

Jonathan Swift. Large collection, first editions, manuscripts, etc.

Oscar Wilde. Collection comprising 1,500 printed works, editions, translations, critical and biographical studies, in addition to some 3,000
manuscripts and typescripts.

COLORADO
Boulder

University of Colorado Libraries. 80302

Edward P. Costigan (1874–1939). Papers of the founder of Colorado's
Progressive (Bull Moose) Party, member of the U.S. Tariff Commission, and U.S. senator.

GEORGIA
Milledgeville

Georgia College, Ina Dillard Russell Library. 31061

Flannery O'Connor (1925–1964). Complete set of the works, including
translations and critical material; plus manuscripts of the works and
correspondence.

ILLINOIS
Carbondale

Southern Illinois University at Carbondale. 62901

Lennox Robinson (1886–1958). Papers include, besides his own manuscripts, letters from W. B. Yeats, Lady Gregory, G. B. Shaw, Sean O'Casey, Sara Allgood, and others associated with the Abbey Theatre.

Brian O'Nolan (1911–1966). Papers, 1939–1966.

Katharine Tynan (1861–1931). Papers, 1887–1929.

W. B. Yeats (1865–1939). Papers, 1894–1935.

Gabriel Fallon. Papers include correspondence relating to the Abbey Theatre.

Chicago

Art Institute of Chicago, Michigan Avenue. 60603.

Louis Henri Sullivan (1856–1924). Typescripts and memorabilia.

Evanston

Northwestern University Library, 1937 Sheridan Road. 60201

Special and first editions and letters of major twentieth-century Irish writers such as James Joyce and W. B. Yeats, as well as minor writers; including the Dublin Gate Theatre Archive.

KANSAS
Lawrence

University of Kansas, Kenneth Spencer Research Library. 66044

P. S. O'Hegarty Collection. Includes Joyce (800 volumes) and Yeats (500 volumes).

MASSACHUSETTS
Amherst

University of Massachusetts/Amherst Library. 01002

W. B. Yeats. The Russell K. Alspach Collection of more than 500 volumes.

Cambridge

Harvard University, Widener Library. 02138

Celtic languages and literatures. Over 8,000 volumes.

LAND WITHOUT RENT TO YOU.
Traditional Irish Toast

Chestnut Hill

Boston College, Bapst Library. 02167.

Irish Collection of over 7,500 volumes covers almost every aspect of Irish history and literature. Papers of Patrick Andrew Collins (1844–1905), president of the Irish Land League. Letters of Jeremiah O'Donovan Rossa (1831–1915), poet, editor, and leader in the Fenian and related organizations.

MINNESOTA
St. Paul
College of St. Thomas. O'Shaughnessy Library. 55105

Celtic collection contains approximately 5000 volumes.

MISSOURI
St. Louis
Washington University Libraries. 63130

Samuel Beckett Collection. First and special editions; copies corrected or inscribed by the author, worksheets comprising manuscripts, typescripts, and notebooks.

NEW HAMPSHIRE
Concord
New Hampshire Historical Society, Manuscripts Library. 30 Park Street. 03301

John Sullivan (1740–1795). Papers of the Revolutionary general, politician, and judge from Durham, New Hampshire. Mostly correspondence for the period 1772–1791.

NEW JERSEY
South Orange
Seton Hall University, McLaughlin Library. 07079.

McManus Room. Extensive collection of books on Irish history and literature.

NEW YORK
Hempstead
Hofstra University. Library. 11550

W. B. Yeats Collection. Microfilms of the author's personal papers, drafts of manuscripts, etc.

Ithaca
Cornell University Libraries. 14850

James Joyce Collection. Manuscripts include short stories, letters to Nora, to Stanislaus Joyce, and to various publishers; letters from Nora, Ezra Pound, Harriet Weaver, Stanislaus Joyce, etc.; Stanislaus Joyce's diary, 1903–1904, etc.

AN ALM FROM HIS OWN SHARE, TO THE FOOL.
Traditional Irish Proverb

New Rochelle

Iona College. Library. 10801.

Michael J. O'Brien Papers. Manuscripts and research notes of leading Irish-American historiographer.

New York

American Irish Historical Society. 991 Fifth Avenue. 10028

Collections of papers relating to the history of the Irish in America, including the papers of the Friendly Sons of St. Patrick and the Friends of Irish Freedom. Library contains about 10,000 volumes on Irish and Irish-American subjects.

A MAN WITHOUT DINNER—TWO FOR SUPPER.
Traditional Irish Proverb

Columbia University Libraries, Avery Architectural Library, 201 Avery Hall. 10027.

Louis Henri Sullivan (1856–1924). Large collection of his drawings.

New York Public Library, Fifth Avenue and 42nd Street. 10018.

Henry W. and Albert A. Berg Collection. Includes Lady Gregory papers; Sean O'Casey papers; Fergus O'Connor papers; Louis MacNeice, drafts of plays, poems and lectures, typescripts, books in proof draft or signed copies.

Manuscript and Archives Division

The John Quinn Memorial Collection. 72 letter file boxes, 16 folders, 30 letterpress copybooks of letters, notes, telegrams and cables, 1900–1924.

Charles Patrick Daly (1816–1899). Diaries of the New York City judge, March–April 1851 (tour and social life in London), May–June 1874 (diary of his tour in Ireland).

St. John's University. Library. 11439

Irish-American Collection. Letters and documents relating to the political and fraternal activity of various Irish-American organizations since about 1940.

Walter Hampden Memorial Library at The Players, 16 Gramercy Park. 10003

George M. Cohan Collection. Manuscripts, typescripts, etc.

NORTH CAROLINA
Chapel Hill

University of North Carolina Libraries. 27514

Archibald Henderson Collection of Shaviana, including Henderson-Shaw correspondence and other manuscripts.

PENNSYLVANIA
Philadelphia
Library Company of Philadelphia. 1314 Locust Street. 19107

Mathew Carey (1760–1839) Papers (1823–1829)

Pittsburgh
Historical Society of Western Pennsylvania, 4338 Bigelow Boulevard. 15213

James O'Hara (1752–1819). Papers of the Revolutionary soldier in Denny-O'Hara Papers (1796–1832).

Villanova
Villanova University, Falvey Memorial Library. 19085

Joseph McGarrity Papers. Correspondence relating to American sympathy for Irish independence, 1920–1948.

Washington
Washington and Jefferson College Library. 15301

Molly Maguire Collection, 1875–1878. Materials concerning the violence at Connellsville against the Westmoreland and Pennsylvania Gas Company and the Pennsylvania Railroad.

TEXAS
Austin
University of Texas, Mirabeau Lamar Library. 78712

Louis MacNeice. Manuscripts of published and unpublished works, radio and television scripts, lectures, plays, letters.

THOUGH NEAR TO A MAN HIS COAT, HIS SHIRT IS NEARER (I.E., BLOOD IS THICKER THAN WATER).
Traditional Irish Proverb

St. Patrick's Day Parade Cities in the United States

California
Beverly Hills
Mission Viejo
Oakland
Sacramento
San Diego
San Francisco

Colorado
Denver

Connecticut
Greenwich
Hartford
Meriden
New Haven

Delaware
Wilmington

Florida
Delray Beach
Fort Lauderdale
Jacksonville
Miami

Georgia
Atlanta
Dublin
Savannah

Hawaii
Honolulu

Illinois
Chicago
Decatur
Waukegan

Iowa
Cedar Rapids
Dyersville
Emmetsburg

Kentucky
Lexington
Louisville

Louisiana
New Orleans

Maryland
Baltimore

Massachusetts
Boston
Holyoke
Lawrence

Michigan
Bay City
Detroit

Minnesota
Belle Plaine
Minneapolis
St. Paul
Waseca

Missouri
Kansas City
Rolla
St. Louis
Springfield

Montana
Anaconda

Nevada
Las Vegas

New Jersey
Belmar
Jersey City
Kedasborg
Kearny
Newark
Norwood
Nutley
South Amboy
West Orange
Wharton
Woodbridge

New Mexico
Albuquerque

New York
Albany
Binghamton
Brentwood
Buffalo
East Islip
Elmira
Garden City
Greenville
Huntington
Mahopac
Mid-Hudson
   (Monroe)
New Paltz
New York
   Brooklyn
   Manhattan
   Staten Island
Pearl River
Rochester
Syracuse
Troy
Utica
Westhampton
   Beach
Yonkers

Ohio
Akron
Cincinnati
Cleveland
Columbus

Pennsylvania
Allentown
East Stroudsburg
Freeland
Philadelphia
Pittsburgh
Pottsville

Scranton
Springfield
Upper Darby
Wilkes-Barre

Rhode Island
Newport
Providence
West Warwick

South Dakota
Clear Lake
Deadwood
Sioux Falls

Texas
Corpus Christi
Dublin
Houston
San Antonio
Shamrock

Utah
Salt Lake City

Virginia
Richmond

Washington
Seattle
Spokane

Wisconsin
Beloit
La Crosse
Milwaukee

**District of
   Columbia**

Puerto Rico
San Juan

IMPORTANT DATES IN IRISH HISTORY

c. 400 B.C.   Celtic tribes invaded Ireland.

c. 432 A.D.   St. Patrick brought Christianity to Ireland.

c. 795 A.D.   Vikings began raiding Ireland.

1014   Brian Boru defeated the Vikings at Clontarf.

1541   Henry VIII of England forced Ireland's Parliament to declare him king of Ireland.

1592   Foundation of Trinity College in Dublin

1601   Spanish forces landed at Kinsale. Defeat of O'Neill.

1603   Death of Queen Elizabeth. Surrender of O'Neill at Mellifont. English law extended over all of Ireland for the first time.

1607   Flight of the earls

1609   The Ulster Plantation begins.

1649   Oliver Cromwell crushed an Irish revolt against England and took land and many political rights away from Irish Catholics.

1690   The English defeated James II and Irish forces in the Battle of the Boyne.

1691   Treaty of Limerick

1695   Beginning of Penal Laws against Catholics

1760   Catholic Committee founded

1793   An important Catholic Relief Act gave Catholics the vote.

1801   Ireland became part of the United Kingdom of Great Britain and Ireland.

1845–1847   A potato famine in Ireland killed about 1,000,000 persons.

1916   The Easter Rebellion against British rule broke out in Dublin.

1921   Ireland became a dominion of Great Britain called the Irish Free State.

1949   Ireland declared itself a republic.

1955   Ireland joined the United Nations.

1973   Ireland became a member of the European Community (ECM).

AISLING: A poetic form common in eighteenth-century Gaelic literature. In a dream the poet meets a beautiful woman who tells him that she is Ireland waiting for the return of the Stuarts.

AMERICAN WAKE: A ceremony held before emigrants set out from Ireland.

ASCENDANCY: The name given to the small ruling class in eighteenth-century Ireland.

BOG: Soggy area in which a semicarbonized turf called peat is found.

BREHON: The judge who administered the Gaelic legal system.

CASHEL: The hill which was the site where the king of Munster was crowned.

CELTS: Tribes of Gaelic-speaking people who came to Ireland from western Europe beginning in the sixth century B.C.

CESS: A tax or rate collected within the counties.

COIGN AND LIVERY: This was the system by which Gaelic and Old English lords forced their tenants to give the lords' soldiers food and lodging without payment.

CURRACH: Boat made by stretching tarred canvas over a wooden frame.

DRUIDS: Members of pagan Celtic religious orders in ancient Britain, Gaul, and Ireland.

EMANCIPATION: Freeing: The term *Catholic Emancipation* was used at the end of the eighteenth century to mean the freeing of Catholics from the last of the Penal Laws and their admission to Parliament.

FENIANS: the Irish Republican Brotherhood, a secret organization that was simultaneously founded in Dublin and New York in 1858.

GAELTACHT: The western enclaves in modern Ireland where Gaelic is still spoken as the mother tongue.

HEDGE SCHOOLS: Small country schools that in summer were often held in the open. Few of them taught more than reading, writing, and elementary arithmetic.

LOUGH: The Gaelic word for "lake."

THERE NEVER CAME A GATHERER BUT A SCATTERER CAME AFTER HIM.
Traditional Irish Proverb

NEW ENGLISH: The name given to Englishmen who came to Ireland from the reign of Henry VIII to the end of the Cromwellian period. They were usually Protestant in religion. Their descendants came to be called Anglo-Irish.

OGHAM ALPHABET: An ancient system of writing that was used before Latin letters were adopted. Groups of short lines were incised on stones at various positions in order to stand for certain sounds.

OLD ENGLISH: The name given to the descendants of the early Norman and English settlers in Ireland. The terms "English by blood" or "Anglo-Norman" are sometimes used. They were usually Catholic in religion. The term ceased to be used after the Cromwellian period.

ORANGE ORDER: A secret society of Protestants pledged to maintain Ireland's links with England and Protestant supremacy. It was founded in 1795.

PALE: The district in eastern Ireland over which the Anglo-Normans and later the "New" English exercised direct rule.

PEAT: A spongy, partly carbonized sod or turf that is used as fuel in parts of Ireland.

PENAL LAWS: Regulations against Irish Catholics that were passed by English-controlled Parliaments in the late seventeenth and early eighteenth centuries.

PLANTATION: The settlement of groups of English or lowland Scottish Protestant farmers on estates obtained by the British in Ireland.

PIKE: A long spearlike weapon widely used in the Rebellion of 1798. It was cheaply and easily made.

RAPAREE: An outlaw in seventeenth- and eighteenth-century Ireland. Raparees, also known as tories, were sometimes dispossessed landowners who stayed near their old homes and attacked the settlers.

PUTTING ON THE MILL THE STRAW OF THE KILN (I.E., ROBBING PETER TO PAY PAUL).
Traditional Irish Proverb

RECUSANT: One who refused to attend the services of the Established Church. By the act of Uniformity all recusants had to pay a fine of twelve pence every week.

SASSANACH: A Gaelic word of contempt for the Saxon or Englishman that later was applied to any Protestant.

SCATHLAN: A simple thatched open shelter where the Roman Catholic Mass could be celebrated for the people when official churches had been prohibited by the British authorities in Ireland.

SEPT: A social grouping based on the notion that everyone in it is descended from a common ancestor.

SINN FEIN: An Irish movement begun in 1899 that advocated separate parliaments for England and Ireland as had been provided for by the Constitution of 1782 prior to the Legislative Union in 1800.

STATUTES OF KILKENNY: Regulations that were imposed by the English rulers of Ireland in 1366 making it a crime for any non-Irish to use Gaelic customs, language, or laws or to associate with the Gaelic Irish.

TARA: The place where the overkings of Meath and, after the tenth century, the "high" king of Ireland were crowned.

TRANSPORTATION: The British policy in the seventeenth and eighteenth centuries of exiling troublesome or indigent Irish to the American colonies or Australia as bonded servants.

UNDERTAKERS: British who were granted large estates in Ireland as a reward for their services to the Crown on the condition that they would settle specified numbers of colonists on the land.

WILD GEESE: Irish students and soldiers who went to France and served in the army of Louis XIV after the Treaty of Limerick in 1691 believing that they might spearhead an invasion to drive out the Protestant regime and restore Stuart rule to Ireland. ◆

WHEN YOUR HAND IS IN THE DOG'S MOUTH, DRAW IT OUT GENTLY.
Traditional Irish Proverb

PHOTO SOURCES

PERMISSIONS ACKNOWLEDGMENTS

Index

THE QUILLS OFTEN
TOOK THE FLESH
WITH THEM.
*Traditional Irish
Proverb*

A HEAVY LOT ARE
YOUR EMPTY GUTS.
*Traditional Irish
Proverb*

AFTER THEIR FEEDING, THE WHELPS BEGIN TO FIGHT.
Traditional Irish Proverb

THEY ARE NOT ALL
BIG MEN WHO REAP
THE HARVEST.
*Traditional Irish
Proverb*

A RING ON THE
FINGER AND NOT A
STITCH OF CLOTHES
ON THE BACK.
*Traditional Irish
Proverb*

AN UNLEARNED KING IS A CROWNED ASS.
Traditional Irish Proverb

TIME IS A GOOD
STORYTELLER.
*Traditional Irish
Proverb*

BETTER THE GOOD
THAT IS THAN THE
DOUBLE GOOD THAT
WAS.
*Traditional Irish
Proverb*

THE MAN WITHOUT A RESOURCE IS HANGED.
Traditional Irish Proverb

DEATH IS THE POOR MAN'S DOCTOR.
Traditional Irish Proverb

'TIS A BAD HEN THAT WON'T SCRATCH FOR HERSELF.
Traditional Irish Proverb

I WOULD TAKE AN
EYE OUT OF MYSELF
TO TAKE TWO OUT
OF ANOTHER.
*Traditional Irish
Proverb*

NOT WORRIED TILL MARRIED.
Traditional Irish Proverb

FAIR WORDS WON'T
FEED THE FRIARS.
*Traditional Irish
Proverb*

NEVER POOR TILL
ONE GOES TO HELL.
*Traditional Irish
Proverb*

BETTER RIDING A GOAT THAN THE BEST MARCHING. *Traditional Irish Proverb*

SHE BURNT HER COAL AND DID NOT WARM HERSELF (SAID WHEN A WOMAN MAKES A BAD MARRIAGE).
Traditional Irish Proverb

MELODIOUS IS THE CLOSED MOUTH.
Traditional Irish Proverb